*Major
Problems
in
American
Foreign
Policy*

Major Problems in American Foreign Policy

DOCUMENTS AND ESSAYS

VOLUME I: TO 1914

Edited by
Thomas G. Paterson
University of Connecticut

D. C. HEATH AND COMPANY Lexington, Massachusetts   Toronto

For Rebecca Virginia Paterson

Cartography by Russell H. Lenz

Cover photograph adapted from "American Commissioners of the Preliminary Peace Negotiations with Great Britain" by Benjamin West. Courtesy, The Henry Francis du Pont Winterthur Museum.

Printed in the United States of America.

International Standard Book Number: 0-669-00475-8

Library of Congress Catalog Card Number: 77-79496

Preface

The goal of this volume is to provide students and instructors with the most distinguished writing in American diplomatic history. Each chapter addresses a major theme or question on which contemporary statesmen and later scholars have conspicuously differed. The primary documents in each chapter help to identify the problem, outline the issues, and reveal the flavor of the times. The essays, or secondary accounts, have been selected for their differing points of view, their provocative and intelligent reasoning, and their recognized high quality as scholarship. Studies by past masters, which have been applauded by their colleagues as being significant, are combined with the recent works of scholars and publicists who also speak with authority. The introductions and headnotes set the readings in historical and interpretive perspective; the maps supply a valuable dimension; and the Further Reading sections suggest additional books and articles for continued research on the topics at hand.

I am grateful to Melvyn Leffler, Paul A. Varg, J. Garry Clifford, Jean-Donald Miller, and Kenneth J. Hagan for their helpful comments on the choice of selections. Their sense of proportion was precise and their standards were high. Don Miller was especially helpful, and I thank him as a friend and colleague in the history of American foreign policy. Holly Izard Paterson, as always, helped in countless ways. The dedication is to my daughter Becki, whose good humor and independent mind make a father proud—and alert.

THOMAS G. PATERSON
University of Connecticut

Contents

Maps

1

Diplomatic Historians and Their History

It is a truism that history is as much the historian as the body of facts the historian weaves together to tell the story of the past. Historians, like all human beings, have their viewpoints that are shaped by parents, by personal experiences, by ideological preferences, and by myriad philosophers, scholars, politicians, and others. It is rare historical writing, indeed, that is free from the personal bias of the author. This does not make the writing less significant as a work of scholarship or as a viable interpretation. On the contrary, readers of history are enriched by knowing about and learning from an author's subjectivity. To overlook the historian's role in creating our image of the past is to miss an exciting part of the quest for knowledge and understanding.

ESSAYS

The following three essays, all by prominent diplomatic historians who have exerted considerable influence upon generations of scholars, help us to illustrate this truism. For example, Samuel Flagg Bemis, ardent nationalist, long-time professor of history at Yale University, mentor of talented students, and author of such major books as *Jay's Treaty* (1923) and *John Quincy Adams and the Foundations of American Foreign Policy* (1950), recalls his early days at Harvard as a graduate student undertaking historical research. Dexter Perkins, whose books on the Monroe Doctrine are considered classics, surveys his own life as a citizen as well as the events and leaders of his time that helped mold his "Wilsonian" view. And, finally, William Appleman Williams of Oregon State University, who has spoken in a powerful, critical voice through such works as *The Tragedy of American Diplomacy* (1959) and *The Roots of the Modern American Empire* (1969), delineates the influences that moved him toward a leftist, "revisionist" perspective.

Bemis, Perkins, and Williams have enjoyed different backgrounds, read different books, studied under different professors, argued with different students, and reached contrasting conclusions about the history of American diplomacy. The questions their autobiographies raise should be raised for every essay in this volume. It is debatable whether one has "to live through a period to understand it," as Professor Perkins claims in his essay, but certainly one must know about the viewpoint of the scholar to understand historical writing about any period.

A Nationalist Education

SAMUEL FLAGG BEMIS

Right away I found myself in Professor Channing's research seminar in American history. Edward Channing was then at the zenith of his lifework, his *History of the United States*. It remains the best attempt at a one-man, multi-volume history of the republic and its colonial background, documented by the best of published scholarship and his own research. As conceived by Channing, it was to cover the period from the discovery to the beginning of his own adult lifetime, that is, to the end of the nineteenth century. Channing died early in 1931 after finishing Volume VI that ended with the close of the Civil War. It was his method to organize his seminar about some central theme or period and to assign problems relating to that general subject to each student—I believe there were six of us that term. He had enough applicants so he didn't have to take in anyone who didn't want to work in this manner. Really it is the ideal way: teacher and disciples working together as fellow students on aspects of the same subject, each able to give and take; of course the instructor gave and the students took, but the latter could stimulate and occasionally rasp one another. It was all to the good for everybody.

I noticed that it was the custom of old students who dropped into the library to greet Channing by asking him what volume of the "great work" he was now working on. At my time he was writing Volume IV on the Federalist Period—dictating it little by little, so he would tell us casually, "after a cigar in the evening." For my seminar exercise I got the subject of Jay's Treaty with Great Britain of 1794, of which I had scarcely heard. Realizing that the subject had no adequate monograph based on investigation in the public and private archives of the negotiating countries, he thought that somebody some-

Samuel Flagg Bemis, "Harvard, 1913–1916." First published in *The New-England Galaxy,* Volume XI, Winter 1970, pp. 13–15. "A Worcester County Student in Wartime London and Paris (via Harvard): 1915–1916." First published in *The New-England Galaxy,* Volume XI, Spring 1970, pp. 15–16, 17–18, 19–23.

day should at least make a start in the foreign sources. It was my great luck that he threw that bone to me. Whether he realized how far it would take me, I often doubt.

Channing, Hart, and Turner were then the American history triumvirate at Harvard, joint compilers of the widely-known pioneer *Guide to American History.*

Channing would affect a singular, almost strutting pose (if one can strut in an armchair), and liked with students to take a poke at Hart now and then. But he never took a dig at Turner. Channing never wholly accepted Turner's famous frontier and sectional interpretation of American history and society; he took occasion to challenge it with other ideas, such as the pervasive centripetal and unifying force of nationalism overcoming sectionalism and states rights from colonial times to the present. I once unavoidably heard Channing and Haskins worrying about how they would keep Turner from going back to Wisconsin.

Channing would begin his seminar, which met only once a week, with a few informal lectures, or rather remarks. They were of a discursive and frequently personal nature—never reflecting any discredit on himself. (I never knew a teacher, including myself, who did. We are all vain.) These talks were mostly designed, I suspect, to take up time and keep the class together while the neophytes were getting immersed in their several researches. The most instructive feature of his teaching was the half-hour conference he had every week with each member of the seminar at his little desk in the library stacks, where he could reach for a special book or direct a student around the corner to a series in the stacks. Even in these conferences one had to hold Channing to one's own track of study: if you didn't he would get to worming personal information out of you, instead of imparting historical knowledge. As one of my friends who later took Channing's seminar said: "You had to knock it out of him." All this, I suspect, was the most subtle type of teaching. It was helping people to help themselves. Education is self-education: teachers and libraries are the means by which one educates oneself. Channing knew that; if his students didn't yet know it, they came to realize it.

The other principal feature of his seminar was the report of each student to the group. Channing wouldn't let you read it: all he would allow was a one-page outline of what you wanted to say, and no surreptitious glances at notes under the table. This required you to be so soaked up in your subject that you would have it at the end of your tongue. . . .

By the time I returned to Harvard in 1915 from my summer tutorial employment, my parents and younger brothers had moved down to Medford. I now enjoyed the Ozias Goodwin Memorial Fellowship and could devote all my time to my studies and preparation for my "generals." I could walk the three miles at least one way: across the Medway, over Winter Hill to East Cambridge, and to Harvard Square. After a hard day I could ride back on the subway and elevated to Sullivan Square and home, all still for a nickel, but it took, with changes, almost as much time as walking. More questionable exercise was walking for hours at night in the Fellsway, rehearsing and memorizing for my oral examination, an ordeal so dreaded by students that some of them collapse out of sheer anxiety.

At last came the day when I was to prove myself, whether I would be dropped out of the University or permitted to go on and present a thesis for the doctorate. I was not too scared or nervous until I saw Assistant Professor Johnston and Dr. Lord around the examiners' table; the others, as I remember, were Channing, Merriman, and McIlwain. Somehow I got through with McIlwain and Merriman. Then came R. M. Johnston's turn.

He asked a few questions about the significance of the French Revolution; then he wondered whether I might review the historiography of that great upheaval. I had read Mignet and Taine, a lot of Aulard, and some of Jaurès. Mr. Johnston himself had published a short volume for the aid of students summing up the subject, so I was able to run over the whole gamut of historians, not neglecting to mention Albert Sorel. The committee was impressed and Professor Johnston's eyes brightened. I should have stopped there, for he didn't seem to have any more to ask. "Then, of course," I added by way of a crowning touch, "there is your own little volume if I may mention it in the same list with these masters." Too late I realized what I had said, but my chagrin was lost in general laughter that went around the table; even R. M. Johnston joined in. "You may," he said, and I came back from the edge of the abyss and smiled sheepishly myself.

Then Channing turned to the youngest examiner, who had been called in as a man who had never had anything to do with my instruction and could size me up impersonally! "Any questions, Dr. Lord?" Dr. Lord had not gone to sleep during the session, as I had once done in my visit to his seminar, not for one second! He asked me a few questions, not at all vindictive, but I was by then so terrified by remembrance of my own snooze that I didn't field them very well, whatever they were. I knew by then I must be sunk.

It was Channing who ended the exam and came to my rescue. He asked me some questions as easy for me as pop flies for a third baseman, though perhaps a little recondite to the committee.

I passed—over Dr. Lord's dissenting vote. His negative voice was not undeserved, if only on the basis of my answers to his questions.

"What did you have against *me?*" Channing asked me a little gruffly, next time I saw him. "We were only trying hard to pull you through."

I had nothing but the greatest gratitude! I guess that I must have looked a little truculent after Lord had got through with me. . . .

At first glance Jay's Treaty, that Channing had assigned me, must seem to be a rather unattractive and uninspiring subject. Actually it lay at the very heart of the new nationality of the United States under the Constitution of 1787, when American foreign policy was taking shape and party politics were crystallizing under the rival leadership of Alexander Hamilton and Thomas Jefferson during the administrations of President George Washington. It was, in fact, the first treaty, aside from a consular convention with France, to be ratified by the Senate of the United States. The negotiation involved the whirlpool of international politics during the wars of the French Revolution and the attitude of the United States toward them: isolation and neutrality under sufferance of the British navy for the benefit of American commerce and tariff revenues so indispensable to the support and credit of the new national government of the United States under the Hamiltonian system. Jay's Treaty of 1794 with Great Britain therefore exposed the very foundations of American foreign policy soon to be spelled out in Washington's Farewell Address of 1796.

Though I did not realize it then, the preparation of this doctoral dissertation launched me on a career at home and abroad of historical writing and teaching nothing less than the history of the foreign policy of the United States, from the beginning, where I started my research, to—I will not say to the end— to the present year 1970 of this terrible yet magnificent twentieth century. Before the First World War it was quite possible for a young man to encompass everything that had been written on the diplomatic history of the United States up to and including his own times. Channing had hitched me up to something big while I was still in my early twenties.

At the time of Jay's Treaty, and indeed until the end of the Napoleonic Wars, foreign policy ruled American politics. For a century afterward American domestic politics ruled foreign policy, so far as the Old World was concerned, during a hundred years of peace on the great oceans. As I set forth for Europe, in October 1915, on the neutral Dutch liner *Nieuw Amsterdam,* Europe was again convulsed on the Continent and engulfed in war at sea. Foreign policy again was agitating and would soon dominate American politics during the Great War of 1914–1918. Another passenger on the *Nieuw Amsterdam* was the Austrian Ambassador Constantine Dumba, whom President Wilson had just expelled from the United States for saying that the President's *Lusitania* notes to Germany were only intended for domestic consumption.

Where I spent the first night in darkened London I cannot remember, but next day an advertisement in the *Times* took me to a boarding house in Finsbury Park at 30 Adolphus Road, the home of a Mr. and Mrs. Kay and their two amiable daughters, Jennie and Lettie, one of whom, Jennie, the elder, succeeded in advancing my German to an imperfect speaking ability. The elder Kays were naturalized British subjects born in Germany, as Mrs. Kay was careful to explain before I engaged room and board. The family, with the possible exception of Mrs. Kay, were violently anti-German. They had changed their names legally from Kaiser to Kay, just as our good neighbors back in Worcester were to change Hamburg St. to Genesee St. after the United States entered the war, and American schools dropped the German language from their curricula. Probably, this was one reason why I obtained such reasonable rates at the Kay's, the sterling equivalent of about five dollars a week. I lived pleasantly with this family all the time I was in London. It was within twenty minutes by tube from the Public Records Office and the British Museum.

Next morning I betook myself to the Records Office, equipped with the required introduction from the American Ambassador. At the head of Chancery Lane was a huge hole, the size of my bedroom, in the street, about six or eight feet deep, made by a Zeppelin bomb dropped the night before I arrived in London. A recruiting officer was signing men up from a scaffolding that had been erected over the hole. The Zeppelins did not do much real damage during the First World War—aerial bombardment was in its infancy and the huge ships were easy targets for anti-aircraft guns. There was not another raid all that winter, but there was many an alarm and blackout, the night sky constantly crisscrossed by searchlights, and much toing and froing in the obscured streets by clanging fire apparatus and mobile artillery, bedlam on foggy nights. . . .

The solemn music and grave ceremony of a wartime service at Westminster Abbey still haunts my mind. . . .

In a few months I finished my work in London and mailed to Professor Channing a typescript of my dissertation. It could still be touched up by some investigation in the archives of the French Foreign Office at the Quai d'Orsay. That part of my requirement for the degree was over, as I booked passage for France and checked my steamer trunk through to Paris. With me I carried a suitcase and a leather Boston bookbag stuffed with the notes I had taken in England.

Those were the days of diplomatic debate between President Wilson and the German Imperial Government over submarine warfare, which had subsided a little, at least in respect to "unarmed passenger vessels."

"Any trouble lately with submarines?" I asked at the London ticket office.

"Not on this line," replied the impassive agent at the window.

The cross-Channel ship *Sussex,* on which I embarked early on the afternoon of March 24, 1916, was a small, unarmed passenger vessel flying the flag of France, on the route Dover to Calais. I had a second-class ticket. For such a short passage I could wait for dinner until we got in to Calais, although the *Sussex* had a dining room up forward, where some passengers were already taking tea. I had not become wholly addicted to the English custom of afternoon tea, so I went back to the stern deck.

The sea was very calm. The flag had been taken down from the rear mast. As I looked out over the water from the port side, I noticed that we were wallowing through drifting bales and flotsam that looked like remnants of wreckage. Suddenly a passenger exclaimed, excitedly, "What's that?"

I was looking in the right direction. "That" was the straight and swirling wake of something just beneath the surface, rapidly shooting toward the ship. I realized what it meant, but before I could shout "torpedo!" it had crashed into the port bow. The submarine never surfaced. According to the log of the submarine commander, preserved in the German archives, it was exactly 2:55 p.m. European time.

A tremendous explosion threw to the deck some of those who happened to be standing. The entire bow was blown off and with it the people who were in the dining room. The ship began slowly to sink forward. Crew and passengers scrambled toward the lifeboats. The boats had not been swung out on their davits to be let down quickly in case of emergency. There had been no lifeboat drill. The ropes were all gummed up and difficult to loosen. I and others tore at them in vain with our cold fingers. Finally the crew were able to lower some boats, loaded principally with women. I don't remember having seen any children about. In one case the ropes stuck at a davit, letting one end of the boat go down while holding up the other. The occupants simply slid into the sea, some with lifebelts that could hold them up for possible rescue.

By this time I began to look about for a lifebelt for myself. All those stored in and about the deck had been taken during the rush, but inside the second-class saloon I found a rotten fragment of one and managed to tie on that much with a chance piece of rope. The boats were all away by now. I resolved to get into a position from which I could swim for something as the ship went down bow first. I took off my shoes, climbed over the rail, and found a temporary perch above the propeller on a cleat that ran around the stern just above the water line. A few minutes before I had seen a man in the sea clinging to the end of the log-line like a fish on a hook; he was no longer there; the rope payed out slack behind the slowly sinking ship. In a moment a lifeboat crowded with people warped around the stern and I stepped off into it. I stepped from the lifeboat to an emergency life-raft, good for one person, that was floating along in touch. Astride this thing, about the size of a child's coffin, I gradually floated out to sea. After a while the ship stopped sinking. The lifeboats remained clustered around her, their occupants waiting to see what would happen. By a miracle the explosion that blew away the bow and perhaps the forward third of the vessel had blasted the remainder inwards, so that it kept afloat in the calm weather. But there was I, drifting farther and farther away from a chance of rescue. I caught hold of some wreckage including a steamer chair, from which with my jackknife I cut the canvas into strips and tied things together to make a raft of sorts, big enough to hold me mostly out of the chilling water.

Riding along in this jolly way, I noticed a singular, almost ridiculous, little coincidence of traffic in the English Channel. Floating close along, bobbing up and down in the easy sea, never quite within reach, was one of my shoes that I had abandoned on the deck of the ship, sailing quite upright, nicely enough to please Old Mother Hubbard herself. I never did recover it, nor its mate wherever that was.

As I looked back at the slowly receding *Sussex* and its cluster of lifeboats I saw on the horizon another ship: a three-masted, full-rigged sailing vessel, sails spread wide to catch the breeze. It soon disappeared. Soon I met a fellow navigator, not too lucid, a Swiss about my own age, who like me was astride a raft of his own. We came within reach of each other and I tied our two seahorses together, so that in that quiet sea we were fairly well out of the water.

It was now getting dusk. We were perhaps a mile or so from the ship. Suddenly we spied a lifeboat making our way. The captain of the *Sussex* had sent it out, manned by two sailors, to pick up anybody still afloat. What a noble Frenchman, to whom we certainly owed our lives!

"Gee!" said my new-found companion, in impeccable English, "I hope they see us. If they pick us up I'll give them five dollars in gold each."

As I have suggested, he was a little delirious.

Back on the *Sussex* when we arrived, people were cheering up. The vessel was floating securely, at least for the time being, though nobody knew for how long, or whether to expect another torpedo; and the wireless was busy. Several bodies were laid out on the starboard deck.

I found my suitcase and bookbag of notes intact where I had left them. From the suitcase I got a pair of beaded Indian moccasins, put them on my cold wet feet, and sat down on the bench inside the saloon, to wait and see. Beside me was a young woman, sad and still dry-eyed. Just before the crash her husband had left her momentarily for some purpose forward. He never came back. Forlornly in her lap she held his Belgian officer's cap. They had just been married and were on their way to Belgium for their honeymoon.

Presently some of the lights turned on, enough to see about the cabin. I began to shiver in my wet clothing. A woman with a lunchbox offered me a leg of chicken, which I accepted, not knowing where or whether the next meal was coming from. Attracted by a warmer current of air, I found my way to the boiler room. The boilers were still warm and I sat down above them. My clothes dried and I stopped shaking.

Some hours after dark we survivors were all rescued. Some eighty-four lives were lost, including that of the famous composer, Granados, whom I had seen walking about the ship in his coat and cap of Astrakhan fur. A British minesweeper came alongside to take us off. What crisp and rapid commands that officer snapped out, how the crew responded promptly: "Aye, aye, sir!"

"Passengers will come on without baggage!"

I had my bag of precious notes in my hand when I joined the line to go down the ladder. It was only a little bag, but I treasured it more than my trunk and suitcase. I stepped out of line, went a few yards to the right or left, and tossed it, well strapped up, down to the deck of the minesweeper. In the pre-occupation and excitement of the moment nobody noticed, and I stepped back to another place in line. Later I found the bag safe and intact on the rescue ship and hugged it to myself all the way into the port of Boulogne.

How and when we passed the rest of the night ashore I forget completely, and indeed everything until we got off the train at the *Gare du Nord* in Paris. At the platform to greet us was a young attaché from the American Embassy. Me he taxied in my dishevelment, wet moccasins and all, to the American Embassy, where Ambassador William Graves Sharp took me into his own residence. I have been a guest in many embassies since, but this first experience was the most welcome of all. A valet conducted me to a guest room on the top floor and equipped me with shoes from the wardrobe of the Ambassador's own son. They fitted just fine.

"The Ambassador will be expecting you down to lunch right away," said the valet, as he left me to my own devices for a moment.

I didn't know what to do with those soggy moccasins. The room opened on an inside balcony that ran around an ornamental central hallway rising four stories from the first floor below, where the dining room and reception parlors were. I stepped to the banister and dropped the moccasins overboard, hoping some servant would pick them up and take care of them. They hit the marble floor below with a squishy sound. When I got downstairs they were nowhere to be seen, but the Ambassador was standing by the entrance to the dining room. "I know what that plomp was," he said jovially, as he took me in to luncheon and introduced me to Mrs. Sharp. "It was those moccasins!"

The Wilsonian Influence

DEXTER PERKINS

As I look back and reflect upon the evolution of my views in the field of foreign policy (a field which has, as the reader knows, occupied much of my teaching and writing), what impresses me is how typical of many an American my own development has been. The innocence of youth has faded; faith in a simple remedy for the appeal to violence has been dimmed; the magnitude of the problem becomes apparent. Above all, and this I shall have to say frankly at the outset, pacifism as gospel seems to me illusory and dangerous. Peace, if it comes, will rest upon organized force, not upon innocent good will. Reinhold Niebuhr has put the matter in a nutshell: "Love without power" (I paraphrase) "will in the long run, or perhaps the short run, be overcome by power without love." I was a long time coming to this view; I reproach myself, student that I was of international affairs, that I awakened slowly to this essential truth; but perhaps just because this is true, what I have to say here may have some value for my readers.

I grew up in an era when the dominant mood of America was peace. Since 1815 there had been no large-scale conflict in Europe. Since 1865 there had been no large-scale conflict in the Americas, save for a bloody struggle in Paraguay—hardly noticed in the United States. True, we had fought a war with Spain in 1898, but this was hardly more than a military picnic. In Europe in the first decade of the twentieth century there were ominous signs for those who knew how to read them, most especially, the growth of German nationalism. But at the time of the first Moroccan crisis (1905) the possibility of a European war on a grand scale seemed to have been exorcised by the Conference of Algeciras. Austria's annexation of the Turkish province of Bosnia Herzegovina in 1908 passed without a conflict, despite the hostility it aroused among the South Slavs. When I graduated from college in 1909, men were dwelling on the folly of war. They were preparing not long after to celebrate a century of peace between the United States and Great Britain. The Hague Conferences of 1899 and 1907, however little they may have accomplished, seemed another happy augury. Norman Angell's *The Great Illusion,* which was published in 1910 and which I read not very long after, confidently predicted that the economic interest of the world in stability would prevent armed conflict. Leading Americans like Charles William Eliot and David Starr Jordan exuded confidence in the pacific character of the future.

It was easy for me, an idealistic youth, to believe in goodness and to mini-mize the forces of evil in the world. In these years I dreamed that a way might be found to abolish war between civilized nations. And in my senior year in college I took a course in international law, and in an immature way came to the conclusion that here was an answer to the problem of power and that I wanted to teach the subject. Part of my graduate work was in this field. When I got my fellowship to study in France in the fall of 1911, one of the induce-ments was that at the École des Sciences Politiques, which I was to attend, was Louis Renault, one of the most renowned international lawyers of the period. When I got my first job in Cincinnati in 1914, I stipulated that I was to have an opportunity to teach a half-course in the law of nations.

In the summer of 1914 came the First World War. I remember very well the day that the newspaperman came up the drive with the Sunday papers, the first of August, 1914, and the look on my father's face as he read that Germany had declared war on Russia. He looked as if the skies had fallen in. And what is striking to me now is that though I had taken an interest in contemporary diplomacy, although indeed I had been in France in 1911 and 1912, and had an opportunity to observe the growth of the war spirit in France, I was by no means prepared for the outburst of hostilities. I resembled most Americans in believing that we had progressed beyond the point where a world war was possible.

In the policy of neutrality which Wilson followed I was strongly behind the President. As I look back, I think I saw the struggle through his eyes. As we now know, Wilson was not indifferent to the idea of a German victory. But he cherished the hope that the war might be brought to an end through American mediation, and he placed in the forefront of his thought the maintenance of legal principle. Did he, as later critics were to insist, discriminate in favor of the Allies? In one sense, yes. He avoided a sharp challenge to Great Britain and France; he responded sharply to German violations of law. But there was a world of difference between Allied and German conduct. The Western powers were interfering with trade; the Germans, in initiating the submarine warfare against merchant vessels, were infringing on the long-established principle that such vessels, whatever their cargo, could not be sunk without making provision for the safety of their passengers and crew. This infringement, to one trained in international law as I had been, seemed a serious breach in the legal order, on a wholly different plane than interference with commerce, with regard to which it is fair to say that the principles of law were somewhat cloudy.

It is not strange, then, that I supported the President, at the same time cherishing the hope that he could avoid a direct confrontation with Germany. When the *Lusitania* went down in May 1915, with the loss of over one hundred American lives, I was behind Wilson in his protest, and also in his exercise of patience. It is not always remembered that after a long period of note-writing that provoked the scorn of such nationalists as Theodore Roosevelt, the President secured the actual suspension of the U-boat war in the spring of 1916.

One day that spring Dr. Rhees called me in and asked if I wanted to attend a dinner meeting at Washington of a new organization called the League to Enforce Peace. The principle on which this organization was based was that the nations of the world would act collectively to put down an aggressor. We have learned today that things do not work out just that way. Very regretfully, but entirely clearly, I have come to the conclusion that collective security, in the broadest sense, is impracticable, that so varied are the interests of nations, and so widespread the desire to keep out of trouble if one can, that it has not been possible to rally all governments against a law-breaking state. But fifty years ago the idea did not seem impractical; it seemed an excellent specific for the evil of war. You may imagine, then, my feelings that evening when I sat in the great ballroom on the top floor of the Willard, and heard the President, in a dry, thin voice, but in precise language, commit himself and his administration to the central idea of the League to Enforce Peace. I can see that scene now. Former President Taft presided. And as the President came to the crux of his argument, while cheers broke out all over the room, Taft lifted his huge bulk, and waved his napkin enthusiastically. It was easy to believe that a new and great idea had been born.

I have already indicated my passionate interest in the election of Wilson in the campaign of 1916. After the election I continued to hope for peace. And I read with enthusiasm the "peace without victory" address of January 1917.

Then came the breach with Germany, the severance of diplomatic relations as Berlin declared unrestricted submarine warfare. Even then, my fundamental aversion to war led me to hope that an all-out conflict could be avoided. Events, of course, were to prove me wrong.

There are two incidents in the winter of 1917 that deserve recollection. Though my father was an orthodox Republican, he and my mother generously offered to take my fiancée and me to the inauguration. When we got to Washington we learned that the President's request to Congress to authorize the arming of the merchant ships of the United States had been filibustered to death in the Senate. And that night, as we were having dinner in our hotel, Senator Robert La Follette, one of the filibusterers, came in with a company of friends and sat down at the table near us. The band struck up the Star-Spangled Banner. At La Follette's table most of his friends remained seated. But the Senator, with the saddest and grimmest expression that I have ever seen, rose while the strains of the national anthem died away.

In the middle of March came the first Russian Revolution. One afternoon I bought the newspaper and read that the tsar had been dethroned. I cannot remember my own reaction, but writing in the historical vein, I have often wondered whether this was not a substantial factor in leading the President to the decision for war. It seems to me that ideologically it cleared the air. It had been difficult to depict the war as an out-and-out struggle of democracy against autocracy with the Russians fighting on the allied side. But the March revolution changed all that, and I know that Wilson, no doubt naively but surely, felt that a new and democratic Russia might rise from the ruins of the old. Another point. The chances of allied victory, it could be perceived, were diminished with the change of government in Russia. Could she, would she, continue the war? Was it not more than ever necessary for the United States to enter the struggle, if the democratic nations of the West were to win? These thoughts were not stressed by the President in that eventful period. But for many Americans, I am sure, they constituted a reason for entering a conflict which these same Americans had been anxious to avoid.

In April came war. I was in Boston visiting my parents at the time. I read the President's request for a declaration of hostilities with complete conviction that he had done all he could to avoid the struggle. It was hard to believe that it had come, and that not improbably I would be in it, but the issue seemed to me inescapable. . . .

The events which I have just described suggest some analysis of my later historical judgment of the period. No one of our wars has left behind more divergent interpretations among the historians. There are those who hold that Wilson's attitude was too rigid, and that war might have been avoided had he been more flexible. On the other hand, with the passage of time the view has been put forward that the United States had a profound security interest in preventing the victory of Germany, and that since the President's policy tended to that end it is to be commended. And there are those, including the most distinguished students of the Wilson period, who believe that no chief executive could possibly have failed to defend the rights which Germany challenged.

No one can tell what would have been the outcome had the United States not entered the war. Time and time again I have had occasion in my teaching to assert that confident judgment on the history that never happened is risky business for the historian. The events in the international scene are so complicated that it is best not to be dogmatic. We simply cannot reconstruct history by hypothesis.

Without our intervention would Germany have won an all-out victory? Would she have dominated the Continent, but failed to bring British seapower to its knees? Would a stalemate have postponed revolution in Russia with all its tremendous consequences? These are all important questions to which a definitive answer is impossible. But recently a young scholar in a noteworthy book has underlined, more strikingly than ever before, the scope of German ambition, and therefore the dangers of German success.

In my interpretation of the period, on which I have lectured for many years, I am thrown back on the facts, as distinguished from the speculations. What are these facts? In taking his stand on the submarine issue the President was supported by the majority opinion of the nation. This was true partly because the legal issue bulked important in the thought of many people, and because it was fortified by the disposition of the majority of the American people to sympathize with the cause of the Allies. The issue of national safety did not bulk large in people's minds by comparison. On this question the nation was divided. There were powerful elements who did not accept it, large numbers of German-Americans as well as large numbers of Irish-Americans who had their eyes on the repression practiced by Britain in Ireland at the same time that she was defending the principles of democracy in war. There were also large numbers of Americans who hoped fervently that the United States could avoid involvement, who remembered, perhaps vaguely but nonetheless with conviction, the principle of nonentangling alliances, and who would have seen direct intervention on the allied side as a violation of American tradition. Wilson acted from conviction, in choosing the ground that he did choose, and his position was, in my judgment, that position which best maintained the unity of the American people, and made it possible, when war came, to enter the struggle with the maximum amount of national unity. This I have maintained for many years.

Nonetheless, subsequent generations, and especially the college generation of the twenties and thirties, often found it hard to accept the necessity of enforcing a legal principle. Why not warn Americans off the merchant ships of the Allies? Why contend for a principle in view of the risks involved? The question has been asked me time and time again, and, as we shall see, it was reflected in wide segments of opinion in the nineteen thirties. It provides an interesting example of the inability of one generation to understand the motives and rationale of another. Intellectually, it is easy for men in time of peace to recoil from the kind of decision that may mean war. Such people cannot reconstruct the emotional suppositions that actually governed action, or the feelings of horror, to make the point more concrete, that filled many American breasts at the time of the sinking of the *Lusitania*. You have to live through a period to understand it. . . .

In the early twenties one leading theme was reduction of armaments. This was not only an obeisance to the peace spirit generated by Wilson, but it was also dictated by prevailing economic notions as to the necessity of frugality in government, and of reduction of swollen expenditures.

At the outset there was what looked like a brilliant success in this field at the Washington Arms Conference of 1921 and 1922. Secretary Hughes managed to bring about an agreement for the restriction of capital ships and aircraft carriers based on existing ratios. The longer view was to prove this achievement a very temporary one. In the second place, the reparations question, which had seemed vexing at the time of the Treaty of Versailles, yielded to treatment. By the terms of the treaty, impossible burdens were assessed on Germany. But in the agreements of 1924 (the Dawes Plan) and 1929 (the Young Plan) progress seemed to have been made in dealing with the problem. Thereby the Locarno treaties and the admission of Germany to the League were other happy omens for the future. The proposal of the Harding and Coolidge administrations for American adhesion to the protocol creating a World Court, though not accepted by the Senate in satisfactory form, nonetheless made it appear that the United States was moving in the right direction. With these various steps I, of course, sympathized, and used my editorial pen to support them.

In two respects, however, I was not in accord with the trend of the times. I did not share the increasing body of opinion which was sharply critical of the Treaty of Versailles. The reparation clauses I thought harsh, and I severely condemned the French occupation of the Ruhr in 1923. But the longer view suggested that these terms would be modified. As to the territorial arrangements in Europe, they seemed to me, on the whole, to be based upon the principle of nationality, and therefore acceptable. I would have admitted that there were exceptions—the prohibition of Austrian union with Germany except by vote of the Council of the League, the incorporation in the newborn state of Czecho-Slovakia of the large German-speaking area of the Sudetenland, and the Italian occupation of the Tyrol. But at the time these did not seem to threaten peace.

What I overlooked was the climate in which the peace treaty was negotiated, a climate which little recognized the necessity for considering German pride and German feeling. The manner in which the Versailles pact was imposed on the new Reich was humiliating. The attempt to fix Germany with total responsibility for the war was bound to be resented. And the territorial terms, however judged, were not likely to be accepted if Germany regained her military power. In not taking account of this latter possibility, the peace treaty was based on sand. None of these things did I see at the time.

On the other hand, I was not captivated by the negotiation in 1928 of that extraordinary document known as the Kellogg-Briand Pact, for the outlawry of war, which was negotiated by Secretary Kellogg, and signed with great fanfare by most of the nations of the world in a great meeting at Paris in the summer of 1928. . . .

What was my own view at the time? I was, I repeat, not a bit seduced by the pact. I was far too good a Wilsonian for that. But I nourished the hope (an extravagant hope, as appeared in the sequel) that it might be the stepping stone to some closer association with the League. In part, therefore, I shared the euphoria with which this extraordinary document was surrounded. . . .

To revert to the period of the thirties, these years provide an interesting example of the way in which foreign policy is—or at any rate may be—formed in the United States. People have the idea, some people, at any rate, that the President is all-powerful. But in the first six years of the Roosevelt administration, one of the strongest of our chief executives was compelled to accept policies which he secretly deprecated, and which were contrary to his own view of the national interest. Perhaps one of the reasons why I never developed for Roosevelt the enthusiasm that I had had for Woodrow Wilson may lie in the fact that he proved so ineffectual in guiding public opinion during these years.

The story of revisionism, as it was called, has often been told, but deserves recapitulation. One of the first important books which hinted at the idea that Wilson was lured into a war which might have been avoided was C. Hartley Grattan's *When War Came*. A famous article in *Fortune* in 1934 laid the foundation for the widening belief that wicked war profiteers had had a good deal to do with American policy. An arms investigation in the Senate, headed (for reasons difficult to explain), by a North Dakota Senator, Gerald P. Nye, fed the flames of the revisionist movement, condemning Wilson for failure to observe the true principles of neutrality. A Yale law professor, Edwin Borchard, wrapped the argument in legal phraseology. And in 1935 Walter Millis, in a book disastrously well written—and therefore quite influential—presented in appealing fashion the thesis that it was all a muddle from beginning to end.

This indictment I never accepted, and do not accept today. That the history of the First World War should be rewritten was perhaps to be expected; every generation sees the problems of the past in a different perspective from that of the generation preceding. To repeat what I have already said, there is a fundamental reason for this, especially when it comes to the history of war. War is passion; it springs from passion and ends in passion. Thus it is not strange that a new generation fails to understand the emotions and the accompanying rationalizations out of which the conflict sprang. This much, it seems to me, is to be admitted.

Nonetheless, there are things strangely wrong with regard to the revisionist judgment of the war period, and of the treaty which followed it. A capital error in revisionism is the assumption that had another course been followed, a happier and better world would have resulted. To make such a judgment ought to be deemed impossible for a mind disciplined to rigorous thinking. The facts of history are far too complicated to permit *any* confident generalization as to what would have happened if that which did not happen had happened! We cannot project with mathematical certainty an alternative course of action. It is foolish to try.

How seriously the revisionist gospel affected the course of politics in the thirties it is, of course, impossible to say. It has been argued that it encouraged Hitler in his ambitious projects, giving him assurance that the United States would keep out of a world struggle. But this is by no means certain. Though sometimes ignorant of and contemptuous of American power, Hitler knew enough not to provoke the American government, and it was only with the Japanese attack on Pearl Harbor that he accepted a direct confrontation with the United States.

In the repeal of the neutrality legislation of the thirties I had a small part. But I was no militant, even in 1940 and 1941. As a teacher, as a radio commentator, by participation in such agencies as the Foreign Policy Association, I sought to do my bit to enlighten public opinion. In general I supported the Roosevelt administration in its European policy and was lukewarm in its attempts to bring pressure on Japan. With Pearl Harbor, of course, I became a complete supporter of the war.

There has been a revisionist movement with regard to the policy of Roosevelt, as there was one with regard to Wilson. It has been claimed that he wished war with Japan, and that he wilfully exposed the American fleet at Pearl. This is nonsense. Roosevelt's object was to "baby" the Japanese along. He did, indeed, give aid to the Nationalists in China, and he gradually restricted, and finally cut off aid to Nippon. In this he was propelled by public opinion. But to him the European struggle was the central matter. And rightly so. Just imagine the kind of world that would have been born if the psychopath who led the German people had attained victory, had found the secret of the bomb, and had made the whole world the object of his ruthless ambition!

I cannot say that in the period of the war I was one who foresaw the kind of world that would come after. I was overoptimistic of the possibilities of understanding with the Soviet Union. I still hoped, more than time has justified, for a major role for the United Nations. But many people felt that way. It was only with 1945 that the international climate began to change, and that there was ushered in one of the most extraordinary periods in the history of mankind. For the last quarter of a century my task, as writer and teacher, and as citizen, has been to try to describe that world, and on occasion, to add my voice to others in the formulation of policy. Twice I have been offered important posts in Washington; but always I have preferred the role which I have just described. Rightly or wrongly, my choice has always been the classroom, the press, and the forum rather than government service.

The Open Door Interpretation

WILLIAM APPLEMAN WILLIAMS

Allow me first to comment directly on the prospects of revisionism.

Go back fifty years.

You will find a youngish doctor in New Jersey who is writing poems, essays, and novels during the moments between-and-after treating his patients. One of his books is a collection of subtle Freudian commentaries on key figures in early American history; and perhaps the best of those pieces, entitled "The Virtue of History," is a revisionist interpretation of Aaron Burr.

The doctor's name is William Carlos Williams. The work is called *In the American Grain.*

Now return to the present.

Go across the river from New Jersey. There you will find an extremely talented gentleman named Gore Vidal who has platinum-plated his literary reputation by offering a brilliant revisionist novel about Aaron Burr. Mr. Vidal does not mention the once-young-and-now-dead poet in New Jersey.

So go the prospects of revisionism.

Well, not quite.

After all, Korea, Cuba, Vietnam, Cambodia, and Chile did happen. So did Jackson State and Kent State. And now we have Watergate and San Clemente, and the cruel games being played in the name of national security and the energy crisis. There is no way to deny the revisionist insight into any of those issues.

Beginning with my first appearance before this honorable trade association as a freshman PhD, I have responded to many critics in candor and in length: orally and in writing, and directly and indirectly. I have not answered others because they have been redundant or incidental; because their primary thrust has been non- or anti-intellectual; or because in general I have been more concerned with getting on with my life.

I am here today in the hope that we can open a dialogue about History, as well as about particular parts of history: a dialectic involving our different strategies of intellectual inquiry. I have chosen the idiom of confession because it offers the most direct way of confronting three important matters: acknowl-

William Appleman Williams, "Confessions of an Intransigent Revisionist," *Socialist Revolution,* 17 (1973), 89–98.

edging mistakes, bearing witness to the truth, and stating one's considered view of the world.

Having taken notes on thousands of primary and secondary documents (and during interviews with hundreds of protagonists), and having many times revised my first drafts, I assume as part of being human that I have made these kinds of mistakes:

1. I have miscopied, or incorrectly transcribed, such documents;

2. In making summaries or abstracts, I have used language that became unclear or ambivalent when I returned to my notes; and

3. I have not always perfectly transferred an initially accurate note or summary into my final draft.

I am also certain, for two reasons, that I have not corrected all those mistakes during the process of publication:

1. I respect my own typing, linotype operators, computer print-outs, and copy editors, but I also know that each make their own kind of mistakes; and that all of them make mistakes correcting mistakes (and thereby produce some very strange results).

2. I am a poor proofreader. By the time I receive galley proof (let alone page proof) I am satiated with the sight of my mind as it existed eight to twelve months earlier. I cope with that situation as I learned to deal with the blindness of the egg checker. After you have candled so many eggs, they all look good or they all look bad. So you turn the job over to someone else while you go off to plow a field, lay in the hay, or catch some catfish. But all of us are susceptible to the blindness of the egg checker—thus there are some mistakes in my work that can be interpreted by those who do not understand such human frailty as proof of crimes that never entered my head, and would in any event be utterly beyond my interest or my patience.

I have always become intellectually excited in the course of any project— researching and writing history has been one of my favorite highs. That has probably led to a higher incidence of the kind of mistakes that I have just described, and has certainly prompted me to present much of my work too cryptically. I have too often written to myself, so to speak, during moments of intellectual exhilaration.

Moving on to a different kind of mistake, and given the orthodoxy that guides this trade, I have erred in not devoting my life to one subject or to one period. Thus all that I have written is subject to modification simply because I do not know everything about everything that I have written about. I have wandered as an historian because I explored many aspects of life before I became an historian, and because I think that it is only rarely that the belated discovery of new documents revolutionizes some part of history.

Here we come in a preliminary way to the heart of the matter about re-visionism. *The revisionist is one who sees basic facts in a different way and as interconnected in new relationships.* He is a sister and a brother to those who use old steel to make a zipper, as contrasted with those who add new elements to make a better steel.

I have also mistakenly assumed that everyone engaged in the serious study of human affairs understands that the urge to power is a significant, but nonetheless routine, element of life. Hence I have considered it more important to concentrate on why individuals or groups want power, what happens when they get it and use it for their purposes, and how they respond to changes in order to keep power. It is of course important to study the special case of those who seek power for its own sake; but neither my personal nor historic experience has convinced me that mankind—and hence History—can be understood in those terms.

In a similar way, I have mistakenly assumed that we all know that some psychological orientation informs the work of every historian; but that if psychology is your thing, then you become a psychologist. I am obviously a Gestaltian who does not think that Freud or Jung or Adler wiped the slate clean of Dilthey or James—or even Marx.

I have likewise been mistaken in assuming that my personal dedication to freedom and equality *within a community* is unequivocally documented in my teaching, my writing, and in the way that I live my life. I disagree with those who assert that such a commitment can only be established by perpetual outrage against the faults of other societies. It is easy to construct an academic (even public) career by moralizing about the failures of other countries. It is also a cheap shot—*bush.* There are moments when serious protest promises consequences, and in those instants I have signed my name, written a private letter, walked the streets, or sent my money.

But whether I am writing about American History, or trying as a citizen to change America, I must first understand America. And I confess that in my lifetime—from the Great Depression to Watergate—that task has absorbed most of my intelligence, my guts, and my energy. I do not approve of imperial actions by Russia *or* by Israel, and I do not approve of repression in Brazil *or* in France; but most of all I like them least by and in my own America.

Finally, I am sure that I am mistaken, *within my chosen framework,* in some of my reconstructions, analyses, and interpretations. I take it as given that most of you who look at the world from another perspective think that I am mostly wrong. Neither truth traumatizes my ego. I learned a lifetime ago that I could not sink every shot or make every finesse, read every book in every library, memorize every document in every archive, or answer every question that I asked myself in the first light of dawn to the satisfaction of myself—let alone to the plaudits of everyone else.

Yet, granted such mistakes, and speaking very softly, I confess that I must say these things:

1. I do not think that my mistakes subvert the value of my work;
2. My critics have yet to respond to fundamental issues that I have raised; and
3. I am sure that a number of my reconstructions, analyses, and interpreta-

tions—granted their weaknesses—have informed and challenged your minds. I never entertained the slightest thought of doing more.

Here permit me to be blunt.

1. I have never engaged in an intellectual conspiracy.
2. I have never wilfully distorted a document.
3. I have never invented evidence.
4. I have protected the confidentiality of primary sources in the United States, Russia, England, and Cuba. I will continue to protect them until they choose to enter the public arena with their information. . . .

Here we confront the central questions: how one perceives the evidence, and how one presents one's perceptions. For the primary issue between me as a revisionist and my serious critics involves our different theories of knowledge—our antithetical conceptions of reality. An honest and potentially creative conflict.

I came to History after ten years of sustained involvement in mathematics and the physical sciences. That education and experience inherently included the serious study of such giants as Aristotle, Descartes, Spinoza, Leibniz, Kant, Whitehead, and Russell. Confronted with such conflicting theories of knowledge, I was inexorably drawn into the process of choosing how I would make sense of the world.

Surprising as it may seem, I did not follow Descartes into a universe composed of discrete positivistic and atomistic elements sometimes connected to each other in a mechanistic fashion. Instead, I chose Spinoza. I thought he was far more realistic in positing one organic world in which seemingly separate parts are in reality always internally related to each other; a universe in which an ostensibly positivistic fact is in truth a set of relationships with all other facts and therefore with the whole.

From the moment I encountered him, therefore, I responded to Marx. For, despite his extensive empirical research, which gives him the appearance of being a super-positivist, I recognized him as a fellow Spinozian. Hence I read him then, as I read him now, as a genius in social history and political economy—and not at all as an early computer offering the date for the birth of Utopia.

I remain exhilarated by his capacity for seeing in one piece of evidence a set of relationships that reveal an economic truth, a truth about an idea, a social verity, and a political truth. I also think that there is more psychological insight in his analysis of our alienation from our Humanity under western capitalism than there is in all but a one-foot shelf of contemporary psychohistory.

Spinoza and Marx proceed from the assumption that everything is internally related to everything else. Thus the problem is not whether or how a may be related to d or p or v, but instead the question of how a and d and p and v reveal as microcosms the nature of the macrocosm. Or, conversely, how the macrocosm reveals the character of a and d and p and v. Reality is not an issue of economics versus ideas, or of politics versus either; it is not even defined by coefficients of correlation between voting records and geographic location, or by a mathematical model that proves that what was done was wrong. Reality instead involves how a political act is also an economic act, of how an economic decision is a political choice, or of how an idea of freedom involves a commitment to a particular economic system. Lukács said it all in three sentences.

> It is not the primacy of economic motives in historical explanation that constitutes the decisive difference between Marxism and bourgeois thought, but the point of view of totality. Whatever the subject of debate, the dialectical method is concerned always with the same problem: knowledge of historical process in its entirety. This means that "ideological" and "economic" problems lose their mutual exclusiveness and merge into one another.

Granted all that, my confidence in the Spinozian-Marxian strategy of intellectual inquiry was severely tested by Fred Harvey Harrington. He pushed the positivistic, interest-group approach to its furthest limits. He could dissect any decision, event, or movement into its constituent parts with a subtle, loving ruthlessness that earned him the nicknames of Mr. Cold, and The Fish Eye. And he understood the techniques of quantification and statistical correlation, though he chose to translate them into the King's English.

After a time, however, the mathematician in me realized that neither he nor anyone else of his persuasion had developed either a scale for weighting the various atomistic factors, or a system of differential equations that could reintegrate the parts into the whole. In the usual course of events, that is to say, discrete atomism, or sophisticated scientism, does nothing more than turn Carl Becker on his head: every historian becomes his own man, and hence there is no dialectical encounter between theories of knowledge. There is only an endless argument about which factor is most important—or endless evasion in the name of multiple causation.

At this point, Hans Gerth took me by the hand. As a brilliant (though neglected) member of the Frankfurt School, he teased and pushed me into a confrontation with the central problem: how does an historian hone the Spinozian-Marxian theory of reality into a manageable intellectual tool? Which is to say: who mediates between our ordinary selves and genius?

Guided by Gerth, I became deeply involved with Hegel, Dilthey, Adorno, Horkheimer, and Lukács. I enjoyed the ensuing dialectical tension: that coming apart at the seams at midnight, and then the stitching it back together in a sentence or two at 3 A.M. Dilthey ultimately taught me the concept of *Weltanschauungen,* the sense of three dialectically interacting world views: a workable version of Spinoza's organic reality, and a realistic limit on relativism.

Foreign relations seemed to offer the most promising arena for the deployment of that intellectual strategy. Indeed, if there is a Spinozian whole for an historian, then it has to involve foreign policy and the periodization of history. My first book was the result of an effort to lay an empirical foundation for developing a set of internal relations that would make it possible to conceptualize the organic sense of reality entertained by American policy-makers (and, by indirection, by the American body politic). I chose relations with Russia because it struck me that such a *Weltanschauung* was apt to reveal itself with particular clarity during a confrontation with a different view of the world.

Out of that effort came my concept of Open Door Imperialism as the *Weltanschauung* of twentieth-century American foreign policy. I began with three atomistic documents: Secretary of State Hay's circular letters of September 6, 1899, and July 3, 1900, and his note to the Germans of October 29, 1900. I next conceptualized those documents as the basic formulation of a general outlook that was amplified and applied to other areas of the world, as in Secretary of State Root's instructions of November 28, 1905, to the American delegation to the Algeciras Conference.

I concluded, at the end of that intellectual voyage, that the Open Door Policy was a vast network of internal relations in the sense meant by Spinoza and Marx—and therefore a *Weltanschauung* in the sense meant by Dilthey. Viewed in that way, it is a conception of reality that integrates economic theory and practice, abstract ideas, past, present and future politics, anticipations of Utopia, messianic idealism, social-psychological imperatives, historical consciousness, and military strategy.

As formulated by the protagonists at the turn of the century, the *Weltanschauung* of the Open Door was an integrated set of assumptions that guided elitist *and* popular thinking (and responses), and that defined bureaucratic perceptions and actions. It then became an ideology (even theology), and ultimately a reification of reality that is finally being subverted by a new reality.

It is so easy to illustrate this with the likes of Hay, Conant, Root, Wilson, Culbertson, Hughes, Hull, and Stimson that the challenge lies with those like Hoover and Acheson. Hoover is fascinating because of his instinct to transcend the orthodoxy. Acheson is particularly revealing because he crystallized the discussion of the 1890s in his 1944 testimony before the congressional committee on postwar planning and policy.

To avoid "a very bad time," Acheson warned, meaning "the most far-reaching consequences upon our economic and social system," "you must look to foreign markets." True, "you could probably fix it so that everything produced here would be consumed here, but that would completely change our Constitution, our relations to property, to human liberty, our very conceptions of law. And nobody contemplates that. Therefore, you find you must look to other markets and those markets are abroad. . . ."

The issue here is not economic motives, and certainly not the kind of economic determinism that Marx would have scorned as absurdly simplistic. The first point is the network of internal relationships in Acheson's mind between foreign markets and everything that he treasures. Or, conversely, the inability to imagine freedom and welfare in a non-capitalistic framework. Secondly, we have a conception of markets that involves American predominance. That is not trade in the classic sense of give-and-take. It is the imperial dynamic of we need, you give.

Having crystallized, Acheson began to reify. As in National Security Council Document No. 68: freedom and welfare can be secured only through "the virtual abandonment by the United States of trying to distinguish between national and global security." And then the ultimate distillation: "We are willing to help people who believe the way we do, to continue to live the way they want to live." Acheson was not present at the creation of a policy—he merely presided over the reification of a *Weltanschauung*.

All of which brings me back to Spinoza. Acheson provides us with a fact that contains the whole, and a whole that contains every fact. So if I condense the evidence about Russian policy on reparations at Potsdam into one introductory paragraph that summarizes Moscow's comments of earlier years, and at the same time provides a preview of the Kremlin's final posture, I have not distorted history. I have done my best to encapsulate the history that I then explore: that is the definition of an essay.

Just as when I seem redundant in *The Roots of the Modern American Empire,* it is because I am trying to explore and reveal all the internal relationships that give meaning to a group of positivistic facts.

Ah, so.

I make my final confession. I have fallen between upteen stools. So be it. All I can do is to echo Wright Morris: *What A Way To Go!*

But, in a final effort to explicate the text, let me offer you a proposition taken from William Carlos Williams' essay on Aaron Burr.

> Near the end of his life a lady said to him: "Colonel, I wonder if you were ever the gay Lothario they say you were." The old man turned his eyes, their lustre still undiminished, toward the lady—and lifting his trembling finger said in his quiet, impressive whisper: "They say, they say, they say. Ah, my child, how long are you going to continue to use those dreadful words? Those two little words have done more harm than all others. Never use them, my dear, never use them."

That is why, warts and all, I remain, faithfully yours, an intransigent revisionist.

Bibliographical Note

This has been an excursion rather than a monograph. Hence my sources are designed to take you along the same great circle route. Or, in other words, a Bowditch for this voyage.

A. G. A. Balz: *Idea and Essence in the Philosophy of Hobbes and Spinoza.*

K. E. Boulding: *The Image, Knowledge in Life and Society.*

Wilhelm Dilthey: *The Essence of Philosophy.* Translated into English by S. A. Emery and W. T. Emery.

H. F. Hallett: *Benedict De Spinoza: The Elements of His Philosophy.*

H. A. Hodges: *The Philosophy of Wilhelm Dilthey.*

M. Jay: *The Dialectical Imagination: A History of the Frankfurt School and the Institute of Social Research, 1932–1950.*

W. Kluback and M. Weinbarum: *Dilthey's Philosophy of Existence: Introduction to* Weltanschauungslehre.

G. Lukács: *History and Class Consciousness.*

K. Müller-Vollmer: *Towards a Phenomenological Theory of Literature: A Study of Wilhelm Dilthey's* Poetik.

B. Ollman: *Alienation: Marx's Conception of Man in Capitalist Society.*

G. H. R. Parkinson: *Logic and Reality in Leibniz's Metaphysics.*

L. Roth: *Spinoza;* and *Spinoza, Descartes, and Maimonides.*

B. Russell: *A Critical Exposition of the Philosophy of Leibniz.*

FURTHER READING

Thomas A. Bailey, "Confessions of a Diplomatic Historian," *Society for Historians of American Foreign Relations Newsletter,* 6 (1975), 2–11

Barton J. Bernstein, ed., *Towards a New Past* (1968)

Warren I. Cohen, *The Revisionists* (1967)

Marcus Cunliffe and Robin Winks, eds., *Pastmasters: Some Essays on American Historians* (1969)

Simon G. Hanson, "Dexter Perkins on the Caribbean," *Inter-American Economic Affairs,* 1 (1948), 46–54

John Higham, "The Cult of the 'American Consensus': Homogenizing Our History," *Commentary,* 27 (1959), 93–100

John Higham, *History* (1965)

Lester Langley, "The Diplomatic Historians: Bailey and Bemis," *History Teacher,* 6 (1972), 51–70

Richard W. Leopold, "The History of United States Foreign Policy," in Charles F. Delzell, ed., *The Future of History* (1976)

Francis L. Loewenheim, ed., *The Historian and the Diplomat* (1967)

Thomas J. McCormick, "The State of American Diplomatic History," in Herbert J. Bass, ed., *The State of American History* (1970)

Thomas G. Paterson, J. Garry Clifford, and Kenneth J. Hagan, *American Foreign Policy: A History* (1977)

Dexter Perkins, "American Foreign Policy and Its Critics," in Alfred H. Kelley, ed., *American Foreign Policy and American Democracy* (1954)

J. A. Thompson, "William Appleman Williams and the 'American Empire,'" *Journal of American Studies,* 7 (1973), 91–104

Robert W. Tucker, *The Radical Left and American Foreign Policy* (1971)

Arthur P. Whitaker, "Aren't We All Revisionists," *Society for Historians of American Foreign Relations Newsletter,* 4 (1973), 2–10

William A. Williams, *The Great Evasion* (1968)

William A. Williams, *History as a Way of Learning* (1973)

2

Public Opinion and Foreign Policy

How *American foreign policy is formulated and administered, argue some scholars, may be as important as* why *the United States pursues the diplomatic course it does. Within the checks-and-balances system of the national government, the President, the Senate, and the House of Representatives hold constitutional responsibilities in foreign affairs and vie with one another to mold foreign policy. Within the executive branch, different agencies and departments traditionally have competed to shape policy. Outside the government, interest groups representing business, labor, religious societies, and ethnic communities, among others, have attempted to exert influence on the making of foreign policy.*

And there is the general electorate's public opinion, seemingly omnipresent and frequently mentioned as a force controlling the content and conduct of American diplomacy. A common assumption in the United States has been that the public can hold elected officials accountable for their decisions and that the moods and desires of the masses, sometimes whimsical and fickle, compel officials to act in ways they would not otherwise have acted.

ESSAYS

Thomas A. Bailey, professor emeritus at Stanford University, emphasizes the importance of public opinion in his *The Man in the Street* (1948), from which the first essay is selected. A more recent study, by political scientist Bernard C. Cohen of Princeton University, challenges the thesis that foreign policy has been significantly molded by public opinion. They both raise basic questions: What is public opinion?

How is it measured? How does it influence foreign relations? And, historically, how important has it been?

The Foundation Stone

THOMAS A. BAILEY

Nero murdered his mother and his divorced wife and did many other diabolical deeds with complete impunity, but he was forced to give up his ambition to become an actor when the Roman populace reacted unfavorably to his efforts. The Pharisees attempted to lay unfriendly hands on the Apostles, but they were compelled to desist when an angry murmur rose from the multitude. These are but two early examples, and by no means the earliest ones, of the sovereign power of an aroused public.

The British economist John Stuart Mill, writing in 1859 on liberty, concluded: "In politics it is almost a triviality to say that public opinion now rules the world." A year earlier Abraham Lincoln, debating with Senator Douglas on the issue of limiting slavery, declared: "With public sentiment on its side, everything succeeds; with public sentiment against it, nothing succeeds." And a dozen years later Charles Dudley Warner, perhaps with tongue in cheek, opined: "Public opinion is stronger than the Legislature, and nearly as strong as the Ten Commandments." Actually, it is often stronger than the Ten Commandments.

All governments, whatever their nature, rest on the foundation stone of public opinion. The Scottish philosopher David Hume observed as long ago as 1741: "As force is always on the side of the governed, the governors have nothing to support them but opinion." The yellowing scroll of history reveals few if any instances when a ruler flagrantly and persistently defied the will of his subjects without courting disaster. Even dictators are keenly aware of their servitude to public opinion, and this explains why they are at such pains to propagandize their people into supporting arbitrary rule. Hitler had to deceive the German nation through Dr. Goebbels' lie factory, and Mussolini and Stalin and other dictators of recent vintage had to employ similar chicanery. Censorship and propaganda are the unconscious compliments that despots pay to the potency of public opinion.

All this seems like an attempt to prove the obvious, but the truth is that millions of people are still unconvinced. Public opinion is so apathetic and preoccupied, so changeful and impulsive, so ill-informed and misinformed, that critics are apt to sneer at its power. Yet a giant who is fickle and ignorant still has a giant's strength, and may use it with frightful effect.

Another source of skepticism is that public opinion is awkward to describe, elusive to define, difficult to measure, and impossible to see, even

Thomas A. Bailey, *The Man in the Street: The Impact of American Public Opinion on Foreign Policy* (New York: Macmillan Co., 1948), pp. 1–5, 7–10, 11–13, 130–131.

though it may be felt. James Russell Lowell once remarked that popular sentiment was like the pressure of the atmosphere: one could not see it but "all
the same, it is sixteen pounds to the square inch." The British Foreign Secretary Sir Samuel Hoare had never seen public opinion when, in 1935, he plotted
with the French premier to sacrifice Ethiopia on the altar of Italy's imperial
ambitions. But when the backfire of public resentment blew him out of office,
he could not deny its force. An angered electorate is an awesome thing.

In a dictatorship, the masses must be deceived; in a democracy, they must
be educated. In either case, they must be courted if public programs are to
be carried through. If Mr. Average American wants to get a glimpse at the
power behind the officeholder's chair, all he has to do is pick up a mirror and
look into it.

The most powerful nation in the world today is the United States, and consequently the most powerful body of public opinion in existence is formed
by the American people. What the government in Washington does or fails
to do in the field of foreign affairs will depend largely on the wishes of our
citizens, and what our citizens demand or fail to demand will affect mightily
the destiny of this planet.

A vexatious problem here at home, such as housing or unemployment,
touches the Man in the Street more immediately than one abroad. For this
reason there is normally much more popular pressure on Washington for
action regarding internal affairs than foreign affairs.

The sovereign American people may influence their government either
positively or negatively. The classic example of positive action may be found
in 1898, when the masses rose and cried out for war against Spain with such
overwhelming insistence that the amiable McKinley dared not deny their
demands.

Negative pressure is much less obvious but no less potent. Fear as to how
the people may react has often caused the President and the State Department to recoil from a contemplated course. When the United States minister
in Mexico City, James Gadsden, was negotiating in 1853 for the strip of
southwestern territory that bears his name, he suggested that the State Department supply him with money for bribing certain Mexican officials. He
was informed from Washington that such funds could be provided only by
Congressional action, and that the resulting stench would be undesirable.
Similarly, the ingrained distrust of the average American for entangling alliances, combined with his hereditary dislike of England, has repeatedly caused
the State Department to draw back from a closer understanding with Downing
Street, lest the news leak out and recoil disastrously upon the administration.

The Harding landslide of 1920 was falsely interpreted as a tremendous
mandate against the League of Nations, and Republican administrations for
the next decade, paralyzed by their prodigious plurality of 7,000,000 votes,
shunned the League as they would a leper. The cautious Republican politician would invite no similar rebuke from a presumably wrathful electorate.

By the early 1930's it was clear to all discerning students of finance that
the debts owed us by our associates in World War I were uncollectible. The

alternatives were cancellation or just not getting the money. But the almighty taxpayer, knowing that he would have to foot the bill in either case, bristled up at the slightest suggestion of cancellation. The officials in Washington had to keep crying for the moon, many of them knowing perfectly well they were crying uselessly, except in so far as they were usefully placating the public.

How does the citizen actually exert pressure on his government? He may send letters, telegrams, and petitions to his congressman, his senator, or his President, but his most formidable bludgeon is the ballot. As Oliver Wendell Holmes put it,

> The freeman, casting with unpurchased hand
> The vote that shakes the turret of the land.

The President fears the electorate, although he may not respect it. He is the head of a great political party first; the director of foreign affairs second or perhaps third. With a natural desire for the endorsement of reelection, he is bedeviled by his eligibility for a second term and, in the days of Franklin Roosevelt, for a third and a fourth. If he offends or defies the voter, he may be repudiated at the polls.

A war with France in 1800 would have been good for the party but bad for the country, and President John Adams, courageously ignoring the clamor of the crowd for blood, patched up existing disputes and gave the nation peace. He suspected that he was committing political suicide when he boldly put patriotism above party, and the event proved him correct. He was defeated for reelection in 1800, and never thereafter held public office. A century later, in 1898, war with Spain over Cuba was good for the party but bad for the country. President McKinley, yielding to the clamor of the crowd for blood, gave the country war. He was triumphantly reelected in 1900. In all fairness it must be added that the two cases are only roughly parallel, but in each instance there was tremendous pressure from the mob and an awareness in the White House of the political penalties and preferments involved. Someone has urged that we award medals to public servants who show courage above and beyond the call of politics.

Even if the President does not care about his own personal fortunes, as Cleveland notoriously did not, he cannot without the basest ingratitude be indifferent to the fortunes of the party that gave him immortality. Scores of Congressmen and other elected officials ride into office on the coattails of a popular President, and their careers are jeopardized if their titular leader needlessly antagonizes the ballot casters.

The Chief Executive is usually more exposed to public pressure regarding major issues of foreign policy than is the Congress and the State Department. He is one; they are many, and some of them are entrenched behind bureaucratic barriers. His name and White House residence are well known, and the ordinary voter can easily send him a postal card, a letter, or a telegram. The names of the bureaucrats may not be known, and their addresses present difficulties. The President is elected every four years; the bureaucrats often have life tenure under civil service. The pressure may therefore converge upon the Executive Mansion with fearful force, as was notably true when McKinley had to take sleeping powders while pondering the fateful decision of war or peace with Spain.

A Frenchman in the days of the Revolution is supposed to have dashed to his window, when he heard the mob go roaring by, and to have cried: "There go my followers. I must follow them. I am their leader." Like this legendary Frenchman, the President must seem to follow public opinion, or at least not get too far out in front of it, for he will then be sniped at from the rear. Franklin Roosevelt's Quarantine Speech of 1937, defiantly delivered in the isolationist capital of America (Chicago), evoked such an uproar from the noninterventionist camp as to force a hasty retreat.

One British statesman, so it is said, would have made fewer political blunders "if he had only ridden more in omnibuses." The President does not ride the busses at all, and if the people have not indicated their desires, he must anticipate their reaction to his moves. His touch must be sure, for if he guesses wrong, his political life may be forfeited. Franklin Roosevelt had no directive from the American public when in 1938 he boldly declared at Kingston, Ontario, that the United States would help defend Canada against foreign invasion; nor when in the pre–Pearl Harbor days of 1941 he dramatically took over the defense of Iceland from Great Britain. But both of these strokes were aimed at the security of the United States, and the President assumed that the American people would support him, as the Gallup polls later revealed that they did in overwhelming measure. Roosevelt was a successful leader because he was generally clever enough to lead in a direction where the masses were willing to go.

The State Department likewise fears the hands that cast the ballots. If it blunders, the administration may be swept out, including the Secretary of State and other top men in the Department.

William H. Seward, who served with distinction during the Civil War, was the first Secretary of State to conduct foreign relations with a keen eye to the necessity of informing and placating public opinion. He published diplomatic papers with unusual frequency, and inaugurated the annual series of official documents which for recency and completeness far surpasses anything put out by other foreign offices. His master stroke came in 1861 with the handling of the *Trent* affair. The United States naval officer who seized two Confederate commissioners from the British mail steamer *Trent* was clearly in the wrong, but his bold wrenching of the lion's tail was ecstatically popular in the North. The Lincoln administration dared not keep the prisoners, lest England declare war; it was unwilling to turn them loose, lest the populace get out of hand. But after passions had cooled, the Confederate envoys could be released, and public opinion was to some extent mollified when in a clever note Seward congratulated the British on having finally accepted the principles for which we had vainly fought them in 1812. Seward's specious discourse was clearly more of a sop to public opinion than a contribution to international law.

The Secretary of State and his associates need to know at all times what the public is thinking, for a policy cooked up in a closet and served suddenly to the people will often produce indigestion, mild or acute. The Department acknowledged the need of entering into more satisfactory diplomatic relations with the American masses when in 1944 it set up the Division of Public Liaison, which analyzes opinion polls, newspaper editorials, Congressional debates and other indexes of popular thinking. The policy officers of the State Department, rather than make a decision blindly, have on occasion arranged for confidential public opinion polls. The precaution is a wise one, for Congress, responding to the outraged voter, may cripple the Department by slashing the annual appropriation.

The average citizen, instead of complaining that the State Department has no policy, could better say: "Let's give the Department a policy." Public pressure can force a policy upon an unwilling administration, as was true of the neutrality legislation of the 1930's, but the administration can hardly force a major policy upon an unwilling people, as Franklin Roosevelt attempted to do in his Quarantine Speech. When there is a strong and articulate public opinion, the Department may move with the assurance that it will not be left out on the end of a limb. When opinion is confused, or when the issue is minor and no public opinion exists regarding it, the Department must make its decisions more or less blindly, and on a guess-and-pray basis. These are the occasions when it has the greatest latitude, and some seemingly minor decisions, regarding which the people were apathetic, have drawn us deeper and deeper into the international quicksands. Commitments in the 1940's to support the Nationalist government of China against the Communists, while fraught with grave dangers, passed virtually unnoticed in the United States. . . .

A purposeful public has on numerous occasions actually forced the President and the State Department to move, sometimes against their better judgment.

In 1803 a rising tide of Western resentment over the closure of the Mississippi prodded President Jefferson into a course that led to the purchase of Louisiana. In 1809, with public opinion so hostile that the very foundations of government trembled, Jefferson was forced to bring about a repeal of the embargo on shipping. In 1854 an enraged North halted the pro-Southern President Pierce in his design to wrest Cuba from the palsied grasp of Spain. In 1893 an aroused nation compelled Cleveland to abandon his plans to restore the dusky Hawaiian queen to her throne. In 1898 the war-mad masses forced the nation into an unnecessary clash with Spain, in spite of McKinley, Mark Hanna, and Big Business. (It was a victory for Main Street rather than Wall Street.) In 1921 a determined citizenry insisted upon the Washington Disarmament Conference, for which a lackadaisical President Harding received more than his just share of praise. In 1928 an organized and inspired public kicked Secretary Kellogg into immortality by forcing him to negotiate the Kellogg-Briand pact, for which at the outset he revealed little enthusiasm but for which he ultimately received the Nobel Peace Prize.

During the years from 1935 to 1937, a peace-obsessed public opinion drove through Congress and foisted upon the administration "permanent" neutrality legislation, as though one could legislate permanence in a world of change. In 1943, when Franklin Roosevelt shamelessly rewarded the Tammany politician "Ed" Flynn with the nomination of minister to Australia, a scandalized public, usually indifferent to such plum passing, compelled a withdrawal of the appointment. Australia, then defended by American boys and facing a Japanese invasion, was much too vital to be used as a political football; besides, many citizens confused Mr. Flynn with the actor of that name, whose alleged amours were enlivening the headlines of a prurient press.

The sovereign voter may not only compel his elected servants to do his bidding, but by defying his own government he may turn laws and treaties into dead letters, with consequent international friction.

Certain parts of the treaty of peace with England in 1783, specifically those having to do with debts and loyalists, were so unpopular in some sections of the country that they were openly nullified. During the Texas revolution of 1835–1836, the Canadian rebellion of 1837, and the Irish-Fenian invasions of Canada in the 1860's and 1870's, public sympathy was so overwhelmingly favorable to the rebels that the federal officials found it difficult or impossible to enforce the neutrality laws. In some instances government agents brazenly joined with the revolutionists in violating the statutes which they had sworn to uphold. The mid-century American filibustering expeditions, notably those of López in Cuba and Walker in Central America, were warmly applauded in the expansionist and slave-holding South, so much so that the federal officials were unable to secure juries that would convict even the most flagrant violators of our national laws. A half-century later the people of the Pacific Coast, determined to hold the dike against an Oriental inundation, deliberately flouted the treaties and statutes of the United States so as to compel the Washington government to adopt exclusion.

The force of American opinion is felt not only at home but abroad. Foreign statesmen study our national crosscurrents with meticulous care, and not infrequently shorten sail rather than risk shipwreck.

The explosive rising of the Westerners in 1803 against the Spanish and French was not lost on Paris when Napoleon sold us Louisiana. American wrath in 1844 over British machinations in Texas was a clear storm warning that Downing Street had better go more slowly. The swelling demand to throw the French out of Mexico in 1867 presumably hastened their going; and the uproar against German brutality during the Venezuela intervention of 1902 certainly had a similar result. The British whitened their blacklist of American firms in 1916 when they saw how offensive it was to us, and they came to terms with Ireland in 1921 partly, although not primarily, out of a desire to reduce the chronic inflammation of Anglo-American relations resulting from the Irish problem.

World War II came to an end with the American people quite favorably disposed to cooperation with the Soviet Union. But the Kremlin, either not recognizing the importance of American public opinion or not understanding how to deal with it, or possibly both, doggedly pursued a course which rapidly alienated American sympathy. President Truman's sensational proposal, in March, 1947, for support of Greece and Turkey received strong public backing, and the nation embarked upon a course which seemed inimical to the interests of the Soviets and possibly to the cause of world peace.

The President and the State Department have on occasion disregarded or even defied a strong majority opinion, but not frequently, and then not too openly. Such defiance is easier in war time, for the government can then hide behind the shield of secrecy. During World War II our continued relations with Fascist-tainted Vichy France, to say nothing of other dubious dealings, were highly unpopular among American liberals. But Washington apologized for these disturbing bedfellows by pleading military necessity, and as a consequence our people were more tolerant than they otherwise would have been.

If the public is rather evenly divided on a given issue, the government may occasionally support what appears to be a minority group. When President Washington angered the pro-French faction in America by issuing his neutrality proclamation in 1793, and when he infuriated the same partisans by sponsoring John Jay's unpopular treaty with Britain in 1795, he may have sided with the minority, but in any event the issue was close and the clatter great. The earlier incident, so Mark Sullivan surmises, inspired Kipling's immortal "If."

When the American people favor a proposed step by a large majority, but with only weak intensity, they may be disregarded by the State Department with relative impunity. After the Sino-Japanese "incident" flared forth in 1937, American sentiment promptly sided with underdog China, although there was a vast amount of indifference. But by 1939, when the issues had sharpened, the opinion polls showed that our people were only 2 per cent pro-Japanese while 74 per cent pro-Chinese. By 1940 the nation was 90 per cent favorable to an embargo on munitions for the Japanese aggressors.

This overwhelming display of solicitude did not stampede the Roosevelt administration, which stubbornly declined to halt the flow of war materials to Japan until three full years after the Marco Polo Bridge incident. The President reasoned that an invocation of the Neutrality Act of 1937 would cut off munitions from both Japan and China, and we wanted China to get her trickle. Also, as was later revealed, Roosevelt feared that strong measures against Japan would drive her into a premature descent upon the Dutch East Indies. . . .

The dangers of flying in the face of public opinion are so apparent that in time of crisis the administration is strongly tempted to resort to deception rather than to defiance.

Some deception is comparatively harmless. When President Madison, in his message to Congress in 1815, congratulated the nation (and incidentally his own administration) on its glorious prosecution of the inglorious War of 1812, he was merely glossing over one of the most disgraceful episodes in our history. When Secretary Marcy in 1855 deliberately deleted damaging passages from his published correspondence describing the attempt to grab Cuba, he was merely trying to whiten his name with posterity, which he succeeded in doing until 1928, at which time a lynx-eyed scholar sharply blackened it. When President Wilson told an inquisitorial Senate committee in 1919 that he had never heard of the notorious secret treaties before reaching the Paris conference, he was presumably trying to smooth the path for the ratification of the Treaty of Versailles. Presidents have claimed achievements for themselves, such as the results of disarmament conferences, which a candid examination of the facts would not support. Theodore Roosevelt was a past master at leading and misleading public opinion by magnifying minor issues and minifying major ones. But such episodes were usually political gestures, designed to make or at least to save votes.

More serious was the deception practiced by President Polk in 1846. He ordered an armed detachment into an area in southern Texas to which the Texans had a highly debatable claim. The Mexicans were provoked into an attack, as Polk expected and rather hoped they would be, and then he triumphantly announced that "American blood" had been shed on "American soil." The people of the United States, even those of the opposition Whig party, arose to avenge this wanton assault, and we were off for the Halls of the Montezumas. Crude young Representative Abraham Lincoln repeatedly taunted the President for this fraud; he wanted to know the exact spot on *American* soil where blood had been shed. If Polk had been writing history instead of making it, he would have said that the Mexican troops were goaded into shedding the blood of those whom they regarded as invaders of their soil. This would have been a good deal nearer the truth than his wordy misrepresentation.

Franklin Roosevelt repeatedly deceived the American people during the period before Pearl Harbor. When he warned them against the aggressors, he was branded a sensationalist. When he pointed to the perils of storm-cellar neutrality, he was branded an interventionist. When he urged adequate armaments, he was branded a warmonger. He was faced with a terrible trilemma. If he let the people slumber in a fog of isolation, they might well fall prey to Hitler. If he came out unequivocally for intervention, he would be defeated in 1940, or shelved for a candidate more willing to let the masses enjoy their fool's paradise. If he was going to induce the people to move at all, he would have to trick them into acting for their best interests, or what he conceived to be their best interests. He was like the physician who must tell the patient lies for the patient's own good. Congresswoman Clare Boothe Luce missed the point entirely when she violently charged, in the campaign of 1944, that Roosevelt "lied us into a war because he did not have the political courage to lead us into it." The latter course would have been foolhardy rather than courageous. The country was overwhelmingly noninterventionist to the very day of Pearl Harbor, and an overt attempt to lead the people into war would have resulted in certain failure and an almost certain ousting of Roosevelt in 1940, with a consequent defeat for his ultimate aims.

The embattled democracies in 1939 needed our munitions, and it was to our interests as well as theirs to lift the arms embargo. In a memorable message to the special session of Congress, Franklin Roosevelt urged that we return to international law, though actually we had never abandoned it: the arms embargo was purely domestic legislation. He dramatically declared that the embargo policy of Jefferson's day had resulted in the burning of the predecessor of the Capitol building from which he was then speaking, though actually the embargo-nonintercourse policy of that time came within a few days of preventing war. Like Polk in 1846, Roosevelt was making history rather than writing it, and he was doing it effectively. Dr. Gallup found a sharp increase of five points in the majority sentiment for lifting the arms embargo following the President's appearance before Congress.

Roosevelt's spectacular transfer of fifty overage United States destroyers to the British, in September, 1940, was difficult to defend on any legal grounds, but Attorney General Jackson dutifully built up a case, much of which hinged on the placement of a comma in the relevant federal statute. The destroyer deal, to say nothing of other acts of unneutrality, was further defended by a shyster-like appeal to an international law that had largely been trampled to death under the hobnailed boots of the belligerents. When the Lend-Lease Act was being debated in 1941, its foes insisted that the munitions would have to be convoyed and convoy would mean war. But the specter of convoy was then unpopular, and administration spokesmen brushed it aside: one thing at a time. Thus sympathy for the democracies led to Lend-Lease, Lend-Lease led to convoy, convoy led to shooting, and shooting led to war.

The noninterventionists cried out against war, and because they were in a strong majority some color of legality had to be found for every questionable step that was taken. Lend-Lease almost certainly would not have been passed, at least not as it was and when it was, if the people could have foreseen that the scheme would lead so inexorably to hostilities. After the bill was safely approved, Roosevelt himself quietly issued the orders to convoy.

The President was also anxious to make it appear, again with the isolationist masses in view, that the aggression was coming from Germany. After a U-boat had fired two torpedoes at the United States destroyer *Greer,* Roosevelt went on the air and declared that henceforth the Navy would repel the piratical acts of these seagoing "rattlesnakes" and defend freedom of the seas by firing first. (Actually, freedom of the seas in the American tradition was not involved at all.) Again Roosevelt's dramatic methods brought results; Dr. Gallup found a strong majority in favor of shoot-at-sight. Yet more than a month after the event the Navy Department revealed that the *Greer* had been trailing the U-boat for three and one-half hours and broadcasting the latter's position to nearby British destroyers when the submarine turned and attacked.

Roosevelt either knew these facts or he did not know them. If he knew them, he deliberately deceived the American people; if he did not, he handled a critical situation with inexcusable precipitancy.

A president who cannot entrust the people with the truth betrays a certain lack of faith in the basic tenets of democracy. But because the masses are notoriously shortsighted, and generally cannot see danger until it is at their throats, our statesmen are forced to deceive them into an awareness of their own long-run interests. This is clearly what Roosevelt had to do, and who shall say that posterity will not thank him for it?

Deception of the people may in fact become increasingly necessary, unless we are willing to give our leaders in Washington a freer hand. In the days of the horse and buggy we could jog along behind our billowy barriers with relative impunity, but in the days of the atomic bomb we may have to move more rapidly than a lumbering public opinion will permit. Just as the yielding of some of our national sovereignty is the price that we must pay for effective international organization, so the yielding of some of our democratic control of foreign affairs is the price that we may have to pay for greater physical security. . . .

An appalling ignorance of foreign affairs is one of the most striking and dangerous defects of American public opinion. This is not to say that we are thick-witted; there is a world of difference between a stupid person and an uninformed one. Even the most brilliant scholars must necessarily be ignorant of a vast body of knowledge.

The American people have informed themselves very creditably on a number of complex questions, *once their interest was aroused*. The heated nationwide debates on imperialism in the 1890's, on the League of Nations in 1919–1920, on the neutrality issues of the 1930's, on the repeal of the arms embargo in 1939, and on Lend-Lease in 1941, while bringing out specious as well as valid arguments, on the whole gave encouragement to those who have faith in the democratic ideal. But we seldom become aroused to this high pitch, and largely because we are uninterested we lack information. The journalist Raymond Clapper used to say: "Never overestimate the people's knowledge, nor underestimate their intelligence."

As a nation we may be reasonably well informed, yet we are not well enough informed to exercise understandingly our present direct and hence dangerous control of foreign affairs. For many years the average citizen has passed judgment on, and exercised pressure regarding, knotty problems of international law upon which not even the ablest international lawyers could agree. Questions of blockade and maritime rights, which figured so prominently in our history during the nineteenth century, baffled both the jurists of that time and the historians of a later generation. But this did not prevent the layman from expressing his judgment with great vigor, often substituting emotion for reason. A true patriot has been aptly defined as one who is unable to wait for the facts. Sanity indeed receives a setback when interpretations of treaty obligations and international law fall into the hands of the mob.

The same danger is no less evident in international trade and finance. Even if the average citizen had the incentive to make a profound study of these subjects, his intellectual capacity and training are not equal to mastering the intricacies of international exchange, international banking, international debts, international reparations, and reciprocal trade agreements. We are largely and perhaps inevitably a nation of economic illiterates. . . .

Lord Bryce, who was as sympathetic a critic of American democracy as one could hope to find among foreigners, wrote regarding control of foreign policy: "Not one in a thousand of the citizens, not one in ten of the representatives, may have enough knowledge to enable him to form a sound opinion." If this was true in the horse-and-buggy era, it is even more true today. In the nineteenth century, when the Atlantic was a tremendous barrier, the American people could better afford the luxury of being ignorant or apathetic or wrong or late, but even then they had some narrow escapes. Those happy days of blessed ignorance are gone forever; we shall continue in some degree to be ignorant, but in a perilous rather than in a blissful state. Facts cannot be ignored out of existence.

The average American is a self-reliant individual; his forefathers rolled back a wilderness with their own muscular arms and backs. He is too prone to rely on himself for an opinion, whether he is in possession of the facts or not—a not uncommon failing. "Nothing is so firmly believed as that which we least know," wrote the French philosopher Montaigne in the sixteenth century. The ordinary citizen is also inclined to believe most readily that which he hopes for most earnestly, and he is all too often most easily persuaded by arguments which he cannot understand. All these human shortcomings are to be found in a despotism, but in a democracy they are more dangerous, for a democracy is the one system in which the ignorant have the most influence and where they are listened to with the most respect.

A Questionable Impact

BERNARD C. COHEN

Foreign policy is quite obviously singled out from all other areas of public policy for special attention and study from the perspective of public opinion, and it is perhaps worthwhile to speculate, at the outset, why this is so. It seems to me to have its roots in two special characteristics of foreign policy. One is the disturbingly high costs and risks that are now associated with it; and the other is the fact that it seems to be peculiarly beyond our reach as policy-attentive and policy-active citizens. It is ironic, not to say frustrating, that groups of specially affected citizens seem to have ways of getting a grip on limited-impact issue-areas, such as agricultural policy or savings-and-loan regulations or auto safety standards, while the "really important questions" of war and peace, life and death, which belong to us all, seem to have eluded our grasp and to be in the hands of a higher and more mysterious imperative. The special academic interest in the impact of public opinion on the foreign policy maker stems thus from both a civic concern and a professional curiosity over the apparent intractability of foreign policy.

The search for understanding and explanation of the relationship between opinion and foreign policy making (which is implicitly also the search for better access to it) has been intense since World War II. It has also been frag-

Reprinted from "The Relationship Between Public Opinion and Foreign Policy Maker," by Bernard C. Cohen, in *Public Opinion and Historians: Interdisciplinary Perspectives,* ed. Melvin Small, by permission of the Wayne State University Press. Copyright © 1970 by Wayne State University Press, Detroit, Michigan.

mented, and if I may say so, generally not quite to the point of the question of impact. As a result of substantial research, we know quite a bit now about the nature and structure of opinions within the body politic on particular foreign policy issues, about their location in the political and social structure of the nation, and about the dynamics of their development and their change. We know a lot about interest groups, and a considerable amount about the press, as instruments for the presentation and circulation and advocacy of foreign policy views. We have done rather well, in other words, on almost every aspect of public opinion *up to* the point where the relationship with policy makers actually begins. But we know strikingly little, in an assured way, about the impact that the body of nongovernmental opinion has upon the men who formulate and execute American foreign policy—which is, I take it, the essence of the question that concerns us. To explore that relationship, we are of necessity led away from the source and character of the opinions themselves, and towards the objects of those opinions, the policy makers. We want to know, both in general terms and in specific cases, how public opinion widely defined actually bears upon the decisions they make.

To put the problem this way is to make abundantly clear the practical difficulties in our path. There are several ways to turn, to surmount them. One is to study foreign policy officials directly, to observe contemporaneously how nongovernmental opinion is factored into policy. Another and perhaps antecedent way is to examine the history of foreign policy issues—the case studies of foreign policy formulation—to see what they can tell us about the impact of nongovernmental opinions on prior foreign policy decisions. The central concern of this paper is with this latter mode of inquiry. We look to the historian for a larger sample of relevant cases from which to draw information and on which to base generalizations. What can we learn about the relationship between public opinion and foreign policy makers throughout the twentieth century that enlarges our present understanding and gives better focus to our contemporary concern?

The question as I have just formulated it is ambiguous, and deliberately so. The question "what can we learn?" can be answered in two ways: by a substantive interpretation of the opinion-policy relationship, drawn from the historical record itself; and by a literal, evaluative answer that rests on the adequacy of that historical record. I shall try to answer it both ways—not just to stir up trouble, but because I have very large doubts about the essential accuracy of that record. My *operational* questions, then, are as follows: What kinds of generalizations do we have, or can we construct, concerning the relationship between public opinion and foreign policy makers in the twentieth century? What are these generalizations based on? How accurate or valid are they? What do we need to know in order to do a better job of explaining the opinion-policy relationship not only in the past but in the present and future as well?

The sheer volume of twentieth century American historiography makes it impossible to itemize in any detail and with statistical precision the generalizations its pages contain that deal with the connections between public opinion and foreign policy. The impressions of a non-historian, however, are that on the whole rather powerful political force has been attributed to general public opinion, to the press, and to political interest groups in the foreign policy field. Some examples are legendary in any event: that public opinion, whipped up by the "yellow press," swept a reluctant President and Congress into a war with Spain in 1898; that the Kellogg-Briand pact of 1928 was the product of the grassroots, of the growing force of enlightened public opinion; that public opinion, stimulated by Father Coughlin and the Hearst press, forced the Senate into a last-minute rejection of the resolution providing for United States adherence to the World Court in 1935; that public opinion compelled President Franklin D. Roosevelt to back away from his proposal to "quarantine the aggressors" by imposing economic sanctions against Japan in 1937. And in the interstices of these landmark events, American foreign policy makers are said to have been steadily directed by a timorous public opinion which chose neutrality over collective security. The chronicle is not exclusively an inter-war one, either. In the post–World War II period, public opinion is generally reported, *inter alia,* to have forced an unwilling and precipitate demobilization in 1945 and 1946, and to have prevented successive administrations from recognizing Communist China after 1949.

I do not mean to suggest that all historians of this period advance these interpretations; indeed, we will have occasion later to mention some significant exceptions. But this is the thrust of the historical argument, the major theme of historians' overview of the twentieth century American experience in foreign affairs. Dexter Perkins provides an exceptionally vivid example of this in his brief essay on the very topic: "In a sense that is true in no such degree in other nations, American diplomatic action has been determined by the people. . . . Uninstructed though the average citizen may be in the facts of international life, he still has an opinion with regard to them. If he does not know, he thinks he knows. And the conviction on his part is one that cannot be disregarded. Nor do those who conduct our affairs in the main desire to disregard it." Following the logic of this position, Perkins attributes a mysterious power to public opinion in specific cases. At the Washington Disarmament Conference of 1921–22, for example, he states that Secretary of State Hughes "secured that parity with the British which American opinion (for no very clear reason, it must be conceded) demanded." And at the same conference the United States gave up, "in the face of Japanese pressure, the right to fortify Guam and the Philippines. . . . No doubt, as was frequently maintained at the time, because of the state of American public opinion, it would have been impossible to secure funds for such fortification in any case." And again: "As early as 1925, eschewing the very cautious view of the matter expressed by Secretary Hughes, and responding, no doubt, to the pressure of powerful elements in American opinion, Secretary Kellogg permitted the United States to take part in the deliberations of the Preparatory Commission on Disarmament that assembled at Geneva."

These are, I imagine, reasonably familiar arguments to most of us; they are part of the folklore of our time, a central element in the explanation of the vast tragedies that have swept the world in this century. Folly on so grand a scale needs to have its source in some ultimate authority; and in our secular democracy, public opinion has replaced the Gods or the Fates or the Kings as that authority.

Despite the fact that these historical interpretations and explanations come to us from men with impressive professional credentials, I am profoundly skeptical about their accuracy, their validity, their relevance—and I trust I am not alone in that sentiment. My skepticism has three roots:

1. We are in rather substantial ignorance about the public opinion–foreign policy relationship that takes place in specific circumstances and on particular issues before our very eyes today, when "access" to government by scholars and journalists is as good as it has ever been, and when the techniques for assessing the state of public opinion and measuring its impact are no doubt better. We believe we know some *general* things about that relationship, but it has proved to be extraordinarily difficult, if not impossible, to trace the flow of public opinion influence in the development of specific foreign policies with any precision whatsoever. Given that simple yet enormous fact, I find it incredible on the face of it that the task of discovery was easier in the past, or even that the simple passage of time makes this extraordinarily complex relationship any easier to ascertain. In point of fact, reliable evidence bearing on the opinion-policy relationship, hard as it is to come by today, scarcely exists among the historical data of the first third of the century, when even the nature of public opinion had not yet become the subject of systematic scientific inquiry. We are at a loss today to state in reasonably accurate terms the impact of public opinion on something as visible and attention-getting as our policy toward Communist China since 1949; A. T. Steele, for example, asserts that public opinion has restrained successive administrations from a policy of recognition, but he also asserts the contrary—that the foreign policy situation itself restrained the policy makers. Given this fundamental uncertainty in the midst of a book on the subject that marshals large amounts of opinion information, I find it very difficult to accept without fundamental question a greater certainty that comes in the form of simple assertions based on much more fragmentary evidence.

In matters so little subject to documentary or empirical verification as these, it seems to me that sifted truth does not necessarily rise to the surface. What does rise rather more often is the interpretation of him who publishes first— or most! It is astonishing how easy it is for one interpretation to gain legendary stature, without challenge even from contemporaries who, while they may not "know" better in the true sense, at least suspect better. This has happened, for example, in the case of Roosevelt's quarantine speech, which we shall look at more closely below. And in our own day, both Theodore C. Sorensen and Arthur M. Schlesinger, Jr. have given historical credence, and thus sanction, to the notion expressed in an AIPO press release that there was a marked shift in public opinion in favor of the Nuclear Test Ban Treaty that helped to put the treaty over. Given the high long-term support in public opinion polls for a test-ban treaty, there are some grounds for questioning the extent of such a shift in the first place, and even greater grounds—in the pages of Sorensen and Schlesinger alone—for questioning whether any manifestations of such a shift had anything to do with the policy outcome.

In short, the record of contemporary historians and analysts of public opinion does not warrant our putting much—or indeed any—confidence in the judgments of an earlier period that are based, unavoidably, on a selective reading of the press or on the accounts of one or at most a few observers or participants.

2. A second reason for my skepticism about the validity of the conventional historical wisdom lies in the very improbability of its assertions, in the light of what little we do know about public opinion and foreign policy. One needs to repeat at this point that the literature of public opinion and public policy in general, and of public opinion and foreign policy in particular, largely evades the question of the relationship between opinion and policy; it has simply not been the focal point of study. But as I noted in (1) above, we nevertheless believe we know in *general* terms some things about that relationship in the contemporary United States. And what we have learned in diverse ways from diverse sources clearly suggests a foreign policy making establishment that is under very few public opinion constraints. And if these constraints are few in a period of substantial public attention to foreign policy questions, one cannot help asking why they should have been systematically and uniformly more extensive in an earlier period of our history, when there is no evidence that public attention was any greater than it is now, and lots of mythology suggesting that it was less.

Contemporary scholarship on public opinion and foreign policy repeatedly underlines the capacity of leaders to shape the public opinion to which they are supposedly responsive, and to interpret the opinions they hear in ways that support their own views. Gabriel Almond's classic study amply documented the foreign policy ignorance and disinterest of the great mass of the population even in the midst of the historic post-war "revolution" in American foreign policy, and the responsiveness of the small attentive segments of the population to the definitions of issues that emanate from the leadership groups. My own study of the formulation of the Japanese peace settlement in the early 1950s revealed that in the general political-strategic aspects of foreign policy, the administration had a virtually free hand; it was only in dealing with Pacific Ocean fisheries questions that foreign policy makers ran into a constituency that had a sufficiently direct interest in the outcome to warrant active and effective—and congressionally supported—involvement. The study of reciprocal trade renewal by Bauer, Pool and Dexter illuminates in a variety of ways the political and perceptual screens used by officials (in this case, congressmen) to filter public responses so that they hear chiefly what they want to hear, thus attenuating the impact of public opinion even on an issue of economic foreign policy—the very issue-area that has seemed to be the most responsive in the foreign policy field to nongovernmental influence.

The President is especially powerful as a shaper of public opinion, since he is the acknowledged symbol of and spokesman for the country in foreign affairs.

He commands attention from the media whenever he wants it, he formulates policy alternatives with an authority that no one else possesses, and he has a substantial and more or less natural base of sympathy and identification on which he can draw and which he can dissipate only with the greatest difficulty. Every major crisis in American foreign policy in the last generation, including those for which responsibility lies at the door of the White House, such as the U-2 incident and the Bay of Pigs, has been followed by an upsurge in popular support for the President. According to Sorensen, Kennedy clearly understood the freedom that his position gave him: "The final difference in the Kennedy treatment of foreign and domestic affairs was the relative influence of Congressional and public opinion. His foreign policy actions were still constrained within bounds set by those forces, but they operated more indirectly than directly and his own powers of initiative and decision were much wider."

Given the conditions that seem to account for this situation—substantial public disinterest, the expectation of executive authority and initiative, the capacity of the President to be a focal point in the public discussion of foreign policy—it seems reasonable to believe that the same situation would hold at least for the major foreign policy questions of the earlier period in the twentieth century. And for all issues defined as "minor," meaning that they did not heavily engage the interest and energy of the political system, it is at least as reasonable to believe that the President and the secretary of state had no incentive to bend with the pale breezes of special interest as to believe that they had no strength to resist them. On the very face of it, for example, it seems highly improbable that so imprecise, so divided, and so superficial a political force as public opinion could have compelled President Franklin Roosevelt to retreat overnight from his public statement on quarantining aggressors. "Retreat" he may have, at least to the extent of not repeating the suggestion of a quarantine—but the ordinary short-term indicators of public opinion, especially editorial reaction, White House mail, and interest group stands, were on his side, and so substantially as to strengthen one's doubts that it was the united impact or even the majority of nongovernmental opinion that moved him.

3. My third reason for being skeptical about the conventional historical wisdom concerning public opinion and foreign policy is more prosaic, if more fundamental: much of the existing literature, the very basis for the historical judgment as well as the expression of it, simply does not handle public opinion convincingly, no matter what conclusions it comes to about public opinion as a political force. The vast bulk of the literature makes no attempt systematically to prove or disprove a causal relationship between opinion and policy, or even to investigate so simple a proposition as that an observed convergence between opinion and policy may be attributable more to the fluidity of opinion than to the mobility of policy, or alternatively that such a convergence may be the result of independent responses to the same political stimuli. No exhaustive review of the literature is possible here, but two

examples may illustrate the inadequacies of the record that weaken one's confidence in it.

Robert Browder's study of the circumstances leading up to the U.S. recognition of the U.S.S.R. attempts to put a major shift in U.S. foreign policy into a broad public, political and economic context; his conclusion is that the desire for expanded trade did not play the paramount role in American recognition of the Soviet Union, that the arguments for increased trade were a convenient cover making a diplomatic enterprise palatable to public opinion. But his arguments about public opinion, as distinct from his conclusion, are inconsistent, contradictory, and unsupported by his evidence. He repeatedly presents the public statements and positions of individuals on the recognition question parallel to the views of policy makers, with the clear implication—but not the evidence—that they were strongly felt, even where they were ignored. I find it hard to fault Browder on his key observations that President Hoover was determined *not* to recognize the Soviet Union no matter how much agitation he encountered from business groups, and that President Roosevelt came to office equally determined to normalize diplomatic relations with the U.S.S.R. no matter what. But fault him or not, it is hard to give equal credence on the one hand to assertions that Roosevelt was from the very beginning determined to alter an anomalous situation, and on the other hand to statements such as, "Among all the other facts which Roosevelt had taken into account before he sent his historic invitation to Kalinin, none perhaps was more instrumental in deciding him to act when he did than his realization that American public opinion in the main supported a resumption of relations with Russia." And it is also difficult to give equal credence both to the latter observation, and to the repeated references throughout the book to American public opinion as isolationist, anti-Communist, fearful of "international complications," so much so that one could not speak openly of political reasoning or advantage. If one took Browder's generalizations about public opinion at face value, one would have to conclude that recognition could never have taken place.

Steele's study, *The American People and China,* cited earlier, shares these defects of analysis and interpretation of public opinion. On the one hand, Steele argues that Congress and the Executive continue to be immobilized on China policy because the mail, editorial opinion, public opinion soundings, and pressure group activity are all ranged against any change, any softening, in our policy toward Peking. "As one author observes, 'A large part of the history of American foreign policy since World War I might be interpreted as a series of successful intimidations by pressure groups.' The applicability of this statement to the China situation is self-evident." And again, in referring to the hostility of the China lobby and its successor groups, supported even by more respectable national organizations, he states: "Members of Congress are of course well aware of this powerful body of opinion and of the hardened attitude of a large and influential section of the popular press. They consciously or subconsciously take it into consideration in weighing any legislation that involves a change in our relations with Communist countries."

On the other hand, Steele repeatedly acknowledges, as a kind of after-thought, that any reconsideration of our China policy "is of course inhibited also by the Peking regime's chronic truculence." In other words, he argues that the Chinese situation itself offers the United States no reasonable alternative to its present policy. Policy is substantially frozen because very few people, inside the government or outside, think that the prospects for change are bright enough to justify much effort or great risk. U.S. policy thus is very largely a response not to internal opinion pressures but to an international political situation over which, in the short run at least, this country has little control. The ambivalence and confusion in Steele's argument concerning the responsibility of public opinion for our present China policy is well illustrated by the following. While he continues to assert that policy makers in Congress and the executive branch live in fear of hostile public reactions if they so much as mention a reappraisal of our China policy, he also notes that the speech by Assistant Secretary of State Hilsman in December 1963, which held open the door to better relations with the next echelon or generation of Chinese leaders, was initiated in the State Department and was favorably received by the American press—though not by the Chinese! In this case, as in the matter of the recognition of the Soviet Union, it is next to impossible to draw firm conclusions about the actual constraints imposed on policy makers by public opinion; and these two studies are better informed about the public opinion dimension than are most historical narratives.

One can understand how an individual might be misled in the process of trying to reconstruct a single and specific decision; but—assuming there is validity in my rather sweeping criticism—how is one to account for such a general misunderstanding or misinterpretation of the impact of public opinion on foreign policy making? What is wrong with our capacity to understand the processes of foreign policy formulation? Why do contemporary scholars persist in attributing great political force to nongovernmental opinions in the foreign policy field in the absence of direct evidence and when almost everything we know about public opinion and foreign policy, both of a specific and a general character, indicates the contrary? At the risk of oversimplification, a few likely causes can be explored, especially because it is in these possible causes that we may find good guidelines to a more accurate and thus more relevant historiography of foreign policy making.

There seems, in the first instance, to be a general intellectual failure, a failure of political conceptualization or theoretical insight on a grand scale. We are all familiar with the principles of normative democratic theory concerning public opinion; and we have long lacked good empirical theories or even descriptive propositions about the foreign policy making process. As one way out of this difficulty, we have apparently been willing to accept normative theories in explanation of what has happened in specific instances for which we have had no other satisfactory or compelling mode of explanation. Another way of accommodating the normatively derived power of public opinion to concrete situations that are devoid of supporting evidence has been to assert that public opinion is indeed powerful, but at the edges of policy rather than at the center; thus public opinion "sets the boundaries" within which foreign policy operates and—implicitly—beyond which it cannot or must not go. This notion sometimes appears explicitly in the literature of explanation, and it is so common as a general consideration that it could hardly fail to be an implicit factor in conceptualizations of foreign policy making in concrete circumstances. The trouble with this notion is that it can only be taken on faith, never proved or disproved, because the "boundaries" of policy are in principle unknown and undefinable. In practice, however, they can only be defined by the things that policy makers have already *chosen* to do or not to do; and thus to say that public opinion sets those boundaries is in fact to attribute a central role in all policy to public opinion, which is manifestly neither intended as a statement nor true as a fact.

The lack of comprehensive empirically based hypotheses about foreign policy making has also, I believe, given longer life to what we might call the Lippmann fallacy: the view that political executives are the repositories of foreign policy initiative and intelligence (in both senses), and that the mass publics in twentieth century western democracies are the sources of unreasoned restraint, negativism, short-run escape from responsibility and commitment, whether through evasion or its opposite, overresponse. In combination, all of these intellectual and conceptual weaknesses have created a predisposition to believe that, where there was no other ready explanation for foreign policy behavior that did not fit some preconceived and generally implicit notion of political rationality, the deviation must have been caused by public opinion in some manifestation.

These conceptual failures have been sustained and even nourished by statements of policy makers themselves. I appreciate the fact that official pronouncements, and observations and recollections of officials, have a special claim to historical relevance, particularly when other sources of evidence are not readily found. But it is precisely the importance that we are obliged to attach to such statements that should compel us to look at them with a cold and fishy eye, and to ask of them, as we have asked of the historians' accounts, are they reasonable or verifiable? For example, Herbert Feis, an official-turned-historian, wrote the following in partial explanation of the state department's failure to give firm support to League of Nations sanctions against Italy in the Italian-Ethiopian War: "There was in the Department a thin hope . . . that public opinion might finally awaken to what was at issue, and demand further and more decisive action. This hope, however, fed largely upon itself. Officials could not find, either in the mail received at the State Department or in the press, evidence that public opinion was insistent upon more vigorous control of trade with Italy." It seems to me quite unreasonable to claim that officials failed to take "more decisive action" because public opinion did not demand or insist on it; since when has this been the source of initiative in foreign policy?

We are accustomed to being told by our secretaries of state that public opinion shapes foreign policy, that the policy maker is guided by public sentiment, and so forth. One would expect the secretary of state to say such things, if only because he believes they are expected of him; this is, after all, what the most articulate members of his nongovernmental audience really want to hear (though the few I know do not believe it either!). But there are other, more proximate and practical reasons why officials talk this way, which I believe really account for the unreliability of their statements. When a policy maker is attributing a decision to the dictates of public opinion, he is explaining away a variety of complicated, delicate political constraints on his and his colleagues' behavior by passing them off onto the one legitimate political actor that cannot answer back, defend itself, or take offense at the charge. He may have been led to a particular policy step because it was the only action on which he could get any agreement from the interested parties within the state department or the executive branch; or he may have concluded *not* to do something by the clear, if unpublicized, intimation of congressional reprisal, or even because he himself was unwilling to shoulder responsibility for all the risks involved. To explain his decision by blaming himself or his colleagues or Congress would be most unwise; but to lay it all on the shoulders of the public might even be construed as flattering. I do not believe, incidentally, that this is a conscious and deliberate subterfuge; rather, it seems to me to be so automatic a set of euphemisms and rationalizations that it constitutes an institutionalized response to the felt necessity of saying something about ultimate responsibility for decisions, wise or unwise.

The heart of the intellectual failure—and a strong reason why it has been so easy for statesmen to get away with patently absurd remarks—is the absence of theories of foreign policy making based on a realistic understanding of political strategies. For reasons that can be explained if not justified, foreign policy as a subject matter has been treated as a special thing in American political science, substantially divorced from the theories and concepts of the political process that specialists in American politics have developed. Even in American government textbooks, foreign policy is invariably treated, in two or three chapters at the end, as a major *problem area* of American government, and not as a major set of questions and issues that define, shape and illustrate the very way the American government and American politics operate. Thus, while there are now some rather elaborate theories of the political process in areas such as budget making or military policy, for example, foreign policy still appears as a subject that is more appropriately studied from the point of view of international politics than of national politics. This blindness to the political strategies of foreign policy making is no doubt largely a function of the fact that much of the foreign policy making process is invisible to the casual observer, being carried on within the confines of the executive branch and often under the wraps of national security, and that Congress has less of a role to play in comparison with areas of domestic policy. Public opinion, and nongovernmental actors generally, have tended consequently to be conceived of as operating more or less directly on the foreign policy officials, rather than more subtly being engaged in a complex political process that envelops large sections of the national political system. One result of this primitive theory of foreign policy making is that it is a contest between "good guys" and "bad guys," the latter being not those in dark shirts but all the unenlightened people on the outside who presumably impede rational policies.

Before we can ever get a reliable statement of the relationship between public opinion and foreign policy maker, we need a fuller and more accurate set of propositions about the larger political processes of foreign policy making, of which public opinion is just a part. And, more narrowly but equally important, we need to know what the expressions of public opinion look like, not to the historian or the contemporary observer or even the persons who articulate them, but to the foreign policy officials themselves. On this point the evidence from history is very poor indeed; scholars have not often looked for it, and when they have it has been more suggestive than conclusive. But we have good reason to believe that an official's perception of public opinion on foreign policy questions differs substantially from the perceptions that others are likely to have. So it is of more than idle curiosity that we learn how policy makers actually do perceive their total environment, including their opinion environment, in specific cases.

It is not beyond reason to speculate that throughout the twentieth century foreign policy leaders have not generally known how free they were to pursue policies in which they were interested. On an earlier occasion I summarized it as follows: "Seeing, in a shadowy way, chiefly the restrictive elements in a probable political process, the policy-maker often spins around himself an artificial web of constraint." Impressions from the historical literature suggest the proposition that policy makers are as often surprised by the lack of public response to what they have done as they are by the nature of responses that do occur. By way of illustration, Browder depicts Roosevelt as having been determined to proceed with the recognition of the Soviet Union despite an articulate body of opinion that opposed the move; but in the aftermath he concludes that "the volume of protest was evidently considerably less than the Administration had anticipated." Brzezinski and Huntington, in their comparison of the American and Soviet political systems, observe that in the United States post-hoc criticisms of foreign policy "certainly shape the Administration's anticipations of the reactions to its next decision in the same area and thereby also presumably affect the content of that decision." To the extent that administrations do approach new decisions in this fashion, having public reactions to the last decisions uppermost in mind, it is not surprising that they may often be surprised when the expected responses do not materialize.

I do not believe that it is inconsistent to argue, however, that even though foreign policy leaders have widely underestimated their freedom of maneuver in foreign policy, they still perceive that freedom more accurately than many scholars have, and more accurately even than they themselves usually admit openly. Joseph M. Jones' description of the development of the Truman Doctrine and the Marshall Plan is noteworthy for its recognition that the foreign policy leaders had to take the initiative all the way, and that the public had to be "educated" to support the grand venture. H. Schuyler Foster, for many years chief of the State Department's office of public opinion studies, has asserted that on the Truman Doctrine, as on a large number of important foreign policy questions of the period, both the executive and Congress had no hesitation in acting without public approval and support—that public responsiveness has followed in due course. And while Secretary of State Rusk talks about the public limitations on foreign policy, Sorensen writes about Kennedy's clear understanding that, of the various foreign policy constraints he faced, this one was marginal. Furthermore, my own research in the public opinion perceptions of state department officials persuades me that most of their talk about the power of public opinion is ritualistic; when one probes its meaning, it usually either disappears entirely, or transmutes into something else, like congressional politics. In either case, the officials themselves are not deceived by the words they use into believing that their hands are tied by nongovernmental opinions.

We need, finally, a substantial reexamination of the history of American foreign policy making in the twentieth century, along with better studies of contemporary foreign policy making. This should not be read as a call for historical revisionism that makes new and different interpretations with no more substantial evidence than before. Rather, it is a request for systematic and focused attention, in historical research, to such questions as these. In specific situations in the past, what is the best evidence concerning policy makers' perceptions of the domestic policy making environment, including the public opinion environment? And what specific modifications or constraints were *thereby* imposed on their foreign policy preferences or intentions? There are some good historical models that demonstrate what can be done by asking relevant questions of an admittedly imperfect and even intractable body of evidence. George W. Auxier, for example, has questioned the significance of sensational journalism in the events leading up to the Spanish-American War, by examining the press in the Midwest, where the Hearst-Pulitzer circulation war did not reach. He has concluded that to the extent that the press played a part in the development of a war policy, it was more likely the result of press consideration of questions of national interest and of political partisanship, rather than sensational, circulation-induced demands for intervention. And in her impressive study of President Roosevelt and the Quarantine Speech, Dorothy Borg has explored his apparent intentions, the public reactions to the speech, and his perceptions of those reactions; and she has concluded that Roosevelt had no specific sanctions in mind from which he was dissuaded, and that there was quite extensive and respectable public support for his speech, but that so far as future policy was concerned, he was extraordinarily sensitive to the isolationist and pacifist segments of that public opinion (which had resonance in the views of leading senators) rather than to the broad supportive sections of public opinion. One wonders what a comparably insightful study of, for example, the political predispositions of senators and their exposure to lobbying activities against U.S. entry into the World Court, set into the larger political context and issue context of the day, would conclude about the true causes for the rejection of U.S. membership.

A large variety of such studies, better informed by better hypotheses about the political processes of foreign policy making, would make a substantial contribution to our understanding of the public opinion-foreign policy making relationship across the twentieth century to the present day.

FURTHER READING

Gabriel Almond, *The American People and Foreign Policy* (1950)
Max Beloff, *Foreign Policy and the Democratic Process* (1955)
William Chittick, *State Department, Press, and Pressure Groups* (1970)
Bernard C. Cohen, *The Press and Foreign Policy* (1963)
Bernard C. Cohen, *The Public's Impact on Foreign Policy* (1973)
Elmer E. Cornwell, Jr., *Presidential Leadership of Public Opinion* (1965)
Robert A. Dahl, *Congress and Foreign Policy* (1950)
Robert A. Divine, *Foreign Policy and U.S. Presidential Elections, 1940–1960* (1974)
Marian D. Irish and Elke Frank, *U.S. Foreign Policy: Context, Conduct, Content* (1975)
Charles O. Lerche, *Foreign Policy of the American People* (1967)
Richard E. Neustadt, *Presidential Power* (1960)
Dexter Perkins, *The American Approach to Foreign Policy* (1962)
James A. Robinson, *Congress and Foreign Policy-Making* (1967)
James N. Rosenau, *National Leadership and Foreign Policy* (1963)
James N. Rosenau, *Public Opinion and Foreign Policy* (1961)
James N. Rosenau, ed., *Domestic Sources of Foreign Policy* (1967)
Arthur M. Schlesinger, Jr., *The Imperial Presidency* (1973)

3

The Foreign Policy of the Founding Fathers

The United States achieved independence in 1783 in a world war featuring Franco-British hostility. The French, smarting from defeat in the Seven Years War, or French and Indian War (1754–1763), wherein they were forced to relinquish Canada to the British, craved revenge against London. First they secretly aided the rebellious American colonists and then, in 1778, struck a permanent military alliance with the nascent United States. Americans found the French assistance vital to victory. But both the peace with Britain and the alliance with France created troublesome diplomatic issues for the new nation.

Through the 1780s and into the 1790s, the British refused to leave fortified posts on American soil or to negotiate a commercial treaty. The 1778 Alliance with France became an encumbrance in 1792–1793 when the French Revolution entered a violent and stormy stage that initiated war between republican France and monarchical Europe. Conservative Americans recoiled from what they identified as the excesses of republicanism. Alexander Hamilton, Federalist Party leader and Secretary of the Treasury in the administration of George Washington, especially denounced France and sympathized with Great Britain as a bastion of convervatism and as America's chief trading partner. On the other hand, James Madison and Thomas Jefferson led a faction called the Republican Party. They applauded the French Revolution as a notable triumph for freedom from tyranny and for the ideals expressed in the American Revolution. They argued also that the United States, because its foreign trade was so dependent

*upon the British, was compromising its sovereignty by favoring Great
Britain.*

*The Jay Treaty of 1794, signed with Britain, defused Anglo-American
tensions, especially over the occupied forts, but it ignited heated controversy
at home. Not until the Convention of 1800 did France and the United
States temper their relations after years of a quasi-war on the high seas.
That agreement freed the United States from the 1778 Alliance. Overall, the
Founding Fathers helped to launch a major debate about the national interest.*

DOCUMENTS

America's birth certificate, in preliminary form, was signed by British and American
emissaries on November 30, 1782. The final Treaty of Peace was signed in Paris
on September 3, 1783, and ratifications were exchanged on May 12, 1784. Relations
with the former mother country were hardly settled by this document and, when
France and Britain once again engaged in war in the 1790s, Americans began to
debate the merits of neutrality and their obligations to France under the 1778
Treaty of Alliance, which read: "The two parties guarantee mutually from the
present time and forever, against all other powers, to wit, the United States to his
most Christian Majesty the present possessions of the Crown of France in America,
as well as those which it may acquire by the future treaty of peace: and his most
Christian Majesty guarantees on his part to the United States, their liberty,
sovereignty, and independence absolute, and unlimited, as well in matters of
government as commerce and also their possessions. . . ."

At stake in the 1790s, thought many, was the survival of the fledgling republic
itself. President Washington asked Jefferson and Hamilton as department heads to
provide answers to some tough questions: Should the United States proclaim formal
neutrality? Should a minister from republican France be received? Was the United
States still bound by the 1778 Alliance? The articulate Cabinet members responded
vigorously in April 1793 with strikingly different views, as the following documents
demonstrate.

Treaty of Peace, 1783

Article 1st. His Britannic Majesty acknowledges the said United States, viz.
New-Hampshire Massachusetts Bay, Rhode-Island & Providence Plantations,
Connecticut, New York, New Jersey, Pennsylvania, Delaware, Maryland,
Virginia, North Carolina, South Carolina & Georgia, to be free sovereign &
Independent States; that he treats with them as such, and for himself his Heirs
& Successors, relinquishes all Claims to the Government Propriety & Territorial
Rights of the same & every Part thereof.

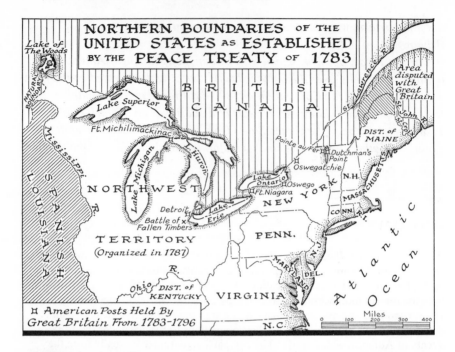

Article 2d. [boundaries]

Article 3d. It is agreed that the People of the United States shall continue to enjoy unmolested the Right to take Fish of every kind on the Grand Bank and on all the other Banks of New-foundland, also in the Gulph of St. Lawrence, and at all other Places in the Sea where the Inhabitants of both Countries used at any time heretofore to fish. And also that the Inhabitants of the United States shall have Liberty to take Fish of every Kind on such Part of the Coast of New-foundland as British Fishermen shall use, (but not to dry or cure the same on that Island) And also on the Coasts Bays & Creeks of all other of his Britannic Majesty's Dominions in America, and that the American Fishermen shall have Liberty to dry and cure Fish in any of the unsettled Bays Harbours and Creeks of Nova Scotia, Magdalen Islands, and Labrador, so long as the same shall remain unsettled but so soon as the same or either of them shall be settled, it shall not be lawful for the said Fishermen to dry or cure Fish at such Settlement, without a previous Agreement for that purpose with the Inhabitants, Proprietors or Possessors of the Ground.

Article 4th. It is agreed that Creditors on either Side shall meet with no lawful Impediment to the Recovery of the full Value in Sterling Money of all bona fide Debts heretofore contracted.

Article 5th. It is agreed that the Congress shall earnestly recommend it to the Legislatures of the respective States to provide for the Restitution of all Estates, Rights and Properties which have been confiscated belonging to real British Subjects. . . . And that Persons of any other Description shall have free Liberty to go to any Part or Parts of any of the thirteen United States and therein to remain twelve Months unmolested in their Endeavours to obtain the Restitution of such of their Estates Rights & Properties as may have been confiscated. . . .

And it is agreed that all Persons who have any Interest in confiscated Lands, either by Debts, Marriage Settlements, or otherwise, shall meet with no lawful Impediment in the Prosecution of their just Rights.

Article 6th. That there shall be no future Confiscations made nor any Prosecutions commenc'd against any Person or Persons for or by Reason of the Part, which he or they may have taken in the present War, and that no Person shall on that Account suffer any future Loss or Damage, either in his Person Liberty or Property; and that those who may be in Confinement on such Charges at the Time of the Ratification of the Treaty in America shall be immediately set at Liberty, and the Prosecutions so commenced be discontinued.

Article 7th. There shall be a firm and perpetual Peace between his Britannic Majesty and the said States and between the Subjects of the one, and the Citizens of the other, wherefore all Hostilities both by Sea and Land shall from henceforth cease: All Prisoners on both Sides shall be set at Liberty, and his Britannic Majesty shall with all convenient speed, and without causing any Destruction, or carrying away any Negroes or other Property of the American Inhabitants, withdraw all his Armies, Garrisons & Fleets from the said United States, and from every Port, Place and Harbour within the same; leaving in all Fortifications the American Artillery that may be therein: And shall also Order & cause all Archives, Records, Deeds & Papers belonging to any of the said States, or their Citizens, which in the Course of the War may have fallen into the Hands of his Officers, to be forthwith restored and deliver'd to the proper States and Persons to whom they belong.

Hamilton on the Alliance with France, 1793

Are the United States bound, by the principles of the laws of nations, to consider the treaties heretofore made with France as in present force and operation between them and the actual governing powers of the French nation? or may they elect to consider their operation as suspended, reserving also a right to judge finally whether any such changes have happened in the political affairs of France as may justify a renunciation of those treaties?

It is believed that they have an option to consider the operation of those treaties as suspended, and will have eventually a right to renounce them, if such changes shall take place as can *bona fide* be pronounced to render a continuance of the connections which result from them disadvantageous or dangerous.

There are two general propositions which may be opposed to this opinion: 1st. That a nation has a right, in its own discretion, to change its form of government—to abolish one, and substitute another. 2d. That *real* treaties (of which description those in question are) bind the NATIONS whose governments contract, and continue in force notwithstanding any changes which happen in the forms of their government.

The truth of the first proposition ought to be admitted in its fullest latitude. But it will by no means follow, that, because a nation has a right to manage its own concerns as it thinks fit, and to make such changes in its political institutions as itself judges best calculated to promote its interests, it has therefore a right to involve other nations, with whom it may have had connections, *absolutely* and *unconditionally,* in the consequences of the changes which it may think proper to make. This would be to give to a nation or society not only a power over its own happiness, but a power over the happiness of other nations or societies. It would be to extend the operation of the maxim much beyond the *reason* of it, which is simply, that every nation ought to have a right to provide for its own happiness. . . .

All general rules are to be construed with certain reasonable limitations. That which has been just mentioned must be understood in this sense, that changes in forms of government do not of course abrogate *real* treaties; that they continue absolutely binding on the party which makes the change, and will bind the other party, unless, in due time and for just cause, he declares his election to renounce them; that in good faith he ought not to renounce them, unless the change which happened does really render them useless, or materially less advantageous, or more dangerous than before. But for good and sufficient cause he may renounce them.

Nothing can be more evident than that the existing forms of government of two nations may enter far into the motives of a real treaty. . . .

Two nations may form an alliance because each has confidence in the energy and efficacy of the government of the other. A revolution may subject one of them to a different form of government—feeble, fluctuating, and turbulent, liable to provoke wars, and very little fitted to repel them. Even the connections of a nation with other foreign powers may enter into the motives of an alliance with it. If a dissolution of ancient connections shall have been a consequence of a revolution of government, the external political relations of the parties may have become so varied as to occasion an incompatibility of the alliance with the Power which had changed its constitution with the other connections of its ally—connections perhaps essential to its welfare.

In such cases, reason, which is the touchstone of all similar maxims, would dictate that the party whose government had remained stationary would have a right, under a *bona-fide* conviction that the change in the situation of the other party would render a future connection detrimental or dangerous, to declare the connection dissolved.

Contracts between nations as between individuals must lose their force where the considerations fail.

A treaty pernicious to the state is of itself void, where no change in the situation of either of the parties takes place. By a much stronger reason it must become *voidable* at the option of the other party, when the voluntary act of one of the allies has made so material a change in the condition of things as is always implied in a radical revolution of government.

Jefferson on the Alliance with France, 1793

I proceed, in compliance with the requisition of the President, to give an opinion in writing on the general Question, Whether the U.S. have a right to renounce their treaties with France, or to hold them suspended till the government of that country shall be established? . . .

I consider the people who constitute a society or nation as the source of all authority in that nation, as free to transact their common concerns by any agents they think proper, to change these agents individually, or the organisation of them in form or function whenever they please: that all the acts done by those agents under the authority of the nation, are the acts of the nation, are obligatory on them, & enure to their use, & can in no wise be annulled or affected by any change in the form of the government, or of the persons administering it. Consequently the Treaties between the U.S. and France, were not treaties between the U.S. & Louis Capet, but between the two nations of America & France, and the nations remaining in existence, tho' both of them have since changed their forms of government, the treaties are not annulled by these changes. . . .

Compacts then between nation & nation are obligatory on them by the same moral law which obliges individuals to observe their compacts. There are circumstances however which sometimes excuse the non-performance of contracts between man & man: so are there also between nation & nation. When performance, for instance, becomes *impossible,* non-performance is not immoral. So if performance becomes *self-destructive* to the party, the law of self-preservation overrules the laws of obligation to others. . . .

But Reason, which gives this right of self-liberation from a contract in certain cases, has subjected it to certain just limitations.

The danger which absolves us must be great, inevitable & imminent. Is such the character of that now apprehended from our treaties with France? What is that danger. . . . Obligation is not suspended, till the danger is become real, & the moment of it so imminent, that we can no longer avoid decision without forever losing the opportunity to do it. . . .

The danger apprehended, is it that, the treaties remaining valid, the clause guarantying their West India islands will engage us in the war? But Does the Guarantee engage us to enter into the war in any event?

Are we to enter into it before we are called on by our allies? Have we been called on by them?—shall we ever be called on? Is it their interest to call on us?

Can they call on us before their islands are invaded, or imminently threatened?

If they can save them themselves, have they a right to call on us?

Are we obliged to go to war at once, without trying peaceable negotiations with their enemy?

If all these questions be against us, there are still others behind.

Are we in a condition to go to war?

Can we be expected to begin before we are in condition?

Will the islands be lost if we do not save them? Have we the means of saving them?

If we cannot save them are we bound to go to war for a desperate object?

Will not a 10 years forbearance in us to call them into the guarantee of our posts, entitle us to some indulgence?

Many, if not most of these questions offer grounds of doubt whether the clause of guarantee will draw us into the war. Consequently if this be the danger apprehended, it is not yet certain enough to authorize us in sound morality to declare, at this moment, the treaties null. . . .

Is the danger apprehended from the 22nd Art. of our treaty of commerce, which prohibits the enemies of France from fitting out privateers in our ports, or selling their prizes here. But we are free to refuse the same thing to France, there being no stipulation to the contrary, and we ought to refuse it on principles of fair neutrality.

But the reception of a Minister from the Republic of France, without qualifications, it is thought will bring us into danger: because this, it is said, will determine the continuance of the treaty, and take from us the right of self-liberation when at any time hereafter our safety would require us to use it. The reception of the Minister at all (in favor of which Col. Hamilton has given his opinion, tho reluctantly as he confessed) is an acknolegement of the legitimacy of their government: and if the qualifications meditated are to deny that legitimacy, it will be a curious compound which is to admit & deny the same thing. But I deny that the reception of a Minister has any thing to do with the treaties. There is not a word, in either of them, about sending ministers. This has been done between us under the common usage of nations, & can have no effect either to continue or annul the treaties.

But how can any act of election have the effect to continue a treaty which is acknoleged to be going on still? For it was not pretended the treaty was void, but only voidable if we chuse to declare it so. To make it void would require an act of election, but to let it go on requires only that we should do nothing, and doing nothing can hardly be an infraction of peace or neutrality.

But I go further & deny that the most explicit declaration made at this moment that we acknolege the obligation of the treaties could take from us the right of non-compliance at any future time when compliance would involve us in great & inevitable danger.

I conclude then that few of these sources threaten any danger at all; and from none of them is it inevitable: & consequently none of them give us the right at this moment of releasing ourselves from our treaties.

ESSAYS

The 1793 debate between Hamilton and Jefferson over the alliance with France was just one of their many verbal skirmishes in the 1790s. As the following essays illustrate, the Founding Fathers grappled with weighty questions about the national interest, and scholars differ in their interpretations of the answers the beleaguered Fathers gave.

Professor Paul A. Varg of Michigan State University gently chides Thomas Jefferson and James Madison for excessive idealism and applauds the tough-minded realism of Hamilton, who saw the economic necessity of amicable ties with Britain. Lawrence Kaplan of Kent State University, on the other hand, finds a healthy blend of realism and idealism in Jefferson and points out similarities with Hamilton. The closing essay by Alexander DeConde of the University of California, Santa Barbara, takes another tack, which is outside the idealism versus realism debate. DeConde stresses the often selfish political partisanship of both Hamiltonians and Jeffersonians and suggests that the inflated, glorified image of the Founding Fathers, especially of the Federalists, as great statesmen requires revision.

All three authors help to identify the Founding Fathers' contributions to the American diplomatic tradition and introduce the questions, contemporary and historical, that help to explain American foreign relations after the era of Washington. What words, in short, should historians use to identify the foreign policy of the Founding Fathers? Nationalist? Idealist? Realist? Isolationist? Partisan? Olympian? Lucky? Self-interested?

The Virtues of Hamiltonian Realism over Jeffersonian Idealism

PAUL A. VARG

Foreign policy questions during the presidency of George Washington became the focal point of political debate and contributed in a major way to the rise of political parties. The Constitution did not envision parties, and George Washington was strongly averse to their becoming a part of the American political scene, but as Joseph Charles has shown in *The Origins of the American Party System,* the debate over foreign policy, culminating in the crisis over the question of ratification of the Jay Treaty, brought about the division of the people into two divergent groups.

It has usually been overlooked that the issues at stake in the debate over that treaty emerged in the first session of the first Congress. James Madison was then a leader in the House of Representatives, and he sought to carry out what he deeply believed had been the mandate of the public in establishing the new government, namely a change from the helpless posture in foreign affairs to a position of effective bargaining. His program centered on commercial relations and sought to extend commerce with nations other than Great Britain and thereby to free the republic from being a mere appendage of the British economy. He viewed British economic influence by means of close commercial ties as exceedingly dangerous to the cherished republican ideals. James Madison is usually associated with the states rights position in domestic

Paul A. Varg, *Foreign Policies of the Founding Fathers* (East Lansing, Mich.: Michigan State University Press, 1963), pp. 70–79, 83, 95–97, 105–107, 111–113, 145–147.

history, but he was a highly sensitive nationalist whose patriotism rested on a deep commitment to the principles of the Revolution.

His opponent in the long controversy was Alexander Hamilton, another nationalist, with whom he had been a colleague in the Constitutional Convention and with whom he joined, along with John Jay, in writing the *Federalist Papers*. They were on cordial terms at the convention and the views they expressed in their written defense of the Constitution show a close harmony. The split between them arose over Madison's foreign commercial policy. Thereafter Madison became an ardent opponent of the views expressed by Hamilton in the famous reports he prepared as Secretary of the Treasury. Hamilton expressed surprise when he found Madison opposing him on the measures he recommended and he recalled that his opponent had expressed sympathy with similar proposals in 1787. There is evidence that Madison's essential disagreement with Hamilton was on foreign policy rather than the domestic measures. A recent writer, E. James Ferguson, raises questions concerning the genuineness of Madison's opposition to Hamilton's funding measures and suggests that political expediency rather than considerations of justice caused Madison to oppose Hamilton's proposal. This conclusion, of course, lends added weight to the view that the basic cause of the split between the two ardent nationalists was a difference in foreign policy.

Their differences on foreign policy are more than adequate to explain the struggle that developed. These differences went down to the very roots where every serious debate over foreign policy issues must inevitably find itself. Hamilton was above all a realist who fatalistically accepted the existing framework, and dedicated himself to obtaining the best bargain possible. He did not object to the *realpolitik* of balance of power diplomacy, chose to regard treaties as convenient arrangements binding on the parties until they no longer served the purposes of one or the other, accepted British dominance as a simple fact of life, and dismissed as dangerous embarking on goals that the limited power of the country could scarcely hope to achieve. His own limited aim in foreign relations was to guarantee access to what he considered the prime need of a nation that desperately needed capital for the development of its tremendous resources so that it might one day emerge as a major power.

James Madison exemplifies the idealist in foreign policy. He spoke often of the rights of the republic and of what was just in international affairs but never felt it necessary to balance goals with the power available. At the base of his nationalism was a moralistic view that the new republic would be false to its mission in the world if it compromised its ideals. To remain true to its mission the nation must free itself from British dominance over the carrying trade and from the marketing of its goods through the British mercantile houses because British influence through these channels would strengthen monarchical principles and jade the lustrous principles of republicanism.

When the administration of George Washington took office in March, 1789, the basic dilemma confronting the nation was not yet clear. The United States was allied to France not only by treaty but by sentiment; it was tied to Great Britain in terms of markets, sources of manufactures, and credit. The rivalry of these two nations, soon to break forth in war, imposed on the new nation issues that threatened to tear it apart. In these issues lies the thread of American diplomacy from 1789 to 1812.

In the first session of Congress Madison presented a program for a commercial system that would give the United States economic independence. He explained that "the commerce between America and Great Britain exceeds what may be considered its natural boundary." British dominance, he said, was due to "the long possession of our trade, their commercial regulations calculated to retain it, their similarity of language and manners, their conformity of laws and other circumstances—all these concurring have made their commerce with us more extensive than their natural situation would require it to be."

Madison's program called for discriminatory tonnage duties on British ships. France and other nations that had entered into commercial treaties were to be rewarded with preferential rates. The opposition quickly pointed out that the higher rates on non-British ships could only mean higher prices on the goods Americans bought. Madison replied that the patriotism of Americans would cause them to make the necessary sacrifice, and that Americans could be induced to build a merchant marine in a short time as American ships would have an advantage over all foreign ships. He admitted that he would much prefer to see a completely free system. "But," he said, "we have maritime dangers to guard against, and we can be secured from them no other way than by having a navy and seamen of our own; these can only be obtained by giving a preference." "I admit it is a tax," he continued, "and a tax upon our produce; but it is a tax we must pay for the national security."

A nationalistic tone pervaded Madison's discourse on commerce. The economic advantages sought seemed at times less important than to command the respect of Great Britain. "We have now the power to avail ourselves of our natural superiority," he said, "and I am for beginning with some manifestation of that ability, that foreign nations may or might be taught to pay us that respect which they have neglected on account of our former imbecility." It was all important to show that "we dare exert ourselves in defeating any measure which commercial policy shall offer hostile to the welfare of America." He defended his program against the charge that it was a tax that the people would pay by asserting that his measures would "secure to us that respect and attention which we merit." Great Britain, he charged, "has bound us in commercial manacles, and very nearly defeated the object of our independence."

Madison's nationalism led him to place a high estimate on the strength of the new nation. He had no fear of British recriminations for "her interests can be wounded almost mortally, while ours are invulnerable." The British West Indies, he maintained, could not live without American foodstuffs, but Americans could easily do without British manufactures. This same faith led him to the conclusion "that it is in our power, in a very short time, to supply all the tonnage necessary for our own commerce."

Enamored with democratic ideals and absorbed with the need for markets for the ever richer flow of agricultural produce, James Madison set forth a foreign policy that would enable the new nation to carry on its experiment in republican principles and promote the economic well being of the farmers who constituted ninety per cent of the population. Like true agrarians they believed that the world lived by the produce of the farm; like true Americans they also believed that American farms were the most important in meeting the needs of the world's markets. Therein, they thought, lay the new nation's opportunity to influence world affairs.

Farmers had an eye for markets that would enter into competitive bidding for their ever expanding supplies. Dependence on Great Britain, they said, reduced them to a hostage of that country. British merchants took almost half of their exports and furnished three-fourths of the imports. Their patriotism rebelled at the sense of dependence that British economic connections fostered. How much better to trade with all the world. That others wanted their wheat, flour, and rice seemed self-evident. The other nations would gladly buy from them if only the dependence on British ships could be overcome. British ships funnelled everything through England's entrepôts, and then redistributed large amounts to other nations. How much better if a direct trade with consuming countries could be opened up. What a great advantage it would be if the United States could have its own merchant marine. That merchant marine would serve as a great nursery for seamen and would enable the nation to build a navy to protect the routes to markets. And what a sense of freedom would be imparted by the absence of the ubiquitous British creditor who stalked through the South collecting his debts. Virginians alone owed British merchants £2,300,000 (pounds sterling).

James Madison, and the new Secretary of State, Thomas Jefferson, who soon joined him, called for legislative measures to emancipate the country from economic bondage to Great Britain and the fostering of closer economic ties with other nations. France naturally attracted attention. Capable of absorbing large amounts of produce both at home and in her West Indies colonies, and also able to supply many of the needed manufactures, France seemed to offer the best counterpoise to England. Together the two nations could break the overwhelming British economic power that held Europe in its control.

The prospect took on a new glow when, in 1789, France embarked on revolution. Now it seemed that the two nations would complement each other politically as well as economically. Thomas Jefferson alone among foreign diplomats in Paris welcomed the event. "I have so much confidence in the good sense of man, and his qualifications for self-government," he wrote, "that I am never afraid of the issue where reason is left free to exert her force; and I will agree to be stoned as a false prophet if all does not end well in this country. Here is but the first chapter of the history of European liberty." To Madison he observed that members of the French Assembly looked to America as their model and viewed American precedents as they would the authority of the Bible, "open to explanation but not to question."

The kinship between the two nations received symbolic expression in Jefferson's assistance in the drafting of the Declaration of the Rights of Man. And in the last days of August, 1789, the leaders of the new government met in Jefferson's apartment to settle their differences on the degree of power to be exercised by the king. Four years later the French Jacobins made James Madison an honorary citizen of France. Madison gloried in the thought that France ignored the traditional national fences that had divided humanity into hostile camps.

On August 28, two days after the French presented to the world the Declaration of the Rights of Man, Jefferson wrote to Madison expressing the hope that the United States would take steps to assist France and not be content to place the French "on a mere footing with the English."

> When of two nations, the one has engaged herself in a. ruinous war for us, has spent her blood and money to save us, has opened her bosom to us in peace, and received us almost on the footing of her own citizens, while the other has moved heaven, earth, and hell to exterminate us in war, has insulted us in all her councils in peace, shut her doors to us in every port where her interests would admit it, libelled us in foreign nations, endeavored to poison them against the reception of our most precious commodities, to place these two nations on a footing, is to give a great deal more to one than to the other if the maxim be true that to make unequal quantities equal you must add more to the one of them than the other.

At first all classes and parts of the country hailed the Revolution. George Washington, after learning of the developments in France in the summer of 1789, expressed fear that it "is of too great a magnitude to be effected in so short a space" but what had taken place struck him as "of so wonderful a nature, that the mind can hardly realize the fact." If it should end as recent events indicated "that nation will be the most powerful and happy in Europe." Gouverneur Morris, who was in Paris, found it difficult "to guess whereabouts the flock will settle, when it flies so wild," but he too approved of the overthrow of the old order. He advised Washington: "I say, that we have an *interest* in the liberty of France. The leaders here are our friends. Many of them have imbibed their principles in America, and all have been fired by our example. Their opponents are by no means rejoiced at the success of our revolution, and many of them are disposed to form connexions of the strictest kind, with Great Britain."

The revolution in France merely strengthened convictions that Jefferson and Madison had held since 1783. As minister to France since 1785 Jefferson had worked industriously to promote commerce between the two countries. And when the new government took office in 1789 Madison earnestly believed that a leading motive in its establishment had been to achieve a degree of reciprocity with England and to extend the trade with other countries.

Congress did establish discriminatory duties on foreign ships, but it rejected Madison's proposal for further discrimination against ships of nations that had failed to enter into a commercial treaty. Those involved in trade saw no great hope of developing a trade with France, a nation they considered as staunch an adherent of the old exclusive mercantile system as the British. Madison would make his proposals another day when the country faced a dangerous foreign situation. By then he faced the hard fact that Alexander Hamilton had committed the nation to a foreign and domestic policy that ran directly counter to the most cherished ideals of the agrarians and tied the United States to England.

Hamilton boldly asserted that foreign policy must serve the ends set forth by national economic policy. Foreign capital constituted the great economic need of the United States, and, true to his principles, Hamilton fought desperately to make foreign policy an instrument for meeting that need. Concerning the value of foreign capital, he wrote that it ought to be "considered as a most valuable auxiliary, conducing to put in motion a greater quantity of productive labor, and a greater portion of useful enterprise, than could exist without it." In an underdeveloped country like the United States, "with an infinite fund of resources yet to be unfolded, every farthing of foreign capital" invested in internal improvements and in industry, "is a precious acquisition."

The value he placed upon it appeared in more eloquent fashion in the measures he put through. Capital would be available if the new nation demonstrated that it was friendly to capitalists and not ready to bend to the whims of an ignorant public guided by passion and by hostility to privileged classes. His program as the Secretary of the Treasury met all the requirements. Foreign, national domestic debts, and state debts were met with an alacrity that invited the fullest confidence of the creditor class. The funding system provided an opportunity for profitable investment guaranteeing to creditors an attractive rate of interest over a long period of time. The United States Bank added to the circulating media and thereby promoted business, but it had the added advantage of providing capitalists with a good investment opportunity. And Hamilton's leadership in the Washington administration approximated that of a British prime minister who steered Congress at will and reduced popular distempers to harmless frustration.

Hamilton's financial system necessitated a policy of friendship toward Great Britain. Only British capital could guarantee the economic leap that the Secretary of Treasury envisioned. Only duties on imports would meet the financial obligations the new government assumed, and three-fourths of the imports came from Great Britain. Any interruption of that trade would deprive the new government of its major source of revenue. National interest, then, dictated good relations with Great Britain.

The great danger facing Hamilton's financial structure lay in the anti-British feelings of the people and their readiness to accept revolutionary France as a sister nation fighting for the rights of man. Of these two hazards, the feeling of kinship for the French revolutionary leaders posed the greatest threat. Hamilton viewed with alarm the French messianic rhetoric and a mass psychological outburst in the name of liberty, equality and fraternity that suggested the immediate emancipation of mankind from the thralldom of the past. The French leaders startled the world with appeals to people everywhere to revolt against their masters. The powerful and deeply ingrained democratic sentiments of Americans provided a fertile soil for such appeals, and Hamilton lived in mortal dread of the excited multitude driving their representatives into a pro-French policy that would alienate the British and perhaps even pull the nation into partnership with France against Great Britain in war. . . .

What had been a rift became a deep cleavage in 1793. Two developments sharpened the differences. In February of that year Great Britain and France went to war and forced the United States to give careful thought to its obligations under the French alliance. The Washington administration no sooner came to grips with that issue than Citizen Genêt arrived with a proposal for a new commercial treaty and instructions to promote the use of American manpower, port facilities, and produce. The merchant group made shrewd use of both to strengthen their political hold.

In April Washington's cabinet debated the question of the relationship of the United States to the two belligerents. The issue was not neutrality as much as it was the kind of neutrality. Hamilton contended that the treaty with France was no longer binding. He argued that the justice of Louis' execution appeared doubtful, that it remained to be seen whether the new government would prove stable, that it was guilty of taking extreme measures and of being the aggressor in the war, that it had violated all rights in seeking to promote revolutions abroad, and that it was undertaking military and naval operations involving risks never contemplated at the time the treaty was negotiated. Hamilton, the advocate of *realpolitik,* held that a nation's first duty was to uphold its own interests and that treaty obligations must always be subordinate to that duty. Jefferson expressed disgust at the expediency of the Secretary of the Treasury. "Would you suppose it possible," he wrote to Madison, "that it should have been seriously proposed to declare our treaties with France void on the authority of an ill-understood scrap in Vattel and that it should be necessary to discuss it?"

Jefferson refused to throw off the treaty, but this did not prevent him from firmly resolving on a policy of neutrality. It must be a "manly neutrality" as opposed to Hamilton's "abject principles" and willingness to offer "our breech to every kick which Great Britain may choose to give." He was equally determined to stand firm against any French violations of American neutrality. "I wish," he wrote to James Monroe, "we may be able to repress the spirit of the people within the limits of a fair neutrality." A "fair neutrality" would yield no more privileges to France than to England. Jefferson gave the treaty with France a strict interpretation and narrowed the rights of that country to a minimum. He confided to Madison, "I fear that a fair neutrality will prove a disagreeable pill to our friends, tho' necessary to keep us out of the calamities of a war."

Jefferson's "fair neutrality" gained the support of President Washington. He issued a proclamation warning citizens against unneutral acts. The tone of the proclamation disturbed the incorruptible Madison whose sense of moral obligation winced at the sacrifice of principle to what appeared to be national self interest. He disliked the use of the term "impartial" in the President's proclamation. "Peace," wrote Madison, "is no doubt to be preserved at any price that honor and good faith will permit." "In examining our own engagements under the Treaty with France," he wrote, "it would be honorable as well as just to adhere to the sense that would at the time have been put on them." "The attempt to shuffle off the Treaty altogether by quibblings on Vattel is equally contemptible." The difference between Hamilton's approach to a treaty and the approach of Jefferson and Madison was symbolic of the wide gulf that separated their broader concept of foreign relations.

The Secretary of State soon complained that his colleagues in the administration leaned toward England. "We are going on here in the same spirit still," he wrote. "The Anglomania has seized violently on three members of our council," said the Secretary of State. Jefferson saw that the "natural aristocrats" of the larger towns, the merchants trading in British capital, the "paper men," and all the "old tories" supported the English side on every question. The farmers, tradesmen, mechanics, and merchants trading on their own capital took the other side. The same groups who supported Hamilton's fiscal policy followed him on the question of foreign affairs. Not all discerned the intimate relation between the recently adopted financial program and the question of what attitude to take toward Great Britain, but the connection by no means escaped such leaders in Congress as William Smith of South Carolina and Fisher Ames and Theodore Sedgwick of Massachusetts. Nor did the fact that domestic policy and foreign policy were essentially one and the same escape Jefferson and Madison. The latter saw in the "errors" of the administration a wound to national honor, a disregard of the obligations to France, and an injury to public feeling "by a seeming indifference to the cause of liberty." But it was not the cause of liberty in Europe alone but in the United States as well that both Jefferson and Madison had in mind. What they did not understand was that Hamilton put national interest above all other considerations. . . .

The debate over relations with Great Britain became inextricably involved with the question of which of the two emerging parties was to control the federal government for the next four years. The Jay Treaty was a reasonable give-and-take compromise of the issues between the two countries. What rendered it so assailable was not the compromise spelled out between the two nations but the fact that it was not a compromise between the two political parties at home. Embodying the views of the Federalists, the treaty repudiated the foreign policy of the opposing party. The Anti-Federalists saw in their party's foreign policy a set of principles of fundamental importance not only in relation to the outside world but also basic to the very nature of the kind of society they were seeking to establish at home. They were likewise intent on taking control of the government in the approaching election. Tied to the question of the ratification of the treaty was the question of the future prospects of the two camps of political leaders.

The British expected their rivals to fight. If they didn't, observed Henry Adams, they looked upon them as cowardly or mean. Alexander Hamilton's determination not to offend Great Britain invited a high handed and callous disregard that nettled the American agrarians. The United States had turned its breeches to receive British kicks. So it seemed to Jefferson.

The list of grievances against Great Britain included retention of the military posts in the Northwest, at least indirect encouragement to the Indians who had launched a costly and troublesome war, the carrying away of several thousand Negro slaves at the close of the Revolution without making compensation, and a policy of extorting the most out of American trade without offering reciprocal advantages. For two years Jefferson invited negotiation of the issues without gaining any response. To this frustrating experience George Hammond, the British minister, added a tone of conversation that convinced Jefferson and Madison that the British planned to make war. A speech by Lord Dorchester, Governor General of Canada, encouraging the Indians to make war, and the building of a new fort at Maumee by Governor Simcoe, strengthened this view.

The British game poorly prepared the way for American acceptance of British rulings as to commerce on the high seas upon the outbreak of hostilities between Great Britain and France in February, 1793. On June 8 Lord Grenville issued orders to naval commanders to seize all ships carrying corn, flour, or meal bound for a port in France or any port controlled by the armies of France. Hammond, the British minister, defended the order with the dubious assertion that the law of nations sanctioned the treatment of all provisions as contraband and subject to confiscation "where the depriving an enemy of these supplies, is one of the means intended to be employed for reducing him to reasonable terms of peace." Jefferson jumped upon the British contention with the eagerness of one who believed that the prospective enemy had overreached himself. In an instruction to Thomas Pinckney, American minister in London, Jefferson damned the measure as "so manifestly contrary to the law of nations, that nothing more would seem necessary, than to observe that it is so."

Jefferson carefully outlined the dangerous implications of the British contention for the United States. "We see, then, a practice begun, to which no time, no circumstances, prescribe any limits, and which strikes at the root of our agriculture, that branch of industry which gives food, clothing and comfort, to the great mass of inhabitants of these States," he stated. "If any nation whatever has a right," he said, "to shut up, to our produce, all the ports of the earth, except her own, and those of her friends, she may shut up these also, and confine us within our limits." "No nation," he proclaimed, "can subscribe to such pretensions; no nation can agree, at the mere will or interest of another, to have its peaceable industry suspended, and its citizens reduced to idleness and want."

The question likewise involved, said Jefferson, the right of the American government to defend itself against involuntary involvement in war. To put the United States into a position in which it furnished supplies to one belligerent and not to the other could only be deemed a cause for war by the latter. There was no difference, he explained, in the United States restraining commerce with France and her suffering Great Britain to prohibit it. France would consider the latter a mere pretext. To permit Great Britain to bar commerce with France would impose on the United States a neutral duty to likewise withhold supplies from Great Britain. "This is a dilemma," he said, "which Great Britain has no right to force upon us, and for which no pretext can be found in any part of our conduct."

Jefferson's firm posture contrasted with the note of supplication that so characterized Hamilton's every intrusion into foreign affairs when these involved Great Britain. Jefferson and Madison meant to demand respect. Privately, Jefferson confessed to Madison that he had no hope of Great Britain revoking her measures. These two architects of the republic aimed at impressing the British with the fact that they could not deal with the United States with impunity. . . .

In April the battle raged on another front. President Washington appointed John Jay special envoy to Great Britain. No appointment would have proved popular with the Republicans who much preferred to take economic measures before entering upon negotiations. The naming of Jay convinced them that further appeasement was to be expected. Jay had been ready to agree to the closing of the Mississippi in 1786 in return for a commercial treaty with Spain. His critics predicted that he would yield to the merchants again and negotiate a treaty that sacrificed the true national interest. The Republican societies engaged at once in a campaign of vilification of the envoy. This did not deter the Senate, always on the side of the executive branch, from confirming the appointment.

The instructions carefully spelled out the grievances, spoliations, violations of the peace treaty, and the restrictions on trade. No commercial treaty should be negotiated unless American ships gained the right to enter the British West Indies. But the firm tone of the instructions did not obscure the fact that the governing group at home desperately needed some kind of a treaty that would put an end to the dangerous tendency to take hostile measures toward England. Jay thought as did Hamilton and the merchants, and one paragraph of his instructions undoubtedly carried a special significance to him. That paragraph read: "You will mention, with due stress, the general irritation of the United States at the vexations, spoliations, captures, &c. And being on the field of negotiation you will be more able to judge, than can be prescribed now, how far you may state the difficulty which may occur in restraining the violence of some of our exasperated citizens." And besides his formal instructions Jay carried with him the letters from Hamilton urging a settlement and outlining its nature. . . .

In July Lord Grenville gave to Jay a draft of the proposed treaty altering somewhat the one submitted by Jay a few days earlier. Grenville's project probably reached Philadelphia in late August. Hamilton examined it and found two major weaknesses. He took strong exception to placing British vessels in American ports on the same basis as American vessels. He objected to Article XII dealing with the right of American vessels to enter the ports of the West Indies because the privilege was limited to two years and because it would have prohibited Americans from transporting produce of any of the West Indies to any other part of the world than the United States.

Edmund Randolph, Jefferson's successor as Secretary of State, scrutinized Grenville's draft with an equally critical eye. The refusal of the British to make compensation for the slaves taken at the close of the Revolution disturbed him more than any other aspect. He too considered Article XII unsatisfactory. He likewise objected to postponing British evacuation of the Northwest posts until June, 1796.

The criticisms of Hamilton and Randolph did not reach Jay until the treaty had been signed. Jay held that the treaty represented the utmost that could be expected in dealing with a nation so proud and so powerful. The fact that Article XII contained a two year limitation and prohibited the United States from engaging in the all important carrying trade from the West Indies struck Jay as less important than the fact that a wedge had been driven into the British barrier against American vessels.

The essence of Jay's defense of the treaty lay in his explanation to Edmund Randolph. "Perhaps it is not very much to be regretted that all our differences are merged in this treaty, without having been decided; disagreeable imputations are thereby avoided, and the door of conciliation is fairly and widely opened, by the *essential* justice done, and the conveniences granted to each other by the parties," he reflected. The treaty removed the most serious apprehensions concerning British intentions in the West. The two boundary disputes in the Northwest and the Northeast were to be settled by commissions. A *modus vivendi* assuring Americans of compensation for the losses on the high seas removed some of the ignitive quality from the controversy over neutral rights. The Hamiltonians, anxious about what war would do to the fiscal system and dreading a war in which they would inevitably become the allies of France considered these two as the great gains of the treaty.

The final treaty arrived in Philadelphia on March 7, 1795. Washington and Randolph decided at once not to make it public. The Senate received it in June and approved the treaty but without a vote to spare and subject to the removal of Article XII. The President delayed ratification, finding serious objections to the document that Jay had signed. During the anxious months of indecision he weighed two notably thoughtful papers prepared by Alexander Hamilton and Edmund Randolph. Both recommended favorable action, but Randolph made his approval subject to the British withdrawal of a recently issued order for the seizure of all corn, grain and flour destined for France. Washington agreed to the condition laid down by his Secretary of State.

Hamilton's paper for the President, *Remarks on the treaty of amity, commerce, and navigation, made between the United States and Great Britain,* placed the treaty under a microscope. With a tough mindedness that deserves notice Hamilton dealt with the objections that had been put forward against the treaty with as much honesty as he did with the advantages. Concerning the first ten articles, the only permanent ones, he concluded: "They close the various matters of controversy with Great Britain, and, upon the whole, they close them reasonably." Article XII was objectionable. Article XVIII left something to be desired, a stricter list of contraband. It likewise suffered from the failure to define clearly by what special circumstances noncontraband might become contraband. This lack of precision, due to a failure to reach agreement, could become "the pretext of abuses on the side of Great Britain, and of complaint on that of France. . . ." "On the whole," wrote Hamilton, "I think this article the worst in the treaty, except the 12th, though not defective enough to be an objection to its adoption."

Hamilton then hammered home the major argument for ratification of the treaty. The "truly important side of this treaty" as he saw it, lay in the fact that it closed the "controverted points between the two countries."

Jefferson contended for the ideal of "free ships make free goods" that had been incorporated in previous treaties of the United States. Both he and Madison held that the ideal was a part of the "law of nations." Hamilton rejected this. A majority of treaties did not incorporate this principle. No nation had gone to war in defense of it. The United States, yet weak, could scarcely find it advisable to contend for it at the price of war entailing economic ruin and probable loss of territory. . . .

The Jay Treaty pinched the Jeffersonians at three points. It committed the United States not to establish discriminatory duties against the British. Thereby it forced the agrarians to lay aside their whole foreign policy program and to accept that of the opposition.

Secondly, the treaty offended the nationalistic and democratic sentiments of the agrarians. Jefferson lamented: "The rights, the interest, the honor and faith of our nation are so grossly sacrificed. . . ." He wrote to Madison: "Where a faction has entered into a conspiracy with the enemies of their country to chain down the legislature at the feet of both; where the whole mass of our constituents have condemned this work in unequivocal manner, and are looking to you as their last hope to save them from the effects of the avarice and corruption of the first agent. . . ." Both Jefferson and Madison believed that a majority of the people opposed the treaty and that the popular will had been denied. When it became clear that the House of Representatives would appropriate the funds for putting the treaty into effect, Madison attributed it to the pressure of business interests.

Jefferson's and Madison's denunciations of the treaty are also better understood if one takes into account that in their eyes the treaty surrendered a major principle in the "Law of Nations." That term—"Law of Nations"—had all the aura of the Age of Enlightenment. It had no well defined meaning and certainly few generally accepted points, but to Jefferson and Madison it connoted justice and reason. They never doubted that their own broad interpretation of neutral rights accorded with the "Law of Nations" and the welfare of mankind.

This approach, one of the central threads of their foreign policy from 1789 to 1812, owed something to the fact that American interests would have benefitted tremendously by a universal acceptance of their interpretation of neutral rights. It owed quite as much to an idealistic view of what would benefit mankind. They desperately wanted a world order in which the innocent by-stander nations would not be made to suffer because a few major powers engaged in the folly of war. Jefferson and Madison overlooked the fact that Great Britain could not accept such an ideal without granting victory to its enemies.

In the situation confronting the United States in the spring of 1796 the surrender of the ideal had an additional and more grievous meaning for Jefferson's followers. To yield to British dictates on control of the seas meant that France would be denied access to American supplies. The United States would provide Great Britain with supplies at a time when the traditional friend, France, was struggling for liberty.

In September, 1796, George Washington delivered his Farewell Address. The President, finding himself amid the dissensions of heated party strife, had striven manfully to avoid falling into the hands of either faction. In 1793 he had, to a great degree, followed Jefferson's advice in meeting the dangers brought on by the war between Great Britain and France. Throughout the heated debates he had retained a sense of gratitude toward France and a sincere desire to deal with her justly. In the summer of 1795, he had resisted the pressure of Hamilton to ratify the Jay Treaty at once and had deliberated long before making his decision to ratify it. To be sure he could not participate in the feelings experienced by Jefferson and Madison because he did not share their philosophical outlook and their intense concern for their particular political ideals. On the other hand, he found it more difficult than Hamilton to make the concessions necessary to preserve harmony with Great Britain. The President found himself in an isolated position.

When the time came to deliver a farewell address, he called on Hamilton to draft it, and the message warned against party spirit and against a passionate attachment to one nation. To the more extreme elements in the more extreme Republican societies the counsel was applicable, but it scarcely applied to Jefferson and Madison whose pro-French feelings were rigorously subordinated to American nationalism.

Their nationalism posed a danger for they confused their American view of the world with their proclaimed universal view of justice and right reason. Their strong desire to make their republic an example of what could be achieved by noble aspiration set free to apply reason made them impatient and particularly so concerning Great Britain's financial influence and arbitrary dicta as to how far the seas were to be open to a free exchange of goods. That they were misunderstood, that their views were dubbed theoretical, is not surprising. Idealists in the realm of foreign affairs trying to establish a program that would reconcile national interests and idealistic considerations were to find themselves in a difficult position many times in the future. . . .

Historians, pointing to the modest changes that ensued in domestic policies, usually reject Jefferson's judgment that his election [in 1800] constituted a revolution. Jefferson's own yardstick, a change in attitude and spirit, does justify the term. It was a revolution in terms of a buoyant spirit unencumbered by traditional fatalism. Jefferson expressed the new attitude as he observed the beginnings of the French Revolution: "I have so much confidence in the good sense of man, and his qualifications for self-government that I am never afraid of the issue where reason is left free to exert her force."

The change from Federalism to Republicanism initiated a new approach to foreign policy of notable significance. Whereas Hamilton was distinguished by a tough-minded realism, by prudence, by a disciplining of the national spirit, and by sober calculation of available power, Jefferson and Secretary of State James Madison exhibited an assertiveness, a keen sensitivity to presumed slights, and a full confidence in the nation's capacity to defend its interests and uphold justice. Hamilton and the Federalists started their formulations with a recognition of the existing system of international relations and were willing to work within the framework of current practice. Jefferson and Madison began by rejecting existing realities and sought to implement an ideal.

To understand Jefferson and Madison in foreign affairs one has to begin by making their full faith in the natural rights political theory central to their approach. In every society man was endowed with the natural rights of life, liberty, and the pursuit of happiness. The ideal government was one which served to uphold these rights and the ideal citizen was one who jealously guarded his rights which rested in the natural order of the universe and were above existing man-made contrivances. Only in the United States had the ideal been transformed into practice and embodied in political institutions. This system had its counterpart in international relations. A nation possessed rights that had their origin in the natural order, and these were no less rights because the existing system ignored them. It was the first duty of an enlightened citizen and of an enlightened nation to uphold these rights against the forces of darkness.

Thereby entered the moralistic approach to foreign policy. What was right and justifiable was to be determined by standards derived from an ideal and not by the standards of existing systems. With it entered the imperious assumption that American concepts of what was right and wrong possessed a universal validity. This is what made the American approach to foreign relations unique and in the light of this we better understand both its strength and weaknesses.

The attitude expressed itself spontaneously and Americans never found it necessary to explain its intellectual basis. An interesting illustration of the approach is found in the report of a committee of Congress drafted in 1803 when it was proposed that two million dollars be appropriated for the purchase of the Floridas. The committee observed:

> The Government of the United States is differently organized from any other in the world. Its object is the happiness of man; its policy and its interest, to pursue right by right means. War is the great scourge of the human race, and should never be resorted to but in cases of the most imperious necessity. A wise government will avoid it, when its views can be attained by peaceful measures. Princes fight for glory, and the blood and the treasure of their subjects is the price they pay. In all nations the people bear the burden of war, and in the United States the people rule.

High purpose and selfish material interests were thereby blended into foreign policy. The upholder of the higher law inevitably became the uncompromising defender of national interests without suffering any wracking doubts concerning the identity of national interests and international justice. Jefferson and Madison gave expression to widely held views and their approach to foreign policy became the American approach that found its culmination in the moralizing of Woodrow Wilson at Versailles and Cordell Hull's moral and legalistic expositions in behalf of an ideal international order based on law rather than force.

Jefferson as Idealist-Realist

LAWRENCE S. KAPLAN

No statesman of the revolutionary and early national periods made a more substantial contribution to the development of American foreign policy than Thomas Jefferson. From his magnificent synthesis of eighteenth-century political theory in the Declaration of Independence to his death fifty years later, Jefferson's idealism, tempered by pragmatic regard for practical realities, played a key role in defining a distinctively American position toward the external world. No one, it might be said, ever blended the moralistic yearnings of the young Republic for a new international order with the practical pursuit of national self-interest more effectively than he.

Examination of Jefferson's amazingly varied career and multiple talents highlights the renaissance quality of his mind and work. For another man any one of his accomplishments would have assured the homage of posterity. Over a span of eighty-three years Jefferson pursued an astonishing range of activities: he was largely responsible for founding the University of Virginia; he was an architectural innovator who helped bring classical forms to the New World; he was an agronomist experimenting with transplantations of rice and silk to the South; he was a theologian who attempted to harmonize Christianity with the temper of the Enlightenment. Above all, he was a scholar in the art of government whose ideas spread through the nation as Jeffersonian democracy. The prestige conferred by authorship of the Declaration of Independence and the power of the presidency ensured dissemination of his ideas in a manner rarely available to political theorists. If his virtuosity did not encompass an appreciation for the intricacies of finance, that shortcoming stemmed less from a lack of understanding the techniques of moneymaking than from a taste that placed spending above getting. Against the bankruptcy of his Monticello estate must be weighed the credit of a life-style that warmed guests in the beautiful mansion with their host's hospitality as much as with fine French wines.

This westerner belonged to an aristocratic family, the Randolphs of Virginia. His father had improved his status by a wealthy marriage. As a member of the governing elite of the colony, Jefferson early experienced British and European influences flowing across the ocean to Tidewater and Piedmont, Virginia. While there may have been few artists or scientists at the College of William and Mary in the colonial capital, there were sufficient men and books to initiate the youthful Jefferson into the life of the eighteenth-century liberal mind. He enjoyed the best of both the Old and the New World, sharing the excitement of European ideas that ranged from Arthur Young's tracts on scientific farming to the disputed poems of Ossian. Books and papers from European centers found their way to Jefferson's library and to the drawing rooms of Williams-

Lawrence S. Kaplan, "Thomas Jefferson: The Idealist as Realist." Reprinted from the book *Makers of American Diplomacy* by Frank Merli and Theodore Wilson with the permission of Charles Scribner's Sons. Copyright © 1974 Frank Merli and Theodore Wilson.

burg and Philadelphia. He was very much a member of the international fraternity of literati that pumped liberal ideas into the courts of Europe and the coffeehouses of America—ideas that ultimately pushed both along the road to revolution. Jefferson's intimacy with such scholarly men as Professor William Small of William and Mary and George Wythe, his law teacher at Williamsburg, and with such sophisticated men of the world as Francis Fauquier, lieutenant governor of Virginia during his student days, were experiences he repeated in Philadelphia and Paris in later years. True, the above names almost exhausted the roster of interesting people in colonial Virginia, but the point is that his circle of acquaintances included some of the broadest intellectual interests there; his six years at the village capital provided him with an extraordinary range of ideas.

At the same time, perhaps more than any contemporary, Jefferson captured the best elements in the transatlantic civilization of the colonies. As an American living close to the frontier he appreciated the richness of his environment and recognized the advantages of a land with few people and abundant resources. The agrarian society he so valued bred equality among its members, fostered self-reliance, and opened opportunities for individual growth that the Old World could never provide; his experiences encompassed facets that Europeans could not share unless they came to America. . . .

For him, as for all the Founding Fathers, the central event of life was the creation of a nation out of thirteen disparate British colonies. Every step in making the Revolution and in securing it afterwards involved foreign affairs. In such a context, conventional divisions between domestic and foreign affairs lost meaning. In the first generation of the Republic no national leader could escape awareness of the hostile outside world. Europe intruded in every way, inspiring fear of reconquest by the mother country, offering opportunity along sparsely settled borderlands, arousing uncertainties over the alliance with a great power. Unless the new nation settled for a subsistence economy its prosperity rested upon trade with the Old World; the European market held the American economy captive, and no political theory could alter that fact of economic life. There could be no escape from such concerns, any more than from the language Americans spoke, the customs they followed, or the ideas they circulated.

Anglo-American relations dominated American history in the early years of the Republic. Despite a successful military separation, the economic links of tradition proved more enduring than the political, even though many people, Jefferson included, wished it to be otherwise. If an alternative to a British connection existed, it was not to be achieved by retreating into autarchy but by shifting the economy toward France, the wartime ally; it was to France that those leaders suspicious or fearful of British designs turned during the administrations of George Washington and John Adams. . . .

The record clearly reveals the Jeffersonian involvement in foreign affairs. His service as delegate to both Continental Congresses, as wartime governor of Virginia, and as commissioner to France at the end of the war were all linked to French and British influences in American life. During the Confederation period he represented the United States in Paris, attempting to mobilize support for its continued independence. Upon [his] return to America he became secretary of state, the first in the revitalized union, absorbed in assuring survival of the nation in a hostile world. The French Revolution and its subsequent wars dominated his years as vice-president and president. The magnificent acquisition of Louisiana, though not wholly his doing, deservedly is credited to him; and the disastrous embargo of 1807, though not wholly his mistake, if mistake it was, appropriately is identified with him. Success or failure, Jefferson the public man was of necessity a maker of diplomacy.

Jefferson's enemies of every generation make much of what they consider his deficiencies in character. Most dwell on his inconsistency, pointing out that he shifted from one position to another at critical moments out of fear of consequences, instability of judgment, or passion for power. Thus, his movement from strict to loose construction of the Constitution, from agrarianism to support of manufacturing, from fear of executive power to abuse of it in office, from a love of France to distrust and finally to dependence upon that country under Napoleon have all been used by enemies who would dismiss him as weak, cowardly, opportunistic, or worse. His Francophilism has been interpreted as a personality quirk with dire consequences for the country.

Much of the familiar Federalist criticism of Jefferson withers in the face of close examination. A far better case may be made of excessive consistency, of an allegiance to a conception of society long after it had become obvious that the ideal could not be sustained, or of reliance upon economic weapons against Europe after those weapons were turned against him. Jefferson never questioned what he wanted for America; he envisioned a society of cultivated, independent men on terms of equality with one another, keeping government as close to the local level as possible, living on farms rather than in cities because the agrarian life best propagated the good life. Expansionism became part of the plan because an American empire would remove the corrupt and dangerous model of Europe, as it would if the pattern of international commerce could also be reorganized to incorporate the American alternative to mercantilism, free trade. He identified urban commercial society with class conflict, with oligarchic manipulation of politics, and with European financial control over America, most especially Great Britain's economic interests in its former colonies. To combat such dangers, he believed that right reason applied to the right environment would create a society embodying the best blend of the Enlightenment with the frontier.

He never abandoned his vision of the good society. Apparent deviations were responses to external pressures or were expedients, temporary tactical retreats. He shared with other Founding Fathers a belief that alliances with European powers were unnecessary and potentially dangerous to American independence. His musings about a relationship with Europe "precisely on the footing of China," while fanciful, were genuine; and he knew that in an imperfect world less desirable choices sometimes had to be made to attain more desirable ends. Thus, an alliance with France might be made if Britain threatened the nation's independence; the danger of a connection with Europe had to be balanced against the greater damage that defeat or accommodation with Britain might bring. . . .

Part of the explanation of Jefferson's flexibility lies in his early recognition of the importance of the external world in American affairs and in his firm belief in the permanent hostility of Great Britain. Preservation of the new nation from the baneful effects of those realities required statecraft; if Jefferson sometimes overrated the efficacy of diplomacy, he seldom underestimated the danger of involvement in transatlantic affairs. Ultimately, of course, Americans sought a solution in withdrawal from the European arena into their own empire, into a peculiarly American isolationism wherein obligations to Europe did not exist. In one way or another nearly every American statesman worked to free the nation from dependence upon Europe.

When Jefferson was secretary of state in the 1790s, his countrymen differed violently about the direction of foreign affairs, especially about the American response to the French Revolution and its subsequent wars. The powerful commercial interests of New England and the seaboard towns looked to Great Britain as a necessary business partner, at least until a viable domestic economy could be created. Many of its leaders equated a pro-British policy with freedom from French ideology and French imperialism. Jefferson and his followers never accepted such views. They believed, at least until after the War of 1812, that Britain intended to reduce America to a position of permanent inferiority in an economic relationship more suffocating than the political connection had been before independence. Like their opponents the Federalists, Jeffersonians responded emotionally to events in France, but they read their import differently. They believed that if the French republic collapsed in its war with monarchical Britain, monarchy if not British rule would return to America.

Jefferson's anti-British animus had deep roots. It grew in part from wartime experiences and received repeated reinforcement during his career. At times his fears approached obsession, but he directed these sentiments more to particular institutions and proponents of policy than to Englishmen per se or to the benign aspects of British culture. However flawed, the British political system surpassed any in Europe; and even when in France desperately seeking help during the Confederation period, Jefferson could in good conscience recommend to French friends that they follow the British political model. If Frenchmen kept in view the example of their cross-Channel neighbor, he told Lafayette, they might advance "step by step towards a good constitution." His feelings for English friends remained as warm as his feelings for Frenchmen. He admired the liberal English reformers whose Anglo-Saxon traditions in law and language he claimed for America—indeed, he who had paraphrased Locke's political philosophy could hardly do otherwise. . . .

To effect a new relationship with France and to break the old one with Britain required a centralized government strong enough to command the respect of its peers in the international arena. In this view Jefferson was at one with John Jay and Alexander Hamilton. Like the former (who had been secretary for foreign affairs under the Confederation) he believed that if Europeans saw an efficient and well-administered national government, with its trade and finances prudently regulated, they would be disposed to cultivate American friendship rather than risk its resentment. This theme, which Jay stressed in the third *Federalist,* found a harmonious response in Jefferson, and he could even join with Hamilton when the New Yorker asserted in the eleventh *Federalist* that "a steady adherence to the Union" might allow the new nation to tip the scales of European competition in the New World for the benefit of Americans. Thus, a commonly recognized impotence in foreign affairs provided a powerful stimulus for strengthening the powers of the central government. The Founding Fathers, even when they could agree on little else, all sought to exploit European disadvantage for America's advantage.

Historians have not always recognized that Hamilton and Jefferson shared belief in a strong executive able to resist congressional encroachments upon its power in foreign affairs. Jefferson earlier had expressed approval of the constitutional device that freed the central government from the interference of state assemblies on matters of taxation; now with the new government in operation, he thought that the federal legislature's natural tendency to interfere with presidential responsibilities must be resisted. In a memorandum to Washington, presented shortly after taking office, the new secretary of state questioned the propriety of presidential consultation with the Senate about diplomatic exchanges. Arguing that there was no constitutional requirement for such solicitation and that the practice would create an unfortunate precedent, Jefferson interpreted senatorial powers as extending no further than approval or disapproval of nominees. Even then, he envisioned the decision as basically presidential—almost exclusively so, "except as to such portions of it as are specially submitted to the Senate. Exceptions are to be construed strictly." Jefferson's rigid construction of the Constitution in 1790 was hardly distinguishable from that of the Hamiltonians around him, including the secretary of the treasury himself.

If the Jeffersonian vision of American foreign policy began with an executive free of congressional constraints and the shortcomings of the Confederation, it included other elements customarily identified with his great rival, Hamilton: repayment of obligations to foreign creditors through assumption of the debts of previous governments and the promotion of American shipping through an effective navigation system. New England merchants and Philadelphia creditors welcomed these facets of the Hamiltonian program, and, to a point, so did Madison and Jefferson. While it is true that from the outset Jefferson had many reservations about his cabinet colleagues, especially when he suspected them of monarchical tendencies, he could work with them during the early years of Washington's administration. He could tolerate Treasury intrusion into his department by Hamilton's involvement in consular affairs, as long as he believed that Jeffersonian views received a fair hearing. His rivals in the cabinet in those early years were "good men and bold men, and sensible men."

Not even the Nootka Sound affair in the summer of 1790 fully revised that judgment. Although Jefferson strongly opposed Hamilton's wish to grant a

British request for the passage of troops through American territory in the event of war between Spain and Britain over the Pacific Northwest, he had no knowledge of Hamilton's intimate connections with British agents. Nor did he adamantly oppose concessions to the British per se. His point simply was that concessions ought to be reciprocal; the United States ought not surrender a bargaining weapon in advance. In their first cabinet debate on foreign affairs Hamilton and Jefferson differed more on tactics than on ideology.

Of course, Hamilton's early hostility to discriminatory legislation against British shipping did evoke criticism from Madison and Jefferson, but not the deep emotional response it was to arouse in 1793–94. Hamilton, after all, had a navigation system, and that was a step in the right direction. It took time before Jefferson's mind converted Hamilton's behavior into a dangerous passion for monarchy and a fatal dependence on Britain.

In part, at least, Jefferson's tolerance for failure of punitive measures against the British may have flowed from the concurrent insensitivity toward America displayed by the liberal regime in France. While the revolutionists had reformed their government under the National Assembly, nothing in those reforms served the interests of the United States. To his chagrin, Jefferson realized that the new bourgeois rulers of France had no more intent than the mercantilists of the old regime to permit liberal terms for American goods in French markets. That realization caught him between anger and embarrassment, for it coincided with a contretemps in relations between the two nations. Madison's navigation law (which failed to discriminate between ships of countries with commercial treaties and those without them) had given rise to a French protest, to which Jefferson normally would have been sympathetic. He recognized that in spirit, if not in letter, it was unfair that British and French ships would receive equal treatment in American ports, and he wished Congress to make special concessions to the French in return for the concessions they had made during his ministry; but French intransigence threatened to undermine support for such an arrangement.

Still, Jefferson sought to exploit the situation. The behavior of the National Assembly freed him from some inhibitions over past French favors and permitted him a degree of flexibility. That France did not see its own advantage in at least removing prerevolutionary restrictions from the West Indian trade seemed incredible to him. His impatience flared into anger when the French consul in New York insisted upon the recall of two consuls whom Congress had sent to the French islands. Jefferson resisted that demand, ultimately winning a minor victory when the American consuls were permitted to remain as "commercial agents." That success signified little and the secretary knew it; he harbored no illusions that an entente had been established between the two countries.

Much of his distress in office, then, stemmed less from the Francophobic character of the Hamiltonians than from the fact that the French refused friendly gestures when they were offered. Neither Madison's persistent attempts in Congress to fashion a navigation system that would benefit French commerce nor Jefferson's illuminating reports on the whale oil and codfish industries (with their clear invitation to France to replace those who had built "their navigation on the ruin of ours") struck responsive chords in Paris. Assuming the impossibility of weaning Americans from British ties, the French middle-class leaders of the Revolution wrote off American commerce. They even revoked the minor concessions that Jefferson had so painfully extracted during his ministry in France. The arrival in 1791 of a new French minister, Jean Baptiste Ternant, did not help matters. Ternant found Hamilton more congenial than Jefferson, so when the latter presented a plan for exchanging with the French full privileges of natives in each other's ports, the negative response did not surprise him. To the minister, free trade seemed to reward Britain at the expense of France.

War in Europe, particularly between France and Britain in 1793, changed the immediate course of Franco-American relations. It revived Jefferson's hopes for a new identity of interests between the two countries, although he recognized the danger of American involvement in the European conflict through obligations incurred in the alliance of 1778. For all his rising anger against Federalists and Britons, Jefferson did not envisage American troops or ships fighting alongside the French in the West Indies or anywhere else any more than did Hamilton. Yet the opportunity for exploiting a new French mood to strike out at British suzerainty over trade and arrogance over maritime claims proved too glittering to resist. The republican government of France opened West Indian ports to American ships and dispatched a more amiable minister to negotiate a liberal commercial treaty based precisely on Jefferson's scheme of mutual naturalization. Small wonder that the secretary's expectations outweighed fears as Europe plunged into the wars of the French Revolution.

There was a link between the worsening of Jefferson's relations with Hamiltonians at home and improvement of his relations with France. From 1793 to the end of the decade, first as secretary of state and then later as vice-president, he saw the Republic in peril in America and the Republic in peril in Europe. France's part as warrior against British monarchy and imperialism sharpened his antagonism toward British agents in America; increasingly, he saw the Federalist faction as a tool of British interests seeking to restore monarchy to America. Such a goal explained the uses to which Hamiltonian power would be put; it explained the failure of his own efforts to reduce British influence and enhance the interests of American democrats. The whole Hamiltonian program—from funding the national debt and establishing a national bank to Anglo-American reconciliation and a pro-British trade policy—became in his mind part of an enormous invisible conspiracy against the national welfare. The European war unmasked Hamilton's real purpose. Such was the Jeffersonian image of Federalism; of course there was a mirror image of Jeffersonians in the minds of their opponents.

Naturally, this Jeffersonian angle of vision enhanced the importance of France as a counterweight to domestic and foreign enemies. While hardly a new position, its urgency intensified after 1793, and introduced a new and ugly dimension into American debates on foreign affairs and domestic politics. The French republic took on symbolic overtones. According to Jeffersonians,

France struggled for more than its own survival—the survival of liberty everywhere was at stake. A British victory would reimpose its rule in America, either directly or through Britain's faithful American servants. Many of Jefferson's friends perished in the struggle for republicanism in France; although he deplored the losses, he endured them stoically, even philosophically, regarding his friends as soldiers fallen in the battle for universal liberty. "My own affections have been deeply wounded by some of the martyrs to this cause," he told William Short on 3 January 1793, "but rather than it should have failed I would have seen half the earth desolated; were there but an Adam to an Eve left in every country. Left free, it would be better than it now is." Written a month before France declared war on Britain, this letter expressed Jefferson's deep commitment to the cause of revolutionary republicanism. Given that predisposition, his fear of counterrevolutionary Britain and its supposed American agents intensified. The mild challenge raised by Britain in the Nootka Sound affair of 1790 had become three years later a matter of the life and death of a society.

The immediate problem for Washington's advisers, however, was the position of the United States toward the belligerents. To resolve that difficulty, Jefferson laid down a precedent for recognition of foreign governments: *de facto* control by the government in power. Possession of domestic power and ability to fulfill international obligations were the tests of legitimacy. Even before Washington raised the question of recognition in the cabinet, Jefferson had spelled out his position in a letter to the American minister in France. "I am sensible," he told Gouverneur Morris on 12 March 1793, "that your situation must have been difficult during the transition from the late form of government to the reestablishment of some other legitimate authority, that you may have been at a loss to determine with whom business might be done. Nevertheless when principles are well understood, their application is less embarrassing. We surely cannot deny to any nation that right whereon our own government is founded, that every one may govern itself according to whatever form it pleases, change these forms at its own will; that it may transact its business with foreign nations through whatever organ it thinks proper, whether King, Convention, Assembly, Committee, President, or anything else it may use. The will of the nation is the only thing essential to be regarded." Jefferson never questioned that the republican government of France should have its minister received, its financial claims honored, and its role as an ally affirmed; when Washington raised these questions after the execution of the French king and the extension of the European war, the secretary of state immediately perceived the mind of Hamilton guiding the president. It outraged him that America seemed more cautious in its support of a republic than it had been in its allegiance to a monarchy. With feeling he asked, "Who is the American who can say with truth that he would not have allied himself to France if she had been a republic?"

In defending the alliance Jefferson marshaled evidence from many authorities on international law of the seventeenth and eighteenth centuries, from Grotius to Vattel. He won his case, at least over recognition and legitimacy of treaties, if not over neutrality. If his position was based on the moral worth of republicans expressing the will of the people rather than on *de facto* control of France by the Girondists, realism needs redefinition. The scholars of international law help little in understanding the Jeffersonian position, for they can be cited either way, as Jefferson himself did when he dismissed that "ill understood scrap in Vattel" that Hamilton had used to deny recognition and then a few months later cited that same Vattel to refute the French minister's demand for a more friendly neutrality. For both Hamiltonians and Jeffersonians the nub of the matter seems to have been the legitimacy of a revolutionary transfer of power. For the former destruction of a hereditary monarchy by revolution stripped from the usurpers all international obligations owed to their predecessors; for the latter, revolutionists merely made legitimate what had been doubtful before by exercising a natural right to alter the form of government. . . .

Belief in Federalist subversion of America's republican experiment dominated Jefferson's mind for the remainder of the decade. Obsession with Hamiltonian maleficence led him at times to startling judgments couched in picturesque language. Washington appeared elliptically as one of the "Samsons in the field & Solomons in the council . . . who have had their heads shorn by the harlot England." On another occasion he prepared to leave Monticello for a visit to London (which he expected to find under French occupation) to "hail the dawn of liberty and republicanism in that island." His conviction that the Federalists had accepted a British definition of neutral rights and an inferior position in the British Empire merged with the conviction that they also planned a monarchical government for America. Washington was their captive, and while John Adams resisted Hamiltonian pretensions, the second president was also an adherent of a form of society inimical to Jeffersonian values. So the world seemed to Jefferson, retired in Virginia from 1794 to 1796 and then isolated in the vice-presidency during Adams's administration. A quasi-war with France coupled with assaults upon the liberties of Republicans lent credence to a nearly paranoid view of America that Jefferson did not alter until he became president.

Yet even in his moments of deepest despair over the direction of American policy under the Federalists, Jefferson resisted his natural impulses to expand the relationship with France, for he knew the limits of counterbalance. Even as he tangled with his rival over neutrality in 1793, Jefferson had no wish to bring the United States into the European war. His opponents were far less fastidious on isolation when Britain was involved. What Jefferson wanted was a benevolent neutrality that would assist France rather than Britain; with it he wished to pressure the British for commercial concessions in return for abstention from the conflict. He failed. Once a proclamation of neutrality had been issued, the possibilities for manipulating it to the advantage of Britain passed to Hamilton, and he made the most of them. There is, however, no evidence that for all his unhappiness Jefferson would have risked a war with Britain. He, rather than Adams, might have reaped the unhappy consequences of Jay's Treaty— and he might have handled them less well.

Jefferson's disavowal of Minister Edmond Genêt during his last year in office and subsequent willingness to let the French alliance lapse at the beginning of his presidency provide an appropriate frame for the comment of France's minister in 1796, Pierre Adet, that Jefferson was an "American and, as such, he cannot be sincerely our friend. An American is the born enemy of all the European peoples." Adet recognized a basic Jeffersonian premise, that in the midst of war and revolution he had given his fervent blessings to the French cause—but France essentially was an instrument of policy rather than an object of it. Its society, its people, its culture all evoked a genuine Francophilism. In Jefferson's statecraft with France, however, there were always *arrières pensées.* . . .

The primacy of American independence from the Old World remained a constant in Jefferson's thinking. He preferred an agrarian society to an industrial one; but if he had to accept the latter, he wished for an industrial America cut loose from British controls, performing the role France had failed to provide. To ensure insulation from Europe's troubles he pressed for westward and southern expansion to free American borders from the anxieties of war and to make room for the growth of the Republic. Jefferson's early encounters with division and disunity in the Revolution and Confederation had qualified his dedication to states' rights; his major involvement with them was when he felt impotent to control the central government. While he never denied the virtues he had celebrated in limited government, his early advice to Washington and his own behavior during his presidency suggest that when opportunities for vital action by the executive offered themselves the president ought not to be inhibited by excessive deference to congressional or state authority.

The pragmatic strain in Jefferson's management of foreign affairs, which permitted him to accept conditions inhibiting his freedom of action, also permitted him to shape those conditions to his ideas of the needs of the nation. If commercial ties with Europe were indispensable—and they were—he wished them to be conducted with minimal political entanglements as he preached in his first inaugural. He shed no tears for the demise of the French alliance. If developments abroad served the interests of a small maritime power, he could exploit them without surrendering either American interests or principles. Philosophers of the Old World might be enlisted in the American cause, just as the conflicts among European states might serve American trade or territorial advances. Such sentiments marked Jefferson's view of France and his policy toward it.

Whether Europe or America derived more gain from his dalliances remains debatable. What is certain is Jefferson's consistent belief in the justice of his policies; they were moral by virtue of their American character. For all his expediency he never separated national self-interest from morality in the management of foreign affairs. His determination to recognize the French republic in 1793 rested on justice as well as on utility. Recognition appeased his moral sense while it appealed to his practical streak, much as did his ideas on neutral rights and free trade. A characteristic American approach to international relations has been the casting of national interests on a moral base; Jefferson's contribution was to shape this conceit and to seek a relationship with the external world that followed from it.

Political Opportunism and Statesmanship

ALEXANDER DECONDE

What significance do the crucial Washington years have in American political and diplomatic history?

If these pages shed any light on the question, they show that the traditional picture of the beginnings of our national history which has heretofore been painted in bold strokes remains firm in the main outline but that some major details should be modified. These first years under the federal government have been depicted as "our Golden Age," as "the classic age of American statecraft," an era which produced men of "heroic stature," particularly among the statesmen who molded foreign policy. While the founding fathers were undeniably men of rare ability, above the average of succeeding generations of politicians, they do not emerge in this study "men of talents and genius on a scale perhaps unexampled in the history of the world." Instead, like all men, they appear mortal, with human strengths and weaknesses, with petty faults, at times with heroic virtues.

The statesmen of the Washington era, to some extent, played their politics and diplomacy by ear. They were marked too often in their attitudes by selfish, irrational behavior; too often they placed political advantage above national welfare. Jefferson, and, to a greater degree, Hamilton, in their political pursuits and in their connivance with agents of foreign powers committed acts which in the mid-twentieth century would appear treasonable.

While recognizing that the Washington administrations were distinguished at times by remarkable foresight and brilliant statesmanship, we should not overlook the political opportunism and partisan strife over foreign policy of the time, seldom if ever equaled in our history. Statesmen of our generation are often compared to the founding fathers of the Washington years as pygmies to giants. Such comparisons are unfair and unjust; recent statesmen in their own context have blundered as badly, but have at times performed just as brilliantly.

Being men, the founding fathers were not infallible. Yet succeeding generations of Americans have, in worship of the past and in seeking guidance for their own pressing problems, glorified them and have accepted them as infallible guides in foreign policy. To assume that Washington's Farewell Address, basically a statement of the partisan political philosophy of Alexander Hamilton, established long-enduring principles to guide the nation in foreign policy for generations to come is to endow Washington with powers reserved for the gods of Olympus. It is to assume that the United States for over a century and

Alexander DeConde, *Entangling Alliance: Politics and Diplomacy under George Washington.* (Durham, N. C.: Duke University Press, 1958), pp. 502–507, 508–510. Copyright © 1958 by Duke University Press.

a half was capable of pursuing a foreign policy of its own choosing, free from the caprices of party and the foibles of other more powerful nations. Actually, in the 1790's the United States was relatively so insignificant in the scale of international power that in any struggle in which the major maritime powers took a real interest it could be little more than a pawn. In relations with the great powers Federalist statesmen were fortunate; they were able to use the opportunities that fell their way. The nation was then led by men who showed real ability in capitalizing on the misfortunes of Europe.

Chance, then as now, played a vital role in the course of our foreign policy. Even though England had most of the advantages in the Washington years, relations with France and England might have gone either way. A stroke of fortune, aided by the vital tie of blood, of culture, and of similar institutions, perhaps more than anything else, thrust us on England's side to the abandonment of the French alliance. Without the support and prestige of Washington and under a more democratic electorate, might not Americans have overthrown the Hamiltonian system and cast America's lot with the French alliance and Republican France? As it was, Federalists and Republicans in their struggle over foreign policy were motivated by self-interest. Each party was convinced that its program, its foreign policy, was in the national interest. The founding fathers were divided on almost every important issue, on the basic philosophies of politics and foreign policy. Who could say, in the context of the times, which side was wrong?

Many students of American foreign policy accept the view that under the American democratic system the orientation and conduct of foreign policy reflects domestic political patterns. To succeed, they say, foreign policy must have the support of the Executive, of the Congress, and of the public. In the Washington years foreign policy conformed to no such criterion. In this period, in relation to the French alliance, we have an example of foreign policy being conducted despite a hostile public opinion until that opinion changed or partially changed. Washington's foreign policy in relation to Great Britain and France was a partisan foreign policy, a foreign policy of one political party, perhaps a minority party.

In assuming that foreign policy reflected the public sentiment of the time, men have often interpreted the Washington era as spawning principles of isolationism. Yet the period was far from isolationist. While it was true that many, regardless of party, nourished the illusion that the United States could isolate and immunize itself from the politics of Europe, other Americans took the opposite view. They tried to thrust the United States into European affairs. Basically, American attitudes toward Europe and toward isolation were, as they have always been, mixed. Some men believed that "the causes which create war among European powers, do not here exist," while others "were too ready to play a part among the nations of Europe; and to involve themselves in the interests of foreign powers, from which nature had most happily separated them."

To quote selected passages from the founding fathers giving voice to hopes and unrealized sentiments without analyzing the actions of the same men, which often were in direct opposition to their isolationist phrases, gives an inaccurate picture of these men and their time. Which best reflects a man's attitudes, his words written to influence other men, or his deeds committed to realize definite objectives?

Although the era of Washington did not in practice set the precedent for a foreign policy of isolationism, there is no denying that it was an age of precedent making in politics and foreign policy. It was not, however, an era in which precedents were established with majority agreement and approval; Washington (even though he may have thought he did) never had a nonpartisan foreign policy. The precedents he left in foreign policy and politics are not clear-cut, having evolved often from political expediency or *ad hoc* diplomatic expediency rather than from exalted principle. As in most periods of stress and storm and as a result of their practical origins, the precedents are mixed and contradictory. What has come to be accepted as binding precedent has gained acceptance because of the authority of time and of the reverence which has blanketed the figure of Washington and also the sacred group denominated founding fathers.

The principle of avoidance of entangling alliances, like most else in Washington's administration, was based on partisan politics, the child of Hamilton's fecund brain. Since the Hamiltonians were anti-French, in their view the French alliance was entangling. Ironically, they saw no evil in close connections with Great Britain; under the circumstances, in Federalist eyes there could be no "entanglement," with its evil connotations, with Great Britain. If cooperation with Great Britain was just and proper, the French alliance alone, as has been maintained, could not have shown by example the danger of entanglement in European international politics. Fears of French entanglement reflected Federalist rationalization, universalized for political consumption.

Whether or not it be entangling has little to do with the real value of an alliance. By definition, an alliance entangles. To have value to both parties, to survive stresses and strains, an alliance should be based on mutual interests; paper bonds alone do not tie effectively. If an alliance is to prove reliable, both parties should continue to fear the contingency or party against whom the alliance was originally directed. There must be, moreover, reasonable hope or assurance that together the allies are capable of meeting the contingency with success. Above all, the alliance should serve the interests of both parties.

After the peace of 1783 the French alliance met none of these conditions. With the exception of the brief war scare of 1793–94 which preceded the Jay treaty, the strength of American animosity toward Great Britain (notably on the part of the Washington administration) was not sufficient to demonstrate the mutual interests of France and the United States under the alliance. The alliance, in fact, became a major source of Franco-American friction. As has often been the case, the stronger party in an alliance usually incites suspicion and jealousy in the weaker country, particularly if the government of the weaker country is antagonistic to it and believes that the alliance entails acceptance of domination by the stronger power. In the Washington period this fear of the French connection was present from the beginning; but more important,

Federalists exploited it for political purposes in support of the Hamiltonian system.

Since French statesmen wished to manipulate their ally, they spoke often of gratitude being the binding cement of the alliance. Yet they recognized that mutual benefits gave real adhesion; they understood the partisan source of American opposition to the alliance. Reflecting eighteenth-century concepts, they believed that an alliance cannot be permanent except among natural allies. The Franco-American alliance, they maintained before consummation of the Jay treaty, was natural because of the position of the two countries; it could do neither country harm. Realizing that the proper measure of an alliance is the importance of its advantages to either party, they came to recognize that to Americans, notably to the Federalists, the alliance had lost its advantages; that Americans under the alliance would defend their own interests, but that they would not make war to succor an ally, particularly one distrusted by the powerful political and financial elements in the community.

When a people take such a stand, the French concluded, it is useless to cultivate their friendship as an ally in time of war. This was one reason why the French never implemented the alliance. In spite of these obstacles, certain French officials believed up to the end of the Washington years that the alliance would triumph in the United States because it had the support of the masses who they believed were still pro-French.

Within the sweep of history, the quarrel with France and the party bitterness in the Washington years had in them the same elements found in similar situations in later years. Undoubtedly, as some have seen it, the conflict with France had in it elements of friction between rival nationalisms. Yet Federalists and Republicans successfully suppressed their national feelings—if they had any independently of their politics—when dealing with the foreign power they preferred. The political struggle over foreign policy had in it elements which later became important factors in our political history: sectionalism, antiforeignism, appeal to the past, and defense of the *status quo* by those in power. . . .

From the beginning, Washington's foreign policy was a partisan policy in keeping with the Hamiltonian system; in sum, it was Hamilton's foreign policy. No important foreign policy decision was made without Hamilton having a part in it. Almost all the important ideas, almost all the significant measures under Washington originated with Hamilton. The Hamilton "engine of government" was all pervasive, touching all aspects of administration and policy. But Washington was essential to the system. Without his unquestioning support, without the backing of his awesome prestige and opposition-smothering popularity, it could never have been carried into effect. Washington the popular hero was far more potent politically than his party or the all-encompassing ideas of Hamilton.

Used as a tool by Hamiltonians and convinced that opposition to Federalism was personal opposition and "faction," Washington in his last years became intensely partisan without knowing it. As Jefferson remarked just before the General retired, "his mind has so long been used to unlimited applause that it could not brook contradiction, or even advice offered unasked." Under the circumstances and in view of Hamilton's *de facto* dominance in the government, Jefferson "long thought therefore it was best for the republican interest to soothe him [Washington] by flattering where they could approve of his measures, & be silent where they disapprove . . . in short to lie on their oars while he remains at the helm, and let the bark of state drift as his will and a superintending providence shall direct."

Since it has long been known that Hamilton, perhaps aided by "a superintending providence," guided the helm of the bark of state during most of the Washington era, it is difficult to account for the efforts of posterity equipped with critical methodology to conjure Washington into a statesman of far-seeing vision and ability. Much easier to understand, but perhaps just as difficult to explain, is the veneration he won from his own people as a statesman. Far from being a statesman of wide grasp, Washington lacked the broad intellectual qualities capable of constructing the all-embracing Hamiltonian program with its sweeping domestic and foreign policy objectives. Slow of mind, he took his ideas and theories, without much question, from Hamilton. Grounded though it was in the broad principles of Hamilton's system, Washington's foreign policy in implementation was *ad hoc* and often governed by political expediency; each policy, while conforming to the over-all philosophy of Alexander Hamilton, was a specific response to a specific situation.

Given the politics, the Hamiltonian theory, and the context of the Washington era, we can see that it was not a period when government on the basis of lofty principle sought to follow a policy of isolation and nonentanglement. It was, instead, a period wherein one party took control of the new national government, supported by men of wealth and position, and successfully attempted to change the foreign policy orientation of the nation. At the end of eight years the government had reversed the basic foreign policy alignment of the nation so that a former enemy was an ally and an ally-in-name was in a state of open hostility, almost of undeclared war. Under the circumstances, the French alliance was doomed from the beginning of the new national government, because of its capture by Washington and Hamilton.

This era of Washington was a crucial time, and Hamiltonians knew it; they knew that in implementing Hamilton's system what they did would form precedents for the future. In giving Hamilton dominance in his government, in accepting the Hamiltonian system as the philosophical foundation of his government, Washington had made his government incompatible with the French alliance. By so doing, from the viewpoint of American responsibility, he planted the seeds of war with France; the roots of the Quasi-War (1797–1800) with France gained nourishment in the Washington administrations.

FURTHER READING

Harry Ammon, *The Genêt Mission* (1973)
Samuel Flagg Bemis, *Jay's Treaty* (1962)
Samuel Flagg Bemis, *Pinckney's Treaty* (1960)

Albert H. Bowman, "Jefferson, Hamilton and American Foreign Policy," *Political Science Quarterly,* 71 (1956), 18–41

Albert H. Bowman, *The Struggle for Neutrality: Franco-American Diplomacy During the Federalist Era* (1974)

Julian P. Boyd, *Number 7: Alexander Hamilton's Secret Attempts to Control American Foreign Policy* (1964)

Joseph Charles, *The Origins of the American Party System* (1956)

Jerald A. Combs, *The Jay Treaty* (1970)

Alexander DeConde, *The Quasi War* (1966)

Lawrence S. Kaplan, *Colonies into Nation* (1972)

Lawrence S. Kaplan, *Jefferson and France* (1963)

Lawrence S. Kaplan, ed., *The American Revolution and "A Candid World"* (1977)

Walter LaFeber, "Foreign Policies of a New Nation," in William A. Williams, ed., *From Colony to Empire* (1972)

Gilbert Lycan, *Alexander Hamilton and American Foreign Policy* (1970)

Dumas Malone, *Jefferson and the Ordeal of Liberty* (1962)

Frederick W. Marks, *Independence on Trial: Foreign Affairs and the Making of the Constitution* (1973)

John C. Miller, *Alexander Hamilton* (1959)

Richard B. Morris, *The Peacemakers* (1965)

Merrill D. Peterson, "Thomas Jefferson and Commercial Policy, 1783–1793," *William and Mary Quarterly,* 22 (1965), 584–610

Charles Ritcheson, *Aftermath of Revolution: British Policy Toward the United States, 1783–1795* (1969)

William Stinchcombe, *The American Revolution and the French Alliance* (1969)

Richard Van Alstyne, *Empire and Independence* (1965)

Richard Van Alstyne, *The Rising American Empire* (1960)

Arthur P. Whitaker, *The Spanish-American Frontier, 1783–1795* (1927)

4

Washington's Farewell Address

George Washington's Farewell Address stands as a key document in the record of American diplomacy, if only because it has been frequently cited by his successors as a landmark. It generally became acknowledged that the first President's words were wise, timeless, and selfless—directed toward future generations of Americans. His valedictory message, it seemed, dictated a policy of isolation from Europe, of abstinence from permanent alliances. Scholars have also attributed other intentions to Washington: to warn Americans against the dangers to sovereignty that were inherent in the French Alliance; to beat back the Republicans in order to promote a Federalist victory in the next presidential election; to expose factionalism as a threat to the nation; and to ensure the continued growth of a rising American empire. Whatever Washington sought or meant, historians agree that in 1796, and for years after, the Farewell Address became a reference point in the making of foreign policy.

DOCUMENTS

The Farewell Address of September 17, 1796, was not delivered as a formal speech. Rather, it was released to the public through the pages of a Philadelphia Federalist newspaper. Though the message was widely applauded as a nationalistic appeal, one Republican Philadelphia editor castigated the retiring President. Benjamin Franklin Bache, grandson of the great Pennsylvania philosopher-politician and nicknamed "Lightning Rod Junior," vented his antagonism in an editorial on March 6, 1797.

The Farewell Address, 1796

The period for a new election of a citizen to administer the Executive Government of the United States being not far distant, and the time actually arrived when your thoughts must be employed in designating the person who is to be clothed with that important trust, it appears to me proper, especially as it may conduce to a more distinct expression of the public voice, that I should now apprise you of the resolution I have formed to decline being considered among the number of those out of whom a choice is to be made. . . .

I have already intimated to you the danger of parties in the State, with particular reference to the founding of them on geographical discriminations. Let me now take a more comprehensive view, and warn you in the most solemn manner against the baneful effects of the spirit of party generally.

This spirit, unfortunately, is inseparable from our nature, having its root in the strongest passions of the human mind. It exists under different shapes in all governments, more or less stifled, controlled, or repressed; but in those of the popular form it is seen in its greatest rankness and is truly their worst enemy.

The alternate domination of one faction over another, sharpened by the spirit of revenge natural to party dissension, which in different ages and countries has perpetrated the most horrid enormities, is itself a frightful despotism. But this leads at length to a more formal and permanent despotism. The disorders and miseries which result gradually incline the minds of men to seek security and repose in the absolute power of an individual, and sooner or later the chief of some prevailing faction, more able or more fortunate than his competitors, turns this disposition to the purposes of his own elevation on the ruins of public liberty.

Without looking forward to an extremity of this kind (which nevertheless ought not to be entirely out of sight), the common and continual mischiefs of the spirit of party are sufficient to make it the interest and duty of a wise people to discourage and restrain it.

It serves always to distract the public councils and enfeeble the public administration. It agitates the community with ill-founded jealousies and false alarms; kindles the animosity of one part against another; foments occasionally riot and insurrection. It opens the door to foreign influence and corruption, which find a facilitated access to the government itself through the channels of party passion. Thus the policy and the will of one country are subjected to the policy and will of another. . . .

Observe good faith and justice toward all nations. Cultivate peace and harmony with all. Religion and morality enjoin this conduct. And can it be that good policy does not equally enjoin it? It will be worthy of a free, enlightened, and at no distant period a great nation to give to mankind the magnanimous and too novel example of a people always guided by an exalted justice and benevolence. Who can doubt that in the course of time and things the fruits of such a plan would richly repay any temporary advantages which might be lost by a steady adherence to it? Can it be that Providence has not connected the permanent felicity of a nation with its virtue? The experiment, at least, is recommended by every sentiment which ennobles human nature. Alas! is it rendered impossible by its vices?

In the execution of such a plan nothing is more essential than that permanent, inveterate antipathies against particular nations and passionate attachments for others should be excluded, and that in place of them just and amicable feelings toward all should be cultivated. The nation which indulges toward another an habitual hatred or an habitual fondness is in some degree a slave. It is a slave to its animosity or to its affection, either of which is sufficient to lead it astray from its duty and its interest. Antipathy in one nation against another disposes each more readily to offer insult and injury, to lay hold of slight causes of umbrage, and to be haughty and intractable when accidental or trifling occasions of dispute occur.

Hence frequent collisions, obstinate, envenomed, and bloody contests. The nation prompted by ill will and resentment sometimes impels to war the government contrary to the best calculations of policy. The government sometimes participates in the national propensity, and adopts through passion what reason would reject. At other times it makes the animosity of the nation subservient to projects of hostility, instigated by pride, ambition, and other sinister and pernicious motives. The peace often, sometimes perhaps the liberty, of nations has been the victim.

So, likewise, a passionate attachment of one nation for another produces a variety of evils. Sympathy for the favorite nation, facilitating the illusion of an imaginary common interest in cases where no real common interest exists, and infusing into one the enmities of the other, betrays the former into a participation in the quarrels and wars of the latter without adequate inducement or justification. It leads also to concessions to the favorite nation of privileges denied to others, which is apt doubly to injure the nation making the concessions by unnecessarily parting with what ought to have been retained, and by exciting jealousy, ill will, and a disposition to retaliate in the parties from whom equal privileges are withheld; and it gives to ambitious, corrupted, or deluded citizens (who devote themselves to the favorite nation) facility to betray or sacrifice the interests of their own country without odium, sometimes even with popularity, gilding with the appearances of a virtuous sense of obligation, a commendable deference for public opinion, or a laudable zeal for public good the base or foolish compliances of ambition, corruption, or infatuation.

As avenues to foreign influence in innumerable ways, such attachments are particularly alarming to the truly enlightened and independent patriot. How many opportunities do they afford to tamper with domestic factions, to practice the arts of seduction, to mislead public opinion, to influence or awe the public councils! Such an attachment of a small or weak toward a great and powerful nation dooms the former to be the satellite of the latter. Against the insidious wiles of foreign influence (I conjure you to believe me, fellow-citizens) the jealousy of a free people ought to be *constantly* awake, since history and experience prove that foreign influence is one of the most baneful foes of republican government. But that jealousy, to be useful, must be impartial, else it becomes the instrument of the very influence to be avoided, instead of a defense against it. Excessive partiality for one foreign nation and excessive dislike of another cause those whom they actuate to see danger only on one side, and serve to veil and even second the arts of influence on the other. Real patriots who may resist the intrigues of the favorite are liable to become suspected and odious, while its tools and dupes usurp the applause and confidence of the people to surrender their interests.

The great rule of conduct for us in regard to foreign nations is, in extending our commercial relations to have with them as little *political* connection as possible. So far as we have already formed engagements let them be fulfilled with perfect good faith. Here let us stop.

Europe has a set of primary interests which to us have none or a very remote relation. Hence she must be engaged in frequent controversies, the causes of which are essentially foreign to our concerns. Hence, therefore, it must be unwise in us to implicate ourselves by artificial ties in the ordinary vicissitudes of her politics or the ordinary combinations and collisions of her friendships or enmities.

Our detached and distant situation invites and enables us to pursue a different course. If we remain one people, under an efficient government, the period is not far off when we may defy material injury from external annoyance; when we may take such an attitude as will cause the neutrality we may at any time resolve upon to be scrupulously respected; when belligerent nations, under the impossibility of making acquisitions upon us, will not lightly hazard the giving us provocation; when we may choose peace or war, as our interest, guided by justice, shall counsel.

Why forego the advantages of so peculiar a situation? Why quit our own to stand upon foreign ground? Why, by interweaving our destiny with that of any part of Europe, entangle our peace and prosperity in the toils of European ambition, rivalship, interest, humor, or caprice?

It is our true policy to steer clear of permanent alliances with any portion of the foreign world, so far, I mean, as we are now at liberty to do it; for let me not be understood as capable of patronizing infidelity to existing engagements. I hold the maxim no less applicable to public than to private affairs that honesty is always the best policy. I repeat, therefore, let those engagements be observed in their genuine sense. But in my opinion it is unnecessary and would be unwise to extend them.

Taking care always to keep ourselves by suitable establishments on a respectable defensive posture, we may safely trust to temporary alliances for extraordinary emergencies.

Harmony, liberal intercourse with all nations are recommended by policy, humanity, and interest. But even our commercial policy should hold an equal and impartial hand, neither seeking nor granting exclusive favors or preferences; consulting the natural course of things; diffusing and diversifying by gentle means the streams of commerce, but forcing nothing; establishing with powers so disposed, in order to give trade a stable course, to define the rights of our merchants, and to enable the Government to support them, conventional rules of intercourse, the best that present circumstances and mutual opinion will permit, but temporary and liable to be from time to time abandoned or varied as experience and circumstances shall dictate; constantly keeping in view that it is folly in one nation to look for disinterested favors from another; that it must pay with a portion of its independence for whatever it may accept under that character; that by such acceptance it may place itself in the condition of having given equivalents for nominal favors, and yet of being reproached with ingratitude for not giving more. There can be no greater error than to expect or calculate upon real favors from nation to nation. It is an illusion which experience must cure, which a just pride ought to discard.

Benjamin Franklin Bache on Washington, 1797

"Lord, now lettest thou thy servant depart in peace, for mine eyes have seen thy salvation," was the pious ejaculation of a man who beheld a flood of happiness rushing upon mankind [Simeon, who had just seen Jesus]. If ever there was a time that would license the reiteration of the exclamation, that time is now arrived. For the man who is the source of all the misfortunes of our country is this day reduced to a level with his fellow citizens, and is no longer possessed of power to multiply evils upon the United States.

If ever there was a period for rejoicing, this is the moment. Every heart in unison with the freedom and happiness of the people ought to beat high with exultation that the name of Washington, from this day, ceases to give a currency to political iniquity and to legalize corruption. A new era is opening upon us—a new era which promises much to the people. For public measures must now stand upon their own merits, and nefarious projects can no longer be supported by a name.

When a retrospect is taken of the Washington administration for eight years, it is a subject of the greatest astonishment that a single individual should have canceled the principles of republicanism in an enlightened people, and should have carried his designs against the public liberty so far as to have put in jeopardy its very existence. Such, however, are the facts, and with these staring us in the face, this day ought to be a jubilee in the United States.

ESSAYS

Was the Farewell Address intended as a partisan campaign document? A timeless declaration about alliances? An immediate warning against the French? A statement of empire? A combination of these? As the following essays demonstrate, historians have come to different conclusions. Samuel Flagg Bemis emphatically states that Washington sought to address the immediate problem of the French Alliance and of French meddling in American internal affairs and thus was once again declaring American independence. Burton I. Kaufman of Kansas State University, on the other hand, thinks the President was articulating a vision of America's destiny as an imperial power.

A Second Declaration of Independence

SAMUEL FLAGG BEMIS

The Farewell Address is often thought of as an expression of abstract ideas of policy looking toward the future, but with little reference to the events of 1796. Its fundamental ideas were, on the contrary, suggested by experience, and very recent and painful experience. To comprehend Washington's point of view and feel the weight of his advice, it is necessary to consider the historical setting, and, for that, to go back to the outbreak of a general European war in February and March, 1793.

In the desperate conflict with the allied monarchies of the First Coalition the French Republic expected to find a valuable counterweight in the independent United States, separated from Great Britain by French diplomacy and arms in the previous war. Thoroughly conscious of the naval impotence of the new American nation, France had preferred not to invoke the *casus fœderis* of the treaty of alliance of 1778—the defense of the French West India Islands. A neutral United States promised greater advantages: (1) as a possible transatlantic base of operations against enemy colonies and commerce, (2) as the largest remaining neutral supply of provisions and naval stores, commodities that perhaps might be passed through the British navy under cover of the neutral flag. To finance both of these objects there was the gradually maturing American debt.

President Washington's proclamation of neutrality and the refusal of his government to lend itself to Genêt's projects soon showed France that her ally did not intend to involve itself in the European war by becoming such a base of belligerent naval and military operations. France perforce acquiesced in that decision, being still unwilling to invoke the letter of the alliance. This was because the actual belligerency of the United States which had no navy was worth nothing in itself and had the really great disadvantage of making American shipping immediately liable to capture and confiscation as enemy property. The neutrality of the United States, even though it could not serve as a base for such projects as Genêt attempted, was far more serviceable than American military assistance. The principal object of France was to secure from neutral America provisions for her beleaguered homeland and colonies, imported in American ships under protection of the principles of the commercial treaty of 1778; free ships free goods; provisions and naval stores not contraband; neutral right to trade in non-contraband goods to and between unblockaded enemy ports.

This Franco-American treaty did not bind France's enemy, Great Britain,

Samuel Flagg Bemis, "Washington's Farewell Address: A Foreign Policy of Independence," *American Historical Review,* 39 (1934), 250–268.

the principal maritime belligerent. The British had never admitted these "novel" principles. They considered them as exceptional articles in particular treaties binding only between the signatory parties. When hostilities commenced in 1793 Great Britain began seizing enemy property right and left wherever it could be found outside neutral territorial waters, whether in enemy or neutral bottoms. British prize courts under orders in council began to apply the Rule of 1756, itself an innovation as late as the Seven Years' War. Secretary of State Thomas Jefferson protested in the name of the United States against this practice, which was contrary to the articles written into the Franco-American treaty and all the other European treaties of the United States. But Great Britain was not bound by those treaties.[1] The United States was powerless to challenge the British navy. American credit, newly established, depended primarily on tariff revenue, and tariff revenue depended principally on imports from Great Britain. The collapse of credit at this time would have meant the collapse of the newly established nationality of the United States. Rather than go to war with Great Britain President Washington took Alexander Hamilton's advice and ratified Jay's Treaty with England which acquiesced in British naval practice for the next twelve years, in effect for the duration of the war.[2] That treaty did not violate the treaties of the United States with France. It recognized a condition which already existed, namely, that the United States could not compel Great Britain to observe the terms of the Franco-American treaty. In 1793 the other maritime powers, which in the War for American Independence had followed principles similar to those of the Franco-American treaty, made treaties with Great Britain agreeing to harass the commerce of France in every possible way. These powers included the old Armed Neutrals of 1780, except Sweden and Denmark. A group of ardent, hateful enemies ringed France about by land and sea to close her frontiers, to sweep her commerce from the seas, to take her colonies from her, and to deprive her of naval supplies and of foodstuffs. The neutral United States, the ally of yesteryear, which France herself had brought into the world, stood aloof and acquiesced in this British naval-diplomatic system of strangulation. Thus were frustrated the advantages of neutral carriage which France had relied on from the American treaty of amity and commerce of 1778.

This situation was aggravated in the eyes of French statesmen by Jay's Treaty. If in the face of that document and of British practice the French were still to adhere to the terms of the American treaty, they would have to stand quietly by and watch British cruisers take French property from neutral American ships, confiscate American-owned naval stores as contraband when *en route* in American vessels to France, and preëmpt (as was the British practice) foodstuffs under similar conditions. Deprived thus by belligerent action of naval stores, foodstuffs, and of the advantages of neutral carriage they would find themselves obliged to abstain from following the British practice; they would have to watch these same goods go unchallenged by French warships into British harbors to feed and strengthen the might of the enemy.

It is not difficult to understand that this seemed unfair to France, and that Jay's Treaty seemed an outrageous, even a treacherous document, made by an ungrateful nation. But one would be more ready to sympathize with France if her own hands were clean. We must remember that when John Jay signed his famous treaty with Lord Grenville on November 19, 1794, France herself was pursuing and had been pursuing, off and on, since May 9, 1793, a maritime policy of retaliation in practice identical with that of Great Britain in the treatment of neutral shipping, and had been applying it to American ships and cargoes,[3] and that notwithstanding her obligations under her treaty with the United States. As in later European wars (1803–1812, and 1914–1917) the force of these belligerent retaliations fell heavily on the neutral United States and developed grave diplomatic problems. Unlike the later wars, in this case the United States was protected by the paper and ink of a treaty against such practice on the part of one belligerent. Nevertheless, French spoliations on American shipping rivaled those of Great Britain. French privateers and naval vessels also vied with the British in violence and outrages against neutral crews and passengers.[4]

The French diplomatic commission, headed by Joseph Fauchet, which in 1794 had succeeded the ruined Genêt in Philadelphia, did not even pretend to reconcile French maritime policy with the obligations of the treaty of commerce of 1778. Nevertheless it claimed for France all the articles of the treaty which were of advantage to her, and requested benevolent interpretations of them. The committee of public safety, in drawing up instructions for these commissioners, anticipated that there would be objections in the United States to the retaliatory French decrees. Admitting deviations from the treaty it became the task of the commissioners to extenuate French policy on the ground of altered circumstances.[5]

Washington and his advisers had foreseen the possible further effect on France of the intended treaty between the United States and Great Britain when John Jay, the Federalist, pro-British diplomatist departed on his famous mission to London. To mask this mission they sent to France the pro-French Republican senator from Virginia, James Monroe, an old opponent of Jay's diplomacy since 1786, who considered Jay's mission as mischievous and in the Senate voted against his confirmation. Monroe never saw Jay's instructions, possibly was not aware of their real scope.

Like an apostle of the rights of man, Monroe set to work to persuade the French government to observe the treaty of amity and commerce of 1778. The restrictions on private trade in French harbors, the embargoes, the delays in payment for purchased cargoes, had already so jeopardized the American provision supply that the Convention admitted the force of the American remonstrances on every point except free ships free goods.[6] The envoy now argued for the full and entire enforcement of the articles of the treaty. He appealed to old friendship and present interest. He contended that it would be good policy for France to repeal her obnoxious decrees before Great Britain should repeal hers. If she did so, it would combine all America in condemnation of the conduct of the British; if she did not, any later repeal would appear merely to be forced by her enemy. At just this time news arrived[7] of the setting aside, by an order in council of August 6, 1794, of the British provision order of June 8, 1793—this had been a means in London of easing the English negotiations with Jay. It reënforced Monroe's argument in Paris. The French law of May 9, 1793, had made the duration of the "retaliatory" maritime measures contingent upon the repeal by the enemy of his illegal procedure. The Convention now (January 2, 1795) availed itself of this provision to yield to the importunities of the ingratiating James Monroe. "As a grand act of honesty and justice", it wiped out at one stroke all the offensive decrees and enjoined the strict observance of the provisions of the treaty of 1778.[8] Orders were immediately given for the adjudication of all claims arising out of violations of that treaty.

Monroe's triumph was short-lived. Before anything very effective could actually be done about the relief of the claimants the significance of Jay's Treaty[9] began to be suspected in Paris. In August, 1795, the text arrived from Philadelphia. It completely undid Monroe's successes. In 1796 Washington recalled the unhappy minister for not having defended with sufficient vigor the new English treaty.[10] In truth Monroe had repeated to the French government the arguments and defenses sent to him by Secretaries of State Randolph and Pickering. They read well, but one may doubt that his heart was in his words. He thought Jay's Treaty a shameful document.[11] There is evidence suggesting that he had confidential conversations with the French Revolutionary leaders about "the real dispositions of his countrymen", conversations which he did not reveal to his own government.[12] He kept up an intimate correspondence with Madison,[13] and other friends of Jefferson, who opposed Jay's Treaty and favored a pro-French policy. He certainly led the French government to believe that any treaty of amity between the United States and Great Britain would never be ratified.[14] When it was known that a treaty had been signed, Monroe repeated this assurance.[15] When Jay's Treaty went through Congress he tried rather lamely to explain its success, and still argued that it would be good policy for the French Republic to observe loyally the terms of its American treaties; the example of that loyalty and the contrasting attitude of the British government would win the good will of the American *people,* from whose eyes the scales of British deception must eventually fall.[16] He led them in Paris to believe that the people would overthrow the administration of President Washington as a result of the treaty, that better things might be expected after the election of 1796.[17] This supposition was reënforced by advice from the French diplomatic representative in the United States, Fauchet, and his successor Adet, and by Americans in Paris like Monroe's friend, Tom Paine.

After Jay's departure from New York Fauchet had become increasingly nervous about the object of the new mission. He sent one of his colleagues to Paris to warn the committee of public safety that something was in the air, and to say that the other two members of the commission, La Forest and Petry, could not be trusted because they hobnobbed with Alexander Hamilton and other Federalists.[18] When news of the signature of the treaty and rumors of its contents began to leak out, the French minister became very much exasperated. His notes of protest against fancied violations of neutral obligations under the treaty of 1778 took on a more rasping tone, full of intimations of American disloyalty. Fauchet tried by fair means and foul, but in vain, to block the ratification of the treaty by the Senate. He hoped with Secretary Randolph that the President might not sign the ratification, even though the Senate had so advised and consented. His successor Adet, encouraged by the widespread popular protests, labored with the House of Representatives to refuse the appropriations necessary to carry it into effect. When the treaty passed unscathed through the House, Adet's last hope was that the people would overthrow the administration of President Washington in the forthcoming election of 1796.[19] Through the agency of organs of the Republican press which he manipulated and inspired to the extent of his limited financial resources, and by means of the democratic societies which had arisen at the wave of Genêt's wand to applaud the French Revolution, the French minister was working with might and main to that end.[20] He did not know, of course, of the President's determination, long since fixed and presently to be announced, to refuse a third term.

In Paris, American affairs had received less attention than they merited. Before the reorganization of the French government under the constitution of the Year III. (1795) the rapidly changing administration of the foreign office failed to give methodical attention. French diplomatists at Philadelphia complained bitterly that their dispatches went unanswered. For months they waited without instructions. None of them had been told what to do about Jay's Treaty. Fauchet, and his successor Adet, had acted on their own responsibility in their protests against that instrument. The new Directory put the conduct of foreign affairs on a more businesslike basis, under a single minister, Charles Delacroix. He straightway brought in a report concerning the United States. Washington must go, he said. "A friend of France must succeed him in that eminent office." He continued:

> We must raise up the people and at the same time conceal the lever by which we do so . . . I propose to the Executive Directory to authorize me to send orders and instructions to our minister plenipotentiary at Philadelphia to use all the means in his power in the United States to bring about the right kind of revolution (*l'heureuse Révolution*) and Washington's replacement, which, assuring to the Americans their independence, will break off treaties [*sic*] made with England and maintain those which unite them to the French Republic.

As in the case of the Netherlands at that time, France and French agents regarded that political party in the United States which was most useful to their purposes as the "patriot" party. Jefferson, Madison, Monroe, Robert R. Livingston, Senator Tazewell of Virginia, Governor Clinton of New York, and Governor Mifflin of Pennsylvania were patriots. Washington, Hamilton, Jay, Rufus King, and John Adams were aristocrats unfriendly to real liberty. The French foreign office looked on the United States as "the Holland of the New World". It hoped for and expected a popular revolution there, on French models, such as did take place in Holland in 1795, to overturn the existing régime of ordered liberty, to cast off the formidable ascendency of President Washington and his Federalist advisers who themselves were esteemed to be beyond the reach of French influence and purpose.[21]

At first the Directory decided on a more positive step to offset Jay's Treaty: to send a special envoy extraordinary to Philadelphia to recall Adet and to announce the end of the Franco-American treaties and then himself to withdraw.[22] Monroe confidentially urged Delacroix against such action: it would please the enemies of both countries. "Left to ourselves", he hinted, "everything will I think be satisfactorily arranged and *perhaps in the course of the present year:* and it is always more grateful to make such arrangements ourselves than to be pressed to it."[23]

Delacroix[24] and the Directory took the advice of President Washington's minister to await the President's overthrow. They blamed Washington, Hamilton, and the Federalist Senate, in short the elected government of the people of the United States, against which, according to French agents and correspondents (including Americans in Paris), the people were now in an uproar, from Boston to Savannah. Well they knew that Monroe's hint referred to the approaching presidential election of 1796.[25] They decided to temporize, to protest, to argue (Monroe had advised them not to abandon their claims for redress), pending the new presidential election, to work up "patriot" sentiment against Washington's administration. To this effect they approved instructions to a new minister.[26] Later came news of the success of Jay's Treaty in the House of Representatives. They then decided not to send any new minister after all, but to keep Adet in Philadelphia for a short while at least, and to follow his advice, and that of the returned Fauchet, to hearten the pro-French "patriots" in America by an unmistakable denunciation of the policy of the executive of the United States, lest by French silence the election should go in Washington's favor.

The inveterate tendency of French policy to stir up the American people against their government had gradually steeled the sympathies of President Washington against the old ally. Though Washington could not know the inner counsels of the French Directory—least of all when he had a minister like Monroe in Paris—the policy of France had been made abundantly apparent by the French diplomatists in Philadelphia. Since Genêt's time they had been openly or covertly attempting to join forces with the anti-Federalist opposition. They had been able to promise themselves much from such strategy because of radical political affinities and because of the memory of French help in the American Revolution. But the French alliance, indispensable as it was to American independence, had always been a great embarrassment to American diplomatists. It was so even during the diplomacy of the Revolution itself, when Vergennes had wavered under the threats of a separate Spanish peace (though his wavering has become known only to scholars in our own day). It was so during the peace negotiations of 1782 in Paris. Experience with it showed the Fathers the danger to independence and sovereignty of any other alliance. Toward the close of the war Congress shrank from committing itself to the Dutch proposal to join the Armed Neutrality. In 1786 John Jay's initialed alliance with Spain (never revealed fully until the twentieth century) collapsed before the opposition of the Southern states who feared for the Mississippi. Soon after, the South united with New England (anxious about its fisheries)[27] and wrote into the Constitution that potent provision that no future treaty could be ratified except by the vote of two-thirds of the senators present in the upper chamber of the national legislature, that Senate in which there must always be exactly two senators from each state. To a certain degree this fixed a constitutional obstacle against European entanglements. More than one delegate supported it for that reason.[28]

The French alliance had become increasingly embarrassing after the French declaration of war on England, February 1, 1793. The proclamation of neutrality was a tangible expression of a sane American policy not of isolation but of diplomatic independence. Washington refused all new foreign alliances. As Hamilton so indiscreetly told the British minister, Hammond, in 1794, he rejected the Swedish invitation to join the second, abortive, armed neutrality of 1794. He also turned down Godoy's famous "propositions for the President", of that same year, for a Spanish alliance, as Pinckney too later repelled them in Madrid. In short, the very life-saving French alliance had long since cured the United States of any hankering for more allies.

The first twenty years of American independence had in fact made American statesmen shy of Europe, and they have remained so ever since. Their writings (with the possible exception of James Monroe, whose name after 1823 was to become so inseparably associated with abstention from European politics and wars!) are full of affirmations that it was the true policy of the United States to steer clear of European politics.[29]

Tom Paine had been the first to express this, in 1776. " 'Tis the true interest of America, to steer clear of European contentions, which she never can do, while by her dependance on Britain, she is made the makeweight in the scale of British politics."[30] "I do not love to be entangled in the politics of Europe", wrote John Adams in 1777.[31] In the Virginia ratifying convention in 1788, Madison, speaking for the adoption of the new Federal Constitution asked: "What is the situation of America?" and answered, "She is remote from Europe, and ought not to engage in her politics or wars."[32] Jefferson in France had written in 1787: "I know too that it is a maxim with us, and I think it a wise one, not to entangle ourselves with the affairs of Europe."[33] Again, in 1790: "At such a distance from Europe, and with such an ocean between us, we hope to meddle little in its quarrels or combinations. Its peace and its commerce are what we shall court . . ."[34] Hamilton repeatedly had used words almost identical with essential portions of the text of Washington's Farewell Address of 1796.[35] So had the President, particularly in 1795.[36]

If George Washington had retired from the presidency in the spring of 1793,[37] as he originally intended when he first consulted James Madison about the draft of a valedictory we may presume that he would never have said anything about foreign affairs. There would have been no Farewell Address of the kind that has become so familiar to us—though we cannot say that the policy itself would not soon have been formulated. Certainly Washington's suggestions, and Madison's draft, for a possible valedictory in 1792, did not touch foreign affairs. In the summer of 1796, however, foreign affairs were uppermost in the mind of the Father of His Country. Then unalterably resolved not to serve another term, he prepared to indite a final message to the American people at large.

It was to remove foreign interference in our domestic affairs, to preserve the nation and the people from Europe's distresses, that the retiring first President, with a particular eye to relations with France, marked out for his now private adviser, Alexander Hamilton, the subjects which he would like to include in his final address. In characteristically familiar and felicitous phrases —many of which we may find already expressed in the *Federalist* and other products of his pen—Hamilton wrote out the President's ideas.[38] Of Washington were the trunk and branches of the sturdy tree. The shimmering foliage dancing and shining in the sunlight was Hamilton's. The President edited several drafts before the address was finished. He cast out at least one extraneous thought which Hamilton tried gratuitously to slip in. Despite Hamilton's principal part in the phrasing of the document, and his previous expression of some of the ideas, we may be sure that in the final text the two men were thinking together in absolute unison. The Address was as directly pointed to the diplomatic problems of the time of the French Revolution as were Woodrow Wilson's Fourteen Points to the intricate diplomacy of the World War. President Wilson and Colonel House worked no more intimately together on that document in 1918, drafting and redrafting its clauses, than did President Washington and Colonel Hamilton in 1796, composing and recomposing the paragraphs of the Farewell Address.

The immortal document, ever since a polestar of American foreign policy, represented the crystallization of the experience of remarkably clear-headed men with foreign affairs since the Declaration of Independence. It was given forthwith to the public in a newspaper.[39] It spoke directly to the great and simple audience of the American people. "The name of AMERICAN", it said to them, putting the word into bold type, "which belongs to you in your national capacity, must always exalt the just pride of Patriotism, more than any appelation derived from local discriminations."

We must keep in mind the involvement of the French alliance in American diplomacy and domestic politics as we read the Farewell Address, even as the authors of the document had that constantly before them.

It began thus with an appeal to support the *National Union*. The orthodox phrase Federal Union does not occur in the document, a very significant omission. It continued with a counsel against the practice of party politics, lest the new nation be undermined by internal dissension assisted by foreign intrigue. The first President and his adviser Alexander Hamilton believed that, with the system of checks and balances in the new government, party politics was unnecessary for the preservation of ordered liberty. The rise of an opposition they identified with a faction opposed not only to the policies of the administration but to the new national government itself. They connected this faction with the French government and its agents.

Turning to the subject of foreign affairs, the Address admonished his fellow citizens to steer clear of European alliances and wars. It justified American neutrality whilst the nation, assisted by the advantages of so peculiar a situation, might grow strong enough to command its own fortune. In these words and these counsels the authors of the Address had continually before them the apparition of the life-giving, but the entangling French alliance, and the distant scene of the great wars engulfing Europe. They had behind them the problems solved by Jay's Treaty and by Pinckney's Treaty, thanks to the occupation of Britain and Spain with those troubles in Europe.

The immediate purpose of the Address was to strike a powerful blow against French intermeddling in American affairs.[40] After the victory of Jay's Treaty in the House of Representatives it had been Adet's advice, and this was also recommended by the returned Fauchet,[41] that some strong and positive action ought to be taken to make the American ally more amenable to French interests. The people, both of those agents had reported—and reported most voluminously—were in favor of France and opposed to their government, but if France did not call Washington's government to terms, and thus support the action of the "good" people to overthrow it, nothing could be hoped from them. Adet advocated[42] that the French Republic proceed to treat American ships precisely as the United States government allowed its flag to be treated by Great Britain, that is, according to the principles of Jay's Treaty. This was, indeed, what France had been doing up to January 3, 1795, when Monroe secured from the Convention the full and entire recognition of the treaty of 1778. But that "grand act of honesty and justice" had not been enforced since the nature of Jay's Treaty had become suspected in France. Nor was it ever to be. It was to be the United States government itself which was finally to pay—throughout a century of litigation—most of the damages to its citizens wrought by the French spoliations in this war.

Jay's Treaty at last having gone into effect, the French Directory prepared its denunciation of the treachery of Washington's government. As a warning to the American people of worse things to follow if President Washington were continued in office it decided to suspend Adet's functions, and with them formal diplomatic relations with the United States. Characterizing Jay's Treaty as equivalent to an alliance between France's principal enemy and her old, ungrateful ally, it proceeded to invoke against American shipping, as a reprisal for that perfidious treaty, the maritime principles of that document itself.[43] If Jefferson should be elected the plan was to restore relations on the old basis, hoping that a new treaty with France might undo Jay's.[44]

To his great satisfaction Adet was able to communicate to the United States government, on October 27, 1796, the text of a decree of the Directory announcing that "All neutral or allied Powers shall, without delay, be notified that the flag of the French republic will treat neutral vessels, either as to confiscation, as to searches, or capture, in the same manner as they shall suffer the English to treat them."[45]

A few weeks later (November 15) he announced the definite suspension of his functions, not, indeed, to indicate a formal rupture between the United States and France, "but as a mark of just discontent, which is to last until the government of the United States returns to sentiments, and to measures, more conformable to the interests of the alliance, and the sworn friendship of the two nations".

It was now the eve of the presidential election of 1796. The several states were choosing their electors. They still had to meet and cast their votes. The precedent had not yet become set which allows the electors no canvass or deliberation among themselves. The French move was studiously calculated to influence the electors to choose Jefferson instead of John Adams.[46] With this in mind, according to his instructions, Adet accompanied his announcement of suspension of his functions with a long and *ex-parte* review (with documents) of the whole quarrel between France and the United States over American neutrality. He included a passionate indictment of Jay's Treaty, all under cover of a fervid manifesto to the American people. A summary in English of the contents of this note appeared in the newspapers before the translation of the French original could be prepared in the Department of State. "Let your Government return to itself", wrote Adet, addressing the people rather than the government to which his note was delivered, "and you will still find in Frenchmen faithful friends and generous allies."[47]

To that uncompromising Federalist, Timothy Pickering, old soldier, negotiator of Indian treaties, professional and capable officeholder, and general utility man in Washington's cabinet, now fell the task of defending the foreign policy laid down in the Farewell Address. Four others had declined the proffered appointment of Secretary of State, with its meager emolument, before he took it. Though Pickering had no special training for the office, he was a facile penman and a sharp-minded debater. These were the qualifications principally in demand from 1795 to 1800.

Space only forbids us to describe and to analyze Pickering's defense of American neutrality, of Jay's Treaty with England, in short of the foreign policy of George Washington. We may be sure that it was inspired by Alexander Hamilton,[48] the man who inspired Jay's Treaty, and who phrased the Farewell Address. The remarkable public disputation took the form of instructions to Charles C. Pinckney, dated January 16, 1797, who had already sailed to France as successor to the recalled Monroe; but its real purpose, as shown by its immediate release to the press on January 19, 1797,[49] was to serve as a counter-manifesto to Adet's passionate attacks on the administration and his undercover efforts to secure the election of Thomas Jefferson rather than John Adams, the champion of Washington's policies. The historian to-day who is privileged to read the archives of France and of the United States can have no serious quarrel with Pickering's eloquent rebuttal of French charges of American ingratitude directed against Washington's government, nor with his blunt conclusion after a long review that France owed fully as much to the United States as the United States to France in the way of service rendered. The day for finesse had passed. It was time that some one put the truth in this way to the American people, at a moment when foreign diplomacy was again trying to reach over the heads of their government to whip them into European complications. Even then in 1795 and 1796 while French diplomatists were accusing the United States of ingratitude and treachery, they themselves were plotting to reëstablish control and tutelage over the American republic by getting Louisiana and West Florida back from Spain, allying France with the southwestern Indians, and tempting the allegiance to the Union of the new western states, to build up thereby a new colonial empire that would be the preponderant power in the New World.[50]

The instructions to C. C. Pinckney,[51] embodying these arguments, rank with Jefferson's rejoinder to Hammond of 1792, with John Quincy Adams's defense of General Jackson's execution of Arbuthnot and Ambrister in 1818, and with Lansing's reply to Austria in 1915 on the question of contraband, as one of the greatest defensive documents in the diplomatic history of the United States. Pickering's paper clinched the case for President Washington's foreign policy.

Before the document was printed the presidential electors had elected John Adams President by a majority of one vote and a margin of three votes over Thomas Jefferson, who became Vice President according to the original constitutional provision. Washington's successor fully recognized that the significance of his election lay in the question whether the American people were to govern themselves or be governed by foreign nations.[52] As President he took over Washington's policies, and, to his later vexation, his entire cabinet.

We cannot conclude that Pickering's instructions to Pinckney decided the election. It had been won already. The dispatch was published after the votes of the electors had been announced on the first Wednesday in January, but before they were formally counted on the first Wednesday in February. The document was rather an appeal to the people to support the foreign policy of Washington—and of Hamilton—and an argument to open the door to an escape from the French alliance, by proving, as Hamilton suggested, that the United States had maintained good faith with its engagements; that if the conduct of the other party released it, the release should not be refused, so far as possible without compromising peace. "This idea is very important", Hamilton wrote to Wolcott, of course for Pickering's benefit.[53]

Despite the high hopes which France had placed on Jefferson's election, both John Adams and his close contestant, the new Vice President, Thomas Jefferson, were equally good Americans (albeit of different political philosophy), and, incidentally, almost equally good friends of France. Nor were they unfriendly to each other. Jefferson had gone so far as to authorize his friend Madison to advise electors, in case of a tie, to vote for Adams as a statesman of senior claims to the presidency.[54] Adet came to sense this relationship before he left. He wrote:[55]

> Mr. Jefferson likes us because he detests England; he seeks to draw near to us because he fears us less than England; but tomorrow he might change his opinion about us if England should cease to inspire his fear. Although Jefferson is the friend of liberty and of science, although he is an admirer of the efforts we have made to cast off our shackles and to clear away the cloud of ignorance which weighs down the human race, Jefferson, I say, is an American, and as such, he cannot sincerely be our friend. An American is the born enemy of all the peoples of Europe.

Such was the historical setting of the famous Farewell Address. Such were the reasons for its pronouncement in 1796, so different a pronouncement from what it would have been if given to the people in 1792. Such was its victory over foreign intrigue within our own country. It did not disown the French alliance, but it taught a patronizing ally that we were an independent and a sovereign nation, and that the French Republic could not use in America the tool that had been so successful with the border satellite states in Europe, the lever of a political opposition to overthrow any government that stood in the way of French policy, purpose, and interest. In Washington's time avoidance of foreign alliances and of foreign entanglement was a question of independence and national sovereignty. What we have generally construed as a policy of "isolation" we ought really to interpret as a policy of vigilant defense and maintenance of sovereign national independence against foreign meddling in our own intimate domestic concerns.

Notes

1. Great Britain had accepted these principles in the treaty of commerce of 1786 with France, but of course that treaty had ceased to exist with the outbreak of war.
2. I have dwelt in detail upon the significance of this in my *Jay's Treaty* (New York, 1923).
3. The various French laws and decrees affecting neutral commerce were:
   May 9, 1793. Law of the National Convention decreeing orders to naval officers and commanders of privateers to bring in "neutral ships laden in whole or in part either with foodstuffs belonging to neutrals and destined to enemy ports, or with goods belonging to the enemy", the former to be purchased at the price they would have commanded at the port of their intended destination, the latter to be confiscated, and an allowance to be fixed by the prize court for freight and detention.
   This act was professedly in retaliation for specified British spoliations on neutral ships, and was retroactive to all prizes brought in since the beginning of the war [which implies that some had been brought in before the occasion for "retaliation"]. Compare it with similar provisions of Article I. of the British order in council of June 8, 1793. The law of May 9 was to cease to have effect when the enemy powers should declare free and nonseizable foodstuffs which were neutral property and destined to the ports of the French Republic, as well as merchandise belonging to the French government or French citizens on board neutral ships. *Lois et actes du gouvernement* (Paris, Imprimerie Royale, 1834), VII. 51–52; the laws and decrees referred to here may also be found in the convenient *Collection complète des lois*, etc., of J. B. Duvergier, under each date. *American State Papers, Foreign Relations* (Washington, 1833), I. 377 [hereinafter cited as A.S.P., F.R., I.].
   May 23, 1793. Law of the National Convention exempting American ships from the operation of the law of May 9, 1793, "conformably to Article XVI. [*sic*] of the treaty of February 6, 1778". [Article XVI. deals with the irrelevant matter of restoration of captures made by pirates. Presumably Article XXIII. was meant.] *Lois et actes,* VII. 82; A.S.P., F.R., I. 365.
   May 28, 1793. Law of the National Convention repealing the law of May 23, 1793, which exempted American ships. *Lois et actes,* VII. 82–83.
   July 1, 1793. Law restoring the exemption of American ships, in phraseology identical with that of May 23, 1793. *Ibid.,* VII. 174.
   July 27, 1793. Law decreeing the full execution of the law of May 9, 1793, relative

to neutral ships loaded with foodstuffs owned by neutrals or with enemy property. *Ibid.,* VII. 241–242.

March 24, 1794 (4 *germinal, an* II.). Law decreeing: "The treaties of navigation and of commerce existing between France and nations with whom she is at peace shall be executed according to their form and tenure." *Ibid.,* VIII. 414–415.

November 18, 1794. Decree of the committee of public safety enjoining French naval officers and commanders of privateers to enforce the law of nations and the stipulations of treaties, "conformably to the terms of the decree of the National Convention of July 27, 1793". A.S.P., F.R., I. 689, 752. This decree does not appear in the *Recueil des actes du Comité de salut public,* edited by Alphonse A. Aulard. Jay's Treaty was signed on November 19, 1794.

4. In addition to an undetermined number of captures at sea, Fulwar Skipwith, American claims agent at Paris in October, 1794, stated that there were nearly 300 vessels in the ports of France suffering from embargoes (a later list showed that the Bordeaux embargo accounted for 103 cases), spoliations, delays, breaches of contract, non-payment of purchased cargoes, etc. The United States Court of Claims, which completed adjudication of the French Spoliation Claims for 1793–1800 (responsibility having been assumed by the convention with France of 1800) awarded a total of $7,149,306.10 for 1853 authentic cases of spoliation. Each case did not, however, represent a particular ship. Congress has appropriated to date only $3,910,860.61, to pay part of these claims. To this may be added $5,000,000 for claims of a special character, assumed by the United States in 1803, in part payment for Louisiana—to wit: embargoes, detention and appropriation of goods in French harbors, money due from the French government for purchases, etc.

5. *Correspondence of the French Ministers to the United States, 1791–1797,* Frederick J. Turner, ed., in *Annual Report* of the American Historical Association, 1903, II. 291.

6. A.S.P., F.R., I. 677.

7. See report of Merlin de Douai, brumaire, an III., Archives du ministère des Affaires étrangères, Correspondance politique, États-Unis, vol. 42, ff. 186–204.

8. Law of 13 nivôse, an III., *Bulletin des lois de la République française,* 1e sér., vol. III., no. 107; decree of the committee of public safety, 14 nivôse, an III. (Jan. 3, 1795), A.S.P., F.R., I. 642 [in English translation; not in Aulard].

9. *Before* the repeal of the retaliatory decrees the committee had asked Monroe about the treaty; and he had conveyed to them information from Jay, to the effect that it contained nothing contrary to the existing treaties of the United States; and had promised that as soon as he might be informed of its contents he would inform the committee. This promise impelled Monroe to refuse to accept from Jay a *confidential* statement of the contents of the treaty. Monroe's *View of the Conduct of the Executive on the Foreign Affairs of the United States, connected with the Mission to the French Republic during the Years 1794, 5, and 6* (Philadelphia, 1797), pp. xvii–xxvii.

10. Monroe's instructions and dispatches are printed in A.S.P., F.R., I., and in his exculpatory *View.* Washington's studied comments on the *View,* written at Mount Vernon on the margin of its pages, are printed in appendix II. to Daniel C. Gilman's *James Monroe* (Boston, 1883, 1898). Beverley W. Bond., jr.'s The Monroe Mission to France, 1794–1796, in The Johns Hopkins *Studies in Historical and Political Science,* XXV. (1907) 9–103, did not have available the valuable sources in the French ministry of foreign affairs. The various deliberations of committees on Monroe's notes, and relevant reports, quite voluminous, are in Arch. Aff., Étr., États-Unis, vol. 42, particularly ff. 17, 141, 186–204.

11. Monroe to Joseph Jones, Sept. 15, 1795. Calendar, in Division of MSS. of the Library of Congress, of the Gouverneur Collection of Monroe Papers, now privately owned. Gilman, p. 62, printed a portion of this letter.

12. Monroe wrote to the committee of public safety a "non-official letter", December 27, 1794, asking that a member of the committee be deputed to have frank conversations with him concerning any propositions about to be made to the American government

"on this subject [*i.e.*, possible propositions] or any other (if you desire) tending to acquaint you [the committees] with the situation and the *real* dispositions of my *countrymen* [italics inserted]. Arch. Aff. Étr., États-Unis, vol. 42, f. 445.

13. *Writings of James Monroe*, Stanislaus Murray Hamilton, ed. (New York, 1898–1903), vol. II., *passim.*

14. Adet to the committee of public safety, 14 thermidor, an III. (Aug. 1, 1795), *Corr. Fr. Min.*, p. 762.

15. "I assured them, generally, as I had done before, that I was satisfied the treaty contained in it nothing which could give them uneasiness; but if it did, and especially if it weakened our connexion with France, it would certainly be disapproved in America." Monroe to the Secretary of State, Apr. 14, 1795, A.S.P., F.R., I. 702. He did convey to the committee of public safety Jay's only statement to him about the treaty, that it contained nothing contrary to the treaty stipulations of the United States with other countries.

16. "Exposé sommaire", etc., dated 1796, in the Monroe Collection of MSS., Library of Congress. Internal evidence proves Monroe to be the writer, and one presumes from the same evidence that it was directed to the French government, although I have not found it in the French archives.

17. Monroe to the minister of foreign affairs, Paris, Feb. 17, 1796 (28 pluviôse, an IV.), Arch. Aff. Étr., États-Unis, vol. 45, f. 146.

18. *Corr. Fr. Min.*, pp. 373, 389, 410, 419; Arch. Aff. Étr., États-Unis, vol. 41, ff. 291, 377, 408.

19. *Corr. Fr. Min.*, p. 894. Neither Fauchet and the commissioners, nor their successor Adet, had any actual instructions concerning Jay's Treaty. Once they left Paris, they received scant attention from the committee of public safety.

20. Bernard Faÿ, *L'esprit révolutionnaire en France et aux États-Unis à la fin du XVIIIe siècle* (Paris, 1925), pp. 254–260. "All these intrigues are sad and displeasing to study when one remembers the sincere enthusiasm which the masses of the American people then testified for France." *Ibid.*, p. 255. John Bach McMaster, *History of the People of the United States* (New York, 1883–1913), vol. II., ch. IX., is in effect a digest of opposing press and pamphlet comment. The arguments of the Republican press against Jay's Treaty, against Washington, against the Farewell Address, and finally against the candidacy of John Adams, reflect the paragraphs of the political correspondence of the French foreign office with its American legation.

21. To this point there is a remarkable analysis of American politics in relation to French policy, by the undersecretary of the sixth division of the foreign office: Memoir on the United States, Florida, and Louisiana, 12 frimaire, an IV. (Dec. 3, 1795). Arch. Aff. Étr., États-Unis, vol. 44, ff. 407–417.

22. Report of the minister of foreign affairs to the Executive Directory, 27 nivôse, an IV. (Jan. 17, 1796), *ibid.*, vol. 45, ff. 41–53.

23. Monroe to the minister of foreign affairs, Paris, Feb. 17, 1796 (28 pluviôse, an IV.), *ibid.*, vol. 45, f. 147 [italics inserted]. This highly significant note was not revealed to his own government and is enough to justify Washington's removal of Monroe. Monroe summarized the arguments he had made to Delacroix in a letter to the Secretary of State of February 20, 1796, but made no reference to any written note of his and said nothing about the hint he had given.

24. Delacroix to Monroe, Paris, 1 ventôse, an IV. (Feb. 20, 1796), *ibid.*, vol. 45, f. 160.

25. Observations on Mr. Monroe's letter to the minister of foreign affairs, not dated, *ibid.*, vol. 45, f. 148.

26. "Memoir of Political Instructions to the Citizen Vincent, to be sent as Minister Plenipotentiary of the Republic to the United States". *Recueil des actes du Directoire exécutif*, A. Debidour, ed. (Paris, 1910), I. 748; II. 621. Some charges against Vincent's integrity apparently stopped his departure. Later Monroe's protest against the appointment of Mangourit, the former French consul at Charleston during Genêt's obnoxious operations, was effective.

27. R. Earl McClendon published a useful note on the Origin of the Two-Thirds Rule in Senate Action upon Treaties, *Am. Hist. Rev.,* XXXVI. 768–772.

28. J. Fred Rippy and Angie Debo, The Historical Background of the American Policy of Isolation, *Smith College Studies in History,* vol. IX., nos. 3 and 4 (Apr.–July, 1924), p. 140.

29. Rippy and Debo, *op. cit.,* have collected numerous expressions of abstention from European politics.

30. *Common Sense* (Philadelphia, 1776, 1st ed.), p. 38.

31. Rippy and Debo, p. 90.

32. *The Writings of James Madison,* Gaillard Hunt, ed. (New York, 1900–1910), V. 151.

33. *The Writings of Thomas Jefferson,* Paul Leicester Ford, ed. (New York, 1892–1899), IV. 483.

34. To Monsieur de Pinto, New York, Aug. 7, 1790. *The Writings of Thomas Jefferson,* Memorial ed. (Washington, 1903–1904), VIII. 74.

35. Over the signature of *Horatius,* arguing for the ratification of Jay's Treaty, Hamilton wrote in 1795: "If you consult your true interest your motto cannot fail to be: 'PEACE AND TRADE WITH ALL NATIONS; beyond our present engagements, POLITICAL CONNECTION WITH NONE.' You ought to spurn from you as the box of Pandora, the fatal heresy of a close alliance, or in the language of *Genet,* a true *family compact,* with France. This would at once make you a mere satellite of France, and entangle you in all the contests, broils, and wars of Europe." The text continues " 'Tis evident that the controversies of Europe must often grow out of causes and interests foreign to this country. Why then should we, by a close political connection with any power of Europe, expose our peace and interest, as a matter of course, to all the shocks with which their mad rivalship and wicked ambition so frequently convulse the earth? 'T were insanity to embrace such a system." *The Works of Alexander Hamilton,* Henry Cabot Lodge, ed. (New York, 1885–1886), IV. 366–367.

36. To Patrick Henry, Oct. 9, 1795; to Gouverneur Morris, Dec. 22, 1795; *The Writings of George Washington,* Worthington Chauncey Ford, ed. (New York, 1889–1893), XIII. 119, 151. Washington refused to lend his official intercession to assist the release from Austrian and Prussian prisons of his dearest friend, Lafayette, for fear of involving the United States in Europe's wars. See my article in *Daughters of the American Revolution Magazine,* vol. LVIII., nos. 6, 7, and 8 (June, July, August, 1924).

37. I have profited from discussions of President Washington's policies with Mr. Frank Louraine of Washington, D. C., particularly on the significance of the Farewell Address in 1796, instead of 1792.

38. Horace Binney in one of the first critical essays in American historiography analyzed the authorship of the document. *An Inquiry into the Formation of Washington's Farewell Address* (Philadelphia, 1859).

39. *Claypoole's American Daily Advertiser* (Philadelphia), Sept. 19, 1796.

40. In closing the document, Adet reported: "It would be useless to speak to you about it. You will have noticed the lies it contains, the insolent tone that governs it, the immorality which characterizes it. You will have had no difficulty in recognizing the author of a piece extolling ingratitude, showing it as a virtue necessary to the happiness of States, presenting interest as the only counsel which governments ought to follow in the course of their negotiations, putting aside honor and glory. You will have recognized immediately the doctrine of the former Secretary of the Treasury, Hamilton, and the principles of loyalty that have always directed the Philadelphia Government." *Corr. Fr. Min.,* p. 954.

41. See Fauchet's long Memoir on the United States of America, 24 frimaire, an IV. (Dec. 15, 1795), Arch. Aff. Étr., États-Unis, vol. 44, ff. 457–529.

42. *Corr. Fr. Min.,* pp. 900–906.

43. The minister of foreign affairs to Adet, 7 fructidor, an IV. (Aug. 24, 1796), Arch.

Aff. Étr., États-Unis, vol. 46, ff. 144–145. See also drafts and reports associated with these instructions, *ibid.,* ff. 133–140.

44. Same to same, 12 brumaire, an V. (Nov. 2, 1796), *ibid.,* ff. 355–358.

45. Translation of an extract from the resolves of the Directory, of the 14th messidor, an IV. (July 2, 1796). A.S.P., F.R., I. 577. This extract is not printed in the proceedings for that date of the *Actes du Directoire exécutif.*

46. *Corr. Fr. Min.,* p. 972.

47. A.S.P., F.R., I. 583.

48. See Hamilton to Wolcott, Nov. 22, 1796, George Gibbs, *Memoirs of the Administrations of Washington and John Adams, edited from the papers of Oliver Wolcott* (New York, 1846), I. 398.

49. It was transmitted to Congress on January 19, 1797, and immediately ordered to be printed. It appeared in the *Aurora* in installments between January 24 and February 3, 1797.

50. Arch. Aff. Étr., États-Unis, vols. 39–42.

51. A.S.P., F.R., I. 559–576.

52. In his Inaugural Address he said: "If the control of an election can be obtained by foreign nations by flattery or menaces, by fraud or violence, by terror, intrigue, or venality, the Government may not be the choice of the American people, but of foreign nations. It may be foreign nations who govern us, and not we, the people, who govern ourselves."

53. Nov. 22, 1796, Gibbs, I. 400.

54. Edward Channing, *A History of the United States,* IV. 173.

55. *Corr. Fr. Min.,* p. 983.

A Statement of Empire

BURTON I. KAUFMAN

When George Washington asked Alexander Hamilton to prepare a farewell statement for him in 1796, he enclosed the draft of a message written four years earlier by James Madison announcing the President's intention to retire at the end of his first term, praising the Constitution, and pleading for the preservation of the Union. To this Washington added his own statement urging a policy of neutrality in the struggle taking place between England and France and calling for a halt to the domestic political battles which threatened to disrupt the new nation. Hamilton incorporated Washington's ideas into the final text of the Farewell Address, which was delivered to the newspapers on September 19, 1796; these ideas have since become the focus of a historical debate over the purpose and meaning of the address.

In the appended statement forwarded to Hamilton, the President also expressed a thought which has been almost completely neglected by historians. This was his conviction that, if his immediate goals were fulfilled, America would become one of the great powers in the world. "While we are encircled in one band," Washington said, "we shall possess the strength of a Giant and there will be none who can make us afraid." This idea was then incorporated into the final address:

> If we remain one people, under an efficient government, the period is not far off when we may defy material injury from external annoyance; when we may take such an attitude as will cause the neutrality we may at any time resolve upon to be scrupulously respected; when belligerent nations, under the impossibility of making acquisitions upon us, will not lightly hazard the giving us provocation; when we may choose peace or war, as our interest guided by justice shall counsel.

Although the President expected America to become an important world power, he did not indicate in his draft to Hamilton how he thought that power would be achieved. Nor were his views made any clearer in the final message; perhaps that is why this particular section has received so little attention. Yet on numerous other occasions Washington elaborated on his vision and charted the path to American greatness.

In his view, the key to the new nation's future was development of its Western lands, ones which he described in 1793 as "a tract of as rich Country for hundreds of miles as any in the world." Washington expected these lands to be settled as far as the northwestern areas around the Great Lakes. To open them up, he planned a number of ambitious inland navigation projects. In combination with other internal improvements, such as bridges and turnpikes, these waterways would constitute an elaborate transportation network not only linking East and West but connecting the seaboard states from Georgia to Rhode Island.

By making possible trade between larger sections of the new nation, these internal improvements would also promote national unity, a goal that Washington considered essential if America was to grow strong. As an ardent nationalist he advocated numerous other measures on which to build a common American identity. He encouraged American contributions in science and literature, and he fostered the creation of American institutions of higher learning in which he hoped to bring together youth from all sections of the nation. He urged giving the central government increased powers at the expense of the states in order to provide for the nation's common needs.

As Washington foresaw it, the country's economy would be based on agriculture; the Western lands would be brought under cultivation and their produce shipped throughout the world. Washington was not, however, narrowly agrarian in outlook. He simply regarded agriculture of paramount importance in the United States' endeavor to become economically self-sufficient. And while he felt that America would continue to be predominantly agricultural, he still encouraged the development of manufacturing and the establishment of a balanced economy.

The President's interest in opening up the West, his promotion of national unity and stronger central government, and his emphasis on self-sufficiency were all related to his vision of the United States as an expanding nation and future world power. Concerning its status in 1796, however, he had no illusions; he realized that the country was then too weak to become involved in international imbroglios. In his farewell address he therefore reiterated his earlier position that the United States follow a policy of neutrality toward European struggles. Aware of the threat which political divisions posed to the country, he also spoke out once more against partisanship and factionalism. But it must be understood that these views were always subordinate to, and directed toward, his larger vision of America's destiny.

Historians who have discussed Washington's valedictory remarks concerning political partisanship and foreign entanglements have usually taken them out of context. Those who have not studied the address in light of ideas previously expressed by the President have failed equally to understand its real significance. That is, the Farewell Address can be properly understood only in relation to Washington's concept of his country's imperial future, a concept whose roots lie in the history of both the country and the man.

Washington was born into a society of tobacco planters whose absorbing interest was land. The number of acres owned by an individual played an important part in determining his financial and social status. By this measurement Virginia, Washington's home, was a prosperous colony. It mattered little that the single-crop system of agriculture wasted the soil and produced poor returns, for vast regions of land lay open to the West. Indeed, planters were great speculators, risking entire fortunes in the purchase of acreage whose value they always expected to rise once it was settled.

Like other planters, Washington became a speculator and real estate promoter. In 1751 he invested in the Ohio Company which, two years earlier, had been granted 500,000 acres of land in the Ohio Valley. Washington continued to purchase land, becoming by the time of the Revolution one of America's largest landowners. His motives were not, however, entirely ones of personal gain. As he traveled beyond the Allegheny Mountains and through the virgin Ohio Valley during his youth and early manhood, he had also developed a lofty sense of the region's future.

A further influence on Washington's concept of America's destiny was the fact that he had grown to maturity within the British mercantile empire whose primary goals were self-sufficiency through economic integration, increased domestic production, and a favorable balance of trade. These goals were to be achieved by careful regulation of the economy and a policy of commercial and territorial expansion under which the British Empire's colonies would both provide the mother country with raw materials and furnish markets for her production. The system was supposed to be complementary; in reality the planters found themselves increasingly in debt to British merchants. . . .

In a real sense it was British unwillingness to allow the colonies to form their own mercantilist system which led Washington to break with the mother country. As England continued to restrict colonial development, Washington encouraged formation of an American system to replace the British imperium. In the Fairfax Resolves of 1774, which he helped George Mason to prepare, he sought an end to trade with England and the establishment of nonimportation agreements, both to be enforced by a strong union of the colonies. Further to make the colonies self-sufficient, he urged that every encouragement be given "to the improvement of arts and manufactures."

During the war with England, Washington's nationalism and vision of American empire emerged clearly. Having broken with the mother country, he now gave more thought to the new nation's future. This direction was evident in his military strategy in which he weighed postwar political and economic objectives with immediate military factors. In a lengthy memorandum of 1780, for example, he reviewed the disposition of British troops in North America and the advantages to be gained by attacking them. Because of the immediate situation he thought his efforts should be directed against enemy forces in New York and the Southern states. Nonetheless, he did not dismiss the possibility of attacking Canada, Halifax, or Bermuda. The capture of Halifax, he remarked,

> would add much weight to the reasons given in support of an Expedition into [Canada]; and in case of success, would be of the utmost importance; as it would add much, not only to the security of the trade of Canada, but the United States in General. Give a well grounded hope of rescuing the Fisheries from Great Britain, which will most essentially injure her Marine, while it would lay a foundation, on which to build one of our own. . . . And lastly, another Provence (Nova Scotia) which sometime ago was very desirous of it, would be added to the Federal Union.

Throughout much of the war, in fact, the general looked toward Canada, cherishing the hope that that huge and relatively unsettled area would join the other former British colonies. The failure of an expedition against the province in 1776 and the apparent unwillingness of its inhabitants to side with the Americans discouraged him from launching a second invasion until he was absolutely certain of victory. Still, he continued to recognize the advantages which would result from Canada's acquisition.

It was because he realized that country's importance to the Union that he reacted strongly against a plan to launch a joint invasion of Canada with France. His close friend, the Marquis de Lafayette, had made the proposal to Congress in 1778, where it met a warm reception. But when that body asked Washington for his opinion he advised against the attack. Publicly he based his opposition on military grounds, but in a private letter to the president of Congress, Henry Laurens, he made it clear that he was really afraid of its political consequences. France had strong ties in Quebec, Washington pointed out, and might desire to remain in the conquered territory indefinitely. "Let us realize for a moment," he continued,

> the striking advantages France would derive from the possession of Canada; the acquisition of an extensive territory abounding in supplies for the use of her Islands; the opening a vast source of the most beneficial commerce with the Indian nations, which she might then monopolize; the having ports of her own on the continent independent of the precarious good will of an ally; the en-grossing of the whole trade of New found land whenever she pleased; the finest nursery of seamen in the world.

At the same time, by controlling Canada the French in alliance with Spain would be able to encircle the new nation and work with the Indians to prevent its growth. On the other hand, American seizure of the province would prevent this danger, and the advantages which France might have gained would accrue to the new nation.

With the war's end the victorious general returned to Mount Vernon, where he spent most of the next five years. During this time he engaged in an enormous correspondence with leading figures of the day on a variety of issues. Of central concern to Washington was the erection of a peace establishment which would assure America's destiny in the world. While others believed the new nation could continue to prosper as a weak union of thirteen states under the Articles of Confederation, the future President held a different view. He had seen the country nearly destroyed during the war by local jealousies and petty prejudices. From Mount Vernon he witnessed additional evidence of the perils of disunion and impotent government: individual states establishing their own commercial systems and competing for trade; Europeans closing their markets to Americans without fear of retaliation; land speculators casting their eyes on the West without thought of the public welfare; the industry which had emerged during the war going into decline; and the value of paper money falling. It was clear to Washington that his vision of America's future could never be attained under these circumstances.

His whole concept of empire, moreover, rested on the assumption of a united people and an integrated economy supported by a government able to provide for the nation's needs. Only by acting together, he wrote in 1783, could the thirteen states find their place in the world. Separately they would be pawns in the hands of European powers, played off against one another as soon as Europe grew jealous of America's "rising greatness as an Empire." Washington therefore urged revision or replacement of the Articles to provide for a governing body able to meet the requirements of a burgeoning—and, he hoped, united—power. "Let us flatter ourselves," he remarked to the Merchants of Philadelphia,

> that the day is not remote, when a wise and just system of policy will be adopted by every State in the Union; then will national faith be inviolably preserved, public credit durably established, the blessings of Commerce extensively diffused, and the reputation of our new-formed Empire supported with as much *Eclat* as has been acquired in laying the foundation of it.

Of those problems which he expected the reconstituted government to handle, none was more important in his mind than orderly Western expansion. As a result of the Treaty of Paris, the United States had secured the entire region from the Alleghenies to the Mississippi River. Almost immediately, emigrants from both the seaboard states and across the Atlantic began to settle and cultivate the frontier. Washington was encouraged by this westward movement. Having made a trip to the area between the Great Kanawha and Ohio Rivers in 1784, he noted in his diary the fertility of the soil, the abundant harvests, and the increasing population. To stimulate further migration he offered the West as an asylum for the poor and oppressed of the world. "I wish to see the sons and daughters of the world in Peace," he remarked,

> and busily employed in fulfilling the first and great commandment, *Increase* and *Multiply;* as an encouragement to which we have opened the fertile plains of the Ohio to the poor, the needy and the oppressed of the Earth; and one therefore who is heavily laden, or who wants land to cultivate, may repair to thither and abound, as in the Land of promise with milk and honey.

It was precisely along the frontier, however, that national feeling was least evident and danger of disunity most threatening. The Alleghenies still posed a natural barrier to trade between the frontier and the Atlantic; to reach the seaboard states, Western settlers were forced to send their goods down the Mississippi to New Orleans. Unless communication could be established with the frontier and its produce easily transported to the coast, Washington realized its people would have no predilection to remain in the Union; they might in fact separate.

To tie these new regions with the old and open the frontier to settlement, the future President proposed his earlier scheme of making the Potomac River navigable and connecting it with the Ohio. For four years he devoted a major part of his time to this project. No longer was it merely a handy tool to tap the resources of the West for Virginia's benefit; now completion of the plan was a matter of political exigency if America were to achieve its destiny in the world. Although, in a letter of 1784, Washington noted the benefits Virginia and Maryland would receive if the Potomac were opened to navigation, he also remarked, "I consider this business in a far more extensive point of view, and the more I have resolved upon the subject, the more important it appears to me; not only as it respects our commerce, but our political interests, and the well being and strength of the union also." He even supported other navigation projects, including a proposal to make the Susquehanna River navigable; the more communications that were opened to the West, the closer it would be bound to the rest of the Union and the stronger the nation would become.

For the very reason that he favored inland navigation projects, Washington was also willing at first to forego the right of free navigation of the Mississippi. Just as trade with the Atlantic States would more tightly bind the Western regions to the rest of the nation, continued commerce down the Mississippi would draw them closer to Spain. He was even willing in 1786, during the Jay-Gardoqui negotiations, to sacrifice the right to navigate the Mississippi for a period of years in return for a commercial treaty with Spain. Only after he realized how divisive an issue the Mississippi question was and how determined the Western settlers were to obtain the right to navigate the river did he change his attitude and come out in favor of their position.

Washington's views on inland navigation projects and free navigation of the Mississippi became part of a long-range plan which he had early formulated for settlement of the West. This plan also called for the creation of one or two states roughly equal in size and shape to present-day Ohio and Michigan. Such an area, Washington felt, would be large enough to accommodate all settlers for the immediate future. Indians would inhabit the area west of the territory and it would be a felony to trespass on their lands. According to this plan, the central government would be able to extend its influence as the nation expanded and unite the frontier regions with the more established areas, thus eliminating the possibility of separation. At the same time speculators would be prevented from grabbing distant lands for their personal profit. Finally, the Indians, safeguarded by law, would not resort to bloodshed to protect their territory. Although obviously concerned with protecting their rights, Washington did not expect the Indians to hamper further white expansion. He hoped that they would eventually become Christians and be absorbed into white civilization. Meanwhile he was confident they could be persuaded to sell their lands as they were needed and move further westward.

By the time Washington became President in 1789, he was hopeful that his vision of America's future was nearing reality—that America would become a "storehouse and granary for the world." The new constitution, which had been ratified in 1788, greatly enhanced the powers of the central government, including the granting of important controls over commerce and the general economy. By the Northwest Ordinance of 1787 the old Confederation had provided for settlement of the West much along the lines suggested by Washington. Construction to make the Potomac navigable had begun, and his dream of making the area between Alexandria and Georgetown the entrepôt for Western goods seemed near fulfillment.

Developments in Europe, on the other hand, appeared particularly foreboding. France was on the eve of revolution, relations between England and Spain remained tense, and war raged between Turkey, Russia, and Austria. To Washington the new nation by comparison seemed blessed by Providence. He noted that no other country had such natural advantages for the growth of agriculture and commerce, and he pointed to the almost unlimited territory which lay open for development. He expected a realization of natural happiness never enjoyed by even the most favored nations. "The natural, political, and moral circumstances of our Nascent empire," he remarked, "justify the anticipation."

He was, however, under no illusion about the current weak internal state of his country. What was needed in his view was time for the United States to develop its natural resources. This could be achieved only by remaining aloof from international affairs. Thus he made the maintenance of peace and noninvolvement in European matters two of his cardinal principles even before he learned of the Treaty of Paris ending the struggle against England. Once he assumed the office of President, he continued to urge application of these policies. . . .

At the end of his first administration, the President appeared generally pleased with the state of the nation and hopeful that his vision of America's destiny would come true. The new government was firmly established, the possibility of Western separation seemed more unlikely, and the country itself was beginning to prosper. Even efforts—including those of Washington—to make the United States more self-sufficient through the promotion of manufacturing seemed to be having some success. If only the nation could continue to develop without interruption for the next several years, the President could see no reason why Americans would not rank among the most powerful and happy people in the world.

Unfortunately, the French Revolution and the Hamiltonian program unleashed forces of dissension within the nation which threatened to tear it apart and destroy its chances for greatness. Having always believed factionalism and internal division to be the greatest dangers facing the young country, Washington strongly deplored these developments. When they resulted in attacks on his administration, he decided to retire from office. In May 1792 he asked Madison to prepare a farewell statement for him, and outlined for the Virginia congressman the points he wanted stressed. In leaving office he desired to "invoke a continuation of the blessings of Providence" upon America. To impress this point, he felt Madison should point out that

> we are *all* the Children of the same country; a Country great and rich in itself; capable, & promising to be, as any the Annals of history have ever brought to our view. That our interest, however diversified in local and smaller matters, is the same in all the great & essential concerns of the Nation. That the extent of our Country, the diversity of our climate & soil, and the various productions of the States . . . are such as to make one part not only convenient, but perhaps indispensably necessary to the other part; and may render the whole (at no distant period) one of the most independant [*sic*] in the world.

Washington's farewell was premature. Madison and other statesmen convinced him to stay in office, and he was reelected without opposition. But political divisions grew worse during the early years of his second administration. They were complicated in February 1793 when England and Spain united in war against France. If Washington regarded internal divisions as the nation's greatest danger, he considered European war, which could lead to American involvement, as its second most serious peril. This was especially true in 1793 when the international struggle only embittered existing political divisions within the United States. He had already made peace and noninvolvement two of his principal objectives. Determined to pursue this policy, he issued in April a proclamation of neutrality. For the remainder of his second administration he tried to steer a strictly neutral course.

Historians have regarded Washington's proclamation of neutrality as an attempt to assert a policy of independence. That it most certainly was, but the interpretation does not go deep enough. Even more than a statement of independence, it was an effort by Washington to assure that the rising empire of the New World would not fall victim to the struggles of the Old. The President was aware of the advantages which war might bring the United States if it did not become involved. As a neutral nation America could develop her commerce by carrying goods between belligerent powers and their possessions. These nations would also need American products, such as ships and naval stores, to meet the requirements of war. Such commerce would lead in turn to increased consideration and respect for the United States. Nonetheless Washington preferred peace to the menace of war. He perhaps best expressed his attitude with regard to neutrality when he remarked, "The present flourishing situation of our affairs, and the prosperity we enjoy, must be obvious to the good Citizens of the United States; it remains, therefore, for them to pursue such a line of conduct, as will insure these blessings, by averting the calamities of war."

Events at home and abroad seemed to conspire against Washington's dream of empire. While Indian forays in the Northwest were finally ended in 1794 as a result of the Battle of Fallen Timbers, Britain continued to hold on to her Western posts, and this, coupled with her violation of American maritime rights, threatened to cause hostilities between the two countries. At the same time, free transit of the Mississippi remained uncertain, and the administration was plagued continually by foreign intrigues along the frontier. Armed rebellion broke out in Pennsylvania against a tax on whiskey. The President's proclamation of neutrality embittered Francophiles who felt the administration was siding with England. When they learned the government had concluded the Jay Treaty with that country, their attacks against Washington became personal and abusive.

The President's reaction was to remind the nation of the destiny it held if neutrality were maintained and internal disunity ended. "Our agriculture, Commerce, and Manufactures, prosper beyond former example," he remarked in his annual message to Congress in December, 1795. "Placed in a situation every way so auspicious," he concluded, "motives of commanding force impel us, with sincere acknowledgment to heaven, and pure love to our country, to unite our efforts to preserve, prolong, and improve, our immense advantages."

The international situation improved somewhat during the first half of 1796, and the future became more hopeful than it had been for the last several years. The successful negotiation of Jay's Treaty momentarily ended the danger of war with England, while Pinckney's Treaty settled major differences with Spain to the great advantage of the United States, particularly by guaranteeing her right to navigate the Mississippi. As his second term drew to a close, Washington could consider retirement without leaving the country facing the dire prospects of war. . . .

As with the proclamation of neutrality, historians have generally interpreted the Farewell Address as the statement of a policy of independence from European affairs. As evidence they have emphasized that part of the address which calls for neutrality with respect to the struggle in Europe. Others have pointed to the section urging an end to political partisanship and have analyzed the address in light of the political war raging between Federalists and Anti-Federalists. Clearly, however, these ideas were subordinate to the larger view of America's future which Washington had outlined in his draft proposal to Hamilton. Commenting on the bitter House struggle over Jay's Treaty at about the time the address was being prepared, the President remarked in words similar to those in his valedictory:

> Every true friend to this Country must *see* and *feel* that [our] policy . . . is
> not to embroil ourselves, with any nation whatever; but to avoid their disputes

and their politics; . . . Twenty years peace with such an increase of population and resources as we have a right to expect; added to our remote situation from the jarring power, will in all probability enable us in a just cause, to bid defiance to any power on earth.

Attainment of this vision of America's destiny which he had first begun to develop as a youth surveying the frontier, which had become more perceptible during the struggle against England, and which he had worked to achieve following the revolution, had become the major objective of his administration. It was only proper that he should leave this vision in his Farewell Address as his legacy to the country.

FURTHER READING

Joseph Charles, *The Origins of the American Party System* (1956)

Alexander DeConde, *Entangling Alliance: Politics and Diplomacy under George Washington* (1958)

Alexander DeConde, "Washington's Farewell, the French Alliance, and the Election of 1796," *Mississippi Valley Historical Review,* 53 (1957), 641–658

Douglas Southall Freeman, *George Washington: A Biography,* 7 vols. (1948–1957)

Felix Gilbert, *To the Farewell Address* (1961)

John C. Miller, *The Federalist Era, 1789–1801* (1960)

Victor Hugo Paltsits, *Washington's Farewell Address* (1935)

Bradford Perkins, *The First Rapprochement: England and the United States, 1795–1805* (1955)

Albert K. Weinberg, "Washington's 'Great Rule' in Its Historical Evolution," in Eric F. Goldman, ed., *Historiography and Urbanization* (1941)

5

The Louisiana
Purchase

*In 1803 the United States purchased from Napoleonic France a territory,
then without precise boundaries, totalling about 828,000 square miles. At a
sale price of $15 million, the vast expanses of land were quite inexpensive—
about 3 cents an acre. Behind the negotiations in Paris lay years of interest
in and worry over Louisiana. In 1800 Spain secretly retroceded Louisiana
to France, although the arrangement was not consummated until 1802.
Americans bristled at this transaction. The administration of Thomas
Jefferson attempted to persuade France to abandon the large colony. On
April 30, French and American emissaries signed a treaty turning Louisiana
over to the United States. "You have made a noble bargain," First Consul
Napoleon Bonaparte remarked, "and I suppose you will make the most of it."*

*Historians differ over the degree to which the United States followed an
active, forceful diplomacy and over whether this purchase was a lucky
windfall made possible by Napoleon's European troubles or a much-pursued,
successful example of America's imperial quest. In either case, the territorial
bargain extended the young nation's border far westward, abutting land
claimed by Spain and Britain.*

DOCUMENTS

The following documents demonstrate the Jefferson administration's profound
concern with Louisiana. Jefferson himself, in a letter of April 1802, appreciated the
value of New Orleans to the American export trade and the detrimental international
consequences of French rule there. Robert Livingston, a New Yorker serving as

American Minister to France, recounted in an April 1803 letter to Secretary of State James Madison the steps leading to the purchase.

Thomas Jefferson on Louisiana, 1802

The cession of Louisiana and the Floridas by Spain to France, works most sorely on the United States. On this subject the Secretary of State has written to you fully, yet I cannot forbear recurring to it personally, so deep is the impression it makes on my mind. It completely reverses all the political relations of the United States, and will form a new epoch in our political course. Of all nations of any consideration, France is the one which, hitherto, has offered the fewest points on which we could have any conflict of right, and the most points of a communion of interests. From these causes, we have ever looked to her as our *natural friend,* as one with which we never could have an occasion of difference. Her growth, therefore, we viewed as our own, her misfortunes ours. There is on the globe one single spot, the possessor of which is our natural and habitual enemy. It is New Orleans, through which the produce of three-eighths of our territory must pass to market, and from its fertility it will ere long yield more than half of our whole produce, and contain more than half of our inhabitants. France, placing herself in that door, assumes to us the attitude of defiance. Spain might have retained it quietly for years. Her pacific dispositions, her feeble state, would induce her to increase our facilities there, so that her possession of the place would be hardly felt by us, and it would not, perhaps, be very long before some circumstance might arise, which might make the cession of it to us the price of something of more worth to her. Not so can it ever be in the hands of France: the impetuosity of her temper, the energy and restlessness of her character, placed in a point of eternal friction with us, and our character, which, though quiet and loving peace and the pursuit of wealth, is high-minded, despising wealth in competition with insult or injury, enterprising and energetic as any nation on earth; these circumstances render it impossible that France and the United States can continue long friends, when they meet in so irritable a position. They, as well as we, must be blind if they do not see this; and we must be very improvident if we do not begin to make arrangements on that hypothesis. The day that France takes possession of New Orleans, fixes the sentence which is to restrain her forever within her low-water mark. It seals the union of two nations, who, in conjunction, can maintain exclusive possession of the ocean. From that moment, we must marry ourselves to the British fleet and nation. We must turn all our attention to a maritime force, for which our resources place us on very high ground; and having formed and connected together a power which may render reinforcement of her settlements here impossible to France, make the first cannon which shall be fired in Europe the signal for the tearing up any settlement she may have made, and for holding the two continents of America in sequestration for the common purposes of the United

British and American nations. This is not a state of things we seek or desire. It is one which this measure, if adopted by France, forces on us as necessarily, as any other cause, by the laws of nature, brings on its necessary effect. It is not from a fear of France that we deprecate this measure proposed by her. For however greater her force is than ours, compared in the abstract, it is nothing in comparison of ours, when to be exerted on our soil. But it is from a sincere love of peace, and a firm persuasion, that bound to France by the interests and the strong sympathies still existing in the minds of our citizens, and holding relative positions which insure their continuance, we are secure of a long course of peace. Whereas, the change of friends, which will be rendered necessary if France changes that position, embarks us necessarily as a belligerent power in the first war of Europe.

Robert Livingston on the Negotiations in Paris, 1803

I have just come from the Minister of the Treasury. Our conversation was so important, that I think it necessary to write it, while the impressions are strong upon my mind; and the rather, as I fear I shall not have time to copy and send this letter, if I defer it till morning.

By my letter of yesterday, you learned that the Minister had asked me whether I would agree to purchase Louisiana, &c. On the 12th, I called upon him to press this matter further. He then thought proper to declare that his proposition was only personal, but still requested me to make an offer; and, upon declining to do so, as I expected Mr. Monroe the next day, he shrugged up his shoulders, and changed the conversation. Not willing, however, to lose sight of it, I told him I had been long endeavoring to bring him to some point; but, unfortunately, without effect: that I wished merely to have the negotiation opened by any proposition on his part; and, with that view, had written him a note which contained that request, grounded upon my apprehension of the consequence of sending General Bernadotte without enabling him to say a treaty was begun. He told me he would answer my note, but that he must do it evasively, because Louisiana was not theirs. I smiled at this assertion, and told him I had seen the treaty recognizing it; that I knew the Consul had appointed officers to govern the country, and that he had himself told me that General Victor was to take possession; that, in a note written by the express order of the First Consul, he had told me that General Bernadotte was to treat relative to it in the United States, &c. He still persisted that they had it in contemplation to obtain it, but had it not. I told him that I was very well pleased to understand this from him, because, if so, we should not commit ourselves with them in taking it from Spain, to whom, by his account, it still belonged; and that, as we had just cause of complaint against her, if Mr. Monroe concurred in opinion with me, we should negotiate no further on the subject, but advise our Government to take possession. He seemed alarmed at the boldness of the measure, and told me he would answer my note, but that it would be evasively. I told him I should receive with pleasure any communication

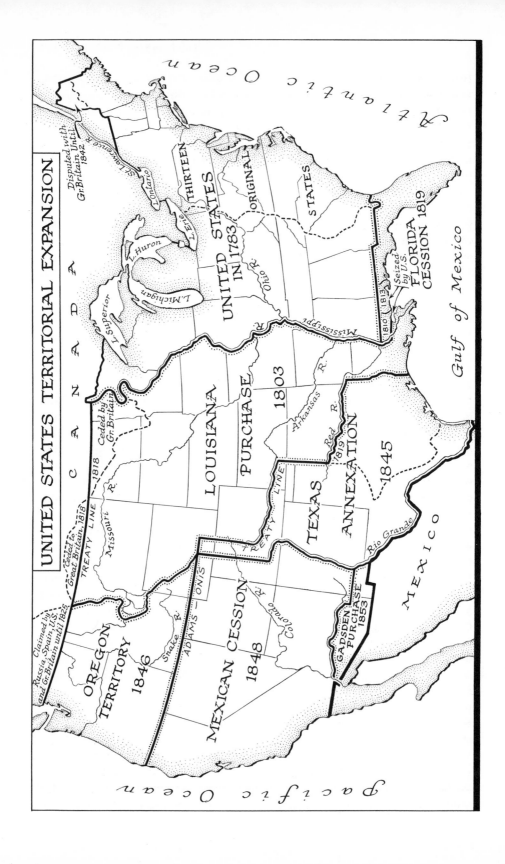

UNITED STATES TERRITORIAL EXPANSION

Atlantic Ocean

Disputed with Gr. Britain Until 1842

St. Lawrence R.

L. Ontario

L. Erie

ORIGINAL THIRTEEN

UNITED STATES IN 1783

L. Huron

L. Superior

L. Michigan

Ohio R.

STATES

Seized by U.S. 1810 1813

FLORIDA CESSION 1819

Mississippi

Gulf of Mexico

CANADA

Ceded by Gr. Britain

Ceded to Great Britain, 1818

TREATY LINE — 1818

Missouri R.

LOUISIANA PURCHASE 1803

Arkansas R.

Red R. 1819

TREATY LINE

TEXAS ANNEXATION 1845

Rio Grande

MEXICO

Claimed by Russia, Spain, U.S. and Gr. Britain until 1825

OREGON TERRITORY 1846

Snake R.

ADAMS — ONIS

MEXICAN CESSION 1848

Colorado R.

GADSDEN PURCHASE 1853

Pacific Ocean

from him, but that we were not disposed to trifle; that the times were critical, and though I did not know what instructions Mr. Monroe might bring, I was perfectly satisfied that they would require a precise and prompt notice; that I was very fearful, from the little progress I had made, that my Government would consider me as a very indolent negotiator. He laughed, and told me that he would give me a certificate that I was the most importunate he had met with. . . .

I told him that the United States were anxious to preserve peace with France; that, for that reason, they wished to remove them to the west side of the Mississippi; that we would be perfectly satisfied with New Orleans and the Floridas, and had no disposition to extend across the river; that, of course, we would not give any great sum for the purchase; that he was right in his idea of the extreme exorbitancy of the demand, which would not fall short of one hundred and twenty-five millions; that, however, we would be ready to purchase, provided the sum was reduced to reasonable limits. He then pressed me to name the sum. I told him that this was not worth while, because, as he only treated the inquiry as a matter of curiosity, any declaration of mine would have no effect. If a negotiation was to be opened, we should (Mr. Monroe and myself) make the offer after mature reflection. This compelled him to declare, that, though he was not authorized expressly to make the inquiry from me, yet, that, if I could mention any sum that came near the mark, that could be accepted, he would communicate it to the First Consul. I told him that we had no sort of authority to go to a sum that bore any proportion to what he mentioned; but that, as he himself considered the demand as too high, he would oblige me by telling me what he thought would be reasonable. He replied that, if we would name sixty millions, and take upon us the American claims, to the amount of twenty more, he would try how far this would be accepted. I told him that it was vain to ask anything that was so greatly beyond our means; that true policy would dictate to the First Consul not to press such a demand; that he must know that it would render the present Government unpopular, and have a tendency, at the next election, to throw the power into the hands of men who were most hostile to a connection with France; and that this would probably happen in the midst of a war. I asked him whether the few millions acquired at this expense would not be too dearly bought?

He frankly confessed that he was of my sentiments; but that he feared the Consul would not relax. I asked him to press this argument upon him, together with the danger of seeing the country pass into the hands of Britain. I told him that he had seen the ardor of the Americans to take it by force, and the difficulty with which they were restrained by the prudence of the President; that he must easily see how much the hands of the war party would be strengthened, when they learned that France was upon the eve of a rupture with England. He admitted the weight of all this: "But," says he, "you know the temper of a youthful conqueror; everything he does is rapid as lightning; we have only to speak to him as an opportunity presents itself, perhaps in a crowd, when he bears no contradiction. When I am alone with him, I can speak more freely, and he attends; but this opportunity seldom happens, and is always accidental. Try, then, if you can not come up to my mark. Consider the extent of the country, the exclusive navigation of the river, and the importance of having no neighbors to dispute you, no war to dread." I told him that I considered all these as important considerations, but there was a point beyond which we could not go, and that fell far short of the sum he mentioned. . . .

I speak now without reflection, and without having seen Mr. Monroe, as it was midnight when I left the Treasury Office, and is now near 3 o'clock. It is so very important that you should be apprized that a negotiation is actually opened, even before Mr. Monroe has been presented, in order to calm the tumult which the news of war will renew, that I have lost no time in communicating it. We shall do all we can to cheapen the purchase; but my present sentiment is that we shall buy. Mr. Monroe will be presented to the Minister to-morrow, when we shall press for as early an audience as possible from the First Consul. I think it will be necessary to put in some proposition to-morrow: the Consul goes in a few days to Brussels, and every moment is precious.

ESSAYS

Lawrence S. Kaplan of Kent State University, an expert on the foreign policy of Thomas Jefferson, places the purchase of Louisiana in the context of a concept made famous by Samuel Flagg Bemis: Europe's distresses worked to America's advantage. In other words, Kaplan tends to emphasize external factors and to suggest a defensive, reactive, even expedient, posture on the part of the United States. France threatened American commerce and security. In his essay, Alexander DeConde, who teaches at the University of California, Santa Barbara, discusses the Louisiana Purchase within the general interpretive framework of American imperial expansion. Thus, to him, the Louisiana "affair" sprang from a self-generated, traditional, ideological American quest for landed empire. He depicts not a defensive reaction, but an aggressive American behavior that followed the dictates of the imperial thrust.

America's Advantage from Europe's Distress

LAWRENCE S. KAPLAN

Although France intended to conceal the fact of the Treaty of San Ildefonso until Louisiana had been fully secured, a secret involving such stakes was impossible to keep for long. Rumors of the transaction flew all over Europe,

Lawrence S. Kaplan, *Jefferson and France: An Essay on Politics and Political Ideas* (New Haven: Yale University Press, 1967), pp. 96–101, 102–103.

notably into the hands of the British enemy, who in turn relayed them to the Americans. Rufus King, the Federalist Minister to England, whom Jefferson was in no hurry to discharge, reported in March, 1801 the news that a double disaster awaited the United States: cession of Louisiana and the Floridas to France, and negotiation of a Franco-British peace which would enable Bonaparte to take advantage of his new property. When these tidings reached the United States, Jefferson confided to his friends the ominous implications that the transfer of Louisiana would have for American security.

From the moment he heard the news he began to wrestle with the problem of living next door to a new neighbor in control of New Orleans. It was an unhappy prospect he faced, filled with opportunities for violence in the event the French attempted to build an empire in America. Even if they did not intend to violate American territory, their probable interference with American commerce on the Mississippi would drive the Westerners either to war or to desertion of the Union. The solution for the United States lay only in Jefferson's ability to thwart fulfillment of the agreement between Spain and France. Such was his object.

War with France was one solution to the problem of Louisiana, but it was an unpalatable response for the President, considering his distaste for the cost of maintaining a large military establishment and considering his fear of a military caste which would thrive on war. The solution had to be a peaceable one, and in order to win time for working out a policy he appeared willing to accept the fiction that Louisiana was still Spanish. If he did not have to recognize the existence of a transfer, he would not have to take any immediate steps until France actually secured possession of the territory. In the meantime, it was conceivable that something could arise that would nullify the Franco-Spanish deal. Hence his annual message to Congress in the fall of 1801 contained no reference to the Louisiana problem. The President in that year had made every effort to maintain friendly ties with France even though it involved the acceptance of Bonaparte's conditions for the ratification of the Convention of 1800 and might require the reception of French envoys Laforest and Otto whom he considered to be anti-republican if not anti-American.

By 1802 the melancholy observations of Robert Livingston on France's imperial plans induced Jefferson to announce not only his knowledge of the Treaty of San Ildefonso but also his opposition to it. Pichon reported the change. Shortly after the President had assured the French Minister of his faith in France's disclaimers about Louisiana, he began to hint at a rupture between the two countries that would take place as soon as war was resumed in Europe. To avoid this state of affairs, Jefferson suggested that France provide Americans with favorable commercial concessions on the Mississippi. He had apparently decided to face the fact of French imperialism without waiting for French troops on American soil to rouse him to action.

The President's aim now was to persuade France by intimidation to give up her ambitions in America. The price of America's friendship would be more than economic favors from the new masters of Louisiana; France would have to cede New Orleans, the Floridas, all the territory that she received from

Spain. If France should refuse his request, he predicted, she would lose the territory the moment the perennial troubles of Europe distracted her attention from the New World. France would be wiser to give up the land voluntarily and retain the good will of the United States. The alternative for Americans was an alliance with Britain. Dramatically, almost theatrically, Jefferson warned that "the day that France takes possession of N. Orleans, fixes the sentence which is to restrain her forever within her low-water mark. It seals the union of two nations, who in conjunction, can maintain exclusive possession of the ocean. From that moment we must marry ourselves to the British fleet and nation."

The President wrote these often quoted words in a letter to the American Minister to France for the beneficial effect he hoped they would have upon its bearer, Pierre Samuel Du Pont de Nemours, a distinguished physiocrat and a friend for almost twenty years. Although Du Pont was then a resident of the United States and was departing for France for what he thought would be only a brief stay, Jefferson saw an opportunity to exploit the economist's contacts with the French government by having him publicize the seriousness with which the United States regarded the Louisiana cession. Lest the Livingston letter fail in its purpose, the President sent Du Pont a note in which he asked him to impress upon his fellow countrymen the importance of ceding all French territory in America, not just New Orleans.

The unofficial emissary of America served faithfully the task which Jefferson had chosen for him, but he did not accept it until his pride as a Frenchman had been appeased. The President's tactics, he thought, would antagonize rather than intimidate the French. It would be better for the United States to help the French win Canada in exchange for the surrender of Louisiana, for such a gesture would permit the arrangement to appear reciprocal. If this plan were impossible, he advised, Jefferson should offer a reasonable price for the territory at issue, in language that would not offend Bonaparte.

While appreciating the spirit of friendship evidenced by Du Pont's reply to his suggestion, the President was not at all pleased with the idea of purchasing Louisiana. He had anticipated France's compliance with his wishes on the strength of his threats and on the hope of new conflicts in Europe. Only when his alternatives seemed to be purchase or war did Jefferson turn to the Du Pont plan. The world situation in general and his political fortunes in particular allowed no other solution in 1802. Abroad, the Peace of Amiens had been made in the very month in which he had made overtures to Du Pont, and Rufus King reported that Britain, despite her interest in the disposition of Louisiana, would not bring the Louisiana question into her negotiations with France. Edward Thornton, the British Chargé d'Affaires in Washington, even suggested that if the French should occupy Louisiana, the British would have greater influence over a frightened United States. Bonaparte was therefore free to complete his plans for the occupation of the territory. At home, the President had to contend with the rising anger of the Westerners over the prospect of having their rights of deposit in New Orleans taken away by the new rulers of the Mississippi. Pinckney's Treaty with Spain in 1795 had given the United States the right to navigate the Mississippi from its source to the sea, and to deposit its goods at New Orleans for transshipment to ocean-going vessels. Spain suspended this right in October, 1802, and France was immediately blamed for the affront. Federalists were able to use Western discontent to embarrass the administration by demanding redress from France and posing as the new champions of the West.

The President responded to these challenges by employing a weapon that his predecessors had used successfully a few years before: a special mission empowered to settle a special problem. He chose James Monroe to be Minister Plenipotentiary and Envoy Extraordinary to France to help Livingston win Louisiana from the French. Jay's mission in 1794 had postponed Republican attacks until a treaty with Britain had been made; Monroe, a popular figure in the West, might have the same success, not only in silencing the Federalists but also in dampening the ardor of the West for war. Jefferson authorized the two envoys to purchase New Orleans and the Floridas alone for a price slightly less than what was finally paid for the entire Louisiana territory, and to guarantee if necessary the rest of the territory to the French. Should France appear hostile, they were to open talks with the British about the possibility of cooperating in a joint venture against French Louisiana. . . .

Inasmuch as France never completed her empire in America, there can be no certainty as to the extent to which Jefferson might have gone to counter the moves of Bonaparte. During the difficult days of 1802 his fears often dented the armor of confidence he had built out of hopes that the troubles of the Old World would in some way prove to be his salvation. On such occasions he would be convinced that France would force the United States into the arms of Britain, and so he took pleasure in noting every manifestation of friendship on the part of the British. But generally Jefferson's dallying with Britain was so half-hearted and so palpably self-seeking that Thornton, with whom he attempted to ingratiate himself in gloomy moments, distrusted his sudden appreciation of British merits and claimed that he seemed to tax "his imagination to supply the deficiency of his feeling." Thornton was right. When Jefferson's mood of despair lifted, he trusted in the intervention of a *deus ex machina*—war in Europe, revolution in the West Indies, or financial difficulties in France—to make France see the light and to keep his country out of the clutches of Britain. Months before he had seen any of his hopes realized, the President railed against those Americans who would have the United States take immediate action on Louisiana. Nothing but dire necessity, he asserted, could force the country out of neutrality and into the orbit of Britain. And such a crisis looked distant as reports began coming in about the restoration of American rights of deposit in New Orleans, the imminence of war in Europe, and the difficulties that Leclerc's French armies were having in occupying the island of Santo Domingo. The President's willingness to guarantee Louisiana to France as well as his talk of a British alliance must be weighed against his knowledge that the future of the territory irrevocably belonged to the rising West and against his conviction that British services should never be used to help obtain it.

When all Louisiana and not just New Orleans fell into the hands of the surprised envoys in May 1803, the event took place in the manner that Jefferson had predicted. Bonaparte had to sacrifice his imperial ambitions in the New World, temporarily at least, before the altar of a new war in Europe. Since British sea power would have prevented him from occupying his American empire, he deemed it advisable to sell the entire territory to the United States, despite the dubious legality of such a transaction, and receive in return funds to carry on his European ventures. Other explanations for the First Consul's actions are available. George Dangerfield has recently pointed out that failure in Santo Domingo made war in Europe inevitable: Bonaparte needed a new arena in which to recoup his losses. Whatever may have been the ultimate factor in the decision, Jefferson had a right to feel that he had won complete success. He had vindicated not only the policy of nonentanglement advocated by Washington and Adams but also the assumption he had made as Secretary of State: America's advantage from Europe's distress.

An American Imperial Thrust

ALEXANDER DECONDE

Imperialism, usually a nation's use of power to acquire territory belonging to others, is an emotionally charged word that implies undesirable behavior. So Americans and their historians have seldom employed the term to describe the growth of their country, and most rarely have they applied it to the formative years of the republic. They have preferred to use *expansion, mission,* or other more flattering terms. According to conventional historical theory, American imperialism or something akin to it developed suddenly in the 1840s under a vague but basically beneficent concept called Manifest Destiny. In the era of the Civil War this imperialism virtually disappeared, but it or something like it came to life again in the 1890s to create an empire overseas.

Modern scholarship has just about demolished the idea that the new Manifest Destiny, or imperialism, of the late nineteenth century was an aberration or something really new in the American experience. In most of the histories dealing with expansion in the early years of the republic, however, the conventional wisdom still prevails. It portrays Americans, at least until mid-nineteenth century, as a peaceful people who shunned the militarism, power politics, and imperialism of European countries but who nonetheless expanded by chance, without much opposition and without causing genuine harm to anyone. They were a people with a sense of mission who when they gobbled territory did so to extend the domain of democracy, to build an empire for liberty, and not to exploit others.

In this interpretation imperialism has no place in the unfolding of early American history. In it the paradigm of peaceful, democratic, fortuitous expansion is the affair of Louisiana. What followed in the nation's history, however, sometimes diverged from the model. In noting this divergence, one scholar argues, for instance, "that Manifest Destiny and imperialism were traps into which the nation was led in 1846 and 1899." This conventional thesis has not reigned without challenge. A diverse group of scholars have depicted imperialism, or expansionism, as a main theme, even as a determining force, in the history of the United States. They contend that from the beginning the leaders of the republic had the imperial urge and that the founding fathers intended the United States to possess adjacent and even distant lands.

In this book the process of analyzing expansionism takes the questioning of the conventional interpretation a step further. It places the origin of the imperial thrust in the colonial period and in Europe, but especially in England, and hence American expansionism fits into a context wider than that depicted in most histories. If we separate rationale from true motivation and from events, or from what happened in the New World since the time of the first European settlements, we can discern the Europeans as venturesome expansionists. We can, in the large context, perceive American expansionism as part of the rise of Western nationalism and imperialism. We can note also that the Anglo-Americans brought with them from England an especially compelling imperialist creed. For example, the eminent English philosopher Francis Bacon stressed the importance of "imperial expansion" as a duty for a people who sought "greatness."

The powerful national states of western Europe pursued imperial greatness in the New World by planting colonies. In the process they systematically reduced, absorbed, or annihilated tribal or other native peoples. In no other people was the racism implicit in this imperial process more deeply rooted than among Anglo-Americans. The sixteenth-century Oxford geographer Richard Hakluyt and others maintained that Englishmen, like the Romans of the ancient world, were predestined to take over, colonize, and rule the New World. Imbued with the concept that native Americans were an inferior people who had to give way before a superior race, Anglo-Americans felt no compunctions in dispossessing Indians. They did all this while using the rationale that they were advancing the frontier of civilization and doing so more capably than any other people.

So it was that descendants of those who settled Jamestown, Plymouth, and Massachusetts Bay inherited an imperialist ideology along with their language, politics, religion, and culture. Motivated by a tough, ruthless acquisitiveness that drove them westward in an unrelenting quest for empire, they accepted territorial expansion in conflict with Indians as an intrinsic part of their experience. Considering themselves a chosen people, the Puritans of New England even rationalized their conquest of Indians in the place of converting them to Christianity as the will of God. Two of the leading Puritan divines, Increase and Cotton Mather, defended wars against Indians and Frenchmen, too, as just and proper. Sometimes these Anglo-American colonists were more aggressively expansionist than were the policy makers of empire in London.

The imperial ideology that accompanied the Anglo-American experience runs through the thinking of a number of pre-Revolutionary leaders, but it stands out most vividly in the thought of Benjamin Franklin, the foremost believer in the idea of an expanding American empire. Another who shared this idea, John Adams, spoke in 1755 while not yet twenty of a time when Anglo-Americans would transfer "the great seat of empire into America. It looks likely to me," he added, "for if we can remove the turbulent Gallicks, our people, according to the exactest computations, will in another century become more numerous than England itself."

Three years later Brigadier General James Wolfe, the British hero of the French and Indian War, was impressed with the presence of this imperial urge and with the general aggressiveness in the Anglo-American colonies. He thought that they had acquired "the vices and bad qualities of the mother country." Nonetheless, he prognosticated that those colonies "will some time hence, be a vast empire, the seat of power and learning, . . . and there will grow a people out of our little spot, England, that will fill this vast space, and divide this great portion of the globe with the Spaniards."

After benefiting from the British conquests in the French and Indian War, Anglo-Americans expanded their horizon in their quest for imperial greatness. Even college students could join in praising such a quest. At the Princeton commencement of 1771 two seniors envisioned the time

> . . . when we shall spread
> Dominion from the north, and south, and west,
> Far from the Atlantic to Pacific shores,
> And people half the convex of the main!—
> A glorious theme!—

The patriot victories of the American Revolution enhanced this imperial view of the future, which now became part of the heritage of the new nation. At the Paris peace negotiations in 1782 and 1783 Benjamin Franklin sought, along with England's recognition of the independence of the United States, acquisition of Canada and the Floridas, or essentially all of continental British North America. He was convinced that eventually all this territory must become part of the empire of the United States. Like Franklin and other Revolutionary leaders, J. Hector St. John de Crèvecoeur, the popular French observer of the American scene, took for granted the indefinite westward expansion of American society. "Who can tell how far it extends?" he wrote. "Who can tell the millions of men whom it will feed and contain?"

Immediately after independence the leaders of the new nation fixed their eyes on Louisiana. They replaced British policy makers and their Anglo-American representatives as the prime imperialists in the Mississippi Valley. Independent Americans were confident that the imperial thrust that had brought them possession of the trans-Appalachian West would make the territory west of the Mississippi the heartland of the American empire.

Those in the ruling establishment, as well as other Americans, unabashedly thought of themselves as expansionists and proudly tried to justify their imperialist ideology with pious assertions of a hazy continental destiny. Their foes, whether Indians, Spaniards, Frenchmen, or Englishmen, also considered them aggressive expansionists, essentially imperialists. Through infiltration, immigration, and trade, American hunters, farmers, and merchants began dominating parts of Spanish Louisiana and West Florida. Retaining their loyalty to the United States, these settlers not only refused allegiance to Spain but also brought with them an undisguised contempt for the Spanish rulers of their new homeland. More than the rhetoric or theories of statesmen, the inexorable pressure of these Americans expanding into the Ohio and Mississippi valleys and then into the territory held by Spain gave substance to the imperial thrust.

While this American vanguard moved across Louisiana's frontiers, prominent and well-to-do men of the republic in 1787 framed a new constitution that could or could not sanction imperialism, depending on the attitude of the interpreter. James Madison, one of the Constitution's most perceptive original interpreters, viewed it as congenial to empire building. In support of this view he advanced a theory that justified American territorial expansion as a means of extending the boundaries of freedom. In discussing the advantages of a republic over a democracy, for example, he argued that "the greater the number of citizens and extent of territory," the less the oppression and the more the security for republican government. "Extend the sphere," he said, "and . . . you make it less probable that a majority of the whole will have a common motive to invade the rights of other citizens." This kind of government required, in his analysis, a strong union or "one great, respectable, and flourishing empire." So he married the idea of freedom with that of expansionism, a duality that American leaders such as Thomas Jefferson used often in the quest for empire.

This theme, taken from the words of the founding fathers themselves, formed a foundation for the conventional wisdom. It gave historians a ready-made analysis based on original sources. They could depict American expansion in moral terms as the peaceful extension of democracy into wilderness or into sparsely settled land and as bringing considerable benefit to lesser peoples. What the expounders of this thesis often overlook or put aside is that early continental expansionism had behind it a thrust of force, a coercive energy, something that its victims—mainly Indians and Spaniards—well understood.

Actually, the thinking of early national leaders as it pertained to empire was less altruistic and tougher than is usually depicted in the conventional analysis. Patrick Henry, for one, argued that "Some way or other we must be a great and mighty empire; we must have an army, and a navy, and a number of things." Publicists stressed the same aggressive theme. Jedidiah Morse, a New Englander, in 1789 published a widely read *American Geography* in which he anticipated American expansion across the Mississippi into Louisiana. Since these were not "merely the visions of fancy," he wrote, "we cannot but anticipate the period, as not far distant, when the AMERICAN EMPIRE will comprehend millions of souls, west of the Mississippi. . . . the Mississippi was never designed as the western boundary of the American empire."

Federalist leaders in the 1790s supported the westward push of "pioneers" and were willing to coerce a weak Spain into relinquishing at least part of Louisiana and the Floridas. A western publicist predicted in 1792 that "posterity will not deem it extraordinary, should they find the country settled quite across to the Pacific ocean, in less than another century."

Eager to extend American dominion toward the Pacific, Federalists debated the various means of acquiring Louisiana. In 1796 Federalist newspapers expressed hope that the United States could someday obtain the province "by purchase or amicable means." Other Federalist shapers of opinion, such as Alexander Hamilton, were willing, even eager, to conquer for empire.

When the Republicans gained control of the federal government, they thought and acted toward Louisiana as had their Federalist predecessors, but they showed more caution in pressuring powerful France than in badgering weak Spain. Despite their periods of restraint, these Jeffersonian leaders, too, were confident expansionists, men with an unquestioning faith in America's destined right to conquer, whether by sword or diplomacy. They played power politics, as they saw it, from a position of strength because they were convinced that the future belonged to them. They viewed the United States as a "rising power," and looked down on rivals such as Spain as "declining powers." Those in decline had no choice. The reality of power compelled them, as it had forced Indian tribes, to recognize the predominance of the United States in North America and to give way before it.

Regardless of the contradictions and inconsistencies in the expansionist ideology, few of the leaders of American society, whether Federalist or Republican, questioned it. They justified their land hunger as the dictate of highest morality. Yet their actions, rather than their rhetoric, indicated that anything goes in constructing an empire for liberty.

According to the conventional view, Thomas Jefferson, the builder of the empire for liberty, was a man who considered war the "greatest scourge of mankind," believed only in defensive measures, and sought peaceful solutions to all foreign problems. Yet historians point out his willingness to use offensive tactics to gain territory. They call him "the greatest of American expansionists," "the architect of orderly expansion," "the first apostle of Manifest Destiny," "the grand agrarian imperialist," the "expansionist of freedom, not of empire," and "America's first great expansionist." Regardless of the accuracy or flaws in the conventional view, he clearly thought in imperial terms.

Unlike contemporaries who often used the rhetoric of expansion without having power, Jefferson as president possessed power; he had the opportunity to act decisively as well as to talk. Continuing desire, ideology, a rhetoric and a program of expansion, no matter how widespread, do not necessarily translate into national policy. A program that becomes policy and a foreign policy that produces imperialist action are shaped by definable forces, usually by men in positions of power.

In the case of Louisiana both external and internal forces, men of power in Europe and America, brought about the acquisition. In the United States Jeffersonians felt the expansionist ideology with such intensity that they considered the transformation of rhetoric and policy into action as the working of Providence. In their thinking the Indians, the French, and the Spaniards held Louisiana temporarily as trustees. Jeffersonians saw themselves as taking rightful possession, regardless of the clouded legal title, of what had been destined to be theirs anyway. With their program of deliberate expansionism, these confident activists merely hastened the work of this inevitable destiny.

In working out this program, Jefferson took over the ideas of Benjamin Franklin, John Adams, James Madison, and other founding fathers, fused expansion with destiny and freedom, and rationalized the whole process as the building of an empire for liberty. Capitalizing on the westward surge of population and using a mixture of threat and restraint in diplomacy, he never lost sight of his desired objective: territory. With the acquisition of Louisiana he converted the idea of empire into reality and made it the finest achievement of his presidency. Henry Adams, a historian often critical of Jefferson, called this affair of Louisiana an unparalleled piece of diplomacy, "the greatest diplomatic success recorded in American history." He ranked its importance "next to the Declaration of Independence and the adoption of the Constitution."

The Jeffersonian concept of empire did not emerge suddenly or haphazardly a full-blown success. It reflected a well-developed expansionist tradition and a conscious vision of a national future. Yet the immediate circumstances of the president's decision to try to buy New Orleans and of Bonaparte's decision to sell Louisiana give the appearance of stemming more from expediency than from plan. So the conventional wisdom usually depicts Louisiana as coming to the Jeffersonians unexpectedly, "out of the blue," as "an accident of fate," a "diplomatic miracle," as being suddenly thrust upon "indifferent hands," virtually "forced on the United States," or tossed "into the lap of Americans." This aspect of conventional history echoes Federalist reactions. Federalists wanted to deny Jefferson credit for the achievement, and so they argued that he really did nothing more than profit from fortuitous circumstances.

Jefferson's political maneuvering lends credence to this thesis. Although committed to a doctrine of expansion, he appeared to act more to placate aggressive Westerners, to preserve his party's power, and perhaps to prevent disunion than to carry out a national mission. Destiny may work in strange, but not necessarily inexplicable, ways. If the president and his advisers had not been heirs of an imperial tradition and believers in an expansionist ideology, they probably would not have acted as they did when they did.

American policy makers and opinion makers and others had long coveted Louisiana, had schemed to obtain it, had within a decade converted at least part of the province into an economic dependent, and had all along assumed that it was destined in the long pull for no hands but their own. When the prize appeared within their grasp, they did not hesitate; they moved swiftly and confidently to possess it.

Bonaparte, too, had a commitment to a concept of western empire. Chance and expediency, according to conventional interpretations, forced him to abandon that commitment. He found it expedient to sell Louisiana to the United

States rather than lose it in war to England. Chance, shaped by the struggle for power in Europe, brought him suddenly to the decision to sell.

Actually, the idea of the sale to the United States had many antecedents. Federalists discussed the possibility of purchase as well as of conquest; Joseph Bonaparte hinted at selling it in 1802; Jefferson alluded to it after hearing of the retrocession to France; and Robert R. Livingston suggested purchase to Bonaparte before Pierre Samuel Du Pont de Nemours and Jefferson had discussed it.

The evidence also suggests that the First Consul decided to sell because of the pressure Americans exerted on him as much as for any other reason. Jefferson, his advisers and diplomats, and Congress all joined the campaign against the French. The Jeffersonians threatened to use force if Bonaparte did not offer concessions in Louisiana, and the evidence indicates they meant it. Bonaparte's own diplomats and advisers, as well as the Jeffersonian leaders, pointed out to him that his plan of empire in North America was turning a friend into an enemy. At the least it was driving the United States into an alliance with England.

Despite this American pressure, according to some scholars, Bonaparte did not have to sell to the United States. He could have disposed of Louisiana in some other way. Actually, he had little real choice. If he had held on, either England or the United States would have conquered the province. Why not turn it over to the United States in exchange for profit and goodwill? He knew that Americans were driven, as much as he was, by a virtually compulsive expansionism. Sooner or later they would take Louisiana anyway. Why not "spare the continent of North America from the war that threatened" to erupt because of clashing French and American imperialisms?

Even the actions of James Monroe and Livingston stemmed more from dedication to the imperial concept than from mere expediency. They committed their government to buy Louisiana, even though they had no authority to do so, because they instantly recognized a great bargain, knew it fitted the American program of empire, and were convinced that the Jeffersonian leadership would support them. They did not think that the affair of Louisiana all hinged on chance. Nor did other Jeffersonian partisans. They gave credit to the president's "wise & firm tho moderate measures," or his masterly statesmanship, as the essential factor that influenced Bonaparte to sell.

Jefferson himself, in retrospect, stressed the inevitability of Louisiana's fate. "I very early saw that Louisiana was indeed a speck in our horizon which was to burst in a tornado," he said. Napoleon's "good sense" in perceiving this as well as the unavoidable sequence between "causes and effects," he added, "saved us from that storm." The acquisition of Louisiana, as the frontier historian Frederick Jackson Turner hypothesized, was thus "no sudden or unrelated episode. . . . It was the dramatic culmination of a long struggle" that began in the colonial era.

The president's shift in constitutional principles can also be viewed as culminating in his desire to gain and hold Louisiana. Since his strict-constructionist principles clashed with his imperial concept, he switched to broad construction, or to the use of implied powers of government to justify the acquisition. This shift, the argument goes, exemplifies gross expediency, or that the end justifies the means. There is truth in this assessment, but in addition the evidence suggests that Jefferson moved as he did not just out of expediency but also because he felt that now he could carry out the imperial idea that had been important in his thinking for years. He never really retreated from his expansionist program; he never questioned the acquisition or considered relinquishing it. He merely sought the best constitutional means of carrying it out, especially a formula that would blunt the criticism of Federalists and anti-expansionists. In doing so, he established a precedent for use of the Constitution as an instrument sanctioning, even sanctifying, expansionism.

This constitutional sanction helped make the Jeffersonian empire for liberty successful and lasting. Independence had given the United States a sound foundation for growth in the trans-Appalachian West. Louisiana provided Americans with room for more growth with a sense of legal and physical security. Its acquisition not only removed "a fearful cause of war with France" and eliminated a powerful barrier to expansion, but also placed the force of the Constitution behind the imperial thrust. American society and institutions, as a result, fashioned no lasting legal barriers to the absorption of nearly a million square miles to the national domain. This area, larger than Great Britain, France, Germany, Italy, Spain, and Portugal lumped together, doubled the size of the nation.

There were, of course, initial difficulties. To the consternation of the Jeffersonians, the Creoles for a while preferred Spanish sovereignty to incorporation within the benevolent empire for liberty. So the president violated the principle he had himself inscribed in the Declaration of Independence—that governments derive "their just powers from the consent of the governed." He used troops in ruling the new empire.

Some critics feared that such tactics, the apparatus of imperial government, or just expansion itself would endanger American democracy as it was evolving within existing geographical limits. In his second inaugural address Jefferson took note of such criticism and restated his old imperial argument. "I know that the acquisition of Louisiana has been disapproved by some from a candid apprehension that the enlargement of our territory would endanger its union," he said. "But who can limit the extent to which the federative principle may operate effectively? The larger our association, the less will it be shaken by local passions; and in any view, is it not better that the opposite bank of the Mississippi should be settled by our own brethren and children than by strangers of another family?"

Disputes within the American family over the governing and status of Louisiana did produce long-lasting political strain and recurring conflicts over constitutional interpretation. Despite these problems, the enlarged nation, as Jefferson hoped, did hold together. Out of the western empire eventually came the states of Louisiana, Arkansas, Missouri, Nebraska, North and South Dakota, Oklahoma, and much of Kansas, Minnesota, Colorado, Montana, and Wyoming. The difficulty of fitting these territories into the nation's previous sectional pattern, however, contributed to the coming of the Civil War.

Regardless of the internal difficulties that Louisiana stimulated, Jefferson considered it—the largest acquisition in the nation's history—a personal and national triumph, a proper monument to the imperial idea. When he left office, he expressed an old desire, expansion into the Floridas, Cuba, Mexico's provinces, and Canada. Then, he said, "we should have such an empire for liberty as she has never surveyed since the creation." He was convinced that his fellow Americans had fashioned an instrument of government uniquely suited for this continuing imperial thrust. "I am persuaded," he added, "no constitution was ever before so well calculated as ours for extensive empire and self-government."

More than a decade later John Quincy Adams, who believed that all of North America was "destined by Divine Providence to be peopled by one *nation*," the United States, looked back upon this affair of Louisiana and expressed similar sentiments. Within it he saw "an assumption of implied power greater in itself and more comprehensive in its consequences than all the assumptions of implied powers in the twelve years of the Washington and Adams Administrations put together."

In even broader perspective, with the acquisition of Louisiana the Jeffersonians carried on the imperial creed of their Anglo-American forefathers. With it they accelerated the dismantling of Spain's New World empire and the emergence of the United States as one of the truly powerful nations in the world. Although the United States did not immediately achieve the status or influence of a great power, its size and wealth after the incorporation of Louisiana were such that other nations could not ignore it or threaten it with impunity in its own North American neighborhood.

While anchored in the past of the Anglo-American imperial tradition, this affair of Louisiana also faced the future. It fitted comfortably within the nationalistic and expansionist ideology of America's political leaders, regardless of party affiliation, and met the desires of the many Americans who felt that sooner or later the entire North American continent must be theirs. With minor variations it gave form to the idea of Manifest Destiny and served as a model for future expansion.

FURTHER READING

George Dangerfield, *Chancellor R. Livingston of New York, 1746–1813* (1960)
Arthur B. Darling, *Our Rising Empire* (1940)
E. Wilson Lyon, *Louisiana in French Diplomacy, 1759–1804* (1934)
E. Wilson Lyon, *The Man Who Sold Louisiana: The Career of François Barbé-Marbois* (1942)
Dumas Malone, *Jefferson the President* (1970)
Merrill D. Peterson, *Thomas Jefferson and the New Nation: A Biography* (1970)
Marshall Smelser, *The Democratic Republic, 1801–1815* (1968)
Richard Van Alstyne, *The Rising American Empire* (1960)
Paul A. Varg, *Foreign Policies of the Founding Fathers* (1970)
Arthur P. Whitaker, *The Mississippi Question, 1795–1803* (1934)

6

The War of 1812

*In 1803 Europe once again exploded in war. England and France battled
furiously and, once again, the United States became ensnarled. As a neutral
trading nation, America was the target of economic warfare as each antagonist
attempted to halt the flow of American goods to the other. France declared a
Continental System to close Europe to British products and to force neutrals to
cease trade with Britain. The British issued Orders in Council to blockade
France and to curb neutral trade with Napoleon's nation. America's neutral
rights and foreign commerce suffered. Jefferson and Madison tried retaliatory
measures—embargo and non-intercourse acts—to no avail. War with England
came in 1812.*

*Historians have offered several explanations for the causes of the War of
1812: national honor, defense of neutral rights, British impressment of
American sailors, injury to commerce, hunger for land (Florida and Canada),
eradication of the Indian menace, and fear of continued economic depression.
Some scholars have emphasized the leadership of James Madison, which
they find inept. The following readings address these issues.*

DOCUMENTS

The importance of maritime issues in the early nineteenth century is well demonstrated by the drastic but unsuccessful Embargo Act of December 1807. This and
other American measures designed to force the European warriors to respect
American neutral rights failed and spawned further diplomatic crises. "War hawk"
Congressman Henry Clay of Kentucky delivered a stirring speech, reprinted here, on
December 31, 1811, which attempted to make the case for war against Britain, a
rival power he considered insolent and arrogant. In June of the following year,

President James Madison asked Congress to declare war. His message, reprinted here, listed a host of reasons. The final document, prepared largely by Josiah Quincy and signed by thirty-four Congressmen, protested the decision for war—a protest shared by many of their dissenting countrymen.

The Embargo Act, 1807

Be it enacted by the Senate and House of Representatives of the United States of America in Congress assembled, That an embargo be, and hereby is laid on all ships and vessels in the ports and places within the limits or jurisdiction of the United States, cleared or not cleared, bound to any foreign port or place; and that no clearance be furnished to any ship or vessel bound to such foreign port or place, except vessels under the immediate direction of the President of the United States: and that the President be authorized to give such instructions to the officers of the revenue, and of the navy and revenue cutters of the United States, as shall appear best adapted for carrying the same into full effect: *Provided,* that nothing herein contained shall be construed to prevent the departure of any foreign ship or vessel, either in ballast, or with the goods, wares and merchandise on board of such foreign ship or vessel, when notified of this act.

Sec. 2. And be it further enacted, That during the continuance of this act, no registered, or sea letter vessel, having on board goods, wares and merchandise, shall be allowed to depart from one port of the United States to any other within the same, unless the master, owner, consignee or factor of such vessel shall first give bond, with one or more sureties to the collector of the district from which she is bound to depart, in a sum of double the value of the vessel and cargo, that the said goods, wares, or merchandise shall be relanded in some port of the United States, dangers of the seas excepted, which bond, and also a certificate from the collector where the same may be relanded, shall by the collector respectively be transmitted to the Secretary of the Treasury. All armed vessels possessing public commissions from any foreign power, are not to be considered as liable to the embargo laid by this act.

Henry Clay on Grievances
Against Britain, 1811

What are we to gain by war, has been emphatically asked? In reply, he would ask, what are we not to lose by peace?—commerce, character, a nation's best treasure, honor! If pecuniary considerations alone are to govern, there is sufficient motive for the war. Our revenue is reduced, by the operation of the belligerent edicts, to about six million of dollars, according to the Secretary of the Treasury's report. The year preceding the embargo, it was sixteen. . . .

He had no disposition to swell, or dwell upon the catalogue of injuries from England. He could not, however, overlook the impressment of our seamen; an aggression upon which he never reflected without feelings of indignation, which would not allow him appropriate language to describe its enormity. Not content with seizing upon all our property, which falls within her rapacious grasp, the personal rights of our countrymen—rights which forever ought to be sacred, are trampled upon and violated. The Orders in Council were pretended to have been reluctantly adopted as a measure of retaliation. The French decrees, their alleged basis, are revoked. England resorts to the expedient of denying the fact of the revocation, and Sir William Scott, in the celebrated case of the Fox and others, suspends judgment that proof may be adduced of it. And, at the moment when the British Ministry through that judge, is thus affecting to controvert that fact, and to place the release of our property upon its establishment, instructions are prepared for Mr. Foster to meet at Washington the very revocation which they were contesting. And how does he meet it? By fulfilling the engagement solemnly made to rescind the orders? No, sir, but by demanding that we shall secure the introduction into the Continent of British manufactures. England is said to be fighting for the world, and shall we, it is asked, attempt to weaken her exertions? If, indeed, the aim of the French Emperor be universal dominion (and he was willing to allow it to the argument,) what a noble cause is presented to British valor. But, how is her philanthropic purpose to be achieved? By scrupulous observance of the rights of others; by respecting that code of public law, which she professes to vindicate, and by abstaining from self-aggrandizement. Then would she command the sympathies of the world. What are we required to do by those who would engage our feelings and wishes in her behalf? To bear the actual cuffs of her arrogance, that we may escape a chimerical French subjugation! We are invited, conjured to drink the potion of British poison actually presented to our lips, that we may avoid the imperial dose prepared by perturbed imaginations. We are called upon to submit to debasement, dishonor, and disgrace—to bow the neck to royal insolence, as a course of preparation for manly resistance to Gallic invasion! What nation, what individual was ever taught, in the schools of ignominious submission, the patriotic lessons of freedom and independence? Let those who contend for this humiliating doctrine, read its refutation in the history of the very man against whose insatiable thirst of dominion we are warned. . . .

He contended that the real cause of British aggression, was not to distress an enemy but to destroy a rival. A comparative view of our commerce with England and the continent, would satisfy any one of the truth of this remark. . . . It is apparent that this trade, the balance of which was in favor, not of France, but of the United States, was not of very vital consequence to the enemy of England. Would she, therefore, for the sole purpose of depriving her adversary of this commerce, relinquish her valuable trade with this country, exhibiting the essential balance in her favor—nay, more; hazard the peace of the country? No, sir, you must look for an explanation of her conduct in the jealousies of a rival. She sickens at your prosperity, and beholds in your growth —your sails spread on every ocean, and your numerous seamen—the foundations of a Power which, at no very distant day, is to make her tremble for naval superiority.

James Madison's War Message, 1812

I communicate to Congress certain documents, being a continuation of those heretofore laid before them on the subject of our affairs with Great Britain.

Without going back beyond the renewal in 1803 of the war in which Great Britain is engaged, and omitting unrepaired wrongs of inferior magnitude, the conduct of her Government presents a series of acts hostile to the United States as an independent and neutral nation.

British cruisers have been in the continued practice of violating the American flag on the great highway of nations, and of seizing and carrying off persons sailing under it, not in the exercise of a belligerent right founded on the law of nations against an enemy, but of a municipal prerogative over British subjects. British jurisdiction is thus extended to neutral vessels in a situation where no laws can operate but the law of nations and the laws of the country to which the vessels belong. . . .

The practice, hence, is so far from affecting British subjects alone that, under the pretext of searching for these, thousands of American citizens, under the safeguard of public law and of their national flag, have been torn from their country and from everything dear to them; have been dragged on board ships of war of a foreign nation and exposed, under the severities of their discipline, to be exiled to the most distant and deadly climes, to risk their lives in the battles of their oppressors, and to be the melancholy instruments of taking away those of their own brethren.

Against this crying enormity, which Great Britain would be so prompt to avenge if committed against herself, the United States have in vain exhausted remonstrances and expostulations, and that no proof might be wanting of their conciliatory dispositions, and no pretext left for a continuance of the practice, the British Government was formally assured of the readiness of the United States to enter into arrangements such as could not be rejected if the recovery of British subjects were the real and the sole object. The communication passed without effect.

British cruisers have been in the practice also of violating the rights and the peace of our coasts. They hover over and harass our entering and departing commerce. To the most insulting pretensions they have added the most lawless proceedings in our very harbors, and have wantonly spilt American blood within the sanctuary of our territorial jurisdiction. The principles and rules enforced by that nation, when a neutral nation, against armed vessels of belligerents hovering near her coasts and disturbing her commerce are well known. When called on, nevertheless, by the United States to punish the greater offenses committed by her own vessels, her Government has bestowed on their commanders additional marks of honor and confidence.

Under pretended blockades, without the presence of an adequate force and sometimes without the practicability of applying one, our commerce has been plundered in every sea, the great staples of our country have been cut off from their legitimate markets, and a destructive blow aimed at our agricultural and maritime interests. In aggravation of these predatory measures they have been considered as in force from the dates of their notification, a retrospective effect being thus added, as has been done in other important cases, to the unlawfulness of the course pursued. And to render the outrage the more signal these mock blockades have been reiterated and enforced in the face of official communications from the British Government declaring as the true definition of a legal blockade "that particular ports must be actually invested and previous warning given to vessels bound to them not to enter."

Not content with these occasional expedients for laying waste our neutral trade, the cabinet of Britain resorted at length to the sweeping system of blockades, under the name of orders in council, which has been molded and managed as might best suit its political views, its commercial jealousies, or the avidity of British cruisers.

To our remonstrances against the complicated and transcendent injustice of this innovation the first reply was that the orders were reluctantly adopted by Great Britain as a necessary retaliation on decrees of her enemy proclaiming a general blockade of the British Isles at a time when the naval force of that enemy dared not issue from his own ports. She was reminded without effect that her own prior blockades, unsupported by an adequate naval force actually applied and continued, were a bar to this plea; that executed edicts against millions of our property could not be retaliation on edicts confessedly impossible to be executed; that retaliation, to be just, should fall on the party setting the guilty example, not on an innocent party which was not even chargeable with an acquiescence in it.

When deprived of this flimsy veil for a prohibition of our trade with her enemy by the repeal of his prohibition of our trade with Great Britain, her cabinet, instead of a corresponding repeal or a practical discontinuance of its orders, formally avowed a determination to persist in them against the United States until the markets of her enemy should be laid open to British products, thus asserting an obligation on a neutral power to require one belligerent to encourage by its internal regulations the trade of another belligerent, contradicting her own practice toward all nations, in peace as well as in war, and betraying the insincerity of those professions which inculcated a belief that, having resorted to her orders with regret, she was anxious to find an occasion for putting an end to them.

Abandoning still more all respect for the neutral rights of the United States and for its own consistency, the British Government now demands as prerequisites to a repeal of its orders as they relate to the United States that a formality should be observed in the repeal of the French decrees nowise necessary to their termination nor exemplified by British usage, and that the French repeal, besides including that portion of the decrees which operates within a territorial jurisdiction, as well as that which operates on the high seas, against the commerce of the United States should not be a single and special repeal in relation to the United States, but should be extended to whatever other neutral nations unconnected with them may be affected by those decrees. . . .

It has become, indeed, sufficiently certain that the commerce of the United States is to be sacrificed, not as interfering with the belligerent rights of Great

Britain; not as supplying the wants of her enemies, which she herself supplies; but as interfering with the monopoly which she covets for her own commerce and navigation. She carries on a war against the lawful commerce of a friend that she may the better carry on a commerce with an enemy—a commerce polluted by the forgeries and perjuries which are for the most part the only passports by which it can succeed.

Anxious to make every experiment short of the last resort of injured nations, the United States have withheld from Great Britain, under successive modifications, the benefits of a free intercourse with their market, the loss of which could not but outweigh the profits accruing from her restrictions of our commerce with other nations. And to entitle these experiments to the more favorable consideration they were so framed as to enable her to place her adversary under the exclusive operation of them. To these appeals her Government has been equally inflexible, as if willing to make sacrifices of every sort rather than yield to the claims of justice or renounce the errors of a false pride. Nay, so far were the attempts carried to overcome the attachment of the British cabinet to its unjust edicts that it received every encouragement within the competency of the executive branch of our Government to expect that a repeal of them would be followed by a war between the United States and France, unless the French edicts should also be repealed. Even this communication, although silencing forever the plea of a disposition in the United States to acquiesce in those edicts originally the sole plea for them, received no attention. . . .

In reviewing the conduct of Great Britain toward the United States our attention is necessarily drawn to the warfare just renewed by the savages on one of our extensive frontiers—a warfare which is known to spare neither age nor sex and to be distinguished by features peculiarly shocking to humanity. It is difficult to account for the activity and combinations which have for some time been developing themselves among tribes in constant intercourse with British traders and garrisons without connecting their hostility with that influence and without recollecting the authenticated examples of such interpositions heretofore furnished by the officers and agents of that Government.

Such is the spectacle of injuries and indignities which have been heaped on our country, and such the crisis which its unexampled forbearance and conciliatory efforts have not been able to avert. It might at least have been expected that an enlightened nation, if less urged by moral obligations or invited by friendly dispositions on the part of the United States, would have found in its true interest alone a sufficient motive to respect their rights and their tranquillity on the high seas; that an enlarged policy would have favored that free and general circulation of commerce in which the British nation is at all times interested, and which in times of war is the best alleviation of its calamities to herself as well as to other belligerents; and more especially that the British cabinet would not, for the sake of a precarious and surreptitious intercourse with hostile markets, have persevered in a course of measures which necessarily put at hazard the invaluable market of a great and growing country, disposed to cultivate the mutual advantages of an active commerce.

Other counsels have prevailed. Our moderation and conciliation have had no other effect than to encourage perseverance and to enlarge pretensions. We behold our seafaring citizens, still the daily victims of lawless violence, committed on the great common and highway of nations, even within sight of the country which owes them protection. We behold our vessels, freighted with the products of our soil and industry, or returning with the honest proceeds of them, wrested from their lawful destinations, confiscated by prize courts no longer the organs of public law but the instruments of arbitrary edicts, and their unfortunate crews dispersed and lost, or forced or inveigled in British ports into British fleets, whilst arguments are employed in support of these aggressions which have no foundation but in a principle equally supporting a claim to regulate our external commerce in all cases whatsoever.

We behold, in fine, on the side of Great Britain a state of war against the United States, and on the side of the United States a state of peace toward Great Britain.

Whether the United States shall continue passive under these progressive usurpations and these accumulating wrongs, or, opposing force to force in defense of their national rights, shall commit a just cause into the hands of the Almighty Disposer of Events, avoiding all connections which might entangle it in the contest or views of other powers, and preserving a constant readiness to concur in an honorable reestablishment of peace and friendship, is a solemn question which the Constitution wisely confides to the legislative department of the Government. In recommending it to their early deliberations I am happy in the assurance that the decision will be worthy the enlightened and patriotic councils of a virtuous, a free, and a powerful nation.

Having presented this view of the relations of the United States with Great Britain and of the solemn alternative growing out of them, I proceed to remark that the communications last made to Congress on the subject of our relations with France will have shewn that since the revocation of her decrees, as they violated the neutral rights of the United States, her Government has authorized illegal captures by its privateers and public ships, and that other outrages have been practiced on our vessels and our citizens. It will have been seen also that no indemnity had been provided or satisfactorily pledged for the extensive spoliations committed under the violent and retrospective orders of the French Government against the property of our citizens seized within the jurisdiction of France. I abstain at this time from recommending to the consideration of Congress definitive measures with respect to that nation, in the expectation that the result of unclosed discussions between our minister plenipotentiary at Paris and the French Government will speedily enable Congress to decide with greater advantage on the course due to the rights, the interests, and the honor of our country.

Congressmen Protest War, 1812

If our ills were of a nature that war would remedy, if war would compensate any of our losses or remove any of our complaints, there might be some alleviation of the suffering in the charm of the prospect. But how will war upon the land protect commerce upon the ocean? What balm has Canada for wounded honor? How are our mariners benefited by a war which exposes those who are free, without promising release to those who are impressed?

But it is said that war is demanded by honor. Is national honor a principle which thirsts after vengeance, and is appeased only by blood? . . . If honor demands a war with England, what opiate lulls that honor to sleep over the wrongs done us by France? On land, robberies, seizures, imprisonments, by French authority; at sea, pillage, sinkings, burnings, under French orders. These are notorious. Are they unfelt because they are French? . . . With full knowledge of the wrongs inflicted by the French, ought the government of this country to aid the French cause by engaging in war against the enemy of France? . . .

It would be some relief to our anxiety if amends were likely to be made for the weakness and wildness of the project by the prudence of the preparation. But in no aspect of this anomalous affair can we trace the great and distinctive properties of wisdom. There is seen a headlong rushing into difficulties, with little calculation about the means, and little concern about the consequences. With a navy comparatively nominal, we are about to enter into the lists against the greatest marine [sea power] on the globe. With a commerce unprotected and spread over every ocean, we propose to make a profit by privateering, and

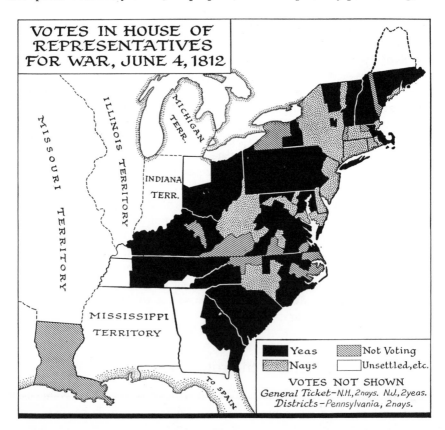

VOTES IN HOUSE OF REPRESENTATIVES FOR WAR, JUNE 4, 1812

Yeas / Nays / Not Voting / Unsettled, etc.

VOTES NOT SHOWN
General Ticket—N.H., 2nays. N.J., 2yeas.
Districts—Pennsylvania, 2nays.

for this endanger the wealth of which we are honest proprietors. An invasion is threatened of the colonies of a power which, without putting a new ship into commission, or taking another soldier into pay, can spread alarm or desolation along the extensive range of our seaboard. . . .

The undersigned cannot refrain from asking, what are the United States to gain by this war? Will the gratification of some privateersmen compensate the nation for that sweep of our legitimate commerce by the extended marine of our enemy which this desperate act invites? Will Canada compensate the Middle states for New York; or the Western states for New Orleans?

Let us not be deceived. A war of invasion may invite a retort of invasion. When we visit the peaceable, and as to us innocent, colonies of Great Britain with the horrors of war, can we be assured that our own coast will not be visited with like horrors? At a crisis of the world such as the present, and under impressions such as these, the undersigned could not consider the war, in which the United States have in secret been precipitated, as necessary, or required by any moral duty, or any political expediency.

ESSAYS

The following essays delineate different causes for the War of 1812. Julius Pratt, noting the desire of Western states and territories for war, emphasizes the Indian menace. Pratt does not deny that maritime issues helped to cause war, but he does argue that without Western grievances there would have been no declaration of war. He suggests, further, a "sectional bargain" between the Northwest, which sought Canada, and the Southwest, which coveted Spanish Florida. Bradford Perkins of the University of Michigan acknowledges Western hawkishness, but he concludes that war came because Americans wished to recover the respect they had lost over the preceding years when the Europeans trampled upon their neutral rights. The war, then, was a question of national honor.

Western Demands and War

JULIUS W. PRATT

That the United States went to war with Great Britain in 1812 at the insistence of western and southern men, and over the opposition of the Northeast, is a fact about which there has never been any doubt. There was a paradox here which apparently gave little concern to the older historians. If the real griev-

Reprinted with permission of Macmillan Publishing Co., Inc. from *The Expansionists of 1812* by Julius W. Pratt. Copyright © 1925 by Macmillan Publishing Co., Inc., renewed 1953 by Julius W. Pratt.

ances which caused the war were interference by Great Britain with American commerce and the rights of American sailors, why was war to redress those grievances opposed by the maritime section of the nation and urged by the inland section, which they scarcely affected? The old answers, that New England was Anglophile, and that the West and South had developed a more aggressive and martial spirit, which felt the humiliation if not the pecuniary loss occasioned by the British measures, were in a measure true, but hardly sufficient. For some years past, historians have been turning to new explanations.

In this field, as in almost every other in American history, it is easy to see the profound influence of Professor F. J. Turner. Before the publication in 1893 of his essay, "The Significance of the Frontier in American History," the frontier had been regarded as little more than a picturesque phase in the national development. Since that event, the frontier—the "West"—has come to be recognized as the source of many aspects of American character and the determining factor in many American policies. It was natural, therefore, that students of the War of 1812 should come to view the West—particularly the Northwest—with more careful scrutiny. The result of such examination has been the placing of new emphasis upon the western demand for the annexation of Canada, which is seen to have arisen in large part from the conviction that the British were in league with the northwestern Indians and that only by destroying that alliance could the Northwest continue its career of expansion.

The war found its sponsors, however, not only in the Northwest but along the whole frontier from New Hampshire round about to Georgia. For the states south of Kentucky, there was little to be gained by the conquest of Canada, and, since the divergence of interests between North and South was already evident, there was reason for southern states to fear the political effect of a large addition to northern territory. Why, then, did the Southwest support the war? The answer to this question has been suggested, but has never been worked out with anything approaching completeness. The examination made in the course of this study reveals an ardent expansionist sentiment already at work along the whole southern and southwestern border, varying in scope from the relatively modest proposal for the annexation of the Floridas to the more visionary idea of seizing all the Spanish possessions on the continent of North America. The link between the designs of the Southwest and those of the Northwest was the existence of the alliance between Great Britain and Spain. It was widely assumed that war with Great Britain would mean war with Spain, and that thus expansion at the north and at the south would proceed *pari passu*.

The purposes of the present study have been: to examine the development in the Northwest of the demand for the conquest and annexation of Canada; to trace the rise in the South and Southwest of the plan to annex the Floridas and possibly Mexico; to discover the relations of these two proposals to each other and to the question of war with Great Britain; to determine the position of the executive branch of the United States government (especially of Madison and his Secretary of State, Monroe) toward the plans for expansion, north and south; and finally, to determine the causes for the failure, all along the line, of the expansionist hopes with which the war began.

The principal conclusions arrived at may be summarized as follows:

1. The belief that the United States would one day annex Canada had a continuous existence from the early days of the War of Independence to the War of 1812. From 1783 to about 1810 such annexation was thought of only as a matter for an indefinite future, the nation during those years having neither the strength, nor any sufficient motive, for taking Canada by force. The rise of Tecumseh, backed, as was universally believed, by the British, produced an urgent demand in the Northwest that the British be expelled from Canada. This demand was a factor of primary importance in bringing on the war.

2. The South was almost unanimous in its demand for the Floridas, for agrarian, commercial, and strategic reasons, and in the spring of 1812 appeared to be in a fair way to accomplish its purpose. In the Southwest, at the same time, there was a lively interest in Mexico and a widely prevalent opinion that it was ready to fall into American hands.

3. Even within the Republican party, there was already a distinct sectional rift between North and South, and neither section was anxious to see the other increase its territory and population. But if both could gain at the same time, and in something like equal proportion, such objections would be obviated on both sides. There is good evidence that, before the declaration of war, northern and southern Republicans came to a definite understanding that the acquisition of Canada on the north was to be balanced by the annexation of the Floridas on the south. Thus the war began with a double-barrelled scheme of territorial aggrandizement.

4. Both Madison and Monroe, especially the latter as Secretary of State, were wholly in sympathy with the proposal for annexing Florida. The invasion of East Florida by General Mathews in March and April, 1812, was effected with the full knowledge of the administration. Special circumstances forced the government to repudiate Mathews, but the territory he had taken from the Spanish was held for over a year, until Congress had twice refused to sanction the occupation. At the same time, Monroe's official correspondence shows that he never really desired or expected the annexation of Canada.

5. It appears that in the all round failure of the expansionist plans, sectional feeling played a larger part than is commonly supposed. The sectional bargain with which the war had begun broke down. Opposition from northern Republicans combined with Federalists forced the abandonment of East Florida. On the other hand, it is evident that in the utter failure of the efforts to take Canada, not only want of skill and preparation, but also a lack of enthusiasm on the part of the administration and of certain southern men in Congress played a part.

6. Finally, in the expansionist program with which the war opened, we have the first general appearance of the idea which later received the name of "Manifest Destiny." Although enthusiasts like Jefferson had dreamed years

before of a nation destined to embrace the continent, the date usually given for the dawn of "Manifest Destiny" is about 1830. Yet both in the Congressional debates of 1812 and in the contemporary press, particularly that of the Southwest, we find the idea repeatedly expressed. "Where is it written in the book of fate," asked the editor of the Nashville *Clarion* (April 28, 1812), "that the American republic shall not stretch her limits from the Capes of the Chesapeake to Nootka sound, from the isthmus of Panama to Hudson bay?"

Two explanations are due, with respect to the scope and proportions of this study. First, it makes no effort to give a full account of the causes of the War of 1812, but deals with one set of causes only. The exclusion from all but briefest mention of the maritime grievances against Great Britain is with no wish to belittle them. Without them, it is safe to say, there would have been no war, just as the writer feels safe in saying that without the peculiar grievances and ambitions of the West there would have been no war. One set of causes was perhaps as essential as the other. . . .

Throughout the year 1811, alarm at the menace of Tecumseh's confederacy and conviction that the British were instrumental in its formation and support grew rapidly among government officials and the people of the West. Governor Harrison wrote in February to the Secretary of War: "If the intentions of the British Government are pacific, the Indian department of Upper Canada have not been made acquainted with them: for they have very lately said every thing to the Indians, who visited them, to excite them against us."

In July a group of citizens of Knox County, Indiana, met at Vincennes and adopted resolutions demanding that the Indian settlement at Tippecanoe—one hundred and fifty miles up the Wabash—be broken up. The wish was natural, in view of the serious menace which the Prophet's town held over the heads of the Knox County settlers; but it was significant that the British were charged with responsibility for the whole situation. "We are fully convinced," said the resolutions, "that the formation of the combination, headed by the Shawanee prophet, is a British scheme, and that the agents of that power are constantly exciting the Indians to hostilities against the United States." Similar views were reflected in resolutions adopted by residents of St. Clair County, Illinois, which mentioned "the seditious village of Peoria, the great nursery of hostile Indians and traitorous British Indian traders."

Meanwhile the *Kentucky Gazette* was warning its readers of the British-Indian menace in outspoken language:

"It would seem from the attitude of the Indians—the combination of the Northern and Southern tribes—the conference at Malden—the circumstances attendant on the mission of *Foster*—the late arrival of regular troops in Canada, that the British ministry were planning '*another expedition.*' . . .

"From the friendly course pursued by Mr. Jefferson, towards our red neighbors, and which has been followed by Mr. Madison, we had supposed the Indians would never more treat us otherwise than as brethren. But we have been mistaken—British intrigue and British gold, it seems, has greater influence with them of late than American justice and benevolence. . . . We have in our possession information which proves beyond doubt, the late disturbances to be owing to the too successful intrigues of British emissaries with the Indians."

Governor Harrison, representative of "American justice and benevolence" toward the Indians, was at this time planning to open the way to a military career by an attack on the Indian village at Tippecanoe. But he knew that war with England was probable, and suspected that the regiment of regular troops now on their way to him from Pittsburgh, were destined "to our frontiers bordering on Upper Canada." More important than his own ideas on the subject was his estimate of the spirit of the western people, whom he knew if any one knew them. "The people of this Territory [Indiana] and Kentucky," he wrote, "are extremely pressing in offers of their service for an expedition into the Indian Country. Any number of men might be obtained for this purpose or for a march into Canada."

Early in September it was reported to Harrison "that defection is evidenced amongst all the Tribes from the Wabash to the Mississippi and the Lakes. That the Indians of the Wabash, Illinois, etc., have recently visited the British agent at Malden. That they are now returning from thence with a larger supply of goods than is ever known to have been distributed to them before. That rifles or fusees are given to those who are unarmed and powder and lead to all. And that the language and measures of the Indians indicate nothing but war." Harrison passed on the information to the War Department a few days later (September 17, 1811), with additional details of the extent of British subsidies: "A trader of this country was lately in the King's store at Malden, and was told that the quantity of goods for the Indian department, which has been sent out this year, exceeded that of common years by £20,000 sterling. It is impossible to ascribe this profusion to any other motive than that of instigating the Indians to take up the tomahawk; it cannot be to secure their trade, for all the peltries collected on the waters of the Wabash, in one year, if sold in the London market, would not pay the freight of the goods which have been given the Indians."

Harrison, however, went on to say that, "although I am decidedly of opinion that the tendency of the British measures is hostility to us, candor obliges me to inform you, that, from two Indians of different tribes, I have received information that the British agent absolutely dissuaded them from going to war against the United States." That the compulsion of candor was necessary to bring the governor to pass on this last bit of information is an interesting commentary on his state of mind; but the information itself is perfectly consistent with the other facts of the situation. General Brock wrote, after Harrison's battle with the Indians, that the latter had been "implicitly told not to look for assistance from us," but the phrase occurs in a letter whose main purpose was to point out how the effective aid of the Indians was to be secured and used against the Americans. Throughout the period of the rise of Tecumseh, the British had dissuaded the Indians from beginning a war against the United States; but the purpose of this policy was to allow time for the consolidation of the confederacy, that the aid of the Indians might be the more effective when needed.

Early in November came Harrison's badly managed campaign ending in the battle of Tippecanoe. From the facts already presented it is clear that the blood there shed would be added to the grievances already existing against the British and would bring the West to an eagerness for war without precedent in the entire controversy. *"The blood of our murdered countrymen must be revenged,"* wrote Andrew Jackson to Harrison. "I do hope that Government will see that it is necessary to act efficiently and that this hostile band which must be excited to war by the secret agents of Great Britain must be destroyed." The battle of Tippecanoe gave inestimable support to the war party in the Twelfth Congress, now assembled in Washington for its first session.

The war party, composed of western men and "radical, expansionist, malcontent politicians of the east," which had existed in Congress since 1810 at least, found itself in full control when the Twelfth Congress met. Clay, the most prominent of the "war hawks," came now to the House of Representatives, where he was at once chosen speaker. He was supported in his warlike policy by members from the frontier sections of the northern states, such as Peter B. Porter of New York and John A. Harper of New Hampshire; by almost the entire delegation of the western states—Worthington of Ohio and Pope of Kentucky, both in the Senate, were the only important exceptions—by a fair proportion of the members from Pennsylvania, Virginia, and North Carolina; and by a very able and aggressive group of young men from South Carolina and Georgia—Calhoun, Cheves, Lowndes, Crawford, Troup, and others—men who had reasons of their own for promoting a war of expansion.

It was soon apparent that the war to which this party was committed was to be no such purely defensive war as the Tenth Congress had contemplated, but that it was to be waged aggressively and with the conquest of Canada as a major object. Some Easterners might agree with Monroe that Canada might be invaded, "not as an object of the war but as a means to bring it to a satisfactory conclusion," but the West was more of the mind of a correspondent of the Philadelphia *Aurora,* "who wrote that if England were to restore all impressed seamen and make compensation for all her depredations we should listen to no terms that did not include Upper Canada."

President Madison's annual message, delivered to Congress on November 5, contained language that could plainly be interpreted as meaning war. After touching upon the obdurate persistence of Great Britain in attacking American commerce, he went on to say: "With this evidence of hostile inflexibility, in trampling on rights which no independent nation can relinquish, Congress will feel the duty of putting the United States into an armor and an attitude demanded by the crisis, and corresponding with the national spirit and expectations." To deal with that part of the message concerned with foreign relations, Speaker Clay appointed a select committee, upon which he placed a group of the most reliable war men—Porter, Calhoun, Grundy, Harper, and Desha. The committee reported on November 29 a set of six resolutions recommending an increase of ten thousand men for the regular army, a levy of fifty thousand volunteers, the outfitting of all vessels of war not in active service, and the arming of merchant vessels.

It was in the House debate on these resolutions that the war party frankly revealed their designs upon Canada. Mr. Porter, chairman of the committee, speaking on December 6, explained that in addition to the injury which American privateers could inflict upon British commerce, "there was another point where we could attack her, and where she would feel our power still more sensibly. We could deprive her of her extensive provinces lying along our borders to the north. These provinces were not only immensely valuable in themselves, but almost indispensable to the existence of Great Britain, cut off as she now in a great measure is from the north of Europe. He had been credibly informed that the exports from Quebec alone amounted during the last year, to near six millions of dollars, and most of these too in articles of the first necessity—in ship timber and in provisions for the support of her fleets and armies. By carrying on such a war as he had described . . . we should be able in a short time to remunerate ourselves tenfold for all the spoliations she had committed on our commerce."

Grundy of Tennessee, three days later, dwelt upon the peculiar advantage to the Westerner to be derived from war. "We shall drive the British from our Continent—they will no longer have an opportunity of intriguing with our Indian neighbors, and setting on the ruthless savage to tomahawk our women and children. That nation will lose her Canadian trade, and, by having no resting place in this country, her means of annoying us will be diminished." Rhea of Tennessee was equally explicit upon the object of the war—"That all that part of North America which joins the United States on the Northeast, North, and Northwest, shall be provided for in a mode which will forever thereafter put it out of the power of Great Britain, or of any British agent, trader, or factor, or company of British traders to supply Indian tribes with arms or ammunition; to instigate and incite Indians to disturb and harass our frontiers, and to murder and scalp helpless women and children."

Two members of the House, one from Kentucky and one from New Hampshire, expounded the doctrine of Manifest Destiny. "I shall never die contented," announced R. M. Johnson, "until I see her [Great Britain's] expulsion from North America, and her territories incorporated with the United States. . . . In point of territorial limit, the map will improve its importance. The waters of the St. Lawrence and the Mississippi interlock in a number of places, and the great Disposer of Human Events intended those two rivers should belong to the same people." "The northern provinces of Britain are to us great and valuable objects," proclaimed Harper of New Hampshire. "Once secured to this Republic, and the St. Lawrence and the Lakes become the Baltic, and more than the Baltic to America; north of them a population of four millions may easily be supported; and this great outlet of the northern world should be at our command for our convenience and future security. To me, sir, it appears that the Author of Nature has marked our limits in the south, by the Gulf of Mexico; and on the north, by the regions of eternal frost."

While Congress debated, reports continued to come in of British agents at work among the Indians. As a matter of fact, it would appear that presents to the Indians, and particularly ammunition, were less at this time than previously.

Claus wrote General Brock from Amherstburg in June, 1812, that during the last six months the Indians had received only 1211 pounds of powder—"nineteen hundred and twenty-one pounds less than at former periods—of lead, not one ounce has been issued to them since last December." But a letter from Fort Wayne in February stated that two British emissaries had recently passed that way on a mission to the Prophet, and that "their business was to invite all the Indians to meet at Malden very early in the spring." Any event of this kind would of course receive the most unfavorable interpretation. The same letter gave other disturbing reports: "The Pottawatomy chief, Marpack, has been in the neighborhood of Malden since August last. . . . He has about one hundred and twenty of the best warriors in this country with him. . . . I know this chief is hostile inclined towards the United States, and have no hesitation in saying, that he is kept at that place by the British agents at Malden."

If their relations with the Indians constituted a standing reason for driving the British from Canada, a special reason was furnished by the publication of the Henry Letters, for Henry had been in the employ of the Governor-General of Canada. "Can any American, after this discovery," wrote Congressman Desha to a friend in Kentucky, "doubt the propriety of ousting the British from the continent, or hesitate in contributing his proportionable part of the expense which will necessarily be incurred in the laudable undertaking."

The West no longer needed any such prompting from its representatives in Washington. The rise of Tecumseh and the Prophet, the battle of Tippecanoe, the outspoken position of their congressmen together with the current belief that the British were behind all their Indian troubles, had resulted in an insistent demand from the Westerners for the conquest of Canada. The Lexington *Reporter* published in January a *"Franklinian Prescription—To cure Indian hostilities, and to prevent their recurrence:* Interpose the American arm between the hands of the English and their savage allies. This done, the occupation of the Canadas, New Brunswick and Nova-Scotia, would give us perpetual concord with the Indians; who would be obliged *to depend upon us* for supplies of Blankets, knives, gunpowder, etc."

The Kentucky Legislature, which in the crisis of 1807–1808 had made no official mention of the border question, in its resolutions of February, 1812, added to Great Britain's violations of American rights at sea her practice of "inciting the savages (as we have strong reasons to believe) to murder the inhabitants of our defenseless frontiers—furnishing them with arms and ammunition lately, to attack our forces; to the loss of a number of our brave men."

Another indication of public opinion in Kentucky is the character of the toasts proposed at a Washington's Birthday dinner in Lexington. The banqueters drank to such toasts as *"Great Britain, when she comes to her senses —If she continues lunatic, Canada and our arms!"* or *"The American Congress—If they barter the nation's honor under the false idea of temporary popularity, may they meet with the just scorn of an indignant people!"*

Public opinion in Ohio paralleled closely that of Kentucky. The Circleville *Fredonian* declared the "indignant spirits" of Americans could be appeased only "by the restoration of our rights, or the conquest of Canada." Correspondents of Senator Thomas Worthington believed that if war came, "we would attack [and] conquer Cannady & humble their overbearing pride," or hoped that American troops would "sever Upper Canada from the British without delay."

As the year advanced, the tone of the press grew even more determined. The *Fredonian* saw no hope of peace and security from the savages until "another WAYNE shall force *them* to become our friends, and another WASHINGTON exterminates from the Canadas, the base remains of royal perfidy." The British "must be for ever driven from all their possessions in America." The same paper professed itself eager to undertake a war against both France and Great Britain when it appeared that neither nation was willing to recognize American rights. In April the *Kentucky Gazette* stated: "Great Britain has determined not to recede, and Congress seem at last to have got in earnest, and appear disposed to prepare for war. . . . The recruiting service has been actually commenced in various places, and large bodies of militia are to be raised to march for Detroit and other parts of our frontier. This is all preparatory to the invasion of Canada, now more than ever necessary, as presenting whilst in the possession of Britain, a never failing source of Indian hostility. Until those civilized allies of our Savage neighbors, are expelled from our continent, we must expect the frequent recurrence of the late scenes on the Wabash."

The same paper could not suppress its wrath when the *National Intelligencer,* reputed to be the administration organ, hinted that war might yet be avoided. "Notwithstanding a mass of evidence of this kind [i.e. as to captures, impressment, Henry plots, etc.], the Intelligencer may talk of *negociation* and *'honorable accommodation'* with England; but when we view the effects of her policy in the *West*—when we hear of the tragic scenes that are now acting on our frontiers, after the slaughter of Tippecanoe, it is really surprising to hear that there is any doubt about the *'active preparations for warlike operations'* . . . We will only add, at this time, that we should much like to know the price which the 'Intelligencer' would receive as a compromise for the scalps of *Western Farmers.*"

On May 26, three weeks before the declaration of war, the *Gazette* gave what appears like a parting injunction to Congress: "Can it be expected that those savage butcheries will have an end until we take possession of Malden and other British forts on the Lakes? And must the settlements in our territories be entirely destroyed, and the blood of the women and children drench the soil before this can be done? . . . What will our Congress say?" In similar tone the *Reporter* of May 30 declared: "Britain has commenced war in the Western Country, equally so as France would have done, was she to burn New York. The citizens of the Eastern States, and members in Congress, may abandon 7,000 seamen—they may term it, a *trifling impropriety* on the part of England, but the old Revolutionary Heroes here are not to be deceived by the misrepresentations of any man whatever. The Government MUST not abandon the Western Country to the British."

Thus by the end of the spring of 1812, the whole frontier country from New

Hampshire to Kentucky was insisting that the British must be expelled from Canada. The demand had been of slow growth. Taking its origin from the ideas of Revolutionary statesmen, it was fed from various sources—from jealousy of the British fur trade, from exasperation at British contempt for the American flag at sea, from the alluring vision of a continent destined to recognize a single sovereignty—but unquestionably most of all from the conviction that the British in Canada were in unholy alliance with the western Indians, and that only by cutting off the Indians from British support could the West gain peace and security. Only thus could the Westerner be free to continue that policy of "justice and benevolence" toward the Indians, which consisted in pushing the boundaries of the white settlements ever farther into the Indian country. Other motives—commercial, political, punitive—played a part; but the overmastering desire of the people of the Northwest was to feel free to develop their country without peril from those Indian conspiracies which were universally believed to have their origin in British Canada. . . .

If the frontiersman of the Northwest demanded war with Great Britain as indispensable, his kinsman of the southern border at least saw in it a means of fulfilling his expansionist dreams. The past two years had done much to give him what he thought his territorial rights, but much remained to be gained. The Spanish still held Mobile and Pensacola, St. Mark's and St. Augustine, and the American troops that held the country between the St. John's and the St. Mary's rivers were, it was supposed, about to be withdrawn.

The demand for the annexation of all Florida was more insistent than ever. Georgians like Floyd, Mitchell, Troup, and Crawford—the last two influential members of the war party in Congress—held the acquisition of East Florida essential to the prosperity, to the very safety, of their state. The Augusta *Chronicle* . . . hoped for "some new measures for the purpose of placing the whole of that colony under the control of the United States." Out in Mississippi Territory, the news of the occupation of East Florida aroused a lively hope of similar action farther west. "There is no doubt," wrote a recent settler at St. Stephens, to a friend in the East, "but Mobille and Pensacola will share the same fate in a few weeks, which no doubt will occasion considerable action in this quarter during this summer, and all the citizens in this part of the country are much gratified at the Idea of the United States getting Possession of this Southern Coast, as it is certainly of all importance to the citizens of this country." The Nashville *Clarion,* quoting at length from the Congressional Report of 1803 on the navigation of the southern rivers, and explaining in detail how Tennessee's transportation difficulties would be solved by the opening of the Alabama and Tombigbee, declared that "No part of the union can be so much interested in the acquisition of West Florida as the State of Tennessee. . . . The Floridas will soon be occupied by American troops."

But if the whole southern border was eager to take what remained of Florida, war with England seemed to afford a perfectly clear occasion for doing so. Spain was England's ally in the European war, and it was safe to assume that Spanish harbors in America would be open to British fleets and armies. As a simple measure of self-defense, the occupation of Florida seemed to many indispensable, and it was commonly assumed at the South that war with England meant war with Spain, or at least the forcible occupation of all Florida.

The notion of a war at once against England and Spain had been broached by Jefferson in 1807, in which case, he declared, "our southern defensive force can take the Floridas." Mathews had alluded to a similar connection when he instructed the "discontents" of East Florida "not to expect that prompt and efficient aid from the United States, if our negotiation with the British Minister terminates auspiciously for us, that they might in the other event expect." Expansionists like Clay and Harper, when they hurled defiance at Great Britain, had spoken in one breath of the nation's prospective conquests on the St. Lawrence and the Gulf of Mexico. Grundy of Tennessee, in the war debate in December, 1811, stated that he felt anxious "not only to add the Floridas to the South, but the Canadas to the North of this empire," and he wrote to Jackson that in case of war "the Canadas & Floridas will be the Theatres of our offensive operations."

Jackson himself, when shortly after the declaration of war he called upon his division of Tennessee militia to be in readiness, assured them that it was in West Florida that their arms should find employment. Jefferson, writing of the mustering of the militia in his Virginia county in June, 1812, said that "the only inquiry they make is whether they are to go to Canada or Florida."

In Georgia it was generally assumed that war with Great Britain would mean the certain seizure of all of Florida that remained unoccupied. "Had we no other claim on Florida or Spain," said the Augusta *Chronicle* in May, "sound policy would dictate the propriety as well as necessity of retaining possession of it till the close of the war we are now on the eve of commencing with an ally of that country." On the day preceding the declaration of war, the Republican citizens of Milledgeville passed resolutions approving the war measures against Great Britain, and declaring their belief that with war in prospect the occupancy of East Florida was "essential to the interests of the country and the safety of our southern frontier." A letter from Milledgeville dated July 8, 1812, reported that Governor Mitchell, who was at St. Mary's, had received news of the declaration of war, and, "considering that the Spaniards and British are in alliance both offensive and defensive, and that the vital interests of this state and the honor of the United States are implicated and will be hazarded by suffering the occupancy of East Florida by the banditti now in possession"— not the "patriots" evidently, to whom the term might have been applied, but the Spanish governor and his negro and Indian auxiliaries—"he will be detained until the reinforcements he has sent for and which are now assembling on the Oconee River, are received." Mitchell himself explained later to the Georgia legislature the light in which, prior to the declaration of war, he had viewed the situation. "The confidence with which I anticipated the declaration of war against Great Britain," said the governor, "led me with equal confidence to anticipate an enlargement of the powers of the President, by congress, as the necessary consequence, having for its object the entire occupancy of East and West Florida."

War with Great Britain, then, meant, to the average Southerner, war also with Spain, and the completion of the annexation of the Floridas. To the people of the Southwest it meant the possibility of even greater things. The old dream of revolutionizing Mexico and, if not actually annexing it to the United States, at least profiting by its agricultural, mineral, and commercial wealth, revived with new vigor. The Southwest tried to persuade itself that the Federal government favored such plans, quoting cryptic passages from "prints known to be in the interest of the administration," and citing the promotion of Colonel Pike, an avowed annexationist, and his position then in command of the troops on the border, as evidence that an invasion was contemplated. A writer signing himself "Americus" contributed to the Nashville *Clarion* of April 28 a long article in which "Manifest Destiny" ran riot.

"The Canadas," wrote Americus, "freed from the chains of an European master, shall take the rank of an independent state; or, too weak for sovereignty, shall hover under the wings of the American eagle. . . . The Floridas will sink into the confederation of American states. . . . Whilst our eastern and southern brethren are purchasing renown in arms, and extending the limits of the republic, are we condemned to remain inactive . . . ? No, citizens of the West! a destiny still more splendid is reserved for you. Behold the empire of Mexico, a celestial region, whose valiant sons are now struggling for their liberties as we struggled for ours thirty years ago. . . . Here it is that the statesman shall see an accession of Territory sufficient to double the extent of the republic; where the merchant shall see commercial resources unrivalled in other countries, the farmer, a luxuriant soil and delicious climate, where the financier shall be dazzled with gold and silver mines; while the ardent and generous mind, in the idea of establishing a new republic . . . shall deliver himself up to an enthusiasm of glory. . . . Besides, where is it written in the book of fate that the American republic shall not stretch her limits from the capes of the Chesapeake to Nootka sound, from the isthmus of Panama to Hudson bay?"

Thus while the Northwesterner expected to take Canada as a result of war with Great Britain, southern men generally expected to complete the seizure of Florida from Great Britain's ally, Spain, while the more ambitious expansionists of the Southwest dreamed of further aggressions upon the Spanish territories, which should end in making the United States coextensive with the continent of North America.

A Question of National Honor

BRADFORD PERKINS

The war continued for two and a half years, and for nearly 150 years it has challenged those who seek to explain its coming. Contemporary Federalists found a simple explanation in alleged Republican subserviency to France.

Bradford Perkins, *Prologue to War: England and the United States, 1805–1812*, pp. 421–437. Copyright © 1961 by The Regents of the University of California; reprinted by permission of the University of California Press.

A New York dominie declared God had brought on war so that the young republic might chastise the British government, "a *despotic usurpation—A superstitious combination of civil and ecclesiastic power—A branch of the grand antichristian apostacy—Erastian in its constitution and administration—*and *Cruel in its policy.*" Actually, neither God nor Napoleon seems an adequate explanation for the war, and historians have sought to establish the importance of more mundane influences.

Most nineteenth-century historians emphasized British outrages against American commerce. Admiral Mahan said that the orders "by their enormity dwarfed all previous causes of complaint, and with the question of impressment constituted a vital and irreconcilable body of dissent which dragged the two states into armed collision." Henry Adams apparently considered this maritime emphasis inadequate, but, as Warren Goodman suggests in an able historiographical article, he modified rather than abandoned the traditional view, although he did hint that Canadian-directed imperialism played a part. Despite a dislike of Jefferson and Madison so bitter that he sometimes doctored the evidence, Adams' volumes remain the most complete, often the best written, and, when used with proper caution, the most useful survey of the entire period. After a lapse of some years, A. L. Burt reëmphasized maritime causes in a graceful summary of the era.

For two decades before the appearance of Burt's work in 1940, scholars sought to explain the motives of the West, the section that most unanimously supported war. Louis M. Hacker, then in a Marxist phase, suggested that a greedy desire for fertile Canadian farm land lay behind the façade of arguments for national honor. Julius W. Pratt contradicted Hacker's position, largely by disproving the central hypothesis, that there was no longer good agricultural land on the American side of the frontier. Then, following a line already sketched by Dice R. Anderson, Pratt in his turn suggested a bargain between frontiersmen and Republicans of the North, who desired Canada, and Southerners, who wanted to absorb Florida. Sectional jealousies, Pratt concluded, broke down this alliance only after it had brought on war. Pratt found it difficult to demonstrate a real bargain, and there is reason to believe that the South did not almost universally desire the acquisition of Florida, as he maintained. But not without merit is Pratt's thesis that Western Anglophobia was stirred by the menace of Indian warfare believed to be inspired by Canadian authorities. Finally, George R. Taylor put forward the argument that the West, economically overextended and suffering from depression from 1808 onward, blamed its troubles on the restrictive edicts of Europe and advocated war to break down this barrier to prosperity. In April, 1812, Augustus J. Foster anticipated this interpretation: "The Western States having nothing to lose by war, . . . [are] clamorous for it, . . . being likely even to gain in the Exports of their produce while the exportation of that of the Atlantic shall be impeded." Moreover, there was always the chance that war, or even the threat of war, would drive England to surrender the orders.

Hacker billed his suggestion "a conjecture," and Pratt and Taylor specifically noted that they were dealing, in the former's words, "with one set of causes only." Still, despite Pratt's coördinate interest in Southern ambitions for Florida, the researches of these scholars concentrated attention upon the West. The war came to bear the mark of the West, although only nine congressmen—a mere one of each nine voting for war—came from Western states. Taylor's suggestion that the West sought war to regain an export market might just as legitimately have been applied to other agricultural areas of the country, particularly the South, as Goodman, Burt, and Margaret K. Latimer have recently noted. Studies of Western motivation, despite the caveats of their authors, have distorted the image of events leading to the War of 1812.

In his biography of the President, Irving Brant attempts to refurbish Madison's reputation. Attention is so narrowly concentrated on the President and on events with which he dealt that many important developments in Europe and America are slighted. Brant clearly shows the President's technical diplomatic ability. He does not equally clearly disprove Henry Adams' contention that, by emphasizing America's right to demand repeal of the orders as a consequence of alleged French repeal,

> Madison had been so unfortunate in making the issue that on his own showing no sufficient cause of war seemed to exist. . . . Great Britain was able to pose before the world in the attitude of victim to a conspiracy between Napoleon and the United States to destroy the liberties of Europe. Such inversion of the truth passed ordinary bounds, and so real was Madison's diplomatic mismanagement that it paralyzed one-half the energies of the American people.

As Brant claims, Madison recognized that peace might become impossibly costly, but in 1812 he abandoned with great reluctance what Samuel Flagg Bemis has perceptively called his "strategy of auctioning the great belligerents out of their respective systems of retaliation." Perhaps Napoleon and Perceval acted foolishly in rejecting the bids Madison put forward during the auction; perhaps the President calculated more accurately the mutual benefits of accommodation. Still, it is one of the supreme functions of the statesman to weigh the intangibles as well as the tangibles, to expect illogical and prejudiced reactions along with coolly calculated ones. When Irving Brant declares that "President Madison to be successful . . . needed to deal with men whose understanding matched his own," he really confesses the political failure of his hero.

Madison never firmly controlled the Congress; he often lost command of his own Cabinet; frequently he seemed to drift rather than to direct policy. John Adams, fiercely challenged during the disintegration of Federalism, at least remained firm. In the spring of 1812 the congressional delegate from Mississippi Territory wrote that "the Executive is much censured by all parties for the tardiness of its advances to meet the *tug of war,* and the tenure of Mr. Madison's continuance in the presidential chair, in my opinion, depends upon the success of our hostile preparations." Yet the President did not forcefully support the cause of those whose loyalty had to be preserved for the impending election, nor did he speak out in favor of a course that might have maintained the peace he cherished. He reigned but he did not rule. After the declaration of war Jonathan Roberts wrote: "The world are pleased to suppose I am on good terms at the White House which by the way is no advantage for the cry of mad dog is not more fatal to its victim than the cry of executive connexion here." Madison won reëlection, but he was the least respected victor the country had yet known.

The war came, not because of the President, but despite him. The war came, not for any single reason, but from the interplay of many. The nation did not want war, and surely it did not embark gleefully on a great crusade. Tired of the self-flagellation and the disgrace that had marked the years since 1805, propelled by the fear of ridicule for inconsistency and by an honest interest in the nation's honor, a sufficient number of congressmen allowed themselves to support war. Justification for a declaration of war was not wanting, and the long-term results were probably beneficial. Still, the war came just when the United States might have enjoyed without a struggle the immense benefits of the neutrality in which so much Christian forbearance (or cowardice) had been invested. Neither side sought the War of 1812, and in the short run it was tragically unnecessary.

The United States did not go to war to add new states to the Union. A very few ebullient men from the North may have desired this. For sectional reasons the South and the West opposed it. A few advance agents of manifest destiny believed, as the Reverend McLeod put it in 1815, that the war was "a contest, not only to prevent the recolonization of these states, but also in the Providence of God for extending the principles of *representative democracy*—the blessings of liberty, and the rights of self-government, among the colonies of Europe." Even McLeod counted more on the imperialism of ideas than on military conquest. For most Americans Canada was but a means to an end, "a blow that might have given a speedier termination to the controversy," as Niles put it. At most, the occupation of the British provinces seemed the best means to reduce the enemy's power. A loyal Republican paper in Virginia commented:

> The great advantages to be derived from the acquisition of those possessions will not accrue so much from the tenure of them as a conquest, . . . but from the very important consequences which their loss will occasion to Britain; and among these consequences we may reckon the suppression of a great deal of smuggling, the curtailment . . . of the British fur trade and the disseverance of the West India Islands from Great Britain.

So feeble was the desire for permanent incorporation of Canada within the Union that within six weeks after the destruction of British power in Upper Canada at the battle of the Thames in 1813, the Western militia had returned to their homes.

From the opening of the war session, both supporters and enemies of war proclaimed that an attack upon Canada would be the principal American offensive. Congress ostensibly tailored the new army to the requirements of this campaign. All the Republicans, at least, believed that even the slightest effort would result in victory. "In four weeks from the time that a declaration of war is heard on our frontier," John C. Calhoun declared, "the whole of

Upper and a part of Lower Canada will be in our possession." When Federalists complained that their opponents sought to establish a standing army that might menace American liberties, Trenton's *True American* replied, "It will be a *moving, fighting, conquering,* army—and as soon as its duty is done, it will be disbanded." Had Bermuda or Jamaica been vulnerable to attack by a flotilla of Jefferson's gunboats, the War Hawks would have been equally satisfied to invade them.

Even Indian warfare did not inspire important demands for Canadian conquest in the winter of 1811–12. "Much of that resentment against the British, which prevailed so strongly in the western states," a Kentucky historian of the war stated, ". . . may fairly be attributed to this source." Even this Western chronicler, however, declared that the Orders in Council became more intolerable than any other source of complaint against England. After Tippecanoe desultory warfare took place along the frontier, but most Indian tribes remained at peace until General Hull surrendered his army to Isaac Brock in the summer of 1812. Although Grundy and the Lexington *Reporter* remained irate, the Indian menace played a comparatively minor part in congressional debates until the very end of the session, when all complaints against Britain were being brought together to support a declaration of war. At that time congressmen emphasized Britain's interference in American affairs rather than the material consequences to one section.

The most important, most justified American complaints against England sprang from Britain's exercise of her maritime power. Substantively, through the loss of seamen, ships, and cargoes, America suffered greatly from impressment, blockades, and the Orders in Council. The sovereign spirit and the self-respect of the American nation suffered perhaps even more every time a seaman was removed from beneath the Stars and Stripes or a merchant vessel was haled to trial before an admiralty court that paid scant heed to international law. The penalties of neutrality are often dear, and perhaps only the weak, the phlegmatic, or the noble are capable of enduring them. Jefferson and Madison might fit into one or the other of these categories. Ultimately the nation felt taxed beyond endurance. However necessary to British prosecution of the contest with Napoleon impressment and attacks upon neutral commerce might be, they finally brought war with America. Fortune rather than justice postponed the outbreak of war beyond the gloomiest days of Britain's struggle, when American entry might well have played an important part.

Impressment, Frank A. Updyke has observed, was "the most aggravating and the most persistent" American grievance. By 1812 the press gangs had been at work for twenty years. In many instances—probably even the majority—the British forcibly recalled a king's subject to his allegiance rather than kidnapped an American. More often than was generally admitted, the Admiralty released mariners mistakenly seized. Still, impressment formed an ultimately intolerable insult to national sovereignty. When, during the war, the Federalist legislature of Massachusetts undertook an investigation to show that very few seamen had been impressed, John Quincy Adams angrily and accurately declared the question irrelevant:

No Nation can be Independent which suffers her Citizens to be stolen from her at the discretion of the Naval or military Officers of another. . . . The State, by the social compact is bound to *protect* every one of its Citizens, and the enquiry how many of them a foreign Nation may be allowed to rob with impunity is itself a humiliation to which I blush to see that the Legislature of my native state could defend. . . . The principle for which we are now struggling is of a higher and more sacred nature than any question about taxation can involve. It is the principle of personal liberty, and of every social right.

Failures of American arms and a European peace that halted impressment caused Adams, along with Madison and Monroe, to accept a peace silent on impressment. In principle, however, he was correct. America might well have gone to war on this issue, perhaps at the time of the *Chesapeake* affair.

Although officially the American government made very little of impressment from 1808 onward, the people could not forget it. During the war session, and particularly in the spring, impressment aroused more and more heat. *Niles' Register,* which began publication in 1811, rallied opinion on this issue. "Accursed be the American government, and every individual in it," an imprecation ran, "who . . . shall agree to make peace with Great Britain, until ample provision shall be made for our impressed seamen, and security shall be given for the prevention of such abominable outrages in the future." A Quid and a Republican who hoped to avoid war told Foster this was the most ticklish problem to explain to their constituents, and even the stanchly antiwar senator, Thomas Worthington, found impressment almost impossible to tolerate. "He says," Foster wrote in his diary, "he would rather live on a Crust in the Interior than live degraded." Foster, who repeatedly suggested that modification of the orders would prevent a declaration of war, nevertheless recognized the renewed importance accorded to impressment. On April 23 he wrote, "Very inflammatory paragraphs and letters on the subject . . . have lately been circulated in the American papers, and as the causes of war become more closely canvassed, that arising out of the practice of impressment seems to be dwelt upon with considerable vehemence." When war approached, the War Hawks had a singularly effective propaganda point in this violation of the rights of individual Americans who deserved better of their country.

Both the British government and the Federalists later complained that the President only resuscitated the impressment issue after the Orders in Council had disappeared. They pointed out that, particularly in the Erskine negotiations, the administration had allowed impressment to pass in silence. In 1813 Lord Castlereagh described it as "a cause of war, now brought forward as such for the first time." These criticisms showed only that the administration had been backward in defending the rights of citizens, or that the President and Congress had been willing for a time to exchange the kidnaping of Americans for the benefit of neutrality. Neither Lord Castlereagh nor Timothy Pickering, who as secretary of state had himself vehemently protested the practice, should have been surprised that the American people considered impressment an insult.

Even more than impressment, with which congressmen and newspaper editors often coupled them, the Orders in Council showed Britain's contemptuous disdain for American protests against her use of sea power. The forcible enlistment of seamen could be expressed in dramatic human terms. The Orders in Council more massively and more selfishly assaulted the United States. Their material cost was impressive. Although the number of seizures actually fell after 1808, the year beginning in October, 1811, saw an increase of nearly 50 per cent. The orders and the *Essex* case had long since reduced the reëxport trade to a shadow of its former size. After a spurt stimulated by Macon's Bill #2 and the Cadore letter, the export of native American produce fell drastically after the spring of 1811. By far the greatest proportion of this decline came in exports to Britain, particularly because return cargoes were forbidden and the United Kingdom suffered from glut. Agriculturists and plantation owners, some shipowners, and the average congressman ascribed the decline to Britain's Orders in Council, which prevented Americans from developing the presumably lucrative Continental market. At the same time, particularly because the British permitted their own subjects to trade with Europe under license, the Orders in Council seemed humiliating. Since at least November, 1807, the English had presumed to legislate not only for their own people but also for the commercial world. Economic necessity and national right alike cried out against the Orders in Council.

Everyone in Washington during the months from November to June placed the Orders in Council at the head of the list of American grievances. Louis Sérurier and Augustus Foster, Federalists and Republicans were in agreement. When the British minister asked Chauncey Goodrich, a Federalist senator, "what was required of us by Men of fair Views, he replied, take off the Orders in Council and come to some Arrangement about Impressment." In November President Madison considered British maritime policy the transcendent issue between the two countries. Porter's report declared that the orders "went to the subversion of our national independence" and were "sapping the foundation of our prosperity." Throughout the winter congressmen assailed the orders, drowning out the "whip-poor-will cry" for Canada of which John Randolph spoke. Repeal, Madison noted years later, would have postponed war and led to renewed negotiations on impressment "with fresh vigor & hopes, under the auspices of success in the case of the orders in council." The orders, he told Jared Sparks in 1830, were the only issue sturdy enough to bear a declaration of war.

The strength of this issue depended in part upon the reinforcement provided by impressment and other grievances, the flying buttresses of the central structure. Had the orders stood alone as a British challenge, war would probably not have come in 1812. But they became the key to the drive for war. No other factor, not even impressment, which most directly affected Northeasterners, struck all sections so impartially. Not even impressment exceeded the orders as a threat to America's position as a sovereign power. The Orders in Council were four years old when the Twelfth Congress met, going on five when America declared war. Why this delay? A natural desire to escape war partly explains it. Unreal faith in the power of trade boycotts, more justified expectations from the Erskine agreement, optimism engendered by the Cadore letter, hope that the Prince of Wales would replace his insane father's ministers with more friendly men, the anticipated impact of American measures of preparedness in Great Britain—all these counseled delay. When war ultimately came in June, 1812, the Orders in Council were the central issue. The requirements of consistency and a growing realization that American honor had been nearly exhausted were the immediate precipitants.

Since at least 1806 the United States government, and more particularly Republican congressmen, had proclaimed that America would not settle for whatever neutral trade the belligerents chose to let her enjoy. Profitable as such trade might be (and it often was extremely rewarding), the United States would demand its rights. Of course Jefferson, and especially Madison, did not demand utter surrender from their opponents, and they did not press certain claims they considered comparatively insignificant. In principle, however, they insisted that Britain and France recognize American rights and tailor their policies to them. Commercial pressure failed, political bargaining did not succeed, pleas for justice rebounded hollowly across the Atlantic. Still America maintained her claims, and the only remaining weapon to secure them was military power. The War Hawk Congress initiated preparedness, and the administration discreetly encouraged it, in the hope that England would surrender to this weapon what she had denied to boycotts, bargaining, and complaint.

Once embarked upon this course it became almost impossible to turn back. Many who voted for military measures without wanting war found it difficult to recede from the ground they had taken. The 10,000-man army proposed by the House of Representatives had an ostensible military purpose, but its supporters valued it chiefly as a demonstration of American determination. "We are not at war yet tho' David R. Williams hopes in god we soon shall be. Till we are at war I shall not go above 10,000 additional troops," Jonathan Roberts wrote in December. As time passed, Roberts became more and more bellicose. In February he wrote, "There seems to be no disposition to relax our war measures but I believe every body would be exceeding glad to remain at peace." A month later he stated, "I am well convinced we have no hope of peace but by vigorous preparations for War," but he added that he was ready to vote for war. As the spring passed, Roberts found his Quaker principles weakening, and he attended meetings very infrequently. In May and June this man, who had come to Washington determined that affairs should be forced to a solution and yet still hopeful war could be avoided, found himself more and more firmly committed to the cause of the War Hawks. The logic of the situation carried the Pennsylvanian and many of his colleagues forward.

In May John Randolph declared that, although many members of the majority would not follow the same course if they had it to do over again, "they have advanced to the brink of a precipice, and not left themselves room to turn." John Smilie admitted as much, arguing that while he would have preferred a further attempt at commercial coercion he now felt it necessary to go on toward war, since "if we now recede we shall be a reproach among nations." Willis Alston of North Carolina told Foster in March that Congress "should have originally taken another Course, now too late. It would have been better to protest against the belligerents & let Commerce thrive, this should have been done from the Beginning." Alston voted with the War Hawks on every important roll call. Speaker Clay and his supporters counted on and made frequent, effective reference to consistency in the closing months of the session. "After the pledges we have made, and the stand we have taken," Clay asked his colleagues, "are we now to cover ourselves with shame and indelible disgrace by retreating from the measures and ground we have taken?" Remembering the reputation of the Tenth Congress, many representatives felt that the answer was as obvious as Clay pictured it. Thus legislators who were really "scarecrow men" came to support a declaration of war. James A. Bayard, one Federalist who had foreseen this danger from the beginning, chided a friend for his shortsightedness, saying, "You have thought the thing all along a jest & I have no doubt in the commencement it was so, but jests sometimes become serious & end in earnest." So it was in 1812.

Consistency in congressmen, in a party, or in an administration became national honor when applied to the country as a whole. Since the acquisition of Louisiana in 1803, America had endured a steady diet of diplomatic humiliation. Jefferson, Madison, and the Congress of their time attempted to reverse European policy by applying economic pressure. This tactic failed because Congress lacked staying power and Republican leaders underestimated the strength of emotions abroad. Defeats continued. Napoleon's announcement of repeal merely worsened the situation, for his cynical contempt and the gullibility of the American administration soon became apparent. Republicans had jeopardized the national character and the reputation of the United States; they had created a situation from which war was almost the only honorable escape; they had encouraged England, where unfortunately such encouragement was too little needed, to act almost as though Lord Cornwallis had won the battle of Yorktown. "We have suffered and suffered until our forbearance has been pronounced cowardice and want of energy," a friend wrote Jonathan Roberts. Although talk of honor perhaps came too easily to the lips of some patriotic orators, the danger was real. When John C. Calhoun asserted that "if we submit to the pretensions of England, now openly avowed, the independence of this nation is lost. . . . This is the second struggle for our liberty," he scarcely exaggerated. When a Republican Fourth of July meeting at Boston toasted "The War—The second and last struggle for national freedom —A final effort to rescue from the deep the drowning honor of our country," the sentiment was apt.

In his first annual message after the outbreak of war, President Madison declared:

> To have shrunk under such circumstances from manly resistance would have been a degradation blasting our best and proudest hopes; it would have struck us from the high rank where the virtuous struggle of our fathers had placed us, and have betrayed the magnificent legacy which we hold in trust for future generations. It would have acknowledged that on the element which forms three-fourths of the globe we inhabit, and where all independent nations have

equal and common rights, the Americans were not an independent people, but colonists and vassals.

A year after the war ended, Henry Clay similarly stressed the theme of national honor and self-respect. "We had become the scorn of foreign Powers, and the contempt of our own citizens," he said. ". . . Let any man look at the degraded condition of this country before the war; the scorn of the universe, the contempt of ourselves. . . . What is our present situation? Respectability and character abroad—security and confidence at home. . . . our character and Constitutions are placed on a solid basis, never to be shaken." Years later, Augustus J. Foster philosophically wrote: "This war was certainly productive of much ill-blood between England and America, but in the opinion of the Speaker, Mr. Clay, and his friends it was as necessary to America as a duel is to a young naval officer to prevent his being bullied and elbowed in society. . . . Baleful as the war has been, I must confess that I think in this respect something has been gained by it." The President, the Speaker, and the envoy, who stood at the center of affairs during the war session, effectively summarized the one unanswerable argument for war. All the insults suffered by the United States, even the most important of them all, the Orders in Council, posed a greater threat in the realm of the spirit than in the world of the accountant and the merchant, the seaman and the frontiersman.

That war became imperative in June, 1812, does not mean that the American people desired it or that it could not have been avoided by greater wisdom in earlier years. Castlereagh's statement, in 1813, that "Great Britain has throughout acted towards the United States of America, with a spirit of amity, forbearance, and conciliation," was simply preposterous. While the policy of England was far less rigid than Americans often suggested, the self-righteous spirit of messianism engendered by the Napoleonic wars and a woeful underestimation of the price of American good will combined to prevent a reconciliation Jefferson and Madison eagerly desired. In America, most of the Federalists served their country ill, for, blinded by their own hatred of Napoleon and their inveterate contempt for the politicians who had displaced them, they sabotaged peaceful American resistance to British outrages and repeatedly declared that the Republicans lacked the fortitude to go to war. Roberts wrote in his memoirs, "There had all along been an idea cherish'd by the opposition, that the majority would not have nerve enough to meet war. This I believe, mainly induc'd Britain to persist in her aggressions. If she could have been made to believe . . . that we were a united people, & would act as such, war might have been avoided." The *Independent Chronicle* complained with a good deal of justice, "In every measure of government, the federal faction have rallied in opposition, and urged the Ministry to persist in their Orders. They forced the United States to the alternative, either to *surrender their independence,* or *maintain it by War.*" American disunion was clear enough, the desire to avoid war quite obvious. Despite the temporary and transparent policy advocated by Quincy, the Federalists contributed to that disunion and to British stubbornness.

Still, the Republican chieftains must bear primary responsibility for the war and the factionalism that made it an almost fatal test of the sturdiness of the nation they themselves had done so much to build. Whereas Washington and Adams kept objectives and means in harmony with one another, their successors often committed the United States to seek absolute right with inadequate weapons. Compromise, when sought, was usually offered at an impossible time. The justice of American demands is nearly undeniable, but the two Virginians, who prided themselves on the coolness of their logic, failed to perceive that justice was not a weapon in itself. They provided it with insufficient support, and they expected warring powers to view collateral problems with the same coolness that America exhibited. Economic warfare rested upon a rigid, mechanical conception of international trade. Although it was, of course, felt by the belligerents, it proved far more harmful to America, economically and morally, and served chiefly to convince Europe of the cowardice of the United States.

The two presidents secured not one important diplomatic objective after 1803. They scarcely challenged the development of factionalism within the Republican party, factionalism that deprived Congress of any real sense of direction. They provided public opinion with far too little leadership. They and their followers often spoke loudly and carried no stick at all. When at last a small group of congressmen declared that the time for half measures had ended and carried a majority with them down the road toward war, neither Great Britain nor the American people believed the destination would be reached. Thus British concession was discouraged and national union made impossible. In a state of military and psychological unpreparedness, the United States of America embarked upon a war to recover the self-respect destroyed by Republican leaders. Old John Taylor of Caroline wrote to the Secretary of State on the day of the declaration of war, "May God send you a safe deliverance."

FURTHER READING

Irving Brant, *James Madison,* 6 vols. (1941–1961)
Roger Brown, *The Republic in Peril: 1812* (1964)
A. L. Burt, *The United States, Great Britain, and British North America* (1940)
Harry L. Coles, *The War of 1812* (1965)
Clifford L. Egan, "The Origins of the War of 1812: Three Decades of Historical Writing," *Military Affairs,* 38 (1974), 72–75
Warren H. Goodman, "The Origins of the War of 1812: A Survey of Changing Interpretations," *Mississippi Valley Historical Review,* 28 (1941), 171–186
Reginal Horsman, *The Causes of the War of 1812* (1962)
Ralph Ketcham, *James Madison* (1971)
Alfred Thayer Mahan, *Sea Power in Its Relations to the War of 1812* (1905)
Bradford Perkins, *The First Rapprochement* (1955)
Bradford Perkins, ed., *The Causes of the War of 1812* (1962)
Norman K. Risjord, "1812: Conservatives, War Hawks, and the Nation's Honor," *William and Mary Quarterly,* 18 (1961), 196–210
Robert A. Rutland, *Madison's Alternatives* (1975)
Marshall Smelser, *The Democratic Republic: 1800–1815* (1968)
Patrick C. T. White, *A Nation on Trial* (1965)

7

The Monroe Doctrine

On December 2, 1823, President James Monroe gave his Annual Message to Congress. Therein he stated principles that became lasting guides to American diplomacy. He declared that the Western Hemisphere was no longer open to European colonization, that the New and Old Worlds were so different that the United States would abstain from European wars, and that the European powers should not intervene forcefully in the two Americas in an attempt to deny them their independence. These three points—non-colonization, two spheres, and non-intervention—were designed to warn the monarchies of Europe against crushing the independence of the new states of Latin America which had broken from the Spanish Empire.

Britain, which had profited commercially from the break-up of the Spanish mercantile system and, therefore, did not welcome a restoration of Spanish rule in South America, approached the United States with the idea of issuing a joint declaration warning against European intervention. North Americans, who also realized economic benefits from the dismantling of the Spanish Empire and who sympathized with the Latin American independence movements, grew worried about the apparent European threat. Monroe's "doctrine" constituted the American answer to this menace.

DOCUMENTS

The first document is British Foreign Secretary George Canning's August 1823 appeal to the American government in Washington to unite with Great Britain in a joint declaration against European intervention in the newly independent Latin American nations. President Monroe consulted his Cabinet about the proposal; he also asked the advice of two former Presidents, Thomas Jefferson and James

Madison. Jefferson's counsel is reprinted here, as is an entry from the diary of Secretary of State John Quincy Adams, who vigorously opposed cooperative action with Britain and won his point. The final selection is Monroe's famous message to Congress in December 1823.

George Canning's Overture for a Joint Declaration, 1823

My Dear Sir: Before leaving Town, I am desirous of bringing before you in a more distinct, but still in an unofficial and confidential, shape, the question which we shortly discussed the last time that I had the pleasure of seeing you.

Is not the moment come when our Governments might understand each other as to the Spanish American Colonies? And if we can arrive at such an understanding, would it not be expedient for ourselves, and beneficial for all the world, that the principles of it should be clearly settled and plainly avowed?

For ourselves we have no disguise.

1. We conceive the recovery of the Colonies by Spain to be hopeless.

2. We conceive the question of the recognition of them, as Independent States, to be one of time and circumstances.

3. We are, however, by no means disposed to throw any impediment in the way of an arrangement between them, and the mother country by amicable negotiation.

4. We aim not at the possession of any portion of them ourselves.

5. We could not see any portion of them transferred to any other Power, with indifference.

If these opinions and feelings are as I firmly believe them to be, common to your Government with ours, why should we hesitate mutually to confide them to each other; and to declare them in the face of the world?

If there be any European Power which cherishes other projects, which looks to a forcible enterprize for reducing the Colonies to subjugation, on the behalf or in the name of Spain; or which meditates the acquisition of any part of them to itself, by cession or by conquest; such a declaration on the part of your government and ours would be at once the most effectual and the least offensive mode of intimating our joint disapprobation of such projects.

It would at the same time put an end to all the jealousies of Spain with respect to her remaining Colonies—and to the agitation which prevails in those Colonies, an agitation which it would be but humane to allay; being determined (as we are) not to profit by encouraging it.

Do you conceive that under the power which you have recently received, you are authorized to enter into negotiation, and to sign any Convention upon this subject? Do you conceive, if that be not within your competence, you could exchange with me ministerial notes upon it?

Nothing could be more gratifying to me than to join with you in such a work, and, I am persuaded, there has seldom, in the history of the world, occurred an opportunity when so small an effort, of two friendly Governments, might produce so unequivocal a good and prevent such extensive calamities.

I shall be absent from London but three weeks at the utmost: but never so far distant but that I can receive and reply to any communication, within three or four days.

Jefferson's Advice to James Monroe, 1823

Dear Sir, The question presented by the letters you have sent me, is the most momentous which has ever been offered to my contemplation since that of Independence. That made us a nation, this sets our compass and points the course which we are to steer through the ocean of time opening on us. And never could we embark on it under circumstances more auspicious. Our first and fundamental maxim should be, never to entangle ourselves in the broils of Europe. Our second, never to suffer Europe to intermeddle with cis-Atlantic affairs. America, North and South, has a set of interests distinct from those of Europe, and peculiarly her own. She should therefore have a system of her own, separate and apart from that of Europe. While the last is laboring to become the domicile of despotism, our endeavor should surely be to make our hemisphere that of freedom. One nation, most of all, could disturb us in this pursuit; she now offers to lead, aid, and accompany us in it. By acceding to her proposition, we detach her from the bands, bring her mighty weight into the scale of free government, and emancipate a continent at one stroke, which might otherwise linger long in doubt and difficulty. Great Britain is the nation which can do us the most harm of any one, or all on earth; and with her on our side we need not fear the whole world. With her then, we should most sedulously cherish a cordial friendship; and nothing would tend more to knit our affections than to be fighting once more, side by side, in the same cause. . . .

But we have first to ask ourselves a question. Do we wish to acquire to our own confederacy any one or more of the Spanish provinces? I candidly confess, that I have ever looked on Cuba as the most interesting addition which could ever be made to our system of States. The control which, with Florida Point, this island would give us over the Gulf of Mexico, and the countries and isthmus bordering on it, as well as all those whose waters flow into it, would fill up the measures of our political well-being. Yet, as I am sensible that this can never be obtained, even with her own consent, but by war; and its independence, which is our second interest, (and especially its independence of England,) can be secured without it, I have no hesitation in abandoning my first wish to future chances, and accepting its independence, with peace and the friendship of England, rather than its association, at the expense of war and her enmity.

I could honestly, therefore, join in the declaration proposed, that we aim not at the acquisition of any of those possessions, that we will not stand in the way of any amicable arrangement between them and the Mother country; but that we will oppose, with all our means, the forcible interposition of any other power, as auxiliary, stipendiary, or under any other form or pretext, and most especially, their transfer to any power by conquest, cession, or acquisition in any other way. I should think it, therefore, advisable, that the Executive should encourage the British government to a continuance in the dispositions expressed in these letters, by an assurance of his concurrence with them as far as his authority goes; and that as it may lead to war, the declaration of which requires an act of Congress, the case shall be laid before them for consideration at their first meeting, and under the reasonable aspect in which it is seen by himself.

John Quincy Adams' Account of the Cabinet Meeting of November 7, 1823

Washington, *November 7th.*—Cabinet meeting at the President's from half-past one till four. Mr. Calhoun, Secretary of War, and Mr. Southard, Secretary of the Navy, present. The subject for consideration was, the confidential proposals of the British Secretary of State, George Canning, to R. Rush, and the correspondence between them relating to the projects of the Holy Alliance upon South America. There was much conversation, without coming to any definite point. The object of Canning appears to have been to obtain some public pledge from the Government of the United States, ostensibly against the forcible interference of the Holy Alliance between Spain and South America; but really or especially against the acquisition to the United States themselves of any part of the Spanish-American possessions.

Mr. Calhoun inclined to giving a discretionary power to Mr. Rush to join in a declaration against the interference of the Holy Allies, if necessary, even if it should pledge us not to take Cuba or the province of Texas; because the power of Great Britain being greater than ours to *seize* upon them, we should get the advantage of obtaining from her the same declaration we should make ourselves.

I thought the cases not parallel. We have no intention of seizing either Texas or Cuba. But the inhabitants of either or both may exercise their primitive rights, and solicit a union with us. They will certainly do no such thing to Great Britain. By joining with her, therefore, in her proposed declaration, we give her a substantial and perhaps inconvenient pledge against ourselves, and really obtain nothing in return. Without entering now into the enquiry of the expediency of our annexing Texas or Cuba to our Union, we should at least keep ourselves free to act as emergencies may arise, and not tie ourselves down to any principle which might immediately afterwards be brought to bear against ourselves.

Mr. Southard inclined much to the same opinion.

The President was averse to any course which should have the appearance of taking a position subordinate to that of Great Britain. . . .

I remarked that the communications recently received from the Russian

Minister, Baron Tuyl, afforded, as I thought, a very suitable and convenient opportunity for us to take our stand against the Holy Alliance, and at the same time to decline the overture of Great Britain. It would be more candid, as well as more dignified, to avow our principles explicitly to Russia and France, than to come in as a cock-boat in the wake of the British man-of-war.

This idea was acquiesced in on all sides, and my draft for an answer to Baron Tuyl's note announcing the Emperor's determination to refuse receiving any Minister from the South American Governments was read.

Monroe's Annual Message, 1823

At the proposal of the Russian Imperial Government, made through the minister of the Emperor residing here, a full power and instructions have been transmitted to the minister of the United States at St. Petersburg to arrange by amicable negotiation the respective rights and interests of the two nations on the northwest coast of this continent. . . . In the discussions to which this interest has given rise and in the arrangements by which they may terminate the occasion has been judged proper for asserting, as a principle in which the rights and interests of the United States are involved that the American continents, by the free and independent condition which they have assumed and maintain, are henceforth not to be considered as subjects for future colonization by any European powers. . . .

It was stated at the commencement of the last session that a great effort was then making in Spain and Portugal to improve the condition of the people of those countries, and that it appeared to be conducted with extraordinary moderation. It need scarcely be remarked that the result has been so far very different from what was then anticipated. Of events in that quarter of the globe, with which we have so much intercourse and from which we derive our origin, we have always been anxious and interested spectators. The citizens of the United States cherish sentiments the most friendly in favor of the liberty and happiness of their fellow-men on that side of the Atlantic. In the wars of the European powers in matters relating to themselves we have never taken any part, nor does it comport with our policy so to do. It is only when our rights are invaded or seriously menaced that we resent injuries or make preparation for our defense. With the movements in this hemisphere we are of necessity more immediately connected, and by causes which must be obvious to all enlightened and impartial observers. The political system of the allied powers is essentially different in this respect from that of America. This difference proceeds from that which exists in their respective Governments; and to the defense of our own, which has been achieved by the loss of so much blood and treasure, and matured by the wisdom of their most enlightened citizens, and under which we have enjoyed unexampled felicity, this whole nation is devoted. We owe it, therefore, to candor and to the amicable relations existing between the United States and those powers to declare that we should consider any attempt on their part to extend their system to any portion of this hemisphere as dangerous to our peace and safety. With the existing colonies or dependencies of any European power we have not interfered and shall not interfere. But with the Governments who have declared their independence and maintained it, and whose independence we have, on great consideration and on just principles, acknowledged, we could not view any interposition for the purpose of oppressing them, or controlling in any other manner their destiny, by any European power in any other light than as the manifestation of an unfriendly disposition toward the United States. In the war between those new Governments and Spain we declared our neutrality at the time of their recognition, and to this we have adhered, and shall continue to adhere, provided no change shall occur which, in the judgment of the competent authorities of this Government, shall make a corresponding change on the part of the United States indispensable to their security.

The late events in Spain and Portugal shew that Europe is still unsettled. Of this important fact no stronger proof can be adduced than that the allied powers should have thought it proper, on any principle satisfactory to themselves, to have interposed by force in the internal concerns of Spain. To what extent such interposition may be carried, on the same principle, is a question in which all independent powers whose governments differ from theirs are interested, even those most remote, and surely none more so than the United States. Our policy in regard to Europe, which was adopted at an early stage of the wars which have so long agitated that quarter of the globe, nevertheless remains the same, which is, not to interfere in the internal concerns of any of its powers; to consider the government *de facto* as the legitimate government for us; to cultivate friendly relations with it, and to preserve those relations by a frank, firm, and manly policy, meeting in all instances the just claims of every power, submitting to injuries from none. But in regard to those continents circumstances are eminently and conspicuously different. It is impossible that the allied powers should extend their political system to any portion of either continent without endangering our peace and happiness; nor can anyone believe that our southern brethren, if left to themselves, would adopt it of their own accord. It is equally impossible, therefore, that we should behold such interposition in any form with indifference.

ESSAYS

Dexter Perkins has traced the origins and evolution of the Monroe Doctrine in a series of scholarly volumes. In the first selection, although acknowledging that Americans were thinking about their commercial stakes when they decided to speak out for the non-colonization principle, he argues that American republican sympathies for the anti-colonial rebellions to the south lay behind the non-intervention clause. William Appleman Williams does not see the Monroe Doctrine in any way as a defensive measure, but as a United States attempt to establish its commercial supremacy in the Western Hemisphere. The third essay, by Ernest R. May of Harvard University, looks not at the question of whether the Doctrine was defensive or expansionist, but rather at the domestic political environment. He suggests that the President and leading contenders for the presidency in 1824, including Adams, reacted to European and Latin American events according to their personal political needs.

The Defense of Commerce and Ideals

DEXTER PERKINS

The famous declaration of December 2, 1823, which has come to be known as the Monroe Doctrine, had a dual origin and a dual purpose. On the one hand, it was the result of the advance of Russia on the northwest coast of America, and was designed to serve as a protest against this advance and to establish a general principle against Russian expansion. Referring to this question of the northwest, President Monroe laid down the principle in his message to Congress that "the American continents, by the free and independent condition which they have assumed and maintain, are henceforth not to be considered as subjects for future colonization by any European powers." On the other hand, the message was provoked by the fear of European intervention in South America to restore to Spain her revolted colonies, and was intended to give warning of the hostility of the United States to any such intervention. "With the governments [that is, of the Spanish-American republics] who have declared their independence, and maintained it," wrote the President, "and whose independence we have, on great consideration and just principles, acknowledged, we could not view any interposition for the purpose of oppressing them, or controlling in any other manner their destiny, by any European power, in any other light than as the manifestation of an unfriendly disposition toward the United States." . . .

Russian interest in the northwest coast of America goes back to the second quarter of the eighteenth century, to the days of the renowned navigator Vitus Behring, who discovered in 1727 the Straits that now bear his name, and fourteen years later the Alaskan coast in the neighborhood of latitude 58. Behring's explorations were followed by the voyages of fur traders and by the establishment of trading posts on the islands off the American mainland. After years of demoralizing competition on the part of private individuals, the Tsar determined to create a commercial monopoly for the exploitation of the rich fisheries to be found in that part of the world. By the ukase of July 8, 1799, the Russian-American Company was constituted, and to this company

Reprinted by permission of the author and publishers from *The Monroe Doctrine, 1823–1826* by Dexter Perkins, Cambridge, Massachusetts: Harvard University Press, Copyright © 1927 by the President and Fellows of Harvard College; renewed 1955 by Dexter Perkins.

were granted exclusive trading rights and jurisdiction along the coast as far south as latitude 55, and the right to make settlements on either side of that line in territory not occupied by other powers.

From an early date the operations of this Russian corporation were impeded by interlopers, very largely American. American vessels sold arms and ammunition to the natives, and secured a considerable part of the fur trade. As early as 1808 and 1810 complaints on the part of the Russian government began to be made to the government at Washington. There was, obviously enough, a situation that might lead to serious friction. . . .

On September 4/16, 1821, the Tsar Alexander I, acting at the instigation of the Russian monopoly, promulgated an imperial decree which renewed its privileges and confirmed its exclusive trading rights. This time the southern limit of these rights on the American coast was set, not at 55, but at 51 degrees. And in addition, all foreign vessels were forbidden, between Behring Straits and 51 degrees, to come within 100 Italian miles of the shore, on pain of confiscation. A Russian warship was dispatched to the northwest coast to enforce this remarkable decree, and every intention was manifested of barring all other nations from any participation whatever in the trade or fisheries of the region. Such a course of action very naturally provoked a protest, not only on the part of the United States, but also on the part of Great Britain. At this time the two Anglo-Saxon powers had joint ownership, under the convention of 1818, of the territory north from 42 degrees to a line yet to be determined, and the Russian claims of exclusive jurisdiction as far south as 51 degrees could hardly fail to be disquieting. Both from London and from Washington, therefore, came strong diplomatic remonstrance, and thus began a controversy which was to have the closest relationship to the famous pronouncement of 1823.

It is neither necessary nor desirable, in connection with this narrative, to trace the negotiations on the northwest question in all their details. What is of special interest here is the evolution of the non-colonization principle in the course of the discussions, the reception which it met at the hands of the interested powers, and the effect which it produced upon the diplomatic interchanges themselves. . . .

These discussions, begun in 1822, assumed little importance till the late spring of 1823. By that time it had been agreed that the question should be threshed out at St. Petersburg. In June the cabinet discussed the instructions which were to be sent to Mr. Middleton, American minister at the court of the Tsar. The Secretary of State declared it to be his conviction that the United States ought to contest the right of the Russian government to any territorial establishment on the American continents. Apparently this point of view did not pass unchallenged. It was pointed out that Russia would have little reason to accept such drastic doctrine. The United States, in maintaining it, would be asking everything, and conceding virtually nothing. A compromise was suggested and agreed upon by which this country would recognize the territorial claims of the Tsar north of 55 degrees. On this basis, the negotiations were actually to be conducted.

But Adams, with a curious inconsistency, did not on this account surrender the principle which was taking shape in his mind. At the very moment when he was perfecting the instructions to Middleton along the lines agreed upon in the cabinet, he declared himself to Tuyll, the Russian minister at Washington, in language very much more sweeping.

> I told him specially [he writes in his diary, alluding to an interview of July 17, 1823], that we should contest the right of Russia to *any* territorial establishment on this continent, and that we should assume distinctly the principle that the American continents are no longer subjects for *any* new European colonial establishments.

In this statement, almost five months before the appearance of the President's message, we have the non-colonization principle full-fledged, no longer merely a subject of cabinet debate, but explicitly put forward to the minister of another power, to the minister of the power perhaps most concerned in denying it. . . .

We have another statement of the non-colonization dogma almost contemporaneous with the interview with Tuyll. This is found in the instructions to Richard Rush, American minister at the Court of Saint James's. As England had an interest in the northwest controversy, it was obviously desirable that the diplomatic representative of the United States at London should be informed of the views of his government on the subject. Accordingly, on July 22, Adams sent forward a long and careful dispatch, in which he set forth his new theory in greater detail than at any other time. That dispatch will claim our special attention later. . . .

Adams secured Monroe's assent to his new principle in July. . . . Whether that assent was cordial and positive, or whether it was given as a mere matter of routine, we have no way of knowing. The President may have warmly approved the non-colonization doctrine; he may, on the other hand, have been little aware of its significance or its implications. On this point his writings provide us with no illumination. But at any rate, he *did* accept it. When, therefore, the Secretary of State drew up in November, the customary sketch of the topics of foreign policy which might interest the President in connection with the preparation of the forthcoming message, he naturally included in the paragraph on the Russian negotiations a reference to the new dogma. That paragraph was taken over almost without verbal change by Monroe, and thus it appeared in his communication to the Congress. These facts are clear, for we have the actual manuscript of Adams's outline of the diplomatic matters which he wished to draw to the attention of the President, and the language of that outline, so far as the non-colonization principle is concerned, corresponds almost exactly with the language of the message itself.

There was, apparently, no consideration of the principle in the cabinet discussion preceding the publication of the President's declaration. On this point Calhoun, then Secretary of War, was to testify many years later, and the silence of Adams's diary at the time confirms this testimony. There is, after all, nothing strange in such a circumstance. For the question of the hour, in November, 1823, was not the dispute with Russia, but the menace offered by the Holy Alliance to the independence of the States of South America. It was on these problems that all the debates turned; so, very naturally, the other problem was crowded out. . . .

Having thus examined the origins of the non-colonization clause in the message of 1823, we must now turn back to discuss the viewpoint and the reasoning which lay behind it. What was the motive in promulgating such a sweeping theory? What was the logic by which it might be supported?

In later interpretations of this part of the President's declaration, the emphasis has frequently been laid on the dangers involved in bringing the intrigues and conflicting territorial ambitions of Europe across the seas and into the New World. The United States, the argument has run, would thus be swept into the vortex of European politics, and exposed to the wicked influences for which those politics are notorious. Or it has been maintained that the new European territorial establishments would endanger American security, and ought to be opposed on these grounds.

These were not the bases, however, on which John Quincy Adams, in 1823, rested his opposition to colonization. The territorial aspects of colonization were not uppermost in his mind. He was thinking (and the point has been all too little emphasized) primarily of the commercial interests of the United States. In the history of American diplomacy, the principle of non-colonization has a certain affinity with the principle of the open door, asserted three quarters of a century later. It was based on immediate economic factors, not on vague fears of the future. It was because the colonial system meant commercial exclusion that the Secretary of State proclaimed its banishment from the American continents.

A close examination of Adams's point of view makes this clear. The principle of equality of commercial opportunity was one for which he contended with the utmost vigor, not only in the northwest controversy, but in other fields. He fought vigorously against the narrow policy of Great Britain in the British West Indies. He instructed the ministers to the South American states, when they set out in 1823, to contend for the principle that the new republics should treat all nations on the same footing, and that they should give no preferences, not even to their former mother country. The right to which he held most tenaciously in the dispute with Russia was not the right to full possession of the territory on the northwest (on this, as we have seen, it had been agreed to compromise on the line of 55 degrees); the right which he deemed of most importance was the right to trade, and this Middleton was instructed stoutly to maintain. In Adams's opinion the notion of European colonization was flatly opposed to the maintenance of these economic interests. The colonizing methods of the Old World, he told Stratford Canning in November, 1822, had always involved a more or less complete commercial monopoly. "Spain had set the example. She had forbidden foreigners from setting a foot in her Colonies, upon pain of death, and the other colonizing states of Europe had imitated the exclusion, though not the rigor of the penalty." From the very beginning, therefore, the Adams doctrine was knit up with the commercial interests of the United States. And so it remained throughout this early period of its development. Nothing shows this more clearly than the important dispatch of July 22, 1823, to Richard Rush, in which the whole theory of the doctrine found most careful expression. After declaring that the American continents will henceforth no longer be subjects for colonization, the American Secretary of State goes on to say:

> Occupied by civilized independent nations, they will be accessible to Europeans and to each other on that footing alone, and the Pacific Ocean in every part of it will remain open to the navigation of all nations, in like manner with the Atlantic. . . . The application of colonial principles of exclusion, therefore, cannot be admitted by the United States as lawful upon any part of the northwest coast of America, or as belonging to any European nation.

In these clear-cut and precise phrases, the innermost connection of the new dogma with American trading rights stands revealed.

It need not be contended, of course, that there was no more to it than this. It would be a clear exaggeration to say that Adams was contending for trading rights alone. He was thinking also of territorial settlement, as the very dispatch just quoted helps to make clear.

> It is not imaginable [he declared] that, in the present condition of the world, *any* European nation should entertain the project of settling a *colony* on the northwest coast of America. That the United States should form establishments there, with views of absolute territorial right and inland communication, is not only to be expected, but is pointed out by the finger of nature.

But these comments were made with an eye to the future. What was interesting in the immediate sense, "the only useful purpose to which the northwest coast of America" had been or could be made "subservient to the settlement of civilized men," was that of trade and of the fishery. The rights of the United States in this regard it was vital to maintain. On the territorial question there might be compromise; this we have already seen. But on the commercial question there ought to be none. "The right of carrying on trade with the natives throughout the northwest coast they [the United States] cannot renounce." Clearly, it was antagonism to commercial restriction that lay at the basis of the Secretary of State's famous dictum. . . .

The revolt of the Spanish-American colonies followed hard upon the Napoleonic conquest of Spain. From the very beginning, the sympathies of the United States appear to have been engaged upon the side of the revolutionists. American sentiment was distinctly favorable to a movement for independence which had at least a superficial resemblance to that of 1776, and which could easily be regarded as an effort to throw off an odious tyranny and establish throughout the greater part of the New World the blessings of republican government. Fellow feeling in a struggle for liberty and independence was an essential element in forming the policy of the United States with regard to South America.

It was indeed, to all appearances, a far more important element than any hope of material gain. In the formative period of this country's relations with the new states of South America, certainly down to 1822, there is little evidence of the working of economic interest. In the absence of exact statistics for much of the period, and in view of the paucity of references to trade with the Spanish colonies, it is difficult to speak with precision. But certain general observations may safely be made. In the first place, the trade with Cuba and with Spain itself was far more important than the trade with the new republics of the South. A diplomatic policy favorable to the South-American states might jeopardize or even sacrifice commercial interests superior to those which it would promote. If economic reasons were to be regarded as shaping political developments, there were more reasons for a cautious than for an active line of policy. In the second place, there was not, as in the case of Great Britain, any powerful pressure from the commercial classes in favor of colonial independence. The evidence on this point is partly negative, it is true, but it is negative evidence of the strongest kind. One can hardly imagine that the existence of such pressure would pass unnoticed in the debates in Congress, and in such contemporary records as the diary and writings of Adams, and the correspondence of Monroe. But it is not necessary to depend upon this fact alone. Statistics indicate that as late as 1821 only 2.3 per cent of American exports and 1.6 per cent of American imports were South American in destination or origin. In March of the same year Adams could tell Henry Clay that he had little expectation of any commercial advantages from the recognition of the new states. And even later, in 1823, the Secretary of State speaks of commercial development as a matter of hope for the future rather than a present accomplishment. That hope may, of course, have counted for something from the beginning. But, all things considered, it seems highly probable that political sympathy, not economic self-interest, lay at the root of American policy so far as it revealed itself as favorable to the new states of South America.

From the very beginnings of the South American struggle this sympathy asserts itself. As early as 1810, the American government, then headed by Madison, sent agents to South America—Joel R. Poinsett to La Plata and Chile, and Robert Lowry to Venezuela. At the end of 1811, James Monroe, then Secretary of State, thought seriously of raising the question of the recognition of the new states, and of exerting American influence in Europe to secure like action from the principal European powers. He also entered into informal relations with agents from at least one of the revolted provinces. And in Congress, at the same time, in response to the sympathetic language of the President's message, a resolution was passed, expressing a friendly solicitude in the welfare of these communities, and a readiness, when they should become nations by a just exercise of their rights, to unite with the Executive in establishing such relations with them as might be necessary. Thus, very early in the course of the colonial struggle, the general bent of American policy was made plain.

But it was some time before the South-American question became a matter of really first-rate importance. In the years 1810 to 1815, the prime concern of the administration at Washington lay in the preservation of American neutral rights, and, from 1812 to 1814, in the prosecution of the war with Great Britain. Moreover, the course of events in the overseas dominions of Spain was for some time hardly favorable to the revolutionists. In 1814 and 1815, indeed, it seemed entirely possible that the revolutionary movements might be snuffed out. In the north, in Venezuela and Colombia, the army of the Spanish general, Morillo, won victory on victory, and drove the leader of the revolutionists, Bolívar, into exile. In the south, in Chile, Osorio reëstablished the power of the mother country, and in Buenos Aires the struggles of contending factions weakened the new government that had been set up. Under such circumstances, prudence would have dictated a policy of reserve on the part of the United States, even if its government had not been preoccupied with other and more pressing matters.

With the year 1817, however, a change takes place in the status of the colonial question. In the case of one, at any rate, of the new states, the struggle was virtually over. The republic of La Plata had declared its independence and successfully maintained it, so that not a Spanish soldier remained upon its territory; even more, it had dispatched its great general, San Martín, across the Andes, and, with the victory of Chacabuca, taken a great step toward the final liberation of Chile. Perhaps as a result of these developments, interest in favor of the recognition of the new state began to develop in the United States; there were numerous newspaper articles in the summer of 1817, notably the discussions of Lautaro in the Richmond *Enquirer;* and the affairs of South America became a matter of debate both in the councils of the administration and in the halls of Congress.

It is interesting, in the light of later events, to examine these developments. So far as the administration was concerned, the point especially to be emphasized is the warm sympathy of the President himself with the South American cause. There has been a tendency in some quarters, in connection with the evolution of the Monroe Doctrine, to ascribe a very slight importance to the views of the very man who promulgated it. Mr. Monroe has been pictured as "slow-moving and lethargic," as prodded forward only by the more vigorous mind and more determined will of John Quincy Adams, his Secretary of State. But as a matter of fact, Monroe was at all times quite as much interested in the colonial cause, and in as full sympathy with it, as Adams. From the very beginning of his presidency, he showed his concern with regard to it. As early as May, 1817, some months before Adams took office, the President had determined upon a mission of inquiry to the provinces of La Plata, and as early as October he questioned his cabinet on the expediency of recognizing the government of that region. He raised the problem again in the succeeding May, even suggesting the possibility of sending an armed force to the coast of South America, to protect American commerce, "and to countenance the patriots." His views, it is true, were to be overruled or modified by his advisers. But his interest in positive action was very real, and is quite consistent with the character of the man whose flaming sympathy with French republicanism had been so obvious in his earlier career. . . .

In the discussions upon the northwest controversy, as has been seen, trading influences contributed very materially to the stand which was taken by the administration. But it would be difficult to prove anything of the kind with regard to the warning given to Europe against intervention in South America. This is not to say that such influences necessarily played no rôle at all. John Quincy Adams, of course, came from the great shipping section of the Union. In his instructions to the American ministers sent out to Colombia and La Plata in the spring of 1823, he had laid a very considerable emphasis upon freedom of commercial opportunity, though he was by no means exuberantly optimistic as to the possibilities of the South American trade. In the cabinet discussions of November, he had, on one occasion, brought forward as a reason for action the fact that if the United States stood aside and Great Britain alone vetoed the designs of the Continental powers, the latter country would gain great commercial advantages. It is worth noting, too, that our commerce with the Spanish-American states was considerably more important in 1823 than it had been two or three years before. But these facts would be a slender foundation on which to base an "economic interpretation" of the Monroe Doctrine. And they are offset by many others. Whoever reads the pages of Adams's diary will find it hard to believe that trading considerations played a very considerable rôle in his mind. The distaste produced by the homilies of the Tsar, a genuine and robust disapproval of the trend of European politics, a desire to set forth the political doctrines of the United States in opposition to those of the Alliance, these are the factors that bulked largest in his thought. Economic considerations there may have been in the background. But it was a profound political antagonism that gave force to the action which he advocated in the councils of President Monroe.

With the President himself, this antagonism was even more keenly felt. The letter to Jefferson, written early in June, seems to express his point of view pretty accurately. He was anxious to strike a blow for liberty, and the situation in the fall of 1823 offered him an excellent opportunity. To this must be added the fact that Monroe, like Calhoun, feared that an assault upon the liberties of the Spanish Americans would be dangerous to the safety of the United States itself. It was these considerations, beyond a doubt, that sharpened his pen as he wrote the declaration of December 2. . . .

Monroe's belief in the superiority of American institutions, his conviction that the extension of European dominion would be dangerous to our peace and safety—these are propositions that are hardly capable of rigorous demonstration. Perhaps their strength lies in just that fact. Yet there is, I think, one thing more to be said for them. In resting his opposition to European intermeddling in Spanish America on the "peace and safety" of the United States, the President was taking up a strong position from the legal and moral point of view. For he was basing American policy on the right of self-preservation, a right that is and always has been recognized as fundamental in international law. If in very truth the interposition of the Holy Alliance in South America imperilled the peace and safety of the United States, then the President's right to protest against it was obvious. Nor was it to be expected that as to the reality of the peril he would accept the conclusions of European statesmen. He stood secure in his own conviction and on his own ground.

Manifesto of the American Empire

WILLIAM APPLEMAN WILLIAMS

Though it is generally treated as the cornerstone of American diplomacy, most analyses of the doctrine emphasize its negative aspects. It is thus presented as a defensive statement of the territorial and administrative integrity of North and South America: no further colonization, no transfer or extension of existing claims, and in return America would not interfere in European affairs. This standard interpretation neglects three major facts: the men who formulated it were concerned as much with European commercial and economic expansion as with its schemes for colonization; they viewed it as a positive, expansionist statement of American supremacy in the hemisphere, and Monroe actually intervened in European politics with the very same speech in which he asserted that Europe should stay out of American affairs.

Aware that the political economy of the United States was established, and properly interpreting the results of the War of 1812 as being fundamentally favorable to its position in the hemisphere, American leaders reached an obvious conclusion. If they could exclude further European penetration as Spain's authority collapsed, then the United States would remain as the predominant power in the hemisphere. Monroe thus reasserted the expansionist thesis at the end of his message of December 2, 1823, which announced the doctrine. Having urged further support for manufactures and internal improvements, as well as warning Europe off Latin America while he encouraged the Greek revolution, he concluded with this well-nigh classic paraphrase of Madison's theory. "It is manifest that by enlarging the basis of our system, and increasing the number of States, the system itself has been greatly strengthened in both its [state and national] branches. Consolidation and disunion have thereby been rendered equally impracticable."

As one who was equally familiar with Madison's theory of expansion (he mentioned it specifically in his eulogy of Madison), Adams fully expected the United States to acquire Cuba, Texas, and other tidbits of territory in North America. But he was at least as concerned with establishing American commercial supremacy as he was with blocking further colonial experiments by European nations. This balanced expansionist sentiment behind the Monroe Doctrine was well revealed in the congressional discussions about Oregon which some thought was threatened by Russia as well as by England. Francis Baylies of Massachusetts might have been expected to concern himself with the "magnificent prospects" of the Pacific commerce, but he also quoted Napo-

From pp. 215–218 in *The Contours of American History* by William Appleman Williams (World Publishing Co., 1961). Reprinted by permission of Thomas Y. Crowell Company, Inc.

leon to emphasize his support for territorial expansion: he "never uttered words of more wisdom than when he said, 'I want ships, commerce, and colonies.'" Robert Wright of Maryland called for expansion because "there is less danger of separatism in a confederacy of 20 or 30 States than in one of a smaller number."

Senator James Barbour agreed. "Our advance in political science has already cancelled the dogmas of theory. We have already ascertained . . . that republics are not necessarily limited to small territories. . . . Whether America is capable of indefinite extent, must be left to posterity to decide." And speaking for a growing consensus, John Floyd of Virginia accurately concluded that "all contemplate with joy" continued westward expansion. It would provide land for farmers, "procure and protect the fur trade," "engross the whale trade," and "control the South Sea trade. . . . All this rich commerce could be governed, if not engrossed, by capitalists at Oregon."

Adams shared such commercial interest in the Northwest, and it contributed to his thinking about the Monroe Doctrine. Even more in his mind, however, was the importance of trade with Latin America. By 1820, when Adams, in his instructions to American agents, described it as "deserving of particular attention," this trade had developed into a significant commerce that vigorous European intervention would curtail and perhaps even destroy. Baltimore specialized in flour and furniture, but Salem, New York, Philadelphia, and even New Orleans, shipped shoes, cotton textiles, fertilizer, pitch, and lumber into such cities as Rio de Janeiro. The carrying trade was also important. American shippers carried Asian goods to Chile, Argentine beef to Cuba, and European items to the entire region. British agents reported to Foreign Secretary George Canning that Americans controlled the Argentine flour market, that their tonnage in Uruguay was "greater than that of any other nation," and that Peru's commerce with Asia "has been entirely engrossed by the North Americans."

Aware of this strong position, Henry Clay predicted that in half a century Americans, "in relation to South America," would "occupy the same position as the people of New England do to the rest of the United States." The implications of Clay's remark unquestionably disturbed some southerners in 1820 as much as the validity of his prediction was to upset Latin Americans in the 20th century. His enthusiastic campaign to establish an American System embracing the hemisphere was important for several reasons. Promising "mercantile profits," an influx of Spanish gold, and markets for the farmers and other entrepreneurs of the Mississippi west, he also assured his countrymen that the expansion of America's ideological principles would provide military as well as economic security. Being like the United States, he argued, the new countries would not be prone to oppose its basic policies.

Adams was wary of Clay's rambunctious ideological assertiveness, but he was fully agreed on the importance of commercial activity. His instructions of May 27, 1823, to an American agent who was being sent to Colombia left no doubt about his basic strategy. The American political economy was now strong enough to take advantage of its great relative superiority over the emerging new nations. "As navigators and manufacturers, *we* are already so far advanced in a career upon which *they* are yet to enter," he explained, "that we may, for many years after the conclusion of the war, maintain with them a commercial intercourse, highly beneficial to both parties, as *carriers* to and for them of numerous articles of manufacture and foreign produce."

The Product of Domestic Politics

ERNEST R. MAY

At latest count, the Library of Congress card catalogue had 359 entries under "Monroe Doctrine." The bibliography includes some of the best works in diplomatic history—among them Samuel Flagg Bemis's *John Quincy Adams and the Foundations of American Foreign Policy,* Bradford Perkins's *Castlereagh and Adams,* Dexter Perkins's *The Monroe Doctrine, 1823–1826,* Harold W. V. Temperley's *The Foreign Policy of Canning,* and Arthur P. Whitaker's *The United States and the Independence of Latin America.* Why, then, another study?

My answer has to start autobiographically. About ten years ago, I went through some of the John Quincy Adams manuscripts in the Massachusetts Historical Society. The supervisor of the Adams Papers project had invited me to edit a definitive edition of John Quincy Adams's diary. In considering the proposal, I examined what the archive contained for the period, 1817–1825, when Adams was secretary of state—his diary, his calendar, his wife's diary, his letterbooks, and his incoming correspondence. Although I decided not to do the editing, I learned a good deal about the man and the period.

Not long afterward, I started to write a short account of the making of the Monroe Doctrine. It was to be for nonscholarly readers, simply recounting the decision. I could not write it. Trying to do so, I found that I could not explain even to myself why the Monroe administration had acted as it did.

Books on the doctrine analyzed the principles which had been announced: European powers should not help Spain regain her former colonies; European monarchies should not impose their ideology on nations in the New World; and there should be no future European colonization in the Americas. Dexter Perkins made a convincing case that the dangers envisioned had been unreal. To the extent that statesmen on the continent contemplated aiding Spain, overturning American republics, or establishing new colonies in the Western Hemisphere, they were deterred by fear of Britain, not by concern about the United States.

It was clear from the record, however, that the American doctrine had been developed in large part because Monroe and his advisers faced issues which

Reprinted by permission of the author and publishers from *The Making of the Monroe Doctrine* by Ernest R. May, Cambridge, Massachusetts: The Belknap Press of Harvard University Press, Copyright © 1975 by the President and Fellows of Harvard College.

seemed to require decisions. They had an invitation to join Britain in resisting the alleged European threat to Latin America. Everyone recognized that acceptance would mean abandonment of the posture previously held and, as Monroe put it, entanglement "in European politicks, & wars." On the other hand, Monroe, and most of those whom he consulted, saw the offer as so advantageous that it should not be turned down. Except for the maxim that there should be no future colonization, the Monroe Doctrine expressed general agreement with British positions.

Coincidentally, the administration faced the question of whether to recognize or aid Greeks who were fighting for independence from the Ottoman Empire. There was loud public demand to do so. The argument for resisting this demand was again to avoid entanglement in European politics. Daniel Webster summarized a popular view, however, when he asked how the United States could defend liberty in Latin America and ignore the same cause in Europe.

In the upshot, the British alliance did not materialize, and the United States did not lead in recognizing Greece. These decisions, even more than the rhetoric that accompanied them, reaffirmed a policy of nonentanglement. But why?

The literature on the Monroe Doctrine did not answer this question—at least not to my satisfaction. Among those who knew of the British alliance overture, everyone except Secretary of State Adams favored acceptance. Adams was the only member of the administration consistently to oppose recognition of Greece. Explaining why the outcomes were victories for Adams, Bemis says simply that his "views by the force of their reason had prevailed over everybody." . . . The same explanation appears in other accounts. In fact, however, there is no evidence that Adams changed anyone's opinion. His own diary records that his colleagues held much the same views at the end as at the beginning. Yet Adams got what he wanted.

When puzzling about what besides Adams's persuasive powers might have produced this outcome, I remembered what had struck me when poring through his manuscripts—the quantity of diary entries and especially correspondence that had to do with the approaching presidential election. It was a preoccupation in his household. His wife characterized the coming contest as "a mighty struggle which arouses alike all the passions and most ardent feelings of mankind." And, as it happened, most of his rivals were in one way or another participants in the foreign debate. William H. Crawford and John C. Calhoun were fellow members of Monroe's cabinet. Henry Clay was the speaker of the house. Andrew Jackson, who had just begun to be talked of as a candidate, was a newly elected member of the Senate. None of the existing accounts of the Monroe Doctrine makes more than passing reference to the "mighty struggle" which filled the mind of Mrs. Adams. Yet the more I thought about it, the more I became convinced that the struggle for the presidency might provide a key to understanding why the foreign policy debates came out as they did. . . .

The week between the two cabinet meetings [in November 1823] brought the dismaying news that Cadiz had fallen and that the French were in control of all Spain. Reportedly, moreover, a French fleet was already preparing to transport across the Atlantic a large contingent of the Spanish troops that had fought for Ferdinand in Spain. The American government, it appeared, no longer had leisure for a long debate.

Monroe seemed on the verge of decision. During the week, he repeatedly summoned Adams to the White House. He said that the fall of Cadiz alarmed him and that he feared all the South American states might be reconquered. Just before the cabinet was to meet, he showed Adams the letters from Jefferson and Madison.

Adams wrote in his diary that he thought the President to be still undecided. Probably, Monroe was exerting himself to get Adams's concurrence in a decision to accept Canning's terms, for he must have recognized that Adams would see the potential political costs to himself, and, if he had not known it before, he had learned from Adams's recent published exchanges with Jonathan Russell about the Ghent negotiations that it was the secretary of state's habit to keep detailed records useful for defending himself in controversies. Monroe could foresee at least a slight possibility that Adams would dissent from a decision to ally with England, make his dissent known through newspapers supporting him and through friends such as Rufus King, the chairman of the Senate Foreign Relations Committee, or perhaps even resign and speak out against the administration. If so, the charge of courting Federalists would be leveled against Calhoun, and Monroe himself might come under attack, losing his cherished position as President of the whole nation and a figure above politics. The whole purpose of accepting Canning's offer might then be undone by a domestic debate which persuaded both the English and the continental powers that Americans were too divided to act effectively. . . .

Since foreign policy is nearly always debated and analyzed in terms of national interests, lofty moral purposes, and the like, it may seem perverse to contend that the actual decisions may be controlled by domestic political factors which the policymakers seldom mention, either at the time or in their later reconstructions. But the character of foreign policy debate is, in fact, indicative of the high uncertainty that shrouds it. National interest is almost as empty a concept as the good of mankind, and standards of right and wrong as applied to nations are equally vague. More specific discussion of issues tends to concern contingencies which are hard to predict and largely uncontrollable—the outcomes of political processes in other governmental systems. In these circumstances, it is not surprising that the positions which men take may be products of rationalization. Indeed, this is probably more likely to be the case with foreign policy than domestic policy, for on domestic issues the interests of specific groups of citizens may be more evident and the criteria for distinguishing right from wrong may be more clear.

In the instance of the Monroe Doctrine, the positions adopted by American policymakers seem to me to be best explained as functions of their domestic ambitions—Monroe's, to leave the presidency without being followed by recrimination and to be succeeded by someone who would not repudiate his policies; Adams's, Calhoun's, and Clay's, to become President; Jefferson's,

Gallatin's, and perhaps Madison's, to see Crawford succeed. Consistently with their fundamental beliefs, any of these men could have taken different positions. Adams, for example, could have reasoned just as easily as Jefferson that concert with England would guarantee America's independence, security, and peace. He actually said as much not long before the specific issues materialized. The processes producing the actual foreign policy decisions are better understood as bargaining encounters among men with differing perspectives and ambitions than as debates about the merits of different policies. And the outcomes are most explicable as ones that equilibrated the competing or conflicting interests of men with differing political assets.

FURTHER READING

Harry Ammon, *James Monroe* (1970)

Samuel Flagg Bemis, *John Quincy Adams and the Foundations of American Foreign Policy* (1949)

George Dangerfield, *The Awakening of American Nationalism, 1815–1828* (1965)

George Dangerfield, *The Era of Good Feelings* (1952)

J. A. Logan, *No Transfer* (1961)

Bradford Perkins, *Castlereagh and Adams* (1964)

Dexter Perkins, *A History of the Monroe Doctrine* (1955)

Armin Rappaport, ed., *The Monroe Doctrine* (1964)

J. Fred Rippy, *Rivalry of the United States and Great Britain over Latin America, 1808–1830* (1929)

E. H. Tatum, Jr., *The United States and Europe, 1815–1823* (1926)

A. P. Whitaker, *The United States and the Independence of Latin America, 1800–1830* (1941)

8

Manifest Destiny and the War with Mexico

The 1840s witnessed an expansionist surge that netted the United States new territories. Texas, Oregon, and the California territory, after the use or threat of force and much debate, became parts of the expanding American empire. Expansionism was certainly not new to the United States in the 1840s. From infancy the nation had been expansionist and, between the Louisiana Purchase of 1803 and the treaty ending the war with Mexico in 1848, the United States had moved steadily westward, enlarging its territory, pushing out its boundaries, and removing Native Americans. The 1840s, however, were particularly active. What caused this burst of territorial acquisitiveness? James K. Polk as President? A cumulative and traditional American expansionism? Idealism? Commercial interest? The answers vary, as the selections in this chapter make evident.

DOCUMENTS

John L. O'Sullivan is credited with having popularized the idea of Manifest Destiny. As editor of the *Democratic Review*, he flamboyantly sketched an unbounded American future of democratic mission and territorial expansion. The first document is selected from his "The Great Nation of Futurity," published in 1839. James K. Polk became President in 1845. An avowed expanionist, he eyed Mexican lands and disputed territories in the Southwest and Northwest. His Inaugural Address of March 4, 1845, made the case for absorbing Texas and Oregon. The third document is Polk's War Message of May 11, 1846, wherein he asked Congress to declare war against Mexico and presented the United States' grievances against its southern neighbor. The outbreak of war and its endorsement by Congress generated spirited debate in the nation. Many critics believed that Polk deliberately provoked hostilities and that expansionists were using war to extend slavery. The final selection is the anti-war resolution drafted by Charles Sumner and passed by the Massachusetts legislature in 1847. This document demonstrates the fact that the nation was hardly united over the means used to acquire new lands and that passions were heated, indeed.

John L. O'Sullivan on Manifest Destiny, 1839

The American people having derived their origin from many other nations, and the Declaration of National Independence being entirely based on the great principle of human equality, these facts demonstrate at once our disconnected position as regards any other nation; that we have, in reality, but little connection with the past history of any of them, and still less with all antiquity, its glories, or its crimes. On the contrary, our national birth was the beginning of a new history, the formation and progress of an untried political system, which separates us from the past and connects us with the future only; and so far as regards the entire development of the natural rights of man, in moral, political, and national life, we may confidently assume that our country is destined to be *the great nation* of futurity.

It is so destined, because the principle upon which a nation is organized fixes its destiny, and that of equality is perfect, is universal. It presides in all the operations of the physical world, and it is also the conscious law of the soul—the self-evident dictates of morality, which accurately defines the duty of man to man, and consequently man's rights as man. Besides, the truthful annals of any nation furnish abundant evidence, that its happiness, its greatness, its duration, were always proportionate to the democratic equality in its system of government. . . .

What friend of human liberty, civilization, and refinement, can cast his view over the past history of the monarchies and aristocracies of antiquity, and not deplore that they ever existed? What philanthropist can contemplate the oppressions, the cruelties, and injustice inflicted by them on the masses of mankind, and not turn with moral horror from the retrospect?

America is destined for better deeds. It is our unparalleled glory that we have no reminiscences of battle fields, but in defence of humanity, of the oppressed of all nations, of the rights of conscience, the rights of personal enfranchisement. Our annals describe no scenes of horrid carnage, where men were led on by hundreds of thousands to slay one another, dupes and victims to emperors, kings, nobles, demons in the human form called heroes. We have had patriots to defend our homes, our liberties, but no aspirants to crowns or thrones; nor have the American people ever suffered themselves to be led on by wicked ambition to depopulate the land, to spread desolation far and wide, that a human being might be placed on a seat of supremacy.

We have no interest in the scenes of antiquity, only as lessons of avoidance of nearly all their examples. The expansive future is our arena, and for our history. We are entering on its untrodden space, with the truths of God in our minds, beneficent objects in our hearts, and with a clear conscience unsullied by the past. We are the nation of human progress, and who will, what can, set limits to our onward march? Providence is with us, and no earthly power can. We point to the everlasting truth on the first page of our national declaration, and we proclaim to the millions of other lands, that "the gates of hell"—the powers of aristocracy and monarchy—"shall not prevail against it."

The far-reaching, the boundless future will be the era of American greatness. In its magnificent domain of space and time, the nation of many nations is destined to manifest to mankind the excellence of divine principles; to establish on earth the noblest temple ever dedicated to the worship of the Most High—the Sacred and the True. Its floor shall be a hemisphere—its roof the firmament of the star-studded heavens, and its congregation an Union of many Republics, comprising hundreds of happy millions, calling, owning no man master, but governed by God's natural and moral law of equality, the law of brotherhood—of "peace and good will amongst men." . . .

Yes, we are the nation of progress, of individual freedom, of universal enfranchisement. Equality of rights is the cynosure of our union of States, the grand exemplar of the correlative equality of individuals; and while truth sheds its effulgence, we cannot retrograde, without dissolving the one and subverting the other. We must onward to the fulfilment of our mission—to the entire development of the principle of our organization—freedom of conscience, freedom of person, freedom of trade and business pursuits, universality of freedom and equality. This is our high destiny, and in nature's eternal, inevitable decree of cause and effect we must accomplish it. All this will be our future history, to establish on earth the moral dignity and salvation of man—the immutable truth and beneficence of God. For this blessed mission to the nations of the world, which are shut out from the life-giving light of truth, has America been chosen; and her high example shall smite unto death the tyranny of kings, hierarchs, and oligarchs, and carry the glad tidings of peace and good will where myriads now endure an existence scarcely more enviable than that of beasts of the field. Who, then, can doubt that our country is destined to be *the great nation* of futurity?

James K. Polk on Texas and Oregon, 1845

I regard the question of annexation as belonging exclusively to the United States and Texas. They are independent powers competent to contract, and foreign nations have no right to interfere with them or to take exceptions to their reunion. Foreign powers do not seem to appreciate the true character of our Government. Our Union is a confederation of independent States, whose policy is peace with each other and all the world. To enlarge its limits is to extend the dominions of peace over additional territories and increasing millions. The world has nothing to fear from military ambition in our Government. While the Chief Magistrate and the popular branch of Congress are elected for short terms by the suffrages of those millions who must in their own persons bear all the burdens and miseries of war, our Government can not be otherwise than pacific. Foreign powers should therefore look on the annexation of Texas to the United States not as the conquest of a nation seeking to extend her dominions by arms and violence, but as the peaceful acquisition of a territory once her own, by adding another member to our confederation, with the consent of that member, thereby diminishing the chances of war and opening to them new and ever-increasing markets for their products.

To Texas the reunion is important, because the strong protecting arm of our Government would be extended over her, and the vast resources of her fertile soil and genial climate would be speedily developed, while the safety of New Orleans and of our whole southwestern frontier against hostile aggression, as well as the interests of the whole Union, would be promoted by it.

In the earlier stages of our national existence the opinion prevailed with some that our system of confederated States could not operate successfully over an extended territory, and serious objections have at different times been made to the enlargement of our boundaries. These objections were earnestly urged when we acquired Louisiana. Experience has shown that they were not well founded. The title of numerous Indian tribes to vast tracts of country has been extinguished; new States have been admitted into the Union; new Territories have been created and our jurisdiction and laws extended over them. As our population has expanded, the Union has been cemented and strengthened. As our boundaries have been enlarged and our agricultural population has been spread over a large surface, our federative system has acquired additional strength and security. It may well be doubted whether it would not be in greater danger of overthrow if our present population were confined to the comparatively narrow limits of the original thirteen States than it is now that they are sparsely settled over a more expanded territory. It is confidently believed that our system may be safely extended to the utmost bounds of our territorial limits, and that as it shall be extended the bonds of our Union, so far from being weakened, will become stronger.

None can fail to see the danger to our safety and future peace if Texas remains an independent state or becomes an ally or dependency of some foreign nation more powerful than herself. Is there one among our citizens who would not prefer perpetual peace with Texas to occasional wars, which so often occur between bordering independent nations? Is there one who would not prefer free intercourse with her to high duties on all our products and manufactures which enter her ports or cross her frontiers? Is there one who would not prefer an unrestricted communication with her citizens to the frontier obstructions which must occur if she remains out of the Union? Whatever is good or evil in the local institutions of Texas will remain her own whether annexed to the United States or not. None of the present States will be responsible for them any more than they are for the local institutions of each other. They have confederated together for certain specified objects. Upon the same principle that they would refuse to form a perpetual union with Texas

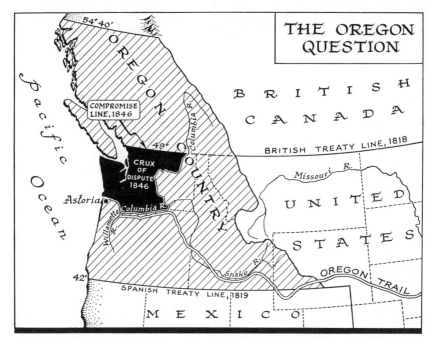

because of her local institutions our forefathers would have been prevented from forming our present Union. Perceiving no valid objection to the measure and many reasons for its adoption vitally affecting the peace, the safety, and the prosperity of both countries, I shall on the broad principle which formed the basis and produced the adoption of our Constitution, and not in any narrow spirit of sectional policy, endeavor by all constitutional, honorable, and appropriate means to consummate the expressed will of the people and Government of the United States by the reannexation of Texas to our Union at the earliest practicable period.

Nor will it become in a less degree my duty to assert and maintain by all constitutional means the right of the United States to that portion of our territory which lies beyond the Rocky Mountains. Our title to the country of the Oregon is "clear and unquestionable," and already are our people preparing to perfect that title by occupying it with their wives and children. But eighty years ago our population was confined on the west by the ridge of the Alleghanies. Within that period—within the lifetime, I might say, of some of my hearers—our people, increasing to many millions, have filled the eastern valley of the Mississippi, adventurously ascended the Missouri to its headsprings, and are already engaged in establishing the blessings of self-government in valleys of which the rivers flow to the Pacific. The world beholds the peaceful triumphs of the industry of our emigrants. To us belongs the duty of protecting them adequately wherever they may be upon our soil. The jurisdiction of our laws and the benefits of our republican institutions should be extended over them in the distant regions which they have selected for their homes. The increasing facilities of intercourse will easily bring the States, of which the formation in that part of our territory can not be long delayed, within the sphere of our federative Union. In the meantime every obligation imposed by treaty or conventional stipulations should be sacredly respected.

Polk's War Message, 1846

The existing state of the relations between the United States and Mexico renders it proper that I should bring the subject to the consideration of Congress. . . .

The strong desire to establish peace with Mexico on liberal and honorable terms, and the readiness of this Government to regulate and adjust our boundary and other causes of difference with that power on such fair and equitable principles as would lead to permanent relations of the most friendly nature, induced me in September last to seek the reopening of diplomatic relations between the two countries. . . . An envoy of the United States repaired to Mexico with full powers to adjust every existing difference. But though present on the Mexican soil by agreement between the two Governments, invested with full powers, and bearing evidence of the most friendly dispositions, his mission has been unavailing. The Mexican Government not only refused to receive him or listen to his propositions, but after a long-continued series of menaces have at last invaded our territory and shed the blood of our fellow-citizens on our own soil.

It now becomes my duty to state more in detail the origin, progress, and failure of that mission. In pursuance of the instructions given in September last, an inquiry was made on the 13th of October, 1845, in the most friendly terms, through our consul in Mexico, of the minister for foreign affairs, whether the Mexican Government "would receive an envoy from the United States intrusted with full powers to adjust all the questions in dispute between the two Governments," with the assurance that "should the answer be in the affirmative such an envoy would be immediately dispatched to Mexico." The Mexican minister on the 15th of October gave an affirmative answer to this inquiry. . . . On the 10th of November, 1845, Mr. John Slidell, of Louisiana, was commissioned by me as envoy extraordinary and minister plenipotentiary of the United States to Mexico, and was intrusted with full powers to adjust both the questions of the Texas boundary and of indemnification to our citizens. The redress of the wrongs of our citizens naturally and inseparably blended itself with the question of boundary. The settlement of the one question in any correct view of the subject involves that of the other. I could not for a moment entertain the idea that the claims of our much-injured and long-suffering citizens, many of which had existed for more than twenty years, should be postponed or separated from the settlement of the boundary question.

Mr. Slidell arrived at Vera Cruz on the 30th of November, and was courteously received by the authorities of that city. But the Government of General Herrera was then tottering to its fall. The revolutionary party had seized upon the Texas question to effect or hasten its overthrow. Its determination to restore friendly relations with the United States, and to receive our minister to negotiate for the settlement of this question, was violently assailed, and was made the great theme of denunciation against it. The Government of General Herrera, there is good reason to believe, was sincerely desirous to receive our minister; but it yielded to the storm raised by its enemies, and on the 21st of December refused to accredit Mr. Slidell upon the most frivolous pretexts. These are so fully and ably exposed in the note of Mr. Slidell of the 24th of December last to the Mexican minister of foreign relations, herewith transmitted, that I deem it unnecessary to enter into further detail on this portion of the subject.

Five days after the date of Mr. Slidell's note General Herrera yielded the Government to General Paredes without a struggle, and on the 30th of December resigned the Presidency. This revolution was accomplished solely by the army, the people having taken little part in the contest; and thus the supreme power in Mexico passed into the hands of a military leader.

Determined to leave no effort untried to effect an amicable adjustment with Mexico, I directed Mr. Slidell to present his credentials to the Government of General Paredes and ask to be officially received by him. There would have been less ground for taking this step had General Paredes come into power by a regular constitutional succession. In that event his administration would have been considered but a mere constitutional continuance of the Government of General Herrera, and the refusal of the latter to receive our minister would have been deemed conclusive unless an intimation had been given by General Paredes of his desire to reverse the decision of his predecessor. But the Government of General Paredes owes its existence to a military revolution, by which the subsisting constitutional authorities had been subverted. The form of government was entirely changed, as well as all the high functionaries by whom it was administered.

Under these circumstances, Mr. Slidell, in obedience to my direction, addressed a note to the Mexican minister of foreign relations, under date of the 1st of March last, asking to be received by that Government in the diplomatic character to which he had been appointed. This minister in his reply, under date of the 12th of March, reiterated the arguments of his predecessor, and in terms that may be considered as giving just grounds of offense to the Government and people of the United States denied the application of Mr. Slidell. Nothing therefore remained for our envoy but to demand his passports and return to his own country.

Thus the Government of Mexico, though solemnly pledged by official acts in October last to receive and accredit an American envoy, violated their plighted faith and refused the offer of a peaceful adjustment of our difficulties. Not only was the offer rejected, but the indignity of its rejection was enhanced by the manifest breach of faith in refusing to admit the envoy who came because they had bound themselves to receive him. Nor can it be said that the offer was fruitless from the want of opportunity of discussing it; our envoy was present on their own soil. Nor can it be ascribed to a want of sufficient powers; our envoy had full powers to adjust every question of difference. Nor was there room for complaint that our propositions for settlement were unreasonable; permission was not even given our envoy to make any proposition whatever. Nor can it be objected that we, on our part, would not listen to any reasonable terms of their suggestion; the Mexican Government refused all negotiation, and have made no proposition of any kind.

In my message at the commencement of the present session I informed you that upon the earnest appeal both of the Congress and convention of Texas I had ordered an efficient military force to take a position "between the Nueces and the Del Norte." This had become necessary to meet a threatened invasion of Texas by the Mexican forces, for which extensive military preparations had been made. The invasion was threatened solely because Texas had determined, in accordance with a solemn resolution of the Congress of the United States, to annex herself to our Union, and under these circumstances it was plainly our duty to extend our protection over her citizens and soil.

This force was concentrated at Corpus Christi, and remained there until after I had received such information from Mexico as rendered it probable, if not certain, that the Mexican Government would refuse to receive our envoy.

Meantime Texas, by the final action of our Congress, had become an integral part of our Union. The Congress of Texas, by its act of December 19, 1836, had declared the Rio del Norte to be the boundary of that Republic. Its jurisdiction had been extended and exercised beyond the Nueces. The country between that river and the Del Norte had been represented in the Congress and in the convention of Texas, had thus taken part in the act of annexation itself, and is now included within one of our Congressional districts. Our own Congress had, moreover, with great unanimity, by the act approved December 31, 1845, recognized the country beyond the Nueces as a part of our territory by including it within our own revenue system, and a revenue officer to reside within that district has been appointed by and with the advice and consent of the Senate. It became, therefore, of urgent necessity to provide for the defense of that portion of our country. Accordingly, on the 13th of January last instructions were issued to the general in command of these troops to occupy the left bank of the Del Norte. This river, which is the southwestern boundary of the State of Texas, is an exposed frontier. From this quarter invasion was threatened; upon it and in its immediate vicinity, in the judgment of high military experience, are the proper stations for the protecting forces of the Government. In addition to this important consideration, several others occurred to induce this movement. Among these are the facilities afforded by the ports at Brazos Santiago and the mouth of the Del Norte for the reception of supplies by sea, the stronger and more healthful military positions, the convenience for obtaining a ready and a more abundant supply of provisions, water, fuel, and forage, and the advantages which are afforded by the Del Norte in forwarding supplies to such posts as may be established in the interior and upon the Indian frontier.

The movement of the troops to the Del Norte was made by the commanding general under positive instructions to abstain from all aggressive acts toward Mexico or Mexican citizens and to regard the relations between that Republic and the United States as peaceful unless she should declare war or commit acts of hostility indicative of a state of war. He was specially directed to protect private property and respect personal rights.

The Army moved from Corpus Christi on the 11th of March, and on the 28th of that month arrived on the left bank of the Del Norte opposite to Matamoras, where it encamped on a commanding position, which has since been strengthened by the erection of fieldworks. A depot has also been established at Point Isabel, near the Brazos Santiago, 30 miles in the rear of the encampment. The selection of his position was necessarily confided to the judgment of the general in command.

The Mexican forces at Matamoras assumed a belligerent attitude, and on the 12th of April General Ampudia, then in command, notified General Taylor to break up his camp within twenty-four hours and to retire beyond the Nueces River, and in the event of his failure to comply with these demands announced that arms, and arms alone, must decide the question. But no open act of hostility was committed until the 24th of April. On that day General Arista, who had succeeded to the command of the Mexican forces, communicated to General Taylor that "he considered hostilities commenced and should prosecute them." A party of dragoons of 63 men and officers were on the same day dispatched from the American camp up the Rio del Norte, on its left bank, to ascertain whether the Mexican troops had crossed or were preparing to cross the river, "became engaged with a large body of these troops, and after a short affair, in which some 16 were killed and wounded, appear to have been surrounded and compelled to surrender."

The grievous wrongs perpetrated by Mexico upon our citizens throughout a long period of years remain unredressed, and solemn treaties pledging her public faith for this redress have been disregarded. A government either unable or unwilling to enforce the execution of such treaties fails to perform one of its plainest duties.

Our commerce with Mexico has been almost annihilated. It was formerly highly beneficial to both nations, but our merchants have been deterred from prosecuting it by the system of outrage and extortion which the Mexican authorities have pursued against them, whilst their appeals through their own Government for indemnity have been made in vain. Our forbearance has gone to such an extreme as to be mistaken in its character. Had we acted with vigor in repelling the insults and redressing the injuries inflicted by Mexico at the commencement, we should doubtless have escaped all the difficulties in which we are now involved.

Instead of this, however, we have been exerting our best efforts to propitiate her good will. Upon the pretext that Texas, a nation as independent as herself, thought proper to unite its destinies with our own she has affected to believe that we have severed her rightful territory, and in official proclamations and manifestoes has repeatedly threatened to make war upon us for the purpose of reconquering Texas. In the meantime we have tried every effort at reconciliation. The cup of forbearance had been exhausted even before the recent information from the frontier of the Del Norte. But now, after reiterated menaces, Mexico has passed the boundary of the United States, has invaded our territory and shed American blood upon the American soil. She has proclaimed that hostilities have commenced, and that the two nations are now at war.

As war exists, and, notwithstanding all our efforts to avoid it, exists by the act of Mexico herself, we are called upon by every consideration of duty and patriotism to vindicate with decision the honor, the rights, and the interests of our country.

Massachusetts Protests the Mexican War, 1847

Resolves. Concerning the Mexican War, and the Institution of Slavery.

Resolved, That the present war with Mexico has its primary origin in the unconstitutional annexation to the United States of the foreign state of Texas while the same was still at war with Mexico; that it was unconstitutionally commenced by the order of the President, to General Taylor, to take military possession of territory in dispute between the United States and Mexico, and in the occupation of Mexico; and that it is now waged ingloriously—by a powerful nation against a weak neighbor—unnecessarily and without just cause, at immense cost of treasure and life, for the dismemberment of Mexico, and for the conquest, of a portion of her territory, from which slavery has already been excluded, with the triple object of extending slavery, of strengthening the "Slave Power," and of obtaining the control of the Free States, under the Constitution of the United States.

Resolved, That such a war of conquest, so hateful in its objects, so wanton,

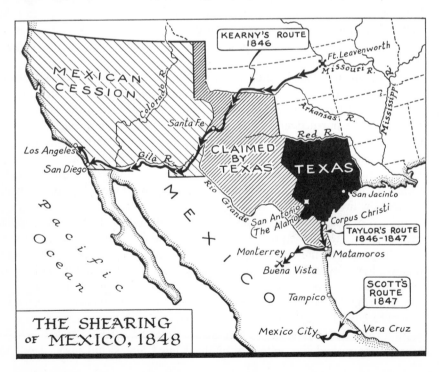

unjust, and unconstitutional in its origin and character, must be regarded as a war against freedom, against humanity, against justice, against the Union, against the Constitution, and against the Free States; and that a regard for the true interests and the highest honor of the country, not less than the impulses of Christian duty, should arouse all good citizens to join in efforts to arrest this gigantic crime, by withholding supplies, or other voluntary contributions, for its further prosecution; by calling for the withdrawal of our army within the established limits of the United States; and in every just way aiding the country to retreat from the disgraceful position of aggression which it now occupies towards a weak, distracted neighbor and sister republic.

Resolved, That our attention is directed anew to the wrong and "enormity" of slavery, and to the tyranny and usurpation of the "Slave Power," as displayed in the history of our country, particularly in the annexation of Texas and the present war with Mexico.

ESSAYS

The causes of the expansionist surge of the 1840s under the mantle of Manifest Destiny have been widely probed by historians. Ephraim D. Adams emphasizes an idealism or emotion that captivated Americans and compelled the nation to reach for territorial greatness. Norman A. Graebner of the University of Virginia, on the other hand, concentrates not on dreams or sentiment, but on the concrete interests American leaders sought and the force they were willing to use to gain them. He studies the means as much as the goals and, in the second selection, explains American efforts to take Texas and California. The closing essay by David M. Pletcher of Indiana University, from his book *The Diplomacy of Annexation,* asks whether the war was necessary and explores alternatives. He appraises the leadership of James K. Polk and assesses the costs and consequences of the President's aggressive diplomacy.

Manifest Destiny—An Emotion

EPHRAIM D. ADAMS

Before attempting a narration of the origin and growth of the ideal of manifest destiny, in its territorial expansion aspect, I find it necessary, in order that its later phases may be understood, to state explicitly what I conceive to be the essence of the ideal of manifest destiny as a force in our history, actively recognized at the time it was exercised. The materialistic historians attribute the westward movement of population to a mere desire for the "gross comforts of material abundance." In answer to this, President Woodrow Wilson, the historian, has written:

Ephraim Douglass Adams, *The Power of Ideals in American History* (New Haven: Yale University Press, 1926), pp. 65–74, 79–92.

The obvious fact is that for the creation of the nation the conquest of her proper territory from Nature was first necessary; and this task, which is hardly yet completed, has been idealized in the popular mind. A bold race has derived inspiration from the size, the difficulty, the danger of the task.

In my opinion both of these interpretations are in error. The purely materialistic historian loses sight of the fact that the people who took part in the westward movement up to 1830, carried with them the ideal of democracy. Mr. Wilson, regarding this wonderful movement from the point of view of later times, himself feeling the joy the pioneer must have had in the mere subjection of the soil, admiring his energy and courage, has depicted the movement in colors that serve to idealize it. But it is an error to assert that our understanding, our idealization, of events and conditions was also the conscious understanding and idealization of the men who were participants in those events and conditions. We of the present age rightly regard as heroic the American migration from East to West, and exalt the personal virtues of the men who led,—and of the women, those "Mothers of a Forest Land, whose bosoms pillowed *Men!*" But an ideal, unless it is consciously held by the actors, can not be considered as a living force on men's minds in their political activities. Now I very much doubt whether a man who "moved west," ever felt any "inspiration from the size, the difficulty, the danger of the task," and I certainly do not believe that before 1830, in thus moving west, he was at all consciously influenced by an ideal of expanding national territory. The inspiration which he did carry west with him was that of democracy, and when by 1830 there had been added the inspiration of nationality, the two operated to create a new element in manifest destiny, and that new element was territorial expansion,—a continent-wide national destiny. The westward movement did not create this new ideal, it was but the necessary preliminary condition in which certain inspirations, already held, took on a new form. It follows from this that I do not consider the mere shifting of population a result of the ideal of manifest destiny. That ideal included, up to about 1830, the sense of democracy and a belief in its superiority; afterwards, a desire to expand it, and to increase national power by territorial acquisition. The ideal of democracy and its manifestations, I reserve for a later lecture. The present lecture is primarily concerned, then, with the emotion of territorial expansion,—the emotion of manifest destiny. But it is to be understood that in each step forward in our territorial growth since 1800, there was a general belief that democracy was expanding as well as national boundaries.

The sense of destiny is an attribute of all nations and all people. If we could penetrate beyond the veil of recorded history, and grasp the emotions of tribes and races, of whom it is known only that they existed, probably we should find that these tribes also felt themselves a people set apart for some high purpose. Possibly even the cannibal, as he sacrifices his victim, satisfies both his physical and his spiritual being,—though it is unlikely that the victim appreciates the service he is rendering. Among civilized peoples, national destiny has frequently been accompanied by cannibalistic rites,—also with an equal ignorance of a service performed by the absorbed. Certainly there is no great nation today that has not a belief in its destiny, both in respect to territory and of peculiar function. The larger nations seek "a place in the sun" for their peoples. The smaller are content to feel that their existence, as now established, is a manifestation of providence, and urge this against absorption threatened by powerful neighbors. But all nations that are worth anything, always have had, and always will have, some ideal of national destiny, and without it, would soon disappear, and would deserve their fate.

America has felt herself destined for various high purposes. In early colonial times, the New England communities felt more than all else that they were destined to occupy and preserve a small section of the earth, where those of like religious faith and practice could realize, without governmental interference, certain religious ideals. There were few who thought of a separate national existence from England, and it was not until shortly before the war of independence that there was any general conception of governmental ideals different from those of Great Britain. Even after independence was won, the eyes of America were still unconsciously turned toward the old world, the colonial instinct was still dominant, and it was only after the war of 1812 that America turned her gaze inward upon herself. At once she felt and expressed her "peculiar destiny,"—at first as the chosen servant of the spreading ideal of democracy, later in terms of territorial greatness. Militant patriotism came to reinforce this sense of a special national function in the cause of civilization, and that patriotism pictured Great Britain as the hereditary foe of America. This was inevitable, since stories of valor or of suffering were necessarily connected with the only nation with whom we had fought. The schoolboy, in selected orations and poetry, was trained in this hostility towards England,—a hostility which was, in fact, merely one expression of nationality. Captain Hall, an Englishman traveling in the United States, in 1827, was both amused and astonished on visiting the Boston public schools, that a boy called up to "speak" for the visitor's pleasure, should recite a "furious philippic" against Great Britain, while a second youth gave an oration beginning:

> For eighteen hundred years the world had slumbered in ignorance of liberty, and of the true rights of freemen. At length America arose in all her glory, to give the world the long desired lesson!

The intolerance of America in thus training its youth in fixed hostility to old England, the arrogance of the young nation, in a new land, assuming to instruct the old world, were truly amusing, yet back of all bombast and back of all crudity of expression was the sincere conviction that America was destined to be the greater nation, that it would accomplish greater things, that it could offer exceptional enlightenment and bestow unusual favors.

The period from 1830 to 1860 is usually regarded as that in which the ideal of manifest destiny most affected our history. During these years the term "manifest destiny" vaguely expressed the sense of the American people that their government gave an example to the world of the success of the democratic principle, and that power went hand in hand with democracy. Previous to 1830 the westward shifting of population did not imply a belief in a continent-wide country. Year after year American citizens laboriously surmounted the Appalachian range, sought the sources of the streams flowing to the west, and followed these to the land of promise. Until the completion of the Erie Canal the bulk of this movement was from the middle and southern states, a poor white population finding in the rich soil of Kentucky, or Indiana, or Ohio, an improved industrial opportunity, and founding settlements marked by extreme simplicity and equality. Gradually the wide domain of the territory east of the Mississippi was dotted with villages and farms, and by 1830 the frontier had moved across the river into the lands of the Louisiana purchase. After 1825, there came an increased northern migration, swelled by a steady stream of British immigrants, though this last was never large and almost ceased temporarily in 1830. The German immigration of the early thirties added to this wave of humanity moving westward. But as yet there was room for all, and save for the uneasy frontiersman, restless if he had any neighbors, there could be no pressing need, for many years to come, of lands beyond the established boundaries of the country.

The controversy with Great Britain in the twenties over Oregon made clear that America, before 1830, had no thought of continental dominion and regarded as a dreamer the man who would still expand the national domain. Benton, senator from Missouri, was such a dreamer, but dared not give expression to his dream. In 1825, Russia, by treaties with England and the United States, had renounced her claims south of 54° 40', leaving the two remaining powers in joint possession. At once a bill was introduced in Congress for the military occupation of Oregon. A few supported it, more were opposed, but the great majority were wholly indifferent. Dickerson of New Jersey made the principal speech against the measure. "We have not," he said, "adopted a system of colonization, and it is to be hoped we never shall. Oregon can never be one of the United States. If we extend our laws to it, we must consider it as a colony. . . . Is this territory of Oregon ever to become a state, a member of this Union? Never. The Union is already too extensive." He then entered upon a calculation to prove the utter impossibility of a representative in Congress for Oregon, since mere distance would prove an effective barrier. Postulating that a representative must visit his constituents at least once a year, he stated the distance from the mouth of the Columbia to Washington as 4650 miles, or 9300 for the round trip. According to federal law granting mileage payment to congressmen, the average rate of travel was then twenty miles per day, but supposing the Oregonian to exceed this rate of speed, and to maintain the high average of thirty miles, "This," continued Dickerson, "would allow the member a fortnight to rest himself at Washington before he should commence his journey home. . . . It would be more expeditious, however, to come by water round Cape Horn, or to pass through Behrings Straits, round the North coast of this Continent to Baffin's Bay, thence through Davis Straits to the Atlantic, and so on to Washington. It is true, this passage is not yet discovered, except upon our maps,—but it will be as soon as Oregon shall be a State."

Benton himself was oppressed by the remoteness of the territory, and standing almost alone in the Senate, did not dare to profess a belief that Oregon could ever be admitted to the Union. He asserted, rather, that "the greatest of all advantages to be derived from the occupation of this country, is in the exclusion of foreign powers from it." He did assert, however, that Oregon would soon be settled, either by European or by American colonists, and declared that it lay with Congress to determine which. Seeking to persuade his hearers to action he pictured American settlement on lines of ultimate separation from the United States. The successive steps would be military occupation, settlements and a civil territorial government, then clamors against the hardship of dependence upon a government so remote as Washington, and finally independence willingly granted by the mother country. Continuing his plea for action, Benton even acknowledged that the Rocky Mountains formed the natural limit of the United States. To the west of that line, this offspring of our institutions would guard our interests, and America would have cause to rejoice in having aided "in the erection of a new Republic, composed of her children, speaking her language, inheriting her principles, devoted to liberty and equality, and ready to stand by her side against the combined powers of the old world."

The long journey to Oregon was indeed a barrier to settlement in the twenties. The next step of the American advance was to the southwest rather than to the northwest, and marks the faint beginnings of the expressed ideal of a territorial manifest destiny, later developed to great proportions. There were several elements merged in the American interest in, and desire for, Texas; the impulsion of the westward movement as lands further west and south became available to settlers; the natural and hopeful interest of Southerners who urged and anticipated annexation; and, in addition, the call of manifest destiny,—the yearning for power and territory. For a time, however, the more cautious and conservative opinion of the older states checked the cry for annexation and Texas was forced to rest under a separate sovereignty. . . .

When, in 1836, Texas declared her independence from Mexico, the Americans who had established that independence strongly desired annexation. The offer was declined, but the migration into this new country rapidly increased, and the newcomers reinforced annexation sentiment both in Texas and in the United States. By 1842, Texas had secured recognition from the stronger powers as an independent state, and to two of these powers, England and the United States, the future of Texas became a matter of great importance. Slavery existed, and cotton seemed destined to be the chief industrial product. England, hoping to free herself from dependence on American cotton, and at the same time establish a barrier to further American expansion, naturally encouraged Texan independence. The United States, while rejoicing over this new Anglo-Saxon nation, was yet in a doubtful position in regard to it. Mexico stubbornly refused to acknowledge Texan independence, and annexation might involve us in a war. Northern feeling was against a new slave state, so large that several slave states seemed then inevitable. In the South there rapidly developed enthusiasm for annexation on the score of Southern political influence, and the sentiment of manifest destiny was appealed to,—an effective appeal, since the hearts of all our Western people beat responsive to the cry. By 1842, the South was determined to have Texas, and the "Texan game," as Northern opponents termed it, was begun.

Manifest destiny was a strong factor in annexation sentiment, but a more specific argument was found in the national jealousy of England. Tyler and Calhoun raised the cry of British opposition, with more justice than the partisans of anti-slavery admitted. Great Britain did indeed hope that in Texas she would find a block to the increasing power of America, and even dreamed of inducing Texas to abolish slavery. Elliot, the British diplomat in Texas, confined his official efforts, however, to a preservation of the independence of Texas. He sought to check annexation sentiment, picturing the future greatness of an independent Texas. British colonists were introduced, but they were few in number compared with the steady stream from the United States, and, as Elliot himself sorrowfully confessed, they were wholly inferior in the art of pioneering. Like Peter Simple, the British colonist "preferred to walk, rather than to run, toward his goal, for fear he would arrive out of breath." Elliot, marveling at the difficulties and crudities of the American push westward, said "they jolt and jar terrifically in their progress, but *on they do get.*" With the coming of new American settlers, it became certain that Texas herself cared more for annexation than for independence. In the United States the sentiment of expansion grew steadily in strength, and though Calhoun, raising the cry of British interference, was at first defeated by the conservative and anti-slavery elements in the Senate, the campaign of Polk in 1844, when the rivalry with England for Oregon was also played upon, settled the destiny of Texas. In that campaign was heard, at last, no mere feeble and isolated assertion of a continent-wide destiny, but a positive and general profession of faith in the inevitable progress of democratic institutions and "Anglo-Saxon" ideals, destined to triumph over monarchical principles and inferior races. The clap-trap political oratory of this campaign is distressing to the patriotic historian, and I refrain from quotation, but it must be recognized that such oratory was used and was effective, simply because it reflected an American emotion. Manifest destiny, in terms of expansion, suddenly revealed itself as a powerful sentiment, against which the conservative minority struggled in vain. Nor was the expression of this sentiment confined to the political orator. Lyman Beecher, in a sermon enumerating the vices threatening American life, yet claimed for America a superior position among nations. "Our very beginning," he said, "was civilized, learned and pious." And even yet America is

> ... still the richest inheritance which the mercy of God continues to the troubled earth. Nowhere beside, if you search the world over, will you find so much real liberty; so much equality; so much personal safety, and temporal prosperity; so general an extension of useful knowledge; so much religious instruction; so much moral restraint; and so much divine mercy, to make these blessings the power of God, and the wisdom of God unto salvation.

If these blessings were indeed peculiar to America, what reasonable opposition could exist to carrying them into new territory?

Polk's election determined the future of Texas, and Great Britain regretfully relinquished her hope of a barrier state, yet consoled herself with the thought that mere territorial weight would break the Union in fragments. But with Oregon it was a different matter. During the campaign, Democratic orators had declared for the extreme American claim,—"fifty-four forty or fight," and to this England would by no means agree. Southern leaders, gratified as to Texas, now sought to quiet the expansion sentiment they had used with so much success. Previously, in 1843, a bill for the organization of Oregon, offering lands to settlers, had been introduced in Congress. Senator McDuffie of South Carolina, who saw in slavery the "bulwark of republican institutions," was against it, saying:

> I would not give a pinch of snuff for the whole territory. I wish to God we did not own it, I wish it was an impassable barrier to secure us against the intrusion of others. . . . Do you think your honest farmers in Pennsylvania, New York, or even Ohio or Missouri, will abandon their farms to go upon any such enterprise as that? God forbid!

At the time McDuffie made this speech, other Southerners were more reserved, but no sooner had Tyler despatched the offer to receive Texas into the Union than the sentiments of McDuffie were revived. But Polk, a determined expansionist, already planning to go far beyond Texas, and to carry American territory to the Pacific in the South as well as in the North, stood firmly for Oregon. Apparently he intended to exact the extreme American claim, and hostilities with England seemed near. At the same time, Mexico, still claiming Texas as her own, threatened war, while Texas unexpectedly delayed a formal acceptance of the annexation proposal. The situation seemed dangerous, and with a prospect of war on both northern and southern borders, wisdom urged caution. Horace Greeley, opposed to slavery expansion, argued in the *New York Tribune* against any expansion, citing Benton's speech of 1825 to prove that the Rocky Mountains formed a natural boundary. Winthrop, in Congress, answered the expansionist dogma, "The finger of God never points in a direction contrary to the extension of the glory of the Republic," by quoting:

> Glory is like a circle in the water,
> Which never ceaseth to enlarge itself,
> Till by broad spreading it disperse to naught.

But Greeley and Winthrop were upheld by the anti-slavery faction alone. The *New York Sun* and the *New York Herald* strongly approved annexation and expansion, the latter asserting, "Our march is *onward* for centuries to come, *still onward*—and they who do not keep up with us, must fall behind and be forgotten,"—apparently a reference to Mexico. According to the *Evening Post,* Greeley stood alone in the North: "With the exception of the *Tribune* . . . there is not a press in the Union which does not say Oregon is ours and must be maintained." Polk had no intention of drifting into war with England, and, after a due amount of bluster, agreed to the forty-ninth parallel as the proper boundary of Oregon; but before this was known, the *Herald,* with an eye on all North America, expressed the hope that war would ensue with both England and Mexico.

> "The destiny of the Republic," it stated, "is apparent to every eye. Texas Annexation must be consummated, and the immediate results of that event may only precipitate the subjugation of the whole continent, despite of all the opposing efforts of the despotic dynasties of Europe."

Thus we were "destined" to have Mexico and Canada sometime;—why not now? The *Washington Union,* the administration paper, while relations with England and Mexico were still undetermined, expressed deep suspicion of Great Britain, and asserted that no nation could thwart American "destiny."

> The march of the Anglo-Saxon race is onward. They must in the event, accomplish their destiny,—spreading far and wide the great principles of self-government, and who shall say how far they will prosecute the work?

Mingled with this emotion of destiny there was evident the appeal which the "West" made as a land of opportunity. A bit of verse appearing in a St. Louis paper was widely reprinted in the East:

> "COME OUT TO THE WEST."
>
> Come forth from your cities, come out to the West;
> Ye have hearts, ye have hands—leave to Nature the rest.
> The prairie, the forest, the stream at command—
> "The world is too crowded!"—pshaw! come and *take*
>   land.
>
> Come travel the mountain, and paddle the stream;
> The cabin shall smile, and the corn-patch shall gleam;
> "A wife and six children?"—'tis wealth in your hand!
> Your ox and your rifle—out West and take land!

Possibly it was by such means that Martin Chuzzlewit was induced to buy a corner lot in "Eden." The West had cast a glamor over the eyes of the nation, and the greater the distance, the more alluring the prospect. But with Oregon secured, and with Texas and California made definitely ours in the progress of the war with Mexico, Polk was satisfied and hastened the peace negotiations, that the fever of expansion should not rise too high. The Southern leaders were accustomed to bewail the fact that they would always be damned in history, since the historical writing was all done in New England. The South has indeed been thus damned for the annexation of Texas and the Mexican War, but in the former case alone can the slavery interest be regarded as an important factor. Manifest destiny was the one great leading force in the war with Mexico.

At the end of the war, except for the extreme anti-slavery faction, there was united glorification in the power, and in the territorial greatness of America. The emotion of manifest destiny was at its height. Foreign observers were astounded by the national self-confidence, and appalled by the actual power of the United States. Warburton, an English traveler, arriving in America "in ignorance," as he himself says, went away astonished and fearful.

"We cannot," he writes, "conceal from ourselves that in many of the most important points of national capabilities they beat us; they are more energetic, more enterprising, less embarrassed with class interests, less burthened by the legacy of debt. This country, as a field for increase of power, is in every respect so infinitely beyond ours that comparison would be absurd." . . . All things "combine to promise them, a few years hence, a degree of strength which may endanger the existing state of things in the world. They only wait for matured power, to apply the incendiary torch of Republicanism to the nations of Europe."

Warburton overstates American desire to meddle in European affairs, yet he expresses American belief in the contagious qualities of the ideal of self-government. Witness our enthusiasm over the European revolutions of 1848, when press, pulpit, and Congress gave credit to American ideals and institutions,—being woefully ignorant of the many sources of the most confused revolutionary movement in history. Yet there is a touch of truth in the theory that the prosperity and power of America, looked upon as a test of the success of her democratic institutions, were an influence in expanding liberalism in Europe. Perhaps this was our most grandiloquent period. Here was this vast country,—its riches untold, seaports on two oceans, the one ideal form of government, and possibilities of power beyond telling. After the absorption of so much territory in so short a time, America summed up her material blessings and was satisfied. But she hoped for dominion even beyond material things. A handful of people as compared with the great powers of Europe, she arrogated to herself leadership in the world of ideas, and proposed to make herself respected and feared in the family of Nations. Clay best expressed it in 1850, saying:

> Our country has grown to a magnitude, to a power and greatness, such as to command the respect, if it does not awe the apprehensions of the powers of the earth, with whom we come in contact.

The ebb of the tide of expansion craze began with the acquisition of the Pacific Coast. The discovery of gold in California drew in a new direction the bulk of that adventurous population which had heretofore worried our neighbors. Before that discovery, Polk, in 1847, had advocated a waterway across the Isthmus of Panama, and Francis Lieber urged America not to be afraid of her future, and to build the canal, writing:

> Let the vastness not appal us;
> Greatness is thy destiny.
> Let the doubters not recall us:
> Venture suits the free.

The gold rush at once forced into prominence the question of transit by the Isthmus, and the Clayton-Bulwer treaty was signed with England, looking toward a canal. A ten-years' dispute as to the interpretation of that treaty followed, and Central America became the scene of a new "American movement," with William Walker, the "grey-eyed man of destiny," as the leading actor in filibustering expeditions, having for their object a tropical expansion, and finding favor in the South. Cuba also was an objective, but all this aftermath of the expansion craze was checked by the political exigencies of the dangerous situation within the United States, when the Kansas-Nebraska controversy arose.

Meanwhile Americans, generally, were proudly conscious of power, and of territorial greatness, and were not unduly modest in expressing this consciousness. Manifest destiny has indeed a characteristic of American humor,—exaggeration. The Englishman defined American humor as "merely a big lie,"—but he missed the fact that, to the American, the "big lie" was never quite an absolute impossibility. It was thus with the expression of the ideal of manifest destiny,—the bombast, however apparently absurd, was never wholly insincere, though it was tinctured with the love of humorous exaggeration for its own sake. This puzzled the English observer and he sometimes took American talk at its face value, as when the House of Lords solemnly recorded its indignation at an American proposal to repudiate all debts to foreign nations, on the ground that such creditors were fully recompensed in having aided in the spread of American civilization. The editorial in a Dubuque, Iowa, paper that inspired this British protest was a mere blatant absurdity and the editor must have been gratified, if he knew of it, to find his effort perpetuated in the pages of Hansard's Parliamentary Debates. Charles Dickens, in "Martin Chuzzlewit," revelled in the opportunity to caricature our assumption of superiority, and of the all-pervading influence of our institutions. Martin, under the guidance of Colonel Diver, editor of the *New York Rowdy Journal,* has made the acquaintance of several of "the most remarkable men of the country, sir," and has been astounded by their youth. At the dinner table in the boarding house, he is equally astounded to learn that the "little girl, like a doll," seated opposite, is the mother of two children. He expresses his wonder to Colonel Diver, who replies, "Yes, Sir, but some institutions develop human nature; others re-tard it." More serious English writers, accepting American estimate of the power and future expansion of the United States, struck the note of "hands across the sea," and declared a common destiny for the two nations, each in its own field. Charles Mackay, the "Ayrshire Poet," read at a banquet in Washington a poem called "John and Jonathan," disclaiming for John any wish to interfere with Jonathan's destiny:

> Take you the West and I the East,
>   We'll spread ourselves abroad,
> With Trade and Spade, and wholesome laws,
>   And faith in Man and God.

> Take you the West and I the East,
>   We speak the self-same tongue
> That Milton wrote and Chatham spoke,
>   And Burns and Shakespeare sung;
> And from our tongue, our hand, our heart,
>   Shall countless blessings flow
> To light two darkened hemispheres
>   That know not where they go.

The Civil War put a sudden end to the clamor for territorial expansion. The purchase of Alaska, in 1867, awoke no enthusiasm in American hearts. It was generally spoken of as "Seward's Folly," and regarded as a recompense to Russia for her friendly attitude during the war. For thirty years America was occupied with industrial development, satisfied to retain for herself the blessing of her institutions, with no inclination to confer them by force on other nations. Then came the Spanish-American war. Whatever its origin, the war awoke again, but only for the moment, the emotion of manifest destiny. President McKinley, in a message to Congress, following the cession of the Philippines by Spain, expressed the national sentiment:

> "The war," he said, "has brought us new duties and responsibilities which we must meet and discharge as becomes a great nation on whose growth and career from the beginning the Ruler of Nations has plainly written the high command and pledge of civilization. Incidental to our tenure in the Philippines is the commercial opportunity to which American statesmanship cannot be indifferent."

A shrill voice from the East protested, but these words express briefly the true inwardness of manifest destiny at all times in our history. Even more briefly put they might be condensed to, "God directs us,—perhaps it will pay."

Concrete Interests and Expansion

NORMAN A. GRAEBNER

Manifest destiny, a phrase used by contemporaries and historians to describe and explain the continental expansion of the United States in the 1840's, expressed merely a national mood. The belief in a national destiny was neither new nor strange; no nation or empire in history has ever been totally without it. But for its proponents of the 1840's the meaning conveyed by the phrase was clearly understood and peculiarly American. It implied that the United States was destined by the will of Heaven to become a country of political and territorial eminence. It attributed the probability and even the necessity of this growth to a homogeneous process created by certain unique qualities in American civilization—the energy and vigor of its people, their idealism and faith in their democratic institutions, and their sense of mission now endowed with a new vitality. It assigned to the American people the obligation to extend the area of freedom to their less fortunate neighbors, but only to those trained for self-government and genuinely desirous of entering the American Union. Expansionists of the forties saw this self-imposed limitation on forceful annexation as no serious barrier to the Republic's growth. It was inconceivable to them that any neighboring population would decline an invitation to enter the realm of the United States. Eventually editors and politicians transformed the idea of manifest destiny into a significant expression of American nationalism.

Such convictions of destiny came easily to the American people in the mid-

From *Manifest Destiny,* edited by Norman Graebner, copyright © 1968, by The Bobbs-Merrill Company, Inc., reprinted by permission of the publisher.

forties, for they logically emerged from the sheer size and dramatic achievements of the young Republic. From New England and Pennsylvania, reaching on into the Ohio Valley and the Great Lakes region, an industrial revolution was multiplying the productive resources of the United States. New forms of transportation, made possible by the efficient application of steam, rendered the national economy greater than the sum of its parts. Steamboats transformed the Mississippi and Ohio rivers—with their many tributaries—into a mighty inland system of commercial and human traffic. Railroads had long since left the Atlantic seaboard and were, by the forties, creeping toward the burgeoning cities of the Middle West. Asa Whitney had already projected a railroad line from Lake Michigan to the Pacific Northwest. Samuel F. B. Morse's successful demonstration of the magnetic telegraph in 1844 assured almost instantaneous communication across the entire continent. "What mighty distances have been overcome by railroads," exclaimed the *Southern Quarterly Review* (October, 1844), "and, stranger than all, is the transmission of intelligence with the speed and with the aid of lightning!" . . .

Never in history could a people more readily accept and proclaim a sense of destiny, for never were a people more perfectly situated to transform their whims into realities. Expansion was rationalized so effectively at each point of conflict that it seemed to many Americans an unchallengeable franchise. Confronted by problems neither of conscience nor of extensive countering force, the American people could claim as a natural right boundaries that seemed to satisfy the requirements of security and commerce. Expanding as they did into a vacuum—vast regions almost devoid of population—they could conclude that they were simply fulfilling the dictates of manifest destiny. For them the distinctions between sentiment and action, between individual purpose and national achievement, appeared inconsequential.

Historians, emphasizing the expansive mood of the forties, have tended to identify the westward extension of the United States to the Pacific with the concept of destiny itself. Such identifications are misleading, for they ignore all the genuine elements of successful policy. Those regions into which the nation threatened to expand were under the legal jurisdiction of other governments. Their acquisition required the formulation of policies which encompassed both the precise definition of ends and the creation of adequate means. Manifest destiny doctrines—a body of sentiment and nothing else—avoided completely the essential question of *means,* and it was only the absence of powerful opposition on the North American continent that permitted the fallacy that power and its employment were of little consequence. Occupying a wilderness created the illusion that power was less important than moral progress, and that expansion was indeed a civilizing, not a conquering, process.

Jeremy Bentham once termed the concept of natural right pure nonsense, for the claims of nations were natural only when supported by superior force. The natural right of the United States to a continental empire lay in its power of conquest, not in the uniqueness of its political institutions. American expansionism could triumph only when the nation could bring its diplomatic and military influence to bear on specific points of national concern. What created the easy victory of American expansion was not a sense of destiny, however widely and dramatically it was proclaimed, but the absence of powerful competitors which might have either prevented the expansion entirely or forced the country to pay an exorbitant price for its territorial gains. The advantages of geography and the political and military inefficiency of the Indian tribes or even of Mexican arms tended to obscure the elements of force which were no less real, only less obtrusive, than that employed by other nations in their efforts at empire building. It was no wonder that British and French critics concluded that the American conquest of the continent was by pick and shovel.

Concepts of manifest destiny were as totally negligent of *ends* as they were of means. Expansionists agreed that the nation was destined to reach its natural boundaries. But what were these natural frontiers? For Benjamin Franklin and John Adams they comprised the Mississippi River. But when the United States, through the purchase of Louisiana, crossed the Mississippi, there was no end in sight. Expansionists now regarded Florida as a natural appendage—belonging as naturally to the United States, declared one Kentucky newspaper, as Cornwall did to England. John Quincy Adams observed in his diary that the acquisition of Florida in 1819 "rendered it still more unavoidable that the remainder of the continent should ultimately be ours." Eventually Europe would discover, he predicted, that the United States and North America were identical. But President James Monroe revealed no more interest in building a state on the Pacific than had Jefferson. Equally convinced that the distances to Oregon were too great to be bridged by one empire, Thomas Hart Benton of Missouri in 1825 defined the natural boundary of the United States as "the ridge of the Rocky Mountains. . . . Along the back of this ridge, the Western limit of this republic should be drawn, and the statue of the fabled god, Terminus, should be raised upon its highest peak, never to be thrown down." President John Tyler, in his message of December, 1843, perpetuated this limited view of the nation's future. And as late as 1845 Daniel Webster continued to refer to an independent republic along the distant Pacific coast. Meanwhile expansionists could never agree on the natural boundaries of Texas. Representative C. J. Ingersoll of Pennsylvania found them in vast deserts between the Rio Grande and the Nueces. For others they comprised the Rio Grande itself, but James Gadsden discovered in the Sierra Madre mountains "a natural territorial boundary, imposing in its Mountain and Desert outlines." . . .

If the ultimate vision of American destiny in the forties comprised a vast federal republic that boasted continental dimensions and a government based on the principle of states rights, the future boundaries of the United States, as determined by the standards of geographical predestination, never seemed to possess any ultimate logic. Boundaries that appeared natural to one generation were rejected as utterly inadequate by the next. It was left for Robert Winthrop, the conservative Massachusetts Whig, in January, 1846, to reduce the doctrine of geographical predestination to an absurdity:

> It is not a little amusing to observe what different views are taken as to the indication of "the hand of nature" and the pointings of "the finger of God," by the same gentlemen, under different circumstances and upon different sub-

jects. In one quarter of the compass they can descry the hand of nature in a level desert and a second-rate river, beckoning us impatiently to march up to them. But when they turn their eyes to another part of the horizon the loftiest mountains in the universe are quite lost upon their gaze. There is no hand of nature there. The configuration of the earth has no longer any significance. The Rocky Mountains are mere molehills. Our destiny is onward.

Democratic idealism was even less precise as a guide to national action than the doctrine of geographical predestination. By 1845 such goals of reaching the waters of the Pacific were far too limited for the more enthusiastic exponents of the new expansionism. As they interpreted the expression of democratic idealism, the dogma represented an ever-expanding force. Indeed, for some it had no visible limit at all. It looked beyond the North American continent to South America, to the islands of the Pacific, and to the Old World itself. One editorial in the New York *Herald* (September 15, 1845), declared, "American patriotism takes a wider and loftier range than heretofore. Its horizon is widening every day. No longer bounded by the limits of the confederacy, it looks abroad upon the whole earth, and into the mind of the republic daily sinks deeper and deeper the conviction that the civilization of the earth—the reform of the governments of the ancient world—the emancipation of the whole race, are dependent, in a great degree, on the United States." This was a magnificent vision for a democratic purpose, but it hardly explains the sweep of the United States across the continent. It bears no relationship whatever to the actual goals which the Tyler and Polk administrations pursued in their diplomacy with Texas, Mexico, and England.

Texas provided the necessary catalyst which fused all the elements of manifest destiny into a single national movement. When, in 1844, the annexation issue suddenly exploded on the national scene, the expansionist front had been quiescent for a full generation. The twenties and thirties had been years of introspection. The changing structure of American political and economic life had absorbed the people's energies and directed their thoughts inward. Yet the same inner-directed concerns which rendered the country generally oblivious to external affairs promoted both the sense of power and the democratic idealism which, under the impetus of expansionist oratory, could easily transform the nation's mood and forge a spirit of national destiny. . . .

California no less than Oregon demanded its own peculiar expansionist rationale, for its acquisition confronted the United States with a series of problems not present in either the Texas or Oregon issues. If the government in Mexico City lacked the energy to control, much less develop, this remote province, its title was still as clear as its hold was ephemeral. The annexation of this outpost required bargaining with its owner. Even that possibility seemed remote in 1845, for the Mexican government had carried out its threat to break diplomatic relations with the United States rather than condone the American annexation of Texas. For a decade American citizens had drifted into the inland valleys and coastal villages of California, but in 1845 they still comprised an infinitesimal number, even when compared to the small Mexican and Indian population.

Obviously the United States could not achieve its continental destiny without embracing California. Yet this Mexican province had never been an issue in American politics; its positive contribution to American civilization had scarcely been established. California, moreover, because of its alien population, was by the established principles of American expansion less than acceptable as a territorial objective. American acquisitiveness toward Texas and Oregon had been ethnocentric; it rejected the notion of annexing allegedly inferior peoples. "There seems to be something in our laws and institutions," Alexander Duncan of Ohio reminded the House of Representatives early in 1845, "peculiarly adapted to our Anglo-Saxon-American race, under which they will thrive and prosper, but under which all others wilt and die." He pointed to the decline of the French and Spanish on the North American continent when American laws had been extended to them. It was their unfitness for "liberal and equal laws, and equal institutions," he assumed, that accounted for this inability to prosper under the United States.

Such inhibitions toward the annexing of Mexican peoples gradually disintegrated under the pressure of events. The decision to annex Texas itself encouraged the process by weakening the respect which many Americans held for Mexico's territorial integrity, and thus pointed the way to further acquisitions in the Southwest. Having, through the annexation of Texas, passed its arm "down to the waist of the continent," observed the *Dublin Freeman,* the nation would certainly "not hesitate to pass it round." That the United States was destined to annex additional portions of Mexican territory seemed apparent enough, but only when its population had been absorbed by the Anglo-Saxons now overspreading the continent. As early as 1845 the rapid migration of pioneers into California promised to render the province fit for eventual annexation. In July, 1845, the *Democratic Review* noted that Mexican influence in California was nearing extinction, for the Anglo-Saxon foot was on its border.

American acquisitiveness toward California, like that displayed toward Texas and Oregon, progressed at two levels—that of abstract rationalization and that of concrete national interest. Polk alone carried the responsibility for United States diplomacy with Mexico, and interpreted American objectives in the Southwest—like those in Oregon—as precise and determined by the sea. Travelers and sea captains of the early forties agreed that two inlets gave special significance to the California coast—the bays of San Francisco and San Diego. These men viewed San Francisco harbor with wonderment. Charles Wilkes assured the readers of his *Narrative . . .* that California could boast "one of the finest, if not the very best harbor in the world." It was sufficiently extensive, he added, to shelter the combined navies of Europe. Thomas J. Farnham, the American traveler and writer, called it simply "the glory of the Western world." All who had visited the bay observed that it was the unqualified answer to American hopes for commercial greatness in the Pacific. To the south lay San Diego Bay—the rendezvous of the California hide trade. Here, all Boston firms maintained their coastal depots for cleaning, drying, and storing the hides until a full cargo of thirty to forty thousand had been collected for the long journey to Boston. The processing and storing of hides required a warm port,

free from rain, fog, and heavy surf. San Diego alone met all these requirements. This beautiful bay, so deep and placid that ships could lie a cable's
length from the smooth, hard-packed, sandy beach, became the chief point of
New England's interest on the California coast. The bay was exposed to neither
wind nor surf, for it was protected for its entire fifteen-mile length and possessed
a narrow, deep entrance. Richard Henry Dana observed in *Two Years Before
the Mast* (1840) that San Diego harbor was comparable in value and importance to San Francisco Bay. The noted sea captain, Benjamin Morrell, once
termed San Diego "as fine a bay for vessels under three hundred tons as was
ever formed by Nature in her most friendly mood to mariners."

During the autumn of 1845, even before his administration had disposed of
the Oregon question, Polk embarked on a dual course to acquire at least a portion of California. English activity in that distant province convinced him that,
in Great Britain, the United States faced a strong and determined competitor
for possession, in particular, of San Francisco Bay. Thomas O. Larkin, an American merchant at Monterey, reported that the French and British governments
maintained consuls in California although neither nation had any commercial
interests along the Pacific coast. "Why they are in Service their Government
best know and Uncle Sam will know to his cost," Larkin warned in July,
1845. Larkin's reports produced a wave of excitement in the administration.
"The appearance of a British Vice Consul and French Consul in California at
this present crisis without any apparent commercial business," Secretary of
State James Buchanan answered Larkin, "is well calculated to produce the
impression that their respective governments entertained designs on that country...." On October 17, 1845, Buchanan drafted special instructions to Larkin:

> The future destiny of that country is a subject of anxious solicitude for the
> government and people of the United States. The interests of our commerce
> and our whale fisheries on the Pacific Ocean demand that you should exert the
> greatest vigilance in discovering and defeating any attempts which may be
> made by foreign governments to acquire a control over that country.... On all
> proper occasions, you should not fail prudently to warn the government and
> people of California of the danger of such an interference to their peace and
> prosperity; to inspire them with a jealousy of European domination, and to
> arouse in their bosoms that love of liberty and independence so natural to the
> American continent.

Polk appointed Larkin as his confidential agent in California to encourage
the Californians, should they separate from Mexico, to cast their lot with
the United States. "While the President will make no effort and use no influence
to induce California to become one of the free and independent states of the
Union, yet," continued Buchanan's instructions, "if the people should desire
to unite their destiny with ours, they would be received as brethren, whenever
this can be done without affording Mexico just cause of complaint." Larkin
was told to let events take their course unless Britain or France should attempt to take California against the will of its residents.

During November, 1845, Polk initiated the second phase of his California
policy—an immediate effort to purchase the province from Mexico. On No-

vember 9, William S. Parrott, a long-time resident of Mexico now serving as Polk's special agent at the Mexican capital, returned to Washington with confirming information that the officials in Mexico City would receive an American envoy. As early as September Polk and his cabinet had agreed to tender such a mission to John Slidell of Louisiana. In his instructions to Slidell, dated November 10, Buchanan clarified the administration's objectives in California. In a variety of boundary proposals Polk was adamant only on one—the Rio Grande. Those that applied to California were defined solely in terms of Pacific ports. They started with San Francisco and Monterey, the capital of the province, but they included also a suggested boundary line which would reach westward from El Paso along the 32nd parallel to the Pacific, this extended as far as the harbor of San Diego. Unfortunately Slidell was not received by the Mexican government. The administration's program of acquiring at least one of the important harbors along the California coast by purchase from Mexico had failed.

From the defeat of their diplomacy to achieve a boundary settlement with Mexico Polk and his cabinet moved early in May, 1846, toward a recommendation of war, employing as the immediate pretext the refusal of the Mexican government to pay the claims of American citizens against it for their losses in Mexico. Before the cabinet could agree on such a drastic course of action, Polk received word that a detachment of General Zachary Taylor's forces stationed along the disputed Rio Grande boundary of Texas had been fired upon by Mexican forces. Armed with such intelligence, the President now phrased his message to obtain an immediate and overwhelming endorsement for a policy of force. Mexico, he charged, "has passed the boundary of the United States, has invaded our territory and shed American blood upon American soil." War existed, in short, by act of Mexico. Polk explained that his action of stationing Taylor on the Rio Grande was not an act of aggression, but merely the attempt to occupy a disputed territory. Yet the possibility that the President had sought to provoke a clash of arms left sufficient doubt in the minds of his Whig opponents to permit them to make the Mexican War the most bitterly criticized in American history.

During the summer of 1846 the rapid American conquest of California quickly crystallized the expansionist arguments for the retention of the province. Indeed, California suddenly appeared totally satisfactory as a territorial addition. Amalgamation of the Mexican population no longer caused anxiety, for, as Andrew J. Donelson predicted, within five years the Anglo-American people would be dominant in the province. Lewis Cass in February, 1847, still believed any amalgamation between Americans and Mexicans quite deplorable. "We do not want the people of Mexico either as citizens or subjects," he warned, but then he added reassuringly with special reference to California, "all we want is a portion of territory which they nominally hold, generally uninhabited, or, where inhabited at all, sparsely so, and with a population which would soon recede or identify itself with ours." Buchanan, opposing the extension of the United States to the Sierra Madre Mountains, asked: "How should we govern the mongrel race which inhabit it?" Like Donelson and Cass, he harbored no fear of annexing California, for, he added, "The Californias are comparatively uninhabited and will therefore be almost exclusively colonised by our own people."

There was little sentimentality in the *Democratic Review*'s prediction in March, 1847, that American pioneers in California would dispossess the inhabitants as they had the American Indians. It declared that evidently "the process which has been gone through at the North of driving back the Indians, or annihilating them as a race, has yet to be gone through at the south." Similarly the *American Review* that same month saw Mexicans giving way to "a superior population, insensibly oozing into her territories, changing her customs, and out-living, out-trading, exterminating her weaker blood...."

California's immense potential as the seat of a rich empire, contrasted to its backwardness under Mexican rule, added a new dimension to the doctrine of manifest destiny—the regeneration of California's soil. . . .

Polk, adequately supported by the Democratic expansionists in Congress, rationalized the American retention of California, not with references to the doctrine of regeneration, but with the principle of indemnity. "No terms can . . . be contemplated," O'Sullivan argued in July, 1846, "which will not require from [Mexico] indemnity . . . for the many wrongs which we have suffered at her hands. And if, in agreeing upon those terms, she finds it more for her interest to give us California than to satisfy our just demands in any other way, what objection can there be to the arrangement . . . ?" Unfortunately for the President, indemnity, clearly recognized as a legitimate fruit of victory by the law of nations, was acceptable to only those Americans who placed responsibility of the war on Mexico. To those Whigs who attacked the war California constituted conquest, not indemnity, and therefore was scarcely an acceptable objective to be pursued through the agency of war. . . .

During December and January, with Congress in session, Democratic orators seized control of the all-of-Mexico movement and carried this new burst of expansionism to greater heights of grandeur and extravagance. Their speeches rang with appeals to the nationalism of war and the cause of liberty. Cass observed that annexation would sweep away the abuses of generations. Senator Ambrose Sevier of Arkansas pointed to the progress that awaited the most degenerate Mexican population from the application of American law and education. In January, 1848, the Democratic Party of New York, in convention, adopted resolutions favoring annexation. The new mission of regeneration was proclaimed everywhere in the banquet toasts to returning officers. At one Washington dinner in January Senator Daniel Dickinson of New York offered a toast to "A more perfect Union: embracing the entire North American continent." In Congress that month Senator R. M. T. Hunter of Virginia commented on the fever annexationism had stirred up. "Schemes of ambition, vast enough to have tasked even a Roman imagination to conceive," he cried, "present themselves suddenly as practical questions." Both Buchanan and Walker of the cabinet, as well as Vice President George M. Dallas, openly embraced the all-of-Mexico movement.

That conservative coalition which had upheld the Oregon compromise combined again early in 1848 to oppose and condemn this new crusade. This powerful and well-led group feared that the United States, unless it sought greater moderation in its external policies, would drift into a perilous career of conquest which would tax the nation's energies without bringing any commensurate advantages. Its spokesmen doubted that the annexation of Mexico would serve the cause of humanity or present a new world of opportunity for American immigrants. Waddy Thompson, the South Carolina Whig who had spent many years in Mexico, warned in October against annexation: "We shall get no land, but will add a large population, aliens to us in feeling, education, race, and religion—a people unaccustomed to work, and accustomed to insubordination and resistance to law, the expense of governing whom will be ten times as great as the revenues derived from them." Thompson, joined by Calhoun and other Southern antiannexationists, warned the South that no portion of Mexico was suitable for slavery. Mexico's annexation would merely endanger the South's interests with a new cordon of free states. In Congress Calhoun acknowledged the dilemma created by the thoughtless decision to invade Mexico and recommended that the United States withdraw all its military forces to a defensive line across northern Mexico and maintain that line until Mexico chose to negotiate a permanent and satisfactory boundary arrangement with the United States.

Neither the mission of regeneration nor its rejection by conservatives determined the American course of empire. The great debate between those who anticipated nothing less than the achievement of a continental destiny and those who, in the interest of morality or from fear of a bitter controversy over slavery expansion, opposed the further acquisition of national territory, was largely irrelevant. Polk and his advisers pursued a precise vision, shared by those expansionists who searched the Mexican borderlands for the American interest. In the mid-forties, when the nation's agricultural frontier was still pushing across Iowa and Missouri, the concern of those who knew California lay less in land than in the configuration of the coastline and its possible relationship to America's future in the entire world of the Pacific. If American continentalism during the war years provided a substantially favorable climate for the acquisition of Mexican lands, it contributed nothing to the actual formulation of the administration's expansionist program.

During the early weeks of the Mexican War the President noted repeatedly in his diary that he would accept no treaty which did not transfer New Mexico and Upper California to the United States. It was left only to hammer out his precise war aims. Initially, Polk and his cabinet were attracted to San Francisco and Monterey. Several days after the outbreak of war George Bancroft, Secretary of the Navy, assured the Marblehead merchant, Samuel Hooper, that by mid-June the United States flag would be floating over these two northern California ports. "I hope California is now in our possession, never to be given up," he added. "We were driven reluctantly to war; we must make a solid peace. . . ."

But Hooper did not rest at Bancroft's promise. He prodded the administration to look southward along the California coast. Settlement at the thirty-second parallel, Hooper informed Bancroft, would secure both Los Angeles and the bay of San Diego. Such a boundary, moreover, would encompass all the Anglo-American population in the province and remove future annoyance by leaving a barren wilderness between Upper California and the larger Mexican cities to the south. Should the United States acquire San Diego as well as Monterey and San Francisco, continued Hooper, "it would insure a peaceful state of things through the whole country and enable [the Americans] to continue their trade as before along the whole coast. . . ." Thereafter the administration looked to San Diego. Bancroft assured Hooper in June, 1846, that the administration would accede to New England's wishes. "If Mexico makes peace this month," he wrote, "the Rio del Norte and the Parallel of 35° may do as a boundary; after that 32° which will include San Diego." This harbor remained the ultimate and unshakable territorial objective of Polk's wartime diplomacy.

Eventually the President achieved this goal through the efforts of Nicholas P. Trist. Unable after almost a year of successful fighting in Mexico to force the Mexican government to sue for terms, Polk, in April, 1847, dispatched Trist as a secret diplomatic agent to join General Winfield Scott's army in Mexico and await any sudden shift in Mexican politics. Trist's official baggage contained detailed instructions and the *projet* for a treaty which aimed pointedly at the acquisition of the entire coast of California to San Diego Bay. Trist's subsequent negotiations secured not only a treaty of peace with Mexico which terminated the war but also the administration's precise territorial objectives. Manifest destiny fully revealed itself in the Mexican War only when it clamored for the whole of Mexico, but even that final burst of agrarian nationalism was killed effectively by the Treaty of Guadalupe Hidalgo. American victories along the road to Mexico City were important only in that they created the force which permitted the President to secure through war what he had once hoped to achieve through diplomacy alone. It was Trist, working alone and unobserved, who in the final analysis defined the southern boundary of California. . . .

Manifest destiny, in its evolution as a body of American thought, expressed a spirit of confidence and a sense of power. It set forth in extravagant language a vision of national greatness in territorial, political, or diplomatic concerns. It proclaimed a national mission to the downtrodden and oppressed, designed to rationalize in terms of a higher good the nation's right, and even its duty, to dispossess neighboring countries of portions of their landed possessions. But whatever its form and strength, manifest destiny was purely the creation of editors and politicians, expounded to churn the public's nationalistic emotions for the purpose of reaping larger political harvests. Those who preached the crusade created fanciful dreams of the Republic's future; they ignored specifics and were unmindful of means. They were ideologues, not statesmen.

Even their success in converting the nation to the wisdom or feasibility of their views was doubtful. It was the consideration of national interest alone that carried the annexations of the forties through Congress. In the case of Texas, where the final decision conformed to the will of the expansionists, the victory came hard. The Senate overwhelmingly rejected the Texas treaty of 1844, and only after months of intense party and sectional maneuvering—during which time the Texas issue became nationalized—was the joint resolution of annexation adopted by the narrow vote of 27 to 25. Where the nation would expand after Texas was the business of the national executive as the wielder of the nation's diplomacy, and the territory which the United States opened up across the continent to the Pacific satisfied a series of traditional and limited national interests. National growth itself had little or no connection with the continentalism which dominated the language of manifest destiny in the forties and which cloaked American expansionism with universal goals —abstract rather than precise. Manifest destiny created the sentiment that would underwrite governmental policies of expansion; it could not and did not create the policies themselves.

The Senate approved the Oregon Treaty of 1846 with an ample margin, but it was the minority of fourteen senators—the die-hard proponents of the whole-of-Oregon movement—who represented the cause of manifest destiny. The Oregon Treaty was a triumph for the moderates. Again, in 1848, the Senate agreed to the nation's expansion by accepting the Treaty of Guadalupe Hidalgo. But the Senate resolution which demanded more than California and New Mexico from the defeated enemy represented a futile effort to convert the all-of-Mexico sentiment into policy. It lost by eleven votes. The persistent failure of Democratic orators to achieve their declared political and diplomatic goals with appeals to both the emotions of patriotism and the actual record of American expansion culminated in their inability to elect their leading expansionist, Lewis Cass, to the White House in 1848.

Except for the Gadsden Purchase in 1853, a quiet transaction that responded to the needs of railroad building, the nation failed to expand between 1848 and 1860. However, manifest destiny suffered one last and glorious revival when, as late as 1859, James Buchanan sparked another burst of expansionism toward Cuba. But whatever the appeal of such sentiment in Washington, it had no influence in Madrid. Without the physical coercion of Spain there could be no expansion, and even those Americans who would accept the doctrine that the ends justified the means could not discover the "occasion"—at least one acceptable to the majority of United States citizens—for bringing the overwhelming power of the United States to bear on the weakening Spanish rule in Cuba.

American expansion before the Civil War, like all successful national action abroad, required specific and limited objectives, totally achievable within the context of diplomacy or force, whether that force be displayed or merely assumed. After national interest and diplomatic advantage combined, during the forties, to carry the United States to the Pacific, the necessary elements of policy and policy formulation never reoccurred to extend boundaries further. Perhaps it mattered little. The decade of the fifties—for the United States a decade of unprecedented internal development—amply proved the contention of the antiexpansionists that the country's material growth was not dependent upon its further territorial advancement.

Polk's Aggressive Leadership

DAVID M. PLETCHER

Shortly after the Mexican War the American Peace Society offered a $500 prize for the best study of the recent conflict "on the principles of Christianity, and an enlightened statesmanship." Abiel A. Livermore, a Unitarian minister from New Hampshire, won the prize with a manuscript setting forth the thesis that the war and the preceding annexation of Texas had been parts of a plot by Polk, Tyler, Calhoun, and the South for the extension of slavery. Another entry in the contest by the Rev. Mr. Philip Berry, a Presbyterian, was less to the judges' liking, perhaps because it criticized the war not as immoral but as unnecessary: "Tested by the principles which have ordinarily governed the civilized world in its international relations [it] was . . . one of the most *just* wars that have blotted with gore the history of man—a war that might nevertheless have been avoided by the United States, had they been so disposed, probably without diminution of an inch of territory."

Livermore's blast was an opening gun in a long historiographical battle over the legal and moral validity of American actions, which lasted well into the twentieth century, but Berry's arresting statement drew no answering fire from the defenders of the war and the annexations. Was the war, in fact, necessary? More broadly expressed, did Tyler, Polk, and other policy makers of the mid-1840s carry through their program of territorial expansion in such a way as to minimize dangers, loss, and general tension? Did the annexations cost the United States too much? Speculative questions such as these cannot be finally answered, but they may serve as a point of departure for appraising policies and actions.

The first step in such an appraisal is to draw up a balance sheet of American gains and losses resulting from the war and from the Texas and Oregon treaties. Some gains are obvious to anyone who can read a map. Between 1845 and 1848 the United States acquired more than 1,200,000 square miles of territory, just over a third of its present area, including Alaska and Hawaii—a vast domain almost as large as all the countries of Free Europe after World War II. During the Mexican War some Whigs were inclined to write off California and Oregon as worthless, save for a few Pacific harbors, but the gold rush of 1849 quickly put an end to such skepticism. After the news of the gold strikes reached Mexico City, Consul John Black, once more at his old post, overheard a Mexican in a restaurant remark bitterly, "Ah, . . . the Yankees knew full well before they commenced the war, what they were going to fight for, they knew the value of that country better than we did."

Other American gains were more intangible—for example, the increasing respect of Europeans. Impressed by the show of power, Old World statesmen and publicists recognized that the United States would now dominate the north Pa-

Reprinted from *The Diplomacy of Annexation: Texas, Oregon, and the Mexican War* by David M. Pletcher, by permission of the University of Missouri Press. Copyright © 1973 by the Curators of the University of Missouri.

cific coast and the Gulf of Mexico. After the American occupation of California was confirmed, the London *Times* commented, "From so favorable a harbour the course lies straight and obvious to Polynesia, the Philippines, New Holland, and China, and it is not extravagant to suppose that the merchants of this future emporium may open the commerce of Japan."

To be sure, European efforts against American expansion did not entirely cease after 1848, but never again did their agents act so boldly and so close to American borders as had Captain Charles Elliot, the British consul in Texas. Indeed, in 1848, as revolution spread over Europe, the democratic republicanism that most persons identified with the United States seemed close to a final triumph on both sides of the Atlantic. The irrepressible George Bancroft rejoiced that "the struggles of Europe . . . will not rest, till every vestige of feudal nobility is effaced; and the power of the people shall have superseded that of hereditary princes." In these struggles, he added, the United States would be the model. To Bancroft's dismay, reaction soon triumphed over the Revolution of 1848, but American successes in the New World remained to raise the discouraged spirits of Old World liberals and democrats.

More immediately important to the United States, the Mexican War helped to shift the balance of power in the Western Hemisphere. In January 1848 the Earl of Ellenborough, who had wanted San Francisco for a British naval base, wrote gloomily to his former chief, Sir Robert Peel, that the only hope for Anglo-American peace was the indefinite occupation of Mexico by the United States, since this would keep the Americans too busy to seize Canada. Probably to his surprise, when the war ended a few weeks later the troops were immediately brought home and mustered out. Nevertheless, the American lodgement on Puget Sound and the American performance in the Mexican War emphasized more firmly to succeeding British administrations that Her Majesty's Canadian subjects were hostages to American good will.

As a result of the war, the British government also gave up any remaining hopes of political influence around the Gulf of Mexico. In 1848 it declined to guarantee the new Mexican boundaries, sponsor a Tehuantepec transit route, or set up a protectorate over Yucatán. The Americans then pursued the British into Central America, which became a field of intrigue for rival diplomatic agents during the late 1840s. Both sides accepted a temporary stalemate in the Clayton-Bulwer Treaty of 1850, which placed the United States for the first time on an equal basis with Great Britain in that area. During the following decade the British gradually abandoned political aspirations in Central America too, content to compete for economic gains with the potent but unmilitary weapons of their factory system and their merchant marine. If the Mexican War alone did not accomplish this contraction of British influence in the Western Hemisphere, it surely hastened the process.

Against these American gains of territory and prestige, however, the appraising historian must charge certain losses. Some of these were the familiar costs of all wars: about 12,800 men dead out of 90,000 under arms and about $100 million in expenses, to which might be added the $15 million paid to Mexico under the peace treaty. The families and friends of the dead soldiers were the chief sufferers, for the growing nation hardly felt the expenditure of men and money. But, as with the gains, some of the most serious losses caused by the Western annexations and the war are impossible to measure exactly.

One part of this intangible deficit was a rising spirit of "lick all creation," an overblown chauvinism with strong hints of militarism and racism that coarsened democratic sensibilities and laid American ideologues open to charges of hypocrisy. Two examples of this national hubris will suffice. The last Texan secretary of state, Ashbel Smith, who had opposed annexation in 1845, saw in the Mexican peace treaty three years later only the first chapter of a long story:

> The Mexican War is part of the mission, of the destiny allotted to the Anglo Saxon race on this continent. It is our destiny, our mission to Americanize this continent. No nation once degenerate has ever been regenerated but by foreign conquest; and such is the predestined fate of degenerate Mexico. The sword is the great civilizer, it clears the way for commerce, education, religion and all the harmonizing influences of morality and humanity. . . . Palo Alto and Buena Vista, Cerro Gordo and Churubusco . . . will be the talismanic watchwords of freedom and security.

A little later, as Lieutenant Raphael Semmes USN looked back on his wartime service, he agreed:

> The passage of our race into Texas, New Mexico, and California, was but the first step in that great movement southward, which forms a part of our destiny. An all-wise Providence has placed us in juxtaposition with an inferior people, in order, without doubt, that we may sweep over them, and remove them (as a people) and their worn-out institutions from the face of the earth. We are the northern hordes of the Alani, spreading ourselves over fairer and sunnier fields, and carrying along with us, beside the newness of life, and the energy and courage of our prototypes, letters, arts, and civilization.

The rest of the world, long accustomed to American strutting, might well have discounted these predictions but for the amazing victories of Zachary Taylor and Winfield Scott and the persistent filibustering expeditions that Americans launched during the 1850s against Mexico, Cuba, and Central America. To Latin Americans the events of 1843–1848 revealed, perhaps for the first time, the aggressive potential of the United States. Sympathy for Mexico encouraged a widespread but disorganized sentiment for some sort of congress to unite Spanish-speaking peoples against their external enemies. The press of many South American countries reprinted the Whigs' speeches and editorials attacking Polk as evidence that the war was unpopular with the American people, but the onward march of the troops suggested that even public opinion could not halt the *yanqui* government. A stereotype began to take shape in Latin American writing about the United States—the Colossus of the North.

But the most alarming effects of Western annexations and the Mexican War developed within the United States. By the early 1840s many Whigs had come to believe that further expansion in any direction would place intolerable strains on national unity. For that reason Daniel Webster opposed acquiring Texas, and even the expansionist James Buchanan eventually came to think of it as a

Trojan horse, for its annexation widened the sectional gap between North and South. To abolitionists Texas became a moral issue; as Charles Sumner put it, "By welcoming Texas as a Slave State we make slavery our own original sin."

In debating the Oregon question, Webster's Whigs also discouraged annexation, expecting that the American emigrants would form an independent, friendly nation on the Pacific coast. To annex it would be as preposterous as annexing Ireland. Nevertheless, the Democratic platform of 1844 and Polk's inaugural address reassured Northern and Western expansionists that the "clear and unquestionable" American title to all Oregon would maintain the balance of sections. The compromise at 49°, however reasonable in legal and practical argument, struck many of them as betrayal by the South. "We have been duped . . . ," declared an Ohioan. "Oregon & Texas should have went [sic] hand in hand, Oregon first."

Northern sectionalism undoubtedly encouraged the nation's desire for California, thereby reinforcing the prowar group within the Democratic party. But it also strengthened Whigs' opposition to the war, especially as the progress of Taylor's army suggested the annexation of territory to the southwest. The Northerners' feeling of betrayal crystallized in the Wilmot Proviso, first introduced by one of Polk's own Democrats, which completed the association of slavery and expansion and made the war seem, like Texas and Oregon before it, both a sectional and a moral issue. "It was conceived in sin . . . ," proclaimed the Albany *Evening Standard,* "not to promote any great principle; . . . but to conquer a neighboring republic to acquiesce in an attempt to extend the borders of slavery." "When the foreign war ends, *the domestic war will begin,*" warned the New York *Gazette and Times.* Ralph Waldo Emerson compared the Mexican War to a dose of arsenic, and he might well have applied the term to the acquisition of Texas and Oregon too.

No one would be so bold as to attribute Latin American Yankeephobia and the Civil War wholly or mainly to the annexations of the 1840s. It would be safer to argue that Texas, Oregon, and the Mexican War hastened and intensified trends that might have led to the same results eventually. But insofar as these annexations inflated American arrogance and spread hemispheric and national disunity, they exacted a heavy price, which a fair appraisal must somehow balance against the material gains and the rise in national prestige.

One may next ask whether the nation might have secured substantially the same territory at smaller cost. Brief examination of this question suggests that the alternatives multiplied as the expansion progressed. Given the situation of the early 1840s, the only way for the United States to acquire Texas was to negotiate an acceptable settlement with the Texan government. After the annexation, the United States had the choice of conciliating Mexico, perhaps by paying a disguised indemnity, or of ignoring her claims to the lost province, secure in the confidence that she would not or could not back them with force.

In the Oregon question the United States faced the alternatives of fighting Britain, negotiating with her, or waiting for American settlers to overrun the disputed territory. Controlling elements in both the American and British governments regarded the first option as a last resort, the unthinkable result of blundering rather than of a deliberate decision by either side. The other two options, both highly plausible, will be discussed later.

In the case of the Mexican War the choice was the most complicated of all, for at various points in their relations with Mexico, American leaders contemplated four different lines of action. One was the course actually followed, that of invading Mexico, compelling her to cede the desired territory in a treaty, and then withdrawing American troops at once. A second was the establishment of a temporary protectorate over all Mexico to regenerate that unhappy nation while the United States detached her northern provinces or even prepared her for total absorption. A third was passive military occupation of California, New Mexico, and parts of Chihuahua, Coahuila, Nuevo León, and Tamaulipas, the Army maintaining a chain of forts along the line of the Sierra Madre until Mexico gave up and recognized the *fait accompli*. The last course of action was not to declare war at all but to wait until American settlers could form a majority in California and possibly also in New Mexico, rebel, create an independent state, and enter the Union in the manner of Texas.

The alternative of establishing a protectorate and regenerating Mexico was a most unlikely one. In the first place, its plausibility was muddied by Americans' envy of Mexican natural resources, so that many who espoused it did so only as a rationalization for annexation. But even if the protectorate plan had been more fully worked out and less burdened with hypocrisy, it would still have been wholly impracticable on several counts. At the most abstract level, no one has ever convincingly demonstrated that democracy can be imposed from above. Waddy Thompson, ex-minister to Mexico and a comparatively enlightened commentator on the war, asked, "But of what avail are free institutions without the spirit of liberty amongst the people; or what avail are both without general intelligence and virtue?" Many Americans believed Mexicans to be sunk so deep in ignorance and reaction that if the United States tried to do more than set a good example, the effort would end by endangering this country's free institutions through militarism, bureaucracy, and executive tyranny.

Descending to more concrete levels, opponents of a protectorate could reasonably doubt that it would command the support of many Mexicans. To be sure, a group of *puros* expressed admiration for American institutions, especially control by the civil government over the military. But at the same time, another part of this faction, the followers of Valentín Gómez Farías, were proclaiming undying hatred of the *yanqui*. Assuming that a sizable group of Mexican liberals had initially supported a protectorate, the detachment of California and New Mexico would have disillusioned many of them.

Also, if a protectorate had been established, the American officials in charge of Mexico would quickly have had to deal with deep-seated internal problems —the powers of the Church, the ownership of land, the role of the army, and others. Whatever they did, these officials would have alienated large blocs of influential citizens. A cursory glance at the French protectorate of the 1860s, the well-meant but blundering leadership of Maximilian, and the everlasting guerrilla warfare fought by the *juaristas* suggests the staggering obstacles confronting even a temporary administration of Mexico. Finally, the protectorate plan would have done nothing to abate destructive sectionalism in the United States. Indeed, the rivalry of conservative and liberal policies in Mexico might have exacerbated the quarrels of North and South.

Another plan of action, somewhat less ambitious than the regeneration of all Mexico, was to occupy the northern territory which the United States wished to annex, establish a line of forts along the proposed new boundary, and wait for Mexico to abandon her efforts at reconquest. This idea seems to have occurred to many Americans at about the same time during the early autumn of 1846. By then Taylor had established his control along the lower Rio Grande, and Stockton and Frémont had taken over the principal settlements along the California coast. Although various versions of the partial occupation plan differed in details, most of them specified a line from Tampico to Mazatlán or San Blas, including several cities such as Monterrey and San Luis Potosí as well as many important silver mines. During the invasion of central Mexico and especially after the impasse had developed at Mexico City, some generals and civilians suggested withdrawal to a northern line. But by this time such a policy would have been most difficult to execute, for the evacuation of any territory whatever would have affronted American patriots, spread war weariness, and encouraged Mexican resistance.

Even if undertaken earlier in the war, the indefinite passive military occupation of northern Mexico would have presented serious obstacles. The advocates of this strategy counted heavily on local separatism and growing friendliness between the inhabitants and the occupying forces. But cities such as Tampico, Monterrey, and San Luis Potosí comprised fully developed Mexican societies and culture, as contrasted to the conglomerate, shallowly rooted settlements of California and the Rio Grande Valley. Sooner or later the relations of long-established Mexican groups with the Protestant, Anglo-Saxon Americans, each despising the strangeness of the other, would surely have produced chronic instability. Arguments over the introduction of slaves, economic and social rivalry between the lower classes of both countries, and differences concerning the position of the Church would probably have intensified sectional and partisan divisions within the United States. At the same time, the indefinite continuation of the war would have stimulated Polk's opposition—Whigs, abolitionists, and those who impatiently demanded bold attack and speedy victory. Once the war had gotten under way, it was hard to refute Thomas Hart Benton's argument that an overwhelming offensive was the surest route to peace.

But was it necessary to fight for the territory at all? The last alternative under consideration was for the United States to maintain "a wise and masterly inactivity" following the annexation of Texas—to parry British proposals for ending joint occupation in Oregon, station a defensive force at the western edge of effective Texan settlement, and wait for the movement of American pioneers to fill up the desired areas. If left to themselves, Californians would presumably declare their independence of Mexico, and the settlers in the Willamette Valley would expand northward to Puget Sound. Meanwhile, in both areas bonds of trade and kinship with the United States would develop. Eventually, the United States government would negotiate an annexation treaty with California; Britain would recognize the *fait accompli* in Oregon by splitting the territory at 49°; and Mexico would abandon her claims, perhaps in return for an indemnity.

This policy assumed that American expansion was inevitable and that the past would continue to repeat itself. Politicians and journalists were fond of proclaiming this assumption; as one of them declared in 1846, "No power on earth . . . can check the swelling tide of American population. . . . Every portion of this continent, from the sunny south to the frozen north, will be, in a very few years, filled with industrious and thriving Anglo-Saxons. . . . This is the irresistible progress of our people. Like the flow of the ocean, it overcomes all opposition." Since its independence the United States had developed a flexible, effective procedure for acquiring territory with a minimum of risk. This procedure was to reinforce the "irresistible progress" with diplomatic and economic pressure or perhaps veiled threats and to exploit fully the disunity among European powers and their tepid interest in North America. In this manner the Americans had won first the navigation of the lower Mississippi, then Louisiana, then the Floridas, and finally Texas without an open declaration of war or serious fighting except against the Indians.

Why not use the time-proven procedure in Oregon and California? In 1843 Calhoun advocated exactly this strategy in Oregon, and he conducted cordial but indeterminate negotiations with Britain during his year in the State Department. The outstanding exponent of the same policy in California was Thomas O. Larkin, the leading American merchant and, after 1843, American consul in Monterey. Always maintaining friendly relations with native inhabitants and local governments, Larkin encouraged a movement for an independent republic in which natives, Europeans, and Americans would enjoy equal status. Eventually, he believed, all three groups would find it to their interest to enter the American Union. For a time Polk approved this policy. After the war began, he experimented with secessionism in northeastern Mexico, hoping to attract the inhabitants peaceably into the United States.

The policy of relying on migration and gradual assimilation of thinly populated areas faced certain obstacles. In northeastern Mexico the boisterousness of the new American arrivals irrevocably antagonized most upper-class Mexicans. In California the Bear Flag revolt showed that many pro-American inhabitants preferred action to persuasion; sometimes Larkin himself leaned in that direction. Another obstacle to gradualism was certain to be the stubbornness of the Mexican government. After resisting the recognition of Texan independence for nine years, it had yielded in 1845 only through British persuasion and in the desperate hope of preventing annexation by the United States. The Mexicans might have resisted for a longer time if California had pulled away from their grasp, and subsequent annexation by the United States might have created a chronic, festering diplomatic problem. Polk might not have come to terms even with the independent Californian republic during his four years as President. Had gradualism won California to the Union, New Mexico might not have attracted enough American settlers to repeat the process, thereby leaving an inconvenient Mexican salient between Texas and the Pacific coast. The chances of delay and of creating an awkward boundary must be weighed against the dangers and cost of precipitate action.

From the viewpoint of Polk and his generation the most serious drawback to gradualism was the risk of British intervention. Persistent rumors throughout 1845 declared that the Mexican government would sell or mortgage California to Britain. British residents were said to be planning an invitation for a protectorate. The British warships that regularly visited the Oregon coast might be carrying on reconnaissance to the south at the same time. Even if Britain did not interfere with an independence movement in California, the partly known story of her activities in Texas furnished a precedent for fearing subsequent intrigue on the Pacific coast. To many Americans a short, decisive war seemed greatly preferable to another long series of negotiations with some Californian Sam Houston, "coquetting" at the same time with the wily Aberdeen or the daredevil Palmerston. . . .

If the Mexican War was indeed an unnecessary gamble, why did Polk undertake it? He and his supporters explained that he did so only as a last resort, in defense of American interests and honor after Mexico had ignored claims, rejected negotiation, and hurled insult and defiance at the United States. Many historians have applied their scholarship to defense of this viewpoint. But a considerable segment of antiwar opinion at the time proclaimed that Polk was waging a war of conquest, pure and simple, which he rationalized with sophistical arguments, so as to legalize the American occupation of California under the law of nations and set up such a barrier as the British would not dare cross. Pursuing the matter further, some of Polk's opponents accused him of "a deliberate contrivance to bring the war about in such a manner as to throw on Mexico the odium of its commencement." Since the 1880s a few historians have accepted this "plot thesis" and have applied it to all his policies from his inauguration to the beginning of the war.

None of these explanations is wholly convincing. The list of American claims and the story of the Slidell mission suggest that American grievances were bearable and that the United States government had not exhausted the possibilities of negotiation. Also, the opening hostilities took place on disputed ground to which Mexico had an arguable claim. But if Polk was waging simply a war of conquest, it is hard to understand why he did not plan it more comprehensively from the beginning and why he conducted it with spurts of action followed by long periods of stagnant delay. As for the "plot thesis," its supporters offer too little evidence and too much surmise in its defense. They ignore the administration's repeated predictions that war was neither likely nor desirable and the administration's failure to enlarge or overhaul the inadequate army until war had begun. Also, they fail to make clear why Polk should have provoked Britain to a war crisis at the same time that he planned to fight Mexico.

A more consistent explanation of Polk's foreign policies appears in several revealing statements he made about Britain and Oregon. Note his account of a conversation with a minor Democratic Congressman on January 4, 1846, during the Oregon debate:

> I remarked to him that the only way to treat John Bull was to look him straight in the eye; that I considered a bold & firm course on our part the pacific one;

that if Congress faultered [*sic*] or hesitated in their course, John Bull would immediately become arrogant and more grasping in his demands; & that such had been the history of the Brittish [*sic*] Nation in all their contests with other Powers for the last two hundred years.

He put it even more succinctly to a friend: "Great Brittain [*sic*] was never known to do justice to any country—with which she had a controversy, when that country was in an attitude of supplication or on her knees before her." Accordingly, when he sent Buchanan or McLane to approach Pakenham or Aberdeen, Polk took a high hand, exaggerated his legal case and his demands, and regarded all suggestions of compromise as probes from Britain or American Anglophiles to find weak points in his armor.

Polk applied the same policy of aggressive negotiation to American-Mexican relations, with the difference that, instead of respectful suspicion toward a tough, tenacious power, he felt contemptuous impatience toward a weak, corrupt, disorganized government, much given to delay and evasion. Tight-mouthed, he let slip no revealing private remarks about the Mexican character such as his comments on Britain, but his public statements in his annual message of 1845 and especially in the war message give some idea of his underlying feelings. "A continued and unprovoked series of wrongs," hope for "a returning sense of justice," "frivolous pretexts," "the subsisting constitutional authorities . . . subverted," a "manifest breach of faith," "a government either unable or unwilling . . . to perform one of its plainest duties," a "system of outrage and extortion" —all these phrases suggest Polk's distaste for Mexico. Such a government, like that of Britain, would respond only to strong words and a show of force. He declared to his cabinet during the last weeks before the declaration of war that "we must treat all nations, whether great or small, strong or weak, alike, and that we should take a bold and firm course toward Mexico."

Thus, when Polk became President, he set forth on a foreign policy of strong stands, overstated arguments, and menacing public pronouncements, not because he wanted war but because he felt that this was the only language which his foreign adversaries would understand. Faced at his inauguration with the delicate final arrangements for the annexation of Texas, Polk had no desire to precipitate an immediate crisis with either Mexico or Britain. Accordingly, he sent a special agent to reconnoiter in Mexico City for a renewal of diplomatic relations and agreed to exchange views on Oregon with Britain. When Pakenham cut short this exchange, Polk, overreacting, jumped to the conclusion that he had been tricked. Breaking off the dialogue, he stiffly notified the British government that it must now make a concrete proposal which he might treat as he chose.

The strong stand toward Mexico was slower to develop. During the summer and autumn of 1845 rumors of Mexico's intentions to attack in the Rio Grande Valley or to reconquer California with British aid provoked Polk to station troops and ships where they would be useful in case of war and also to inaugurate a program of propaganda and intrigue among the natives of California. These preparations made, he sent Slidell to Mexico, with instructions to press Herrera not only for recognition of Texan boundaries but for the sale of California and New Mexico as well. In December his annual message summarized the strong stands toward both Britain and Mexico and added new arguments, such as the Monroe Doctrine, to earlier rationalizations.

Events during the winter of 1845–1846 forced Polk to modify his original plans. He had called on Congress to demonstrate unified support by quickly passing a firm resolution of notice to Britain on Oregon. But before doing so, in late April, the legislators spent four months in rancorous debate, thus threatening Polk's whole legislative program and the unity of his party. Meanwhile, the Mexican government refused even to receive Slidell, who finally returned home empty-handed. At some time during the last stages of the Oregon debate Polk became convinced that an actual war with Mexico would be necessary— not a major conflict, but a limited, short, decisive engagement in the Rio Grande Valley which would convince Mexico that the United States meant business. If the Mexicans began the fighting, their attack could be used to unify the Democratic party and confound the Whigs. If American forces could then occupy California and New Mexico, Mexico would be forced to negotiate and the United States could obtain title to the provinces, perhaps in return for a disguised indemnity to Mexico. By this time Britain would have decided to propose an Oregon settlement which the Senate would accept.

This version of Polk's policies explains his episodic method of waging war. During May and June he carried out much of his program through Taylor's victories in the Rio Grande Valley, the Oregon settlement, and the occupation of California—so much that, when the Mexicans continued to resist, Polk was firmly convinced that one more crushing victory would cause their collapse and bring peace. First, the Americans advanced to Monterrey, then to Tampico, while he let the apparently pliant Santa Anna slip through the blockade to return home. He then pressed Congress for a special fund of $3 million, which might be used as an inducement to Mexico to sign a proper peace treaty.

After waiting in vain for Santa Anna to negotiate, Polk decided to occupy Veracruz and then to advance into the fever-free interior, sending a minor diplomat, Nicholas P. Trist, to accompany the army and transmit correspondence. But even Scott's victory at Cerro Gordo, the most impressive of the entire war, failed to break the Mexicans' amazing will to resist. After pausing three months at Puebla, Scott moved into the Valley of Mexico—a dangerous advance, for he risked being cut off from his base. At this point one setback would have undone the effect of all previous victories. But the Americans continued to win battles. At one point peace talks actually got under way, but again Santa Anna did not choose or dare to submit, and Scott had to occupy Mexico City.

The war now threatened to get out of hand altogether, as a movement spread through the United States for extensive annexations in central Mexico or rule over the entire country as the only acceptable return for American losses. But Polk gave no evidence that he had lost his nerve or had changed his plans. Instead, learning of the fruitless peace talks, he recalled Trist. Apparently the President intended to take over direct control of negotiations and perhaps force the Mexicans to come to Washington if they wanted peace. However, his repudiated envoy spared him the need of testing his assumptions further by an act of courageous insubordination. Urged by British diplomats and merchants, Trist remained in Mexico and with their aid obtained a treaty along the lines of his original instructions. One might add that Polk's luck continued to hold, even in his failure to acquire Yucatán and Cuba after the war, for he was able to leave office without bequeathing to his successor half-realized annexations which were beyond the country's capacity at that time.

To the retrospective eye of the historian Polk's alarums and excursions present an astonishing spectacle. Impelled by his conviction that successful diplomacy could rest only on a threat of force, he made his way, step by step, down the path to war. Then, viewing the war as a mere extension of his diplomatic scheme, he proceeded as confidently as a sleepwalker through a maze of obstacles and hazards to the peace settlement he had calmly intended from the beginning.

Despite his boldness and his unshakable determination, Polk was at heart a cautious leader. His apparently most impetuous acts—the withdrawal of the Oregon offer to Pakenham, the bold stands of his first annual message, the declaration of war, and the occupation of Veracruz—were undertaken only after weeks or even months of meditation and discussion with his advisers. If he thought long and hard about his country's interests, he was even more careful when the interests of his party and himself were concerned, for he tried to associate Congress in some way with every important decision he made, in order to divert and disperse the wrathful lightning of his many opponents.

Nevertheless, for all his prudence, he clearly did not anticipate the rigors of a war crisis with Britain or a long-drawn-out invasion of Mexico. Why did he miscalculate so grossly? One reason was simple lack of up-to-date, accurate information. Dispatches from London or Mexico City required at least three or four weeks to reach Washington, and news from Oregon and California five or six months. Even the most experienced, trusted observers were sometimes highly unreliable. While Everett and McLane presented fairly exact pictures of British attitudes, Consul Black in Mexico City consistently misled the United States government about the Mexicans' support of the war, and Larkin's important dispatch of July 10, 1845, about the British threat to California was wrong on every count. During the critical weeks of April and May 1846 Polk and his cabinet learned about Mexican troop movements from rumors in the New Orleans newspapers or hearsay dispatches from Mexico City and Veracruz. When Taylor marched into the lower Rio Grande Valley, his superiors provided him with an almost useless topographical map put together in Washington and with little more. In effect, both the administration and the general were feeling their way into unknown territory.

Polk's rigid determination to follow a course of aggressive diplomacy and war also rose from traits of his personality. His diary reveals that he could be insensitive to the ideals and convictions of others; this characteristic was dominant when he looked outward toward Europe or Latin America. He lacked a primary qualification of the diplomat—the ability to appreciate a foreign people's hopes, fears, and driving impulses and to see America and himself through their eyes. To him, Britain was a thieving bully, British appeals to national honor mere rationalizations, and British sentiments of democracy and friendship no more than traps for the unwary. Similarly, the Mexicans were a people hardly worthy of self government, unable to develop the borderlands that stood in the way of American expansion, and their clamorous boasts and appeals to patriotism mere mouth honor.

Polk's insensitivity toward Britain, though dangerous to American interests, was eventually nullified by countervailing factors. The more sophisticated Britons understood the President's personality, having seen its traits in some of their own politicians, and they made allowances for it, although they found it distasteful. Webster, Everett, Sturgis, and other American conciliators well known in London assured them by their demeanor that Polk represented only one aspect of the American character. Most important, perhaps, British leaders were perceptive enough to sense some of the possibilities for future Anglo-American cooperation and strong enough to defend British national honor with patience rather than with passion.

If such countervailing factors existed in American-Mexican relations, they are hard to discern. Mexicans had long regarded the United States with a combination of admiration and suspicion, and in the 1840s their rising anger was both complicated and frustrated by profound ignorance concerning American political and social institutions. Weak, disunited, repeatedly humiliated by revolutions, penury, and foreign slights, the Mexicans seemed to have nothing further to lose but national integrity. Remembering his experiences in Mexico City, Pakenham predicted that the Mexicans' sense of honor would require stubborn defense of their boundaries and that an American offer of money would probably intensify their resistance. A high British official, well acquainted with the Spanish character, once observed, "The Mexican is like a mule—if you spur him too much he will back off the precipice with you."

The most enlightened leaders of this quixotic people were far behind Peel and Aberdeen in training, perception, and firmness of purpose. Some, like Herrera and Cuevas, saw the need to restrain a national impulse toward self-immolation but did not know how. Others, like Gómez Farías, plunged into the flames with the rest. The master of Mexico during most of the war, Santa Anna, was even more inscrutable than Polk. Despite his postwar apologies and reams of Mexican writings, no convincing evidence has emerged to indicate that he ever seriously intended to reach an agreement with the United States. The record of his words and deeds suggests only that he was an incorrigible opportunist who improvised his plans from day to day without any guiding principle more sophisticated than self preservation.

Whatever the qualities of the Mexican leaders, their view of Polk and the United States was as simplistic as Polk's view of them, and the intermediaries between the two nations did little to correct the fault. Almonte's abilities might have been comparable to Pakenham's, but the Mexicans recalled him in 1845. Slidell might have been as persuasive as McLane, but the Mexicans would not receive him. As for unofficial go-betweens, Atocha and Beach are not comparable with Everett, Sturgis, or the Baring agents.

Polk's myopia and lack of empathy in relations with Britain and Mexico can also be attributed in large measure to his training and environment. From his mentor Andrew Jackson, he may have derived the models for his British and Mexican policies—the peremptory Jacksonian challenge to France over unpaid debts and the conniving mission of Anthony Butler to Mexico. In the challenge to France the threat of force, though later modified, had brought action; while the heavy-handed Butler was unsuccessful, Polk might reasonably have supposed that a more suave agent would prevail.

In a broader sense, whether Polk received from Jackson his suspicions of other nations and his techniques for dealing with them, he may be said to have epitomized the self-centered, aggressive nationalism prevalent in the Mississippi Valley during much of the nineteenth century. Remembering British-Indian intrigues and the War of 1812, Midwesterners easily envisaged the Hudson's Bay Company, the governor general of Canada, and the cabinet in London as deceitful bullies. Remembering how Spanish dons in Madrid and New Orleans had opposed American expansion, the inhabitants of the lower valley and their cousins, the transplanted Texans, easily attributed to Mexico the same sly, ceremonious evasion they had experienced earlier. During the first fifty years of the United States' national existence Presidents and secretaries of state had frequently displayed a sophisticated cosmopolitanism that mitigated or, in some instances, nullified American xenophobia. This restraining factor, however, almost disappeared with the generation of Madison and Monroe. Post-Jacksonian leaders were not always more free from international involvements than their predecessors, but with few exceptions they were certainly less citizens of the world.

If Polk shared the *Weltanschauung* of his people and times, what may be said of his other blind spot—failure to anticipate the disunity Oregon and the Mexican War spread among the American people? Ideological and sectional rivalry arising from the Texas question had nearly torn the Democratic party asunder in the campaign of 1844. Once in office, Polk could not avoid carrying through the immediate annexation of Texas, since Congress and Tyler had precipitated the action. But why did he not realize that internal suspicions and resentments made it expedient to halt the pressure on Britain and Mexico for the time being?

Polk's abolitionist opponents and some later pro-Northern historians answered this question by labeling him the tool of the blind, recklessly imperialist Southern "slaveocracy." Years ago, American scholars punctured the thesis that the South monopolized or was even united behind southwest expansionism, although many Mexican writers still accept it as sound. Might Polk have wished to avoid a repetition of the sectional struggle over Texas and therefore set out to acquire Oregon, California, and New Mexico directly and quickly, so as to give sectionalism no time to develop? There is no evidence in his correspondence or diary to indicate this line of thought. Like many other Southerners, Polk regarded the "local institutions" of Texas as a matter of concern to the Texans alone. In his diary he had nothing to say about sectional agitation over slavery until the introduction of the Wilmot Proviso in the summer of 1846, when the war had already begun. Thereafter, he clearly looked on all attempts to link slavery and expansion as mischievous, wicked, and foolish —mischievous and wicked because his opponents were using the issues for partisan gain, foolish because the territory to be acquired would never support slavery.

Polk was not alone in his shallow, unenlightened view of the nation's most threatening problem, for other statesmen of the mid-1840s, older and more experienced than he, failed also to understand that sectionalism and expansion had formed a new, explosive compound. John C. Calhoun, deliberate and canny where Oregon was concerned, acted with reckless abandon in the Texas question when he answered Aberdeen's mild defense of abolitionism with a note gratuitously proclaiming what the North already suspected—that Calhoun wanted annexation in order to preserve slavery as a positive good. John Quincy Adams, who had reluctantly surrendered American claims to Texas in the Spanish treaty of 1819, threatened a secessionist movement in 1843 if Texas were annexed. Three years later he shifted back to expansionism and invoked *Genesis* to support the American claim to 54°40'. When one sees elder statesmen like these playing ducks and drakes with American passions, the insensitivity of younger men becomes more understandable.

In the effort to explain and appraise Polk's policies, one final element remains to be considered—his freedom of choice. To what extent were his decisions shaped or forced on him by circumstances beyond his control?

From 1845 to 1848 Polk seems to have experienced a phenomenon that diplomatic and military strategists of the mid-twentieth century have called *escalation*. This phenomenon is a process by which an initial set of decisions starts a chain of causes and effects, each more difficult to control than its predecessor. At the beginning of the chain the decision maker may have been presented with a fairly wide range of acceptable choices. The range is gradually reduced until at the end he has—or seems to have—none. In other words, events close in on him until he finds himself surrounded with dilemmas, all exits blocked.

Even at the beginning of his administration Polk did not have complete freedom of choice, for his party platform, the joint resolution of Congress, and Tyler's last-minute offer to Texas committed him to immediate annexation. This action, in turn, brought an unavoidable break in formal diplomatic relations with Mexico. Nevertheless, since that nation was in no position to launch a concerted attack, Polk could take stock of the situation, send a private observer to Mexico, and wait for the Mexicans' anger to subside. In the Oregon question he was limited only by an extremist plank in the Democratic platform and by the statements of Democratic congressmen during the winter debate of 1844–1845.

Polk might have taken stock of this question too, and perhaps he intended to do so. But he committed his first serious tactical error when he inserted into his inaugural address a restatement of the "clear and unquestionable" United States title—by implication to all Oregon—and thereby stirred up violent argument in Britain and in the American West. After this address, postponement of action was no longer possible, but for a time he considered private negotiations with Britain on the basis laid down by Calhoun in 1844. Pakenham rebuffed him; then, yielding to his own convictions about Britain, Polk committed his second major error by breaking off negotiations altogether and insisting that Britain must take the initiative to resume them. In less than six months he had abdicated nearly all choice concerning Oregon.

Until November 1845 Polk retained, almost unhampered, the power to determine the direction and timing of his Mexican policy. During the next two months, however, he seriously restricted his freedom of choice here as well. His instructions to Slidell and his annual message to Congress announced to Mexico and to the world at large that the United States would take an extreme position regarding its claims and objectives to the southwest. By thus proclaiming his intentions and by sending Taylor's army to the Rio Grande, Polk destroyed any hope of privately persuading Mexico. Meanwhile, his annual message again stimulated Western expectations for all of Oregon and formally transferred to Congress much of the responsibility for settling the question.

After January 1846 events began to drive Polk irresistibly. The long, raucous debate on Oregon encouraged the British government to postpone any useful initiative to resume negotiations. The debate and Mexico's rejection of Slidell induced Polk to plan for a short war with Mexico. But a short war turned into a long one, for the Mexicans now held the power of decision, and although repulsed or routed in every major battle, they determined to resist the invaders, supported by their formidable topography and climate.

Once war had been declared, Polk's policy choices were limited to alternate military strategies, attack of some sort versus a holding action. After the landing at Veracruz there remained only one way forward—up the foothills and across the mountains into the Valley of Mexico. When Scott captured Mexico City, Polk had exhausted the acceptable choices available to him, for further conquest, indefinite occupation, and retreat to a line across northern Mexico all presented insuperable difficulties. Fortunately, at this point conciliation and compromise, so foreign to Polk's nature, saved him.

All in all, an appraisal of the diplomacy of annexation brings the realization that annexation might have been less painful and costly if skillful diplomacy had been allowed to play a more vital role at several points. Diplomats drew up the basic terms for the incorporation of Texas, and the climactic victory of Donelson over Elliot was in large measure a diplomatic one. After a serious Anglo-American war crisis, it was the diplomacy of McLane that pointed the way to a settlement of the Oregon question. Similarly, after nearly two years of costly war with Mexico, it was the diplomacy of Trist, aided by British representatives, that laboriously untied the Gordian knot in Mexico City.

Could Polk have avoided the Oregon and Mexican crises by placing his chief reliance on conventional, professional diplomacy in the spring of 1845? The evidence suggests that he might have done so. In one of Tyler's last special messages, the outgoing President had reassured Congress about Oregon: "Considerable progress has been made in the discussion, . . . [and] there is reason to hope that it may be terminated and the negotiation brought to a close within a short period." Some such bromide, inserted into Polk's inaugural address, would probably have mollified most Western expansionists for the time being and would have allowed him opportunity to examine the files of the diplomatic correspondence before taking a stand.

At Polk's inauguration he had a nine-month period of grace before facing Congress—a period in which distribution of patronage, internal problems, and the Texas question were certain to occupy the public's attention. If he had set diplomats to work privately during this period, he might have been able to announce a viable solution of the Oregon question in his first annual message. The prospect of a peaceful settlement with Britain would then have immeasurably strengthened his hand in further diplomacy with Mexico. As the urgency of the Oregon question faded, Polk might have sent Slidell to Mexico as a special envoy, nominally to discuss Texan annexation but actually to present a confidential offer for boundary adjustments, while Taylor's army, still at Corpus Christi, mounted guard over the disputed zone without offering an overt threat that would goad the Mexicans to cross the Rio Grande.

By avoiding a crisis, Polk might have maintained this indeterminate but not uncomfortable position for a year or more, while the emigrants of 1845 and 1846 settled in central California. Tactful private warnings to Britain and the presence of Sloat's squadron cruising off the Mexican coast could have shielded an independence movement in California, which would establish a new state. At the least, an independent California could have maintained friendly relations for an indefinite period with the government at Washington. Eventually, the United States might have opened negotiations for annexation, choosing a time when Britain was fully involved in European affairs. As events developed, the revolutions of 1848 provided just such an opportunity, and there were others during the succeeding years.

Would this gradualism have satisfied Western expansionists? Probably not, but it is inconceivable that their protests could have been as divisive as the debates that took place over Oregon and the Mexican War. Indeed, their impatient outbursts might have been put to good use, for diplomats such as McLane or Slidell, their cunning sharpened by experience in American politics, would have known how to invoke Western extremism as a stimulus for lagging negotiations. If expansionist pressure became too great to resist, Polk would yet have retained his freedom to speak out; after initiating bona fide efforts toward peaceful settlement, his stirring pronouncements would probably have had more effect than they actually did. They might indeed have strengthened moderates in Britain or Mexico instead of repelling them.

Polk's background and character militated against such reliance on conventional diplomacy. Instead of carefully exploring issues and interests, he chose a policy based on bluff and a show of force. At the time it seemed an easier policy. In its constant appeals to Congress and the people it seemed more democratic. By goading British and Mexican nationalists, however, this policy raised obstacles, and as these obstacles increased, it proved impossible to reverse. No one can deny that Polk achieved his goals, but he was favored by good luck, by the steadfastness of American soldiers, and, at the end, by the long-neglected skill of his diplomats. For many persons his achievements justified themselves. But later generations might reasonably complain that he served his country ill by paying an unnecessarily high price in money, in lives, and in national disunity.

FURTHER READING

Samuel Flagg Bemis, *John Quincy Adams and the Union* (1956)

Ray A. Billington, *The Far Western Frontier, 1830–1860* (1956)

William Goetzmann, *When the Eagle Screamed* (1966)

Norman A. Graebner, *Empire on the Pacific* (1955)

Archie P. McDonald, ed., *The Mexican War* (1969)

Frederick Merk, *Albert Gallatin and the Oregon Problem* (1950)

Frederick Merk, *Manifest Destiny and Mission in American History* (1963)

Frederick Merk, *The Monroe Doctrine and American Expansionism, 1843–1849* (1966)

Frederick Merk, *The Oregon Question* (1967)

Julius W. Pratt, "The Ideology of American Expansion," in Avery Craven, ed., *Essays in Honor of William E. Dodd* (1935)

Glenn W. Price, *Origins of the War with Mexico: The Polk-Stockton Intrigue* (1967)

José Fernando Ramérez, *Mexico during the War with the United States*, ed. Walter V. Scholes (1950)

John H. Schroeder, *Mr. Polk's War* (1973)

Charles G. Sellers, *James K. Polk: Continentalist, 1843–1846* (1966)

Justin H. Smith, *The War with Mexico*, 2 vols. (1919)

Richard Van Alstyne, *The Rising American Empire* (1960)

Charles Vevier, "American Continentalism: An Idea of Expansion, 1845–1910," *American Historical Review*, 65 (1960), 323–335

Albert K. Weinberg, *Manifest Destiny* (1935)

9

Late Nineteenth-Century Expansionism and Economics

The issue of slavery, sectionalism, and the Civil War interrupted the seeming relentlessness of American expansion. After the bitter North-South clash, expansionists once again took up the call. Secretary of State William H. Seward (1861–1869) became their leader and, under his stewardship, the United States acquired the large territory of Alaska and the tiny Midway Islands. Seward's other schemes for acquiring islands in the Caribbean were squelched by Congress. Still, from the 1860s to 1900 the United States became more active in affairs beyond its continental boundaries, participating in international conferences, sending American products into distant lands, enlarging its navy, extending its commercial and missionary interests in Asia, scolding European powers about their intrusions in Latin America by citing the Monroe Doctrine, intervening in inter-American squabbles, and launching Pan-Americanism. The relative importance of economic factors in this conspicuous nineteenth-century expansionism has long been debated by historians.

DOCUMENTS

The following documents represent some of the most prominent voices of late nineteenth-century expansionism. William H. Seward acquired Alaska in 1867. Two years later, on August 12, 1869, he visited his imperial prize and delivered an exuberant speech to the citizens of Sitka. President Ulysses S. Grant tried very hard

231

to annex Santo Domingo, but the Senate eventually blocked his effort. In his message to Congress, dated May 31, 1870, the President itemized the reasons why the Caribbean nation should be attached to the United States.

In 1881 Secretary of State James G. Blaine wanted to hold a Pan American Conference, but he left office within a few months and his dream was foiled. In 1888, however, once again the Secretary of State, he organized a Pan American Conference, which met in Washington, D.C., from October 1889 to April 1890. Blaine's goals are spelled out in the congressional resolution calling for the meeting, reprinted here. Another spokesman for expansion was Captain Alfred T. Mahan. His teaching at the Naval War College and his publications, including *The Influence of Sea Power Upon History,* from which the fourth selection is chosen, encouraged a larger navy and active overseas involvement for the United States.

A voice from the pulpit, the Reverend Josiah Strong, also envisioned American greatness, but largely in religious and racial terms. The Anglo-Saxon race, he preached according to Social Darwinism, was destined to rule a world of inferiors. His book *Our Country,* first published in 1885, made the point in reverent tones, as the fifth selection illustrates. Ten years later a major dispute, the Venezuelan controversy, sparked Secretary of State Richard Olney to send Britain a haughty message, dated July 20, 1895, which President Grover Cleveland called a "twenty-inch gun." Britain and Venezuela had been arguing for years about disputed land near British Guiana. Olney decided to settle the annoying question and, in so doing, declared United States hegemony over the Western Hemisphere, as the last document demonstrates.

William H. Seward on Alaska, 1869

Citizens of Alaska, Fellow-citizens of the United States:—You have pressed me to meet you in public assembly once before I leave Alaska. It would be sheer affectation to pretend to doubt your sincerity in making this request, and capriciously ungrateful to refuse it, after having received so many and varied hospitalities from all sorts and conditions of men. It is not an easy task, however, to speak in a manner worthy of your consideration, while I am living constantly on ship-board, as you all know, and am occupied intently in searching out whatever is sublime, or beautiful, or peculiar, or useful. On the other hand, it is altogether natural on your part to say, "You have looked upon Alaska, what do you think of it?" Unhappily, I have seen too little of Alaska to answer the question satisfactorily. The entire coast line of the United States, exclusive of Alaska, is 10,000 miles, while the coast line of Alaska alone, including the islands, is 26,000 miles. The portion of the Territory which lies east of the peninsula, including islands, is 120 miles wide; the western portion, including Aleutian islands, expands to a breadth of 2,200 miles. The entire land area, including islands, is 577,390 statute square miles. . . .

Of course I speak first of the skies of Alaska. It seems to be assumed in the case of Alaska that a country which extends through fifty-eight degrees of longitude, and embraces portions as well of the arctic as of the temperate zone, unlike all other regions so situated, has not several climates, but only one. The weather of this one broad climate of Alaska is severely criticised in outside circles for being too wet and too cold. Nevertheless, it must be a fastidious person who complains of climates in which, while the eagle delights to soar, the humming-bird does not disdain to flutter. . . .

It is next in order to speak of the rivers and seas of Alaska. The rivers are broad, shallow, and rapid, while the seas are deep but tranquil. Mr. Sumner, in his elaborate and magnificent oration, although he spake only from historical accounts, has not exaggerated—no man can exaggerate—the marine treasures of the Territory. Beside the whale, which everywhere and at all times is seen enjoying his robust exercise, and the sea-otter, the fur-seal, the hair-seal, and the walrus, found in the waters which embosom the western islands, those waters, as well as the seas of the eastern archipelago, are found teeming with the salmon, cod, and other fishes adapted to the support of human and animal life. Indeed, what I have seen here has almost made me a convert to the theory of some naturalists, that the waters of the globe are filled with stores for the sustenance of animal life surpassing the available productions of the land.

It must be remembered that the coast range of mountains, which begins in Mexico, is continued into the Territory, and invades the seas of Alaska. Hence it is that in the islands and on the mainland, so far as I have explored it, we find ourselves everywhere in the immediate presence of black hills, or foot-hills, as they are variously called, and that these foot-hills are overtopped by ridges of snow-capped mountains. These snow-capped mountains are manifestly of volcanic origin, and they have been subjected, through an indefinite period, to atmospheric abrasion and disintegration. Hence they have assumed all conceivable shapes and forms. In some places they are serrated into sharp, angular peaks, and in other places they appear architecturally arranged, so as to present cloud-capped castles, towers, domes, and minarets. The mountain sides are furrowed with deep and straight ravines, down which the thawing fields of ice and snow are precipitated, generally in the month of May, with such a vehemence as to have produced in every valley immense level plains of inter-vale land. These plains, as well as the sides of the mountains, almost to the summits, are covered with forests so dense and dark as to be impenetrable, except to wild beasts and savage huntsmen. On the lowest intervale land the cotton-wood grows. It seems to be the species of poplar which is known in the Atlantic States as the Balm of Gilead, and which is dwarfed on the Rocky Mountains. Here it takes on such large dimensions, that the Indian shapes out of a single trunk even his great war canoe, which safely bears over the deepest waters a phalanx of sixty warriors. These imposing trees always appear to rise out of a jungle of elder, alder, crab-apple, and other fruit-bearing shrubs and bushes. The short and slender birch, which, sparsely scattered, marks the verge of vegetation in Labrador, has not yet been reached by the explorers of Alaska. The birch tree sometimes appears here upon the river side, upon the level next above the home of the cottonwood, and is generally found a comely and stately tree. The forests of Alaska, however, consist mainly neither of shrubs, nor of the birch, nor of the cottonwood, but, as I have already intimated, of the pine, the cedar, the cypress, the spruce, the fir, the larch, and the hemlock. These forests begin almost at the water's edge, and they rise with regular gradation to a height of two thousand feet. The trees, nowhere dwarfed or diminutive, attain the highest dimensions in sunny exposures in the deeper cañons or gorges of the mountains. The cedar, sometimes called the yellow cedar, and sometimes the fragrant cedar, was long ago imported into China as an ornamental wood; and it now furnishes the majestic beams and pillars with which the richer and more ambitious native chief delights to construct his rude but spacious hall or palatial residence, and upon which he carves in rude symbolical imagery the heraldry of his tribe and achievements of his nation. No beam, or pillar, or spar, or mast, or plank is ever required in either the land or the naval architecture of any civilized state greater in length and width than the trees which can be hewn down on the coasts of the islands and rivers here, and conveyed directly thence by navigation. A few gardens, fields, and meadows, have been attempted by natives in some of the settlements, and by soldiers at the military posts, with most encouraging results. Nor must we forget that the native grasses, ripening late in a humid climate, preserve their nutritive properties, though exposed, while the climate is so mild that cattle and horses require but slight provision of shelter during the winter. . . .

After what I have already said, I may excuse myself from expatiating on the animal productions of the forest. The elk and the deer are so plenty as to be undervalued for food or skins, by natives as well as strangers. The bear of many families—black, grizzly, and cinnamon; the mountain sheep, inestimable for his fleece; the wolf, the fox, the beaver, the otter, the mink, the raccoon, the marten, the ermine; the squirrel—gray, black, brown, and flying, are among the land fur-bearing animals. The furs thus found here have been the chief element, for more than a hundred years, of the profitable commerce of the Hudson Bay Company, whose mere possessory privileges seem, even at this late day, too costly to find a ready purchaser. This fur trade, together with the sea fur-trade within the Territory, were the sole basis alike of Russian commerce and empire on this continent. This commerce was so large and important as to induce the Governments of Russia and China to build and maintain a town for carrying on its exchanges in Tartary on the border of the two empires. It is well understood that the supply of furs in Alaska has not diminished, while the demand for them in China and elsewhere has immensely increased. . . .

Alaska has been as yet but imperfectly explored; but enough is known to assure us that it possesses treasures of what are called the baser ores equal to those of any other region of the continent. We have Copper Island and Copper River, so named as the places where the natives, before the period of the Russian discovery, had procured the pure metal from which they fabricated instruments of war and legendary shields. In regard to iron, the question seems to be not where it can be found, but whether there is any place where it does not exist. Mr. Davidson, of the Coast Survey, invited me to go up to him at the station he had taken up the Chilcat River to make his observations of the eclipse, by writing me that he had discovered an iron mountain there. When I came there I found that, very properly, he had been studying the heavens so busily, that he had but cursorily examined the earth under his feet; that it was not a

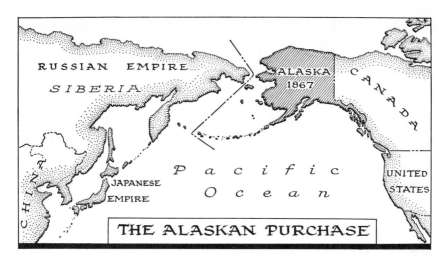

THE ALASKAN PURCHASE

single iron mountain he had discovered, but a range of hills, the very dust of which adheres to the magnet, while the range itself, two thousand feet high, extends along the east bank of the river thirty miles. Limestone and marble crop out on the banks of the same river and in many other places. Coal-beds, accessible to navigation, are found at Kootznoo. It is said, however, that the concentrated resin which the mineral contains renders it too inflammable to be safely used by steamers. In any case, it would seem calculated to supply the fuel requisite for the manufacture of iron. What seems to be excellent cannel coal is also found in the Prince of Wales archipelago. There are also mines at Cook's Inlet. Placer and quartz gold mining is pursued under many social disadvantages upon the Stickeen and elsewhere, with a degree of success which, while it does not warrant us in assigning a superiority in that respect to the Territory, does nevertheless warrant us in regarding gold mining as an established and reliable resource. . . .

It remains only to speak of man and of society in Alaska. Until the present moment the country has been exclusively inhabited and occupied by some thirty or more Indian tribes. I incline to doubt the popular classification of these tribes upon the assumption that they have descended from diverse races. Climate and other circumstances have indeed produced some differences of manners and customs between the Aleuts, the Koloschians, and the interior continental tribes. But all of them are manifestly of Mongol origin. Although they have preserved no common traditions, all alike indulge in tastes, wear a physiognomy, and are imbued with sentiments peculiarly noticed in Japan and China. Savage communities, no less than civilized nations, require space for subsistence, whether they depend for it upon the land or upon the sea—in savage communities especially; and increase of population disproportioned to the supplies of the country occupied necessitates subdivision and remote colonization. Oppression and cruelty occur even more frequently among barbarians than among civilized men. Nor are ambition and faction less inherent in the one condition than in the other. From these causes it has happened that the

25,000 Indians in Alaska are found permanently divided into so many insignificant nations. These nations are jealous, ambitious, and violent; could in no
case exist long in the same region without mutually affording what, in every
case, to each party, seems just cause of war. War between savages becomes the
private cause of the several families which are afflicted with the loss of their
members. Such a war can never be composed until each family which has suffered receives an indemnity in blankets, adjusted according to an imaginary
tariff, or, in the failure of such compensation, secures the death of one or more
enemies as an atonement for the injury it has sustained. The enemy captured,
whether by superior force or strategy, either receives no quarter, or submits for
himself and his progeny to perpetual slavery. It has thus happened that the Indian tribes of Alaska have never either confederated or formed permanent
alliances, and that even at this late day, in the presence of superior power exercised by the United States Government, they live in regard to each other in
a state of enforced and doubtful truce. It is manifest that, under these circumstances, they must steadily decline in numbers, and unhappily this decline is
accelerated by their borrowing ruinous vices from the white man. Such as the
natives of Alaska are, they are, nevertheless, in a practical sense, the only
laborers at present in the Territory. The white man comes amongst them from
London, from St. Petersburg, from Boston, from New York, from San Francisco, and from Victoria, not to fish (if we except alone the whale fishery) or
to hunt, but simply to buy what fish and what peltries, ice, wood, lumber, and
coal, the Indians have secured under the superintendence of temporary agents
or factors. When we consider how greatly most of the tribes are reduced in
numbers, and how precarious their vocations are, we shall cease to regard them
as indolent or incapable; and, on the contrary, we shall more deeply regret than
ever before, that a people so gifted by nature, so vigorous and energetic, and
withal so docile and gentle in their intercourse with the white man, can neither
be preserved as a distinct social community, or incorporated into our society.
The Indian tribes will do here as they seem to have done in Washington Territory, and British Columbia: they will merely serve their turn until civilized
white men come.

You, the citizens of Sitka, are the pioneers, the advanced guard, of the future
population of Alaska; and you naturally ask when, from whence, and how soon,
reinforcements shall come, and what are the signs and guarantees of their
coming? This question, with all its minute and searching interrogations, has
been asked by the pioneers of every state and territory of which the American
Union is now composed; and the history of those states and territories furnishes
the complete, conclusive, and satisfactory answer. Emigrants go to every infant
state and territory in obedience to the great natural law that obliges needy men
to seek subsistence, and invites adventurous men to seek fortune where it is
most easily obtained, and this is always in the new and uncultivated regions.
They go from every state and territory, and from every foreign nation in America, Europe, and Asia; because no established and populous state or nation
can guarantee subsistence and fortune to all who demand them among its
inhabitants.

The guarantees and signs of their coming to Alaska are found in the resources of the territory, which I have attempted to describe, and in the condition of society in other parts of the world. Some men seek other climes for health and some for pleasure. Alaska invites the former class by a climate singularly salubrious, and the latter class by scenery which surpasses in sublimity that of either the Alps, the Apennines, the Alleghanies, or the Rocky Mountains. Emigrants from our own states, from Europe, and from Asia, will not be slow in finding out that fortunes are to be gained by pursuing here the occupations which have so successfully sustained races of untutored men. Civilization and refinement are making more rapid advances in our day than at any former period. The rising states and nations on this continent, the European nations, and even those of Eastern Asia, have exhausted, or are exhausting, their own forests and mines, and are soon to become largely dependent upon those of the Pacific. The entire region of Oregon, Washington Territory, British Columbia, and Alaska, seem thus destined to become a ship-yard for the supply of all nations. I do not forget on this occasion that British Columbia belongs within a foreign jurisdiction. That circumstance does not materially affect my calculations. British Columbia, by whomsoever possessed, must be governed in conformity with the interests of her people and of society upon the American continent. If that territory shall be so governed, there will be no ground of complaint anywhere. If it shall be governed so as to conflict with the interests of the inhabitants of that territory and of the United States, we all can easily foresee what will happen in that case. You will ask me, however, for guarantees that the hopes I encourage will not be postponed. I give them.

Within the period of my own recollection, I have seen twenty new states added to the eighteen which before that time constituted the American Union, and I now see, besides Alaska, ten territories in a forward condition of preparation for entering into the same great political family. I have seen in my own time not only the first electric telegraph, but even the first railroad and the first steamboat invented by man. And even on this present voyage of mine, I have fallen in with the first steamboat, still afloat, that thirty-five years ago lighted her fires on the Pacific ocean. These, citizens of Sitka, are the guarantees, not only that Alaska has a future, but that that future has already begun. I know that you want two things just now, when European monopoly is broken down and United States free trade is being introduced within the territory: These are, military protection while your number is so inferior to that of the Indians around you, and you need also a territorial civil government. Congress has already supplied the first of these wants adequately and effectually. I doubt not that it will supply the other want during the coming winter. It must do this, because our political system rejects alike anarchy and executive absolutism. Nor do I doubt that the political society to be constituted here, first as a territory, and ultimately as a state or many states, will prove a worthy constituency of the Republic. To doubt that it will be intelligent, virtuous, prosperous, and enterprising, is to doubt the experience of Scotland, Denmark, Sweden, Holland and Belgium, and of New England and New York. Nor do I doubt that it will be forever true in its republican instincts and loyal to the American Union, for the inhabitants will be both mountaineers and seafaring men. I am not among those who apprehend infidelity to liberty and the Union in any quarter hereafter, but I am sure that if constancy and loyalty are to fail anywhere, the failure will not be in the states which approach nearest to the North Pole.

Ulysses S. Grant on Santo Domingo, 1870

I feel an unusual anxiety for the ratification of this treaty, because I believe it will redound greatly to the glory of the two countries interested, to civilization, and to the extirpation of the institution of slavery.

The doctrine promulgated by President Monroe has been adhered to by all political parties, and I now deem it proper to assert the equally important principle that hereafter no territory on this continent shall be regarded as subject of transfer to a European power.

The Government of San Domingo has voluntarily sought this annexation. It is a weak power, numbering probably less than 120,000 souls, and yet possessing one of the richest territories under the sun, capable of supporting a population of 10,000,000 people in luxury. The people of San Domingo are not capable of maintaining themselves in their present condition, and must look for outside support.

They yearn for the protection of our free institutions and laws, our progress and civilization. Shall we refuse them?

I have information which I believe reliable that a European power stands ready now to offer $2,000,000 for the possession of Samana Bay alone. If refused by us, with what grace can we prevent a foreign power from attempting to secure the prize?

The acquisition of San Domingo is desirable because of its geographical position. It commands the entrance to the Caribbean Sea and the Isthmus transit of commerce. It possesses the richest soil, best and most capacious harbors, most salubrious climate, and the most valuable products of the forests, mine, and soil of any of the West India Islands. Its possession by us will in a few years build up a coastwise commerce of immense magnitude, which will go far toward restoring to us our lost merchant marine. It will give to us those articles which we consume so largely and do not produce, thus equalizing our exports and imports.

In case of foreign war it will give us command of all the islands referred to, and thus prevent an enemy from ever again possessing himself of rendezvous upon our very coast.

At present our coast trade between the States bordering on the Atlantic and those bordering on the Gulf of Mexico is cut into by the Bahamas and the Antilles. Twice we must, as it were, pass through foreign countries to get by sea from Georgia to the west coast of Florida.

San Domingo, with a stable government, under which her immense resources can be developed, will give remunerative wages to tens of thousands of laborers not now on the island.

This labor will take advantage of every available means of transportation to abandon the adjacent islands and seek the blessings of freedom and its sequence—each inhabitant receiving the reward of his own labor. Porto Rico and Cuba will have to abolish slavery, as a measure of self-preservation to retain their laborers.

San Domingo will become a large consumer of the products of Northern farms and manufactories. The cheap rate at which her citizens can be furnished with food, tools, and machinery will make it necessary that the contiguous islands should have the same advantages in order to compete in the production of sugar, coffee, tobacco, tropical fruits, etc. This will open to us a still wider market for our products.

The production of our own supply of these articles will cut off more than one hundred millions of our annual imports, besides largely increasing our exports. With such a picture it is easy to see how our large debt abroad is ultimately to be extinguished. With a balance of trade against us (including interest on bonds held by foreigners and money spent by our citizens traveling in foreign lands) equal to the entire yield of the precious metals in this country, it it is not so easy to see how this result is to be otherwise accomplished.

The acquisition of San Domingo is an adherence to the "Monroe doctrine"; it is a measure of national protection; it is asserting our just claim to a controlling influence over the great commercial traffic soon to flow from east to west by the way of the Isthmus of Darien; it is to build up our merchant marine; it is to furnish new markets for the products of our farms, shops, and manufactories; it is to make slavery insupportable in Cuba and Porto Rico at once and ultimately so in Brazil; it is to settle the unhappy condition of Cuba, and end an exterminating conflict; it is to provide honest means of paying our honest debts, without overtaxing the people; it is to furnish our citizens with the necessaries of everyday life at cheaper rates than ever before; and it is, in fine, a rapid stride toward that greatness which the intelligence, industry, and enterprise of the citizens of the United States entitle this country to assume among nations.

Call for a Pan American Conference, 1888

The Conference is called to consider—

First. Measures that shall tend to preserve and promote the prosperity of the several American States.

Second. Measures toward the formation of an American customs union, under which the trade of the American nations with each other shall, so far as possible and profitable, be promoted.

Third. The establishment of regular and frequent communication between the ports of the several American States and the ports of each other.

Fourth. The establishment of a uniform system of customs regulations in each of the independent American States to govern the mode of importation and exportation of merchandise and port dues and charges, a uniform method of determining the classification and valuation of such merchandise in the ports of each country, and a uniform system of invoices, and the subject of the sanitation of ships and quarantine.

Fifth. The adoption of a uniform system of weights and measures, and laws to protect the patent-rights, copyrights, and trade-marks of citizens of either country in the other, and for the extradition of criminals.

Sixth. The adoption of a common silver coin, to be issued by each Government, the same to be legal tender in all commercial transactions between the citizens of all of the American States.

Seventh. An agreement upon and recommendation for adoption to their respective Governments of a definite plan of arbitration of all questions, disputes, and differences, that may now or hereafter exist between them, to the end that all difficulties and disputes between such nations may be peaceably settled and wars prevented.

Eighth. And to consider such other subjects relating to the welfare of the several States represented as may be presented by any of said States which are hereby invited to participate in said Conference.

Alfred T. Mahan on Sea Power, 1890

To turn now from the particular lessons drawn from the history of the past to the general question of the influence of government upon the sea career of its people, it is seen that that influence can work in two distinct but closely related ways.

First, in peace: The government by its policy can favor the natural growth of a people's industries and its tendencies to seek adventure and gain by way of the sea; or it can try to develop such industries and such sea-going bent, when they do not naturally exist; or, on the other hand, the government may by mistaken action check and fetter the progress which the people left to themselves would make. In any one of these ways the influence of the government will be felt, making or marring the sea power of the country in the matter of peaceful commerce; upon which alone, it cannot be too often insisted, a thoroughly strong navy can be based.

Secondly, for war: The influence of the government will be felt in its most legitimate manner in maintaining an armed navy, of a size commensurate with the growth of its shipping and the importance of the interests connected with it. More important even than the size of the navy is the question of its institutions, favoring a healthful spirit and activity, and providing for rapid development in time of war by an adequate reserve of men and of ships and by measures for drawing out that general reserve power which has before been pointed to, when considering the character and pursuits of the people. Undoubtedly under this second head of warlike preparation must come the maintenance of suitable naval stations, in those distant parts of the world to which the armed shipping must follow the peaceful vessels of commerce. The protection of such stations must depend either upon direct military force, as do Gibraltar and Malta, or upon a surrounding friendly population, such as the American colonists once were to England, and, it may be presumed, the Australian colonists now are. Such friendly surroundings and backing, joined to a reasonable military provision, are the best of defences, and when combined with decided preponderance at sea, make a scattered and extensive empire, like that of England, secure; for while it is true that an unexpected attack may cause disaster in some one quarter, the actual superiority of naval power prevents such disaster from being general or irremediable. History has sufficiently proved this. England's naval bases have been in all parts of the world; and her fleets have at once protected them, kept open the communications between them, and relied upon them for shelter.

Colonies attached to the mother-country afford, therefore, the surest means of supporting abroad the sea power of a country. In peace, the influence of the government should be felt in promoting by all means a warmth of attachment and a unity of interest which will make the welfare of one the welfare of all, and the quarrel of one the quarrel of all; and in war, or rather for war, by inducing such measures of organization and defence as shall be felt by all to be a fair distribution of a burden of which each reaps the benefit.

Such colonies the United States has not and is not likely to have. As regards purely military naval stations, the feeling of her people was probably accurately expressed by an historian of the English navy a hundred years ago, speaking then of Gibraltar and Port Mahon. "Military governments," said he, "agree so little with the industry of a trading people, and are in themselves so repugnant to the genius of the British people, that I do not wonder that men of good sense and of all parties have inclined to give up these, as Tangiers was given up." Having therefore no foreign establishments, either colonial or military, the ships of war of the United States, in war, will be like land birds, unable to fly far from their own shores. To provide resting-places for them, where they can coal and repair, would be one of the first duties of a government proposing to itself the development of the power of the nation at sea. . . .

The question is eminently one in which the influence of the government should make itself felt, to build up for the nation a navy which, if not capable of reaching distant countries, shall at least be able to keep clear the chief approaches to its own. The eyes of the country have for a quarter of a century been turned from the sea; the results of such a policy and of its opposite will be shown in the instance of France and of England. Without asserting a narrow parallelism between the case of the United States and either of these, it may safely be said that it is essential to the welfare of the whole country that the conditions of trade and commerce should remain, as far as possible, unaffected by an external war. In order to do this, the enemy must be kept not only out of our ports, but far away from our coasts.

Josiah Strong on Anglo-Saxon Predominance, 1891

It is not necessary to argue to those for whom I write that the two great needs of mankind, that all men may be lifted up into the light of the highest Christian civilization, are, first, a pure, spiritual Christianity, and second, civil liberty. Without controversy, these are the forces which, in the past, have contributed most to the elevation of the human race, and they must continue to be, in the future, the most efficient ministers to its progress. It follows, then, that the Anglo-Saxon, as the great representative of these two ideas, the despository of these two greatest blessings, sustains peculiar relations to the world's future, is divinely commissioned to be, in a peculiar sense, his brother's keeper. Add to this the fact of his rapidly increasing strength in modern times, and we have well-nigh a demonstration of his destiny. In 1700 this race numbered less than 6,000,000 souls. In 1800, Anglo-Saxons (I use the term somewhat broadly to include all English-speaking peoples) had increased to about 20,500,000, and now, in 1890, they number more than 120,000,000, having multiplied almost six-fold in ninety years. At the end of the reign of Charles II, the English colonists in America numbered 200,000. During these two hundred years, our population has increased two hundred and fifty-fold. And the expansion of this race has been no less remarkable than its multiplication. In one century the United States has increased its territory ten-fold, while the enormous acquisition of foreign territory by Great Britain—and chiefly within the last hundred years—is wholly unparalleled in history. This mighty Anglo-Saxon race, though comprising only one-thirteenth part of mankind, now rules more than one-third of the earth's surface, and more than one-fourth of its people. And if this race, while growing from 6,000,000 to 120,000,000, thus gained possession of a third portion of the earth, is it to be supposed that when it numbers 1,000,000,000, it will lose the disposition, or lack the power to extend its sway? . . .

America is to have the great preponderance of numbers and of wealth, and by the logic of events will follow the scepter of controlling influence. This will be but the consummation of a movement as old as civilization—a result to which men have looked forward for centuries. John Adams records that nothing was "more ancient in his memory than the observation that arts, sciences and empire had traveled westward; and in conversation it was always added that their next leap would be over the Atlantic into America." He recalled a couplet that had been inscribed or rather drilled, into a rock on the shore of Monument Bay in our old colony of Plymouth:

> The Eastern nations sink, their glory ends,
> And empire rises where the sun descends. . . .

Mr. Darwin is not only disposed to see, in the superior vigor of our people, an illustration of his favorite theory of natural selection, but even intimates that the world's history thus far has been simply preparatory for our future, and tributary to it. He says: "There is apparently much truth in the belief that the wonderful progress of the United States, as well as the character of the people, are the results of natural selection; for the more energetic, restless, and courageous men from all parts of Europe have emigrated during the last ten or twelve generations to that great country, and have there succeeded best. Looking at the distant future, I do not think that the Rev. Mr. Zincke takes an exaggerated view when he says: 'All other series of events—as that which resulted in the culture of mind in Greece, and that which resulted in the Empire of

Rome—only appear to have purpose and value when viewed in connection with, or rather as subsidiary to, the great stream of Anglo-Saxon emigration to the West.' "

There is abundant reason to believe that the Anglo-Saxon race is to be, is, indeed, already becoming, more effective here than in the mother country. The marked superiority of this race is due, in large measure, to its highly mixed origin. Says Rawlinson: "It is a general rule, now almost universally admitted by ethnologists, that the mixed races of mankind are superior to the pure ones"; and adds: "Even the Jews, who are so often cited as an example of a race at once pure and strong, may, with more reason, be adduced on the opposite side of the argument." The ancient Egyptians, the Greeks, and the Romans, were all mixed races. Among modern races, the most conspicuous example is afforded by the Anglo-Saxons. . . . There is here a new commingling of races; and, while the largest injections of foreign blood are substantially the same elements that constituted the original Anglo-Saxon admixture, so that we may infer the general type will be preserved, there are strains of other bloods being added, which, if Mr. Emerson's remark is true, that "the best nations are those most widely related," may be expected to improve the stock, and aid it to a higher destiny. If the dangers of immigration, which have been pointed out, can be successfully met for the next few years, until it has passed its climax, it may be expected to add value to the amalgam which will constitute the new Anglo-Saxon race of the New World. Concerning our future, Herbert Spencer says: "One great result is, I think, tolerably clear. From biological truths it is to be inferred that the eventual mixture of the allied varieties of the Aryan race, forming the population, will produce a more powerful type of man than has hitherto existed, and a type of man more plastic, more adaptable, more capable of undergoing the modifications needful for complete social life. I think, whatever difficulties they may have to surmount, and whatever tribulations they may have to pass through, the Americans may reasonably look forward to a time when they will have produced a civilization grander than any the world has known."

It may be easily shown, and is of no small significance, that the two great ideas of which the Anglo-Saxon is the exponent are having a fuller development in the United States than in Great Britain. There the union of Church and State tends strongly to paralyze some of the members of the body of Christ. Here there is no such influence to destroy spiritual life and power. Here, also, has been evolved the form of government consistent with the largest possible civil liberty. Furthermore, it is significant that the marked characteristics of this race are being here emphasized most. Among the most striking features of the Anglo-Saxon is his money-making power—a power of increasing importance in the widening commerce of the world's future. We have seen . . . that, although England is by far the richest nation of Europe, we have already outstripped her in the race after wealth, and we have only begun the development of our vast resources.

Again, another marked characteristic of the Anglo-Saxon is what may be called an instinct or genius for colonizing. His unequaled energy, his indomitable perseverance, and his personal independence, made him a pioneer. He excels all others in pushing his way into new countries. It was those in whom this tendency was strongest that came to America, and this inherited tendency has been further developed by the westward sweep of successive generations across the continent. So noticeable has this characteristic become that English visitors remark it. Charles Dickens once said that the typical American would hesitate to enter heaven unless assured that he could go farther west.

Again, nothing more manifestly distinguishes the Anglo-Saxon than his intense and persistent energy, and he is developing in the United States an energy which, in eager activity and effectiveness, is peculiarly American.

This is due partly to the fact that Americans are much better fed than Europeans, and partly to the undeveloped resources of a new country, but more largely to our climate, which acts as a constant stimulus. Ten years after the landing of the Pilgrims, the Rev. Francis Higginson, a good observer, wrote: "A sup of New England air is better than a whole flagon of English ale." Thus early had the stimulating effect of our climate been noted. Moreover, our social institutions are stimulating. In Europe the various ranks of society are, like the strata of the earth, fixed and fossilized. There can be no great change without a terrible upheaval, a social earthquake. Here society is like the waters of the sea, mobile; as General Garfield said, and so signally illustrated in his own experience, that which is at the bottom to-day may one day flash on the crest of the highest wave. Every one is free to become whatever he can make of himself; free to transform himself from a rail splitter or a tanner or a canal-boy, into the nation's President. Our aristocracy, unlike that of Europe, is open to all comers. Wealth, position, influence, are prizes offered for energy; and every farmer's boy, every apprentice and clerk, every friendless and penniless immigrant, is free to enter the lists. Thus many causes co-operate to produce here the most forceful and tremendous energy in the world.

What is the significance of such facts? These tendencies infold the future; they are the mighty alphabet with which God writes his prophecies. May we not, by a careful laying together of the letters, spell out something of his meaning? It seems to me that God, with infinite wisdom and skill, is training the Anglo-Saxon race for an hour sure to come in the world's future. Heretofore there has always been in the history of the world a comparatively unoccupied land westward, into which the crowded countries of the East have poured their surplus populations. But the widening waves of migration, which millenniums ago rolled east and west from the valley of the Euphrates, meet to-day on our Pacific coast. There are no more new worlds. The unoccupied arable lands of the earth are limited, and will soon be taken. The time is coming when the pressure of population on the means of subsistence will be felt here as it is now felt in Europe and Asia. Then will the world enter upon a new stage of its history—*the final competition of races, for which the Anglo-Saxon is being schooled*. Long before the thousand millions are here, the mighty *centrifugal* tendency, inherent in this stock and strengthened in the United States, will assert itself. Then this race of unequaled energy, with all the majesty of numbers and the might of wealth behind it—the representative, let us hope, of the largest liberty, the purest Christianity, the highest civilization—having developed peculiarly aggressive traits calculated to impress its institutions upon mankind, will spread itself over the earth. If I read not amiss, this powerful race will move down upon Mexico, down upon Central and South America, out upon the islands of the sea, over upon Africa and beyond. And can any one doubt that the results of this competition of races will be the "survival of the fittest?" "Any people," says Dr. Bushnell, "that is physiologically advanced in culture, though it be only in a degree beyond another which is mingled with it on strictly equal terms, is sure to live down and finally live out its inferior. Nothing can save the inferior race but a ready and pliant assimilation. Whether the feebler and more abject races are going to be regenerated and raised up, is already very much of a question. What if it should be God's plan to people the world with better and finer material?"

Richard Olney on the Venezuelan Controversy, 1895

That America is in no part open to colonization, though the proposition was not universally admitted at the time of its first enunciation, has long been universally conceded. We are now concerned, therefore, only with that other practical application of the Monroe doctrine the disregard of which by an European power is to be deemed an act of unfriendliness towards the United States. The precise scope and limitations of this rule cannot be too clearly apprehended. It does not establish any general protectorate by the United States over other American states. It does not relieve any American state from its obligations as fixed by international law nor prevent any European power directly interested from enforcing such obligations or from inflicting merited punishment for the breach of them. It does not contemplate any interference in the internal affairs of any American state or in the relations between it and other American states. It does not justify any attempt on our part to change the established form of government of any American state or to prevent the people of such state from altering that form according to their own will and pleasure. The rule in question has but a single purpose and object. It is that no European power or combination of European powers shall forcibly deprive an American state of the right and power of self-government and of shaping for itself its own political fortunes and destinies. . . .

Is it true, then, that the safety and welfare of the United States are so concerned with the maintenance of the independence of every American state as against any European power as to justify and require the interposition of the United States whenever that independence is endangered? The question can be candidly answered in but one way. The states of America, South as well as North, by geographical proximity, by natural sympathy, by similarity of governmental constitutions, are friends and allies, commercially and politically, of the United States. To allow the subjugation of any of them by an European power is, of course, to completely reverse that situation and signifies the loss of all the advantages incident to their natural relations to us. But that is not all. The people of the United States have a vital interest in the cause of popular self-government. They have secured the right for themselves and their posterity at the cost of infinite blood and treasure. They have realized and exemplified its beneficent operation by a career unexampled in point of national greatness or individual felicity. They believe it to be for the healing of all nations, and that civilization must either advance or retrograde accordingly as its supremacy is extended or curtailed. Imbued with these sentiments, the people of the United States might not impossibly be wrought up to an active propaganda in favor of a cause so highly valued both for themselves and for mankind. But the age of the Crusades has passed, and they are content with such assertion and defense of the right of popular self-government as their own security and welfare demand. It is in that view more than in any other that they believe it not to be tolerated that the political control of an American state shall be forcibly assumed by an European power.

The mischiefs apprehended from such a source are none the less real because not immediately imminent in any specific case, and are none the less to be guarded against because the combination of circumstances that will bring them upon us cannot be predicted. The civilized states of Christendom deal with each other on substantially the same principles that regulate the conduct of individuals. The greater its enlightenment, the more surely every state perceives that its permanent interests require it to be governed by the immutable principles of right and justice. Each, nevertheless, is only too liable to succumb to the temptations offered by seeming special opportunities for its own aggrandizement, and each would rashly imperil its own safety were it not to remember that for the regard and respect of other states it must be largely dependent upon its own strength and power. Today the United States is practically sovereign on this continent, and its fiat is law upon the subjects to which it confines its interposition. Why? It is not because of the pure friendship or good will felt for it. It is not simply by reason of its high character as a civilized state, nor because wisdom and justice and equity are the invariable characteristics of the dealings of the United States. It is because, in addition to all other grounds, its infinite resources combined with its isolated position render it master of the situation and practically invulnerable as against any or all other powers.

All the advantages of this superiority are at once imperiled if the principle be admitted that European powers may convert American states into colonies or provinces of their own. The principle would be eagerly availed of, and every power doing so would immediately acquire a base of military operations against us. What one power was permitted to do could not be denied to another, and it is not inconceivable that the struggle now going on for the acquisition of Africa might be transferred to South America. If it were, the weaker countries would unquestionably be soon absorbed, while the ultimate result might be the partition of all South America between the various European powers. The disastrous consequences to the United States of such a condition of things are obvious. The loss of prestige, of authority, and of weight in the councils of the family of nations, would be among the least of them. Our only real rivals in peace as well as enemies in war would be found located at our very doors. Thus far in our history we have been spared the burdens and evils of immense standing armies and all the other accessories of huge warlike establishments, and the exemption has largely contributed to our national greatness and wealth as well as to the happiness of every citizen. But, with the powers of Europe permanently encamped on American soil, the ideal conditions we have thus far enjoyed can not be expected to continue. We too must be armed to the teeth, we too must convert the flower of our male population into soldiers and sailors, and by withdrawing them from the various pursuits of peaceful industry we too must practically annihilate a large share of the productive energy of the nation. . . .

Thus, as already intimated, the British demand that her right to a portion of the disputed territory shall be acknowledged before she will consent to an arbitration as to the rest seems to stand upon nothing but her own *ipse dixit*. She says to Venezuela, in substance: "You can get none of the debatable land by force, because you are not strong enough; you can get none by a treaty, because I will not agree; and you can take your chance of getting a portion by arbitration, only if you first agree to abandon to me such other portion as I may designate." It is not perceived how such an attitude can be defended nor how it is reconcilable with that love of justice and fair play so eminently characteristic of the English race. It in effect deprives Venezuela of her free agency and puts her under virtual duress. Territory acquired by reason of it will be as much wrested from her by the strong hand as if occupied by British troops or covered by British fleets. It seems therefore quite impossible that this position of Great Britain should be assented to by the United States, or that, if such position be adhered to with the result of enlarging the bounds of British Guiana, it should not be regarded as amounting, in substance, to an invasion and conquest of Venezuelan territory.

ESSAYS

Although scholars agree that the United States was an important foreign trader and that the late nineteenth century saw increased commercial expansion, they disagree on the relative importance of economic questions in American foreign policy. Put simply, are the nation's leaders influenced at all or primarily in their decision-making by economic considerations such as the exportation of goods, the importation of inexpensive raw materials, and financial investment abroad? Have American businessmen exerted pressure on Washington to intervene abroad in order to expand and protect their economic interests? Basically, how important is foreign trade to the security and prosperity of the United States?

In the first selection, Charles S. Campbell of the Claremont Graduate School suggests that commercial expansionism was quite important in the post–Civil War years, especially when the depression of 1893 struck. Robert L. Beisner of American

University, although acknowledging that foreign trade was one of several induce-
ments to expansionism and that the depression of the 1890s accentuated a drive for
foreign markets, finds fault with a primary emphasis on economics.

Commercial Expansionism and Empire

CHARLES S. CAMPBELL

For several decades the settlement of the west coast had been turning American attention toward territorial expansion overseas—especially in Central
America, the site of a potential canal; in the Caribbean Sea; and in the Hawaiian Islands. Over the same years economic developments were creating pressure for commercial expansion. During the decades after the Civil War the
American economy was growing at a tremendous rate. The gross national product quadrupled, rising from $9,110,000,000 for 1869–1873 to $37,100,000,-
000 for 1897–1901. The gross farm product almost tripled, increasing from a
value of $1,484,000,000 in 1860 to one of $3,799,000,000 in 1900. In 1865,
35,085 miles of railway were under operation; in 1899, 250,143. As for manufacturing, the production index jumped from 17 in 1865 all the way to 100
in 1900.

As one consequence of this extraordinary economic growth, exports mounted
steadily. From 1865 to 1900 total exports increased in value from $281 million
to $1,394 million. Exports to the United Kingdom rose in value from $103
million to $534 million; to Germany, from $20 million to $187 million; to
France, from $11 million to $83 million; to Canada, from $29 million to $95
million; and to Cuba, from $19 million to $26 million. Imports, too, were increasing, though less rapidly. As is to be expected in the case of a new and underdeveloped country, imports had exceeded exports for many years; but the
traditional pattern reversed itself in 1876, the centennial year, when merchandise exports first began to exceed imports consistently.

The historic change meant that the United States was producing a greater
value of goods than she consumed. In the late 1870s and early 1880s informed
people were becoming aware of this unfamiliar situation, a situation seeming
to require the urgent cultivation of foreign markets. Thus as early as 1877
Abram S. Hewitt, a member of Congress from New York, thought that the country needed foreign markets "more than any other thing"; and in 1881 John A.
Kasson (later on, the American delegate at the Samoan conference in Berlin)
warned that if the United States did not find markets for her agricultural and
industrial goods, "our surplus will soon roll back from the Atlantic coast upon
the interior, and the wheels of prosperity will be clogged by the very richness of
the burden which they carry, but cannot deliver." Secretary of State Evarts

found that all thinking people were worrying about "how to create a foreign demand for those manufactures which are left after supplying our home demand"; and in 1880 he inaugurated monthly consular reports giving up-to-date information about trade openings. American participation in international exhibitions testified to the interest in foreign markets. Congress made appropriations for American displays at many exhibitions, at Vienna in 1873, Sydney in 1879, Berlin in 1880, Melbourne in 1880 and 1888, London in 1883, Barcelona and Brussels in 1888, and Paris in 1867, 1878, 1889, 1890, and 1900.

Export promotion was chiefly the occupation not of the government but of thousands of individual producers who turned to foreign markets to absorb the goods they did not sell at home. But increasingly as the post–Civil War years passed, the government, too, concerned itself in the matter; and because of the worry about the surplus (as it was beginning to be called), and also because of an economic depression in 1884, administrations in the late 1870s and especially in the 1880s made unprecedented efforts to expand exports. The worry about overproduction was considerably less than it was to become during the great depression of the 1890s, and consequently these early moves to foster exports occupied a relatively small part of official attention. Nonetheless, already in the 1880s commercial expansion in the New World, in Europe, and even in darkest Africa and little known areas in Asia was an important objective of United States foreign policy.

Some historians have strongly emphasized the agricultural and industrial surplus, with the consequent desire for commercial expansion abroad; they have depicted Washington, responsive to lobbying by special business interests, as preoccupied with commercial expansion—which frequently led also to territorial expansion; and they have argued that the foreign markets which were opened up to the burgeoning American exports constituted just as real an empire as if the Stars and Stripes had flown over these lands. Although throughout the ages commercial expansion has sometimes been the precursor of territorial expansion, it is an oversimplification virtually to equate these two types of expansion. The question of their relationship is a complicated one, but in the present context it is sufficient to say that the political control associated with colonization assures a degree of continuity and certainty in trade and other arrangements that is unobtainable in an informal commercial "empire." Thus the United States, as we shall observe, become dissatisfied with the commercial control of Hawaii given by the reciprocity treaty and decided that outright political control was essential.

At any rate American administrations during the 1880s, which on the whole opposed colonization on principle, did not consider commercial expansion as a substitute for territorial expansion, although a few individuals did, including, probably, Secretary of State Frederick T. Frelinghuysen. For various reasons these administrations looked to Mexico, the west coast of South America, and the Caribbean islands, as New World markets that should be cultivated. Whereas it was mainly for reasons of security and naval strategy (although the influence of trade was already great too) that Washington directed its attention to the potential canal, the Caribbean, Hawaii, and Samoa, the strategic consideration was less significant in policy toward Mexico and South America. As regards Mexico, America's main purpose was simply to protect the Texan border from marauders, but the wish to gain a new market became increasingly strong. As regards South America, both ideology and strategy were important—the feeling, strongly encouraged by the Monroe Doctrine, that by the nature of things, as well as for her national security, the United States rather than Europe should shape Latin American destiny; but for a time in 1881 and 1882 American party politics strongly influenced foreign policy, and at all times export promotion was a major consideration. . . .

It is clear that America's increasing agricultural and industrial output had a marked effect upon her foreign policy in the 1880s. The influence of the so-called surplus, which was already noticeable during the border-crossing dispute with Mexico and, again, during the War of the Pacific, became especially apparent when Arthur was President. So prudent a Secretary of State as Frelinghuysen made vigorous attempts to find markets not only in familiar places like the Caribbean Sea, Hawaii, and Europe, but even in distant Africa. Although, thanks to Cleveland, all his Caribbean reciprocity treaties failed, as well as the Congo General Act, Frelinghuysen's wide-ranging efforts to relieve the surplus must have given rise to an uneasy suspicion throughout the country that the United States was confronting a difficult situation that might soon become critical. When the great panic of 1893 struck the country, the business community had no doubt that overproduction was the root cause. Business leaders and government officials redoubled their efforts to find foreign markets, and this time they were more successful. . . .

By the 1890s the enormous growth in the American economy, which already in the 1880s had aroused considerable interest in commercial expansion, had convinced not only Washington but most business leaders and many publicists that it was essential to cultivate foreign markets. Arthur and Frelinghuysen had favored commercial expansion but had opposed territorial expansion; in the 1890s many Americans came to wonder whether exports could be significantly increased without the acquisition of colonies, which not only would themselves provide markets but, more important, would serve as points of strength for ensuring access to larger markets nearby. The new attention to territorial expansion resulted from the continuing economic growth at home, from changing policies abroad, and from new ideas and outlooks. We must examine these various matters.

The Arthur administration's attempts to boost exports had come to grief, for the most part, when Cleveland shipwrecked Frelinghuysen's reciprocity treaties and the Congo General Act. Under Benjamin Harrison the Republicans again experimented with reciprocity. By authority of the McKinley tariff act of 1890 they concluded reciprocity treaties with Austria-Hungary, Brazil, Santo Domingo, Spain (for Cuba and Puerto Rico), Salvador, Great Britain (for British West Indian islands and British Guiana), Nicaragua, Honduras, and Guatemala. But the familiar story repeated itself: Cleveland, again President in 1893 and still opposed to preferential tariff arrangements, terminated them all in 1894.

If export promotion was so important, why did not American business interests induce Washington to act more resolutely? The fact is that most businessmen were apathetic about exporting until the mid-1890s. The home market was, generally speaking, quite adequate for their needs—although we have observed the considerable interest in Mexican and South American markets, in pork exports to Europe, and in such remote places as Korea and the Congo. Moreover, most exports consisted of agricultural goods, notably wheat and cotton; in 1875 exports of these two items alone had a value of $251 million, as compared with $499 million for total exports; in 1881, $416 million against $884 million. For many years after 1874 crops were poor in Europe, where the great bulk of American agricultural produce went; in the "black year" of 1879 they were catastrophic. A British royal commission of 1879 and another of 1893 foresaw no end to the avalanche pouring in from the American plains and prairies. In these circumstances there was little reason for anxiety about foreign markets. No wonder that American consuls in the 1870s and 1880s were described as being "almost pathetic" in begging business interests back home to wake up to the trade opportunities theirs for the asking. Worry about exporting simply did not exist on a large scale until the 1890s.

During that decade a major change occurred in the trade balance of manufactured goods; and it not only transformed ideas about exporting, but it directly affected industrialists, a group that had much more influence in Washington than agriculturalists had. We have seen that a favorable balance of trade for all kinds of merchandise, agricultural as well as industrial, was first achieved on a continuing basis in 1876; but the balance of manufactures remained on the debit side. Trends of commerce, however, indicated an early reversal; and in 1894 exports of manufactures passed imports; they continued to be greater during the years to come. The reversal came mainly from the staggering increase in American industrial output; this gave rise, in turn, to an equally staggering increase in exports of manufactures: from $89 million in 1865 to $805 million in 1900. Contrasting with this more than ninefold rise was an increase in imports of manufactures from $174 million in 1865 to $470 million in 1900, less than a threefold rise.

It was highly gratifying, of course, to have such a booming economy; but at the same time it was worrying. For where could ever-expanding markets be found for the ever-increasing industrial output? The domestic market, businessmen believed, was not large enough. Nor were the traditional markets in industrialized Europe, which absorbed the American agricultural output, expected to take this quite different, industrial output. The lesson of the rising tide of manufactures seemed clear: somehow, and at all costs, the United States must increase her exports; otherwise the home market would become saturated with a mounting surplus.

Much of the alarm about the surplus is attributable to the panic of 1893 and the great depression that followed. These events rocked the country to its foundations. Not only was the economic distress severe, but social disorders and the rise of the Populist party appeared to portend dire calamity. For conservatives, everything was going alarmingly wrong. Catastrophic business conditions, widespread radicalism, violent strikes—such dreadful happenings seemed to presage the disintegration of the social structure itself. After a century of brilliant success, were American institutions and ideals about to founder in chaos?

What caused the depression? Farmers typically attributed it to a scarcity of money and prescribed the free coinage of silver. Most business leaders, on the other hand, put the blame on overproduction, particularly of manufactured goods, and prescribed not financial tinkering but exporting the surplus. The worst of the distress came during Grover Cleveland's second administration (1893–1897). A strong gold-standard, low-tariff man, the President attempted to restore the plummeting economy by acting on two fronts: one relating to the currency; the other, the tariff. Both had direct implications for exporting. To strengthen the currency he fought hard and successfully for the repeal in 1893 of part of the Sherman Silver Purchase Act, which required the government to buy large quantities of silver every month, and he also replenished the Treasury's gold holdings by selling bonds. Businessmen in general strongly applauded these steps, partly because they accepted the overproduction thesis with its corollary that the surplus must be exported. They and the administration were in full accord that the gold standard, which Cleveland's measures were supporting, provided the stable exchange rates necessary for thriving international commerce—and consequently for export expansion. This was the accepted, orthodox doctrine. It contrasted sharply with the beliefs of free-silverites, who generally put less emphasis on foreign markets because they thought that if more money was created, Americans could themselves purchase enough goods to prevent a surplus from arising. Some silverites, but fewer in number, agreed with the gold-standard advocates on the importance of foreign markets. In many cases highly respectable businessmen, they advocated bimetallism not through free silver but by international agreement; and every President from Hayes through McKinley sent missions to Europe or participated in bimetallic conferences in the vain hope of arranging European and American bimetallism—or at least of quieting the clamor for free silver.

Cleveland's second device for dealing with the depression—the Wilson-Gorman tariff of 1894—also brought up considerations of overproduction and overseas markets. The chief purpose of the McKinley tariff of 1890 had been to protect the home market, but it had also provided for the small measure of reciprocity we have noted. Republicans extolled reciprocity as an ingenious device to gain foreign markets while retaining protection against cheap foreign labor. Democrats scoffed at this view. They agreed, to be sure (at least before 1896), that foreign markets were essential in order to prop up the collapsing economy. But their prescription for exporting the surplus was not reciprocity but duty-free raw materials; and the contention that export promotion depended on cheaper raw materials furnished perhaps the main argument for the tariff of 1894. Thus Representative William L. Wilson, who had charge of the bill in the House, reported for the Ways and Means Committee that every duty on raw materials raised the price of the finished product and thereby narrowed export possibilities; and the Senate's leading supporter of the bill, Roger Q. Mills, argued: "It is the tax on the materials of manufacture alone that keeps us out of foreign markets. . . ."

The tariff measure as passed by the House on February 1, 1894, contained a long duty-free list that included many components of industrial exports. But the Senate, as a result of pressure from special interests, deleted everything on the list except wool, copper, and lumber, an altogether inadequate basis for export promotion. The Senate passed the emasculated bill on July 3, 1894; Cleveland reluctantly signed it the next month.

Cleveland Democrats backed both the gold standard and low tariffs; Republicans, although generally supporting the gold standard, advocated high tariffs and, in some cases, reciprocity. But Cleveland Democrats and Republicans alike typically attributed the depression to surplus production and emphasized the necessity of cultivating foreign markets—although for Republicans, maintaining high tariff rates had first priority. Commercial expansion became a much more important objective of policy than it had been in the 1880s.

Where were foreign markets to be found? For many years Americans had looked to Latin America and, even more, to the great potential market of China with its 400 million supposedly eager customers. And now the depression of the 1890s clarified and intensified these older views. So did other developments. The fact was that Latin America and China were desirable not only on their own merits; they were desirable also because most other large markets seemed in danger of being closed to American exports. In the middle years of the century colonies had been unfashionable in Western countries—a "mill-stone round our necks," Benjamin Disraeli, soon to be a leading British imperialist, had called them as late as 1852. But in the 1880s the great powers of Europe, now including Germany, embarked again upon a race for colonies, and in the 1890s Japan joined them. Two new and powerful navies, the German and Japanese, made their appearance; and Japan's intentions in Hawaii came to seem to Americans as sinister as Germany's in Samoa.

By the late 1890s the slicing up of Africa among the great powers, with the consequent erection of discriminatory tariffs, had been practically completed. There were signs that even America's European markets might soon be walled in. In a much-noticed speech regarding the perils for Europe posed by the colossal American economic machine, Count Agenor Goluchowski, Foreign Minister of Austria-Hungary, warned: "The destructive competition with transoceanic countries...requires prompt and thorough counteracting measures.... The European nations must close their ranks in order successfully to defend their existence." This and other such remarks worried Americans. About that same time the most dynamic public figure in Great Britain, Colonial Secretary Joseph Chamberlain, was campaigning for imperial preference by which the British empire, hitherto open to world commerce, would erect a tariff wall against outside countries. Should the vast British world abandon free trade, American exporters would be hard hit. China, too, seemed in danger of being partitioned, but Americans could hope to influence events there more than in Africa, Europe, and the British empire.

For United States foreign policy, the lesson of these domestic and international economic trends of the 1890s was clear. Everyone agreed that, to be more competitive with her European rivals, the United States needed a shorter sea route between her industrial center in the northeast and her potential markets in China and on the west coast of South America. This an isthmian canal would provide. In short, the economic trends of the 1890s, now reinforcing the older strategic and geographic considerations attendant upon west coast settlement, pointed urgently to a canal and to the Caribbean and Hawaiian bases needed for its protection. As yet, however, there was nothing like a consensus for even these basic objectives, and the old-fashioned repugnance for anything smacking of territorial expansion overseas remained remarkably strong. Notwithstanding the historic shift to an export surplus of manufactured goods, and notwithstanding the depression of the 1890s and the ominous signs of closing markets around the world, both the government and the business community continued to have faith in commercial expansion, unaccompanied by territorial expansion, as adequate to relieve the surplus. The faith was somewhat old-fashioned in a world of high and proliferating tariff walls (outside the British empire); it had in fact been greatly weakened, and a canal and bases in the Caribbean and Hawaii had come much more into national favor. But not until the Spanish-American War did sentiment turn irresistibly to territorial expansion.

The Limits of an Economic Interpretation

ROBERT L. BEISNER

An economic interpretation of American expansionism goes back at least as far as the Englishman John Hobson, who argued in *Imperialism* (1902) that the origins of this impulse were to be found in the efforts of moneylenders to find profitable new areas in which to invest their surplus capital. But the idea that J. P. Morgan singlehandedly got the United States ensconced in Manila has always been too much to swallow, and American historians—aware that the United States was a net borrower of capital until World War I—have tended to emphasize the search for foreign markets for goods, not capital, as the economic impetus to American imperialism. The search was necessary, according to this argument, because American industrialization had led to a productive surplus that must be disposed of abroad if businessmen were to avoid the unpleasant alternatives: decreased production, which would reduce profits and increase unemployment and social unrest, or, worse still because it reeked of socialism, a redistribution of wealth on a scale to permit lower-wage workers to buy the surplus products themselves.

Since neither alternative was attractive, another path was chosen—the government would help businessmen sell their surplus in other parts of the world. Thus, in this view, America's policymakers began the process of shaping U.S.

Robert L. Beisner, *From the Old Diplomacy to the New, 1865–1900* (Arlington Heights, Ill.: AHM Publishing Corp., 1975) pp. 17–26. Reprinted by permission of the publishers, AHM Publishing Corporation, Arlington Heights, Illinois.

diplomacy to these economic ends, haltingly at first right after the Civil War, but more systematically later on when business effectively supplanted agriculture as the dominant political influence in Washington and the need for action became more obvious. The climax came in the mid-nineties, precipitated by a shattering panic and depression and the news of the apparent disappearance of America's safety-valve frontier (Frederick Jackson Turner, "The Significance of the Frontier in American History," *Annual Report of the American Historical Association for the Year 1893*). These blows fell on an already unnerved population that had been nurtured on the story that America's progress would be onward-and-upward-forever. The threats of recurrent crisis or stagnation somehow had to be avoided, and an aggressive search for new markets seemed to provide the way out.

Latin America and the Far East were considered especially suitable areas for the construction of escape routes. Administrations once depicted as presenting a record of unparalleled mediocrity were actually, so the argument goes, establishing a crucial foundation for future developments by using tariff reform, reciprocity agreements, antirevolutionary and anti-European interventions, and other means to insure the increase of American exports. That the process culminated in war and the consequent acquisition of an empire did not mean that American leaders wanted it that way; it meant only that in 1898–99 they saw no other way to get what they did want without adopting such drastic methods.

This economic interpretation of the foreign policy of the period is not burdened with the cruder aspects of "left wing" history that have always been so easy to criticize. Such present-day exponents as Williams, LaFeber, and Thomas J. McCormick have not made the mistake of blaming American imperialism on Wall Street or attributing it to some kind of conspiracy but have argued instead that American foreign policy was the product of a consensus of businessmen, politicians, and intellectuals. They do not brand these men as ideological colonialists, but rather as individuals who, if events had gone the way they hoped, would gladly have settled for a few small island bases of use to American merchants and the navy assigned to protect their trade. The leaders of the United States wanted an "informal empire" created by the demand for American products, not a formal empire dependent on the weapons of war.

Critics of this line of argument are quick to point out the apparently meager results of commercial diplomacy. Although U.S. exports to China rose from $3 million in 1890 to $15 million in 1900, the latter figure represented only 1.1 percent of total American exports, hardly an imperial proportion. It has also been noted that only a small portion of the gross national product in the late nineteenth century was involved in foreign trade, that most of this modest portion was with Canada and Europe and little with the "imperial" areas of Asia and Latin America (e.g., in 1900 about 44 percent of all U.S. exports went to Great Britain and France, while 3 percent went to China and Japan), and that agricultural rather than manufactured products continued to account for the bulk of American exports to the very end of the century.

"Informal empire" historians have made a three-fold response to these criticisms. First, they assert that American trade statistics of the time are not as modest and unimportant as they appear at first glance. Relatively small percentage increases in exports could make the difference between stagnation and prosperity, both for an individual company and the economy at large. For some industries exports to particular regions were cruical; almost 50 percent of the exports of the American cotton textile industry, for example, were shipped to China in the late 1890s. Second, they argued that their thesis does not depend upon massive economic results, but evidence that American leaders *believed* in the urgency of increased exports and the shimmering China market. Third, William A. Williams, in *Roots of the Modern American Empire,* has met the agricultural issue head-on. He points out himself that Americans earned as much in 1869 from the export of animal tallow and butter as from iron and steel, evidence of the continuing vitality of trade in agricultural commodities. Giving this fact its due attention, he concludes that the American obsession with exports started in Jeffersonian times; that wheat farmers, cattle-raisers, cotton farmers, dairymen, food processors, and others in the agricultural sector long pushed for a commercially oriented foreign policy; but that at the end of the century "metropolitan" business and political leaders took control of the export drive and turned it to the needs of an industrial economy. Thus Williams makes a valiant attempt to incorporate both preindustrial pressures for foreign markets and the continuing importance of agricultural exports in his economic interpretation of late-nineteenth-century U.S. diplomacy. And, by focusing attention once more on ordinary farmers and their spokesmen instead of the industrial-political elite, he places renewed emphasis on the popular roots of American imperialism.

The economic approach to American foreign policy from 1865 to 1900 contains many strong points and has found widespread acceptance, in part because of its appeal to the numerous critics of contemporary American foreign policy. But though it is valuable in explaining some specific episodes, this view has serious shortcomings as a key to the whole period. Not only is it simplistic to suppose there was a generation of policymakers invariably motivated by rational and precise calculations of the nation's economic interests, but a thorough sifting of the evidence turns up far too many discrepancies for an endorsement of the economic interpretation.

Much evidence, in fact, points in contrary directions. In 1870 when Secretary of State Fish put before the Grant cabinet a dispatch urging a concerted effort to increase American trade and influence in Hawaii, he was met with total silence and "the subject [was] dropped." In the same era the United States willingly jeopardized prospects for important new trade with China because of hostility at home to Chinese immigrants. No one was more eager for the China trade than Californians, yet, as Alexander DeConde states in his useful textbook, *A History of American Foreign Policy* (2d ed., 1971), "they were willing to sacrifice benefits that trade would bring rather than continue to accept the Chinese." Jobs and racial tensions were more important issues than foreign markets. In 1884 the Arthur administration actively participated in the Berlin conference on the Congo, from which many trade benefits were expected to flow; but the incoming Cleveland administration withdrew the conference treaty from the

Senate in 1885 because it conflicted with American isolation from Big Power affairs, a tradition more deep-rooted than the imperatives of foreign trade. Did President Harrison shake the mailed fist at Chile in 1891–92 . . . to open it up as a market for Connecticut locomotives, or was it to avenge an insult to the American uniform and counterbalance Great Britain's considerable influence in the Latin republic? The fact is that patriotic concerns and fear of European political influence in the hemisphere weighed more in Harrison's mind than commercial ledger sheets. James G. Blaine's vain attempt in 1881 to establish a Pan-American conference is often cited as a pioneering venture in market expansionism, but according to Russell H. Bastert he acted "from a mixture of many motives, probably least of all economic." His desire to be president was perhaps the most important ("A New Approach to the Origins of Blaine's Pan-American Policy," *Hispanic American Historical Review,* XXXIX, August 1959). Grover Cleveland's attempt to lower the tariff during the nineties was not a depression-induced maneuver to stimulate trade but the fulfillment of a political pledge he had made in 1887. He was responding to old Democratic party traditions and the ire of American consumers, not the needs of eastern industrialists (Paul S. Holbo, "Economics, Emotion, and Expansion: An Emerging Foreign Policy," in H. Wayne Morgan, ed., *The Gilded Age* [rev. ed., 1970]). Indeed, despite the calamitous depression of the nineties and the purported "consensus" on the wisdom of supporting all measures that would encourage exports, Congress quashed reciprocity agreements with Brazil, the Central American States, the British West Indies, Austria-Hungary, Germany, and Spain (involving Cuba and Puerto Rico). America's legislators apparently had not gotten the word.

One reason politicians did not take the foreign trade problem too seriously was that businessmen themselves set a bad example. Expansionist Brooks Adams complained bitterly of their "failure . . . to act intelligently and aggressively" in foreign markets. Milton Plesur has argued (*America's Outward Thrust: Approaches to Foreign Affairs, 1865–1890* [1971]) that American trade suffered constantly from plain old sloppiness and ineptitude in business practices—sending products abroad that were not only inferior, poorly packaged, and inappropriate for their designated markets, but in some cases unsafe as well (e.g., celluloid collars and cuffs made of harmful ingredients); poor timing (fur coats sent to Canada in July); and reliance upon incompetent or negligent local representatives. The general problem described by Plesur applied doubly in China, where commercial aspirations were supposedly greatest of all at the end of the century (Paul A. Varg, "The Myth of the China Market, 1890–1914," *American Historical Review,* LXXIII, February 1968). One historian notes that despite the urging of American political officials for special attention to be paid to area conditions, U.S. manufacturers "were slow to meet the trade demands of the Asian market" and "made little effort" to adapt their products to its needs (Marilyn B. Young, "American Expansion, 1870–1900: The Far East," in Barton J. Bernstein, ed., *Towards a New Past: Dissenting Essays in American History* [1968]; Young develops her argument more fully in *Rhetoric of Empire: American China Policy, 1895–1900* [1968]).

It is therefore highly misleading to think in terms of a unified American business community, backed by a determined government, striving unremittingly to break into the markets of Asia and Latin America. Most exporters still regarded trade as a matter between businessmen in any case; and of those who did believe that the government should have an active economic policy, most had in mind the protection of *home* markets by a high tariff wall, a strategy not designed to promote exports either in theory or practice. Protectionist sentiment remained intact throughout the Johnson-McKinley years, and free-trade views virtually disappeared from the expansionist Republican Party. Paul Holbo has pointed out that the annual debates in Congress on the tariff, far more passionate and rhetorical over the years than those aroused by foreign trade, spent their strength in arguments about workingmen's jobs, relief for consumers, and such ideological labels as "Americanism" and "Jeffersonianism"—not export strategy; and Tom E. Terrill, while generally supporting the economic interpretation, makes clear in *The Tariff, Politics, and American Foreign Policy, 1874–1901* (1973) how hard it was to turn attention from protection of the home market to expansion of foreign trade. As to the businessmen who were vitally interested in foreign sales, the great majority directed their attention to the profitable markets of Canada and Europe and failed to concentrate significantly on the undeveloped markets of Asia and Latin America until the era of Theodore Roosevelt and Woodrow Wilson (David E. Novack and Matthew Simon, "Commercial Responses to the American Export Invasion, 1871–1914: An Essay in Attitudinal History," *Explorations in Entrepreneurial History,* 2d ser., III, Winter 1966).

The behavior of American officials and businessmen does not support the carefully measured, symmetrical case put forward by LaFeber, Williams, McCormick, et al. That the United States government should skillfully and knowingly formulate and execute a farsighted economic foreign policy flies in the face of evidence that most American "policymakers," at least until the nineties, were amateurish and often maladroit in their diplomatic conduct, ignorant of and not particularly interested in the affairs of other nations, and much more inclined to react in the accustomed way to outside events than to initiate well-defined new policies. Behavior, not occasional rhetoric, is the crucial test. What, in actual fact, did presidents and secretaries of state do through most of the years from 1865 to 1900? They revealed some interest in the expansion of foreign markets, of course, but they also revealed much faintheartedness or unconcern about such matters and consistently appointed to the field men who were poorly qualified for any grand economic promotional task. And Congress? It raised the tariff and rejected the principle of reciprocal trade treaties, sacrificed quality in the diplomatic service on the altar of thrift, and repeatedly put partisan concerns high above good relations with other nations. And businessmen? They concentrated overwhelmingly on selling to the ever-enlarging domestic market, and, when they did get into the export game, continued to look to the traditional and nonimperialistic markets of neighboring Canada and Europe. Tables I and II illustrate both points.

This criticism does not mean the economic interpretation should be rejected

TABLE I   United States Exports as Percentage of Estimated Gross National Product in Selected Years

Year	Total Exports	Pct. of GNP (est.)
1874	$ 606,000,000	8.1%
1884	752,600,000	7.1
1889	762,700,000	6.4
1891	909,800,000	6.7
1893	862,300,000	6.5
1895	807,500,000	5.8
1897	1,051,000,000	7.5
1899	1,227,000,000	6.9
1900	1,394,500,000	7.5

out of hand, but it must be blended where possible with other views to create a useful synthesis. Historians have always noted, of course, that foreign trade and other economic factors have been important in American diplomacy. The problem has been that few writers, including the recent revisionists, have integrated these factors into a general framework or emphasized their significant political and ideological overtones. Agile politicians throughout the years have manipulated these economic currents for their own purposes; David Healy has argued that many statesmen with power and prestige uppermost in their minds used a rhetoric heavily dosed with "markets" talk to win support from a public more concerned with dollars and cents than glory (*US Expansionism: The Imperialist Urge in the 1890s* [1970]). Even more common than politicians who manipulated economic, political, and ideological issues were those who never dreamed of separating them. They might, for example, have wanted to increase American political influence in China during the 1890s, but for what purpose if not to open doors for U.S. exports? Or, conversely, they might have wanted to increase exports as a means of enhancing American political influence throughout the Far East.

TABLE II   Exports to Canada and Europe Compared with Exports to Asia and Latin America

Year	Exports to Canada and Europe	Pct. of Total	Exports to Asia and Latin America	Pct. of Total
1875	$ 494,000,000	86.1%	$ 72,000,000	12.5%
1885	637,000,000	85.8	87,000,000	11.7
1895	681,000,000	84.3	108,000,000	13.4
1900	1,135,000,000	81.4	200,000,000	14.3

Tables compiled from information in *Historical Statistics of the United States,* 1960; U.S. Department of Commerce, *Long Term Growth, 1860–1965,* 1966; National Bureau of Economic Research, *Trends in the American Economy in the Nineteenth Century,* 1960.

In short, as Marilyn B. Young has written, most Americans merged economics into a broader view "which saw a strong navy, trade, political power, and the territory necessary . . . to maintain both trade and power, as complementary factors contributing to the wealth and strength of the nation." Moreover, since the time of the Revolution, Americans have considered foreign trade to be not only a source of money profits, but a wellspring of social enlightenment and a beneficent bond between distant peoples (James A. Field, Jr., *America and the Mediterranean World, 1776–1882* [1969]). Foreign commerce was, in addition, a source of American pride; Paul A. Varg observes that it "flattered the ego of Americans to think of their country as the supplier of the world's market. . . ." Thus American interest in foreign trade has long transcended exclusively economic horizons, a fact that must be understood if we are properly to appreciate the actual role of economics in late-nineteenth-century American foreign policy.

FURTHER READING

William H. Becker, "American Manufacturers and Foreign Markets, 1870–1900," *Business History Review*, 47 (1973), 466–481

Robert B. Davies, " 'Peacefully Working to Conquer the World': The Singer Company in Foreign Markets, 1854–1889," *Business History Review*, 43 (1969), 299–325

John A. Garraty, *The New Commonwealth, 1877–1890* (1968)

John A. S. Grenville and George B. Young, *Politics, Strategy, and American Diplomacy* (1967)

Kenneth J. Hagan, *American Gunboat Diplomacy and the Old Navy, 1877–1889* (1973)

Paul S. Holbo, "Economics, Emotion, and Expansion: An Emerging Foreign Policy," in H. Wayne Morgan, ed., *The Gilded Age* (1970)

Walter LaFeber, *The New Empire* (1963)

Ernest N. Paolino, *The Foundations of the American Empire: William Henry Seward and U.S. Foreign Policy* (1973)

Thomas G. Paterson, "American Businessmen and Consular Service Reform, 1890s to 1906," *Business History Review*, 40 (1966), 77–97

Milton Plesur, *America's Outward Thrust* (1971)

David M. Pletcher, *Rails, Mines, and Progress: Seven American Promoters in Mexico, 1867–1911* (1958)

Howard B. Schonberger, *Transportation to the Seaboard* (1971)

Tom Terrill, *The Tariff, Politics, and American Foreign Policy, 1874–1901* (1973)

Robert Wiebe, *The Search for Order* (1967)

Mira Wilkins, *The Emergence of the Multinational Enterprise: American Business Abroad from the Colonial Era to 1914* (1970)

William A. Williams, *The Roots of the Modern American Empire* (1969)

William A. Williams, *The Tragedy of American Diplomacy* (1962)

Marilyn Blatt Young, "American Expansion, 1870–1900: The Far East," in Barton J. Bernstein, ed., *Towards a New Past* (1968)

10

The Spanish-American War and Empire

*In 1898 the United States and Spain went to war over Cuba. After the brief
conflict, which saw military action in Asia as well as in the Caribbean, the
United States demanded and achieved from a humiliated Spain the cession of
the Philippines, Guam, and Puerto Rico and independence for Cuba. At about
the same time, the United States annexed Hawaii and Wake Island. Two key
questions arise: Why did the McKinley administration decide in favor of war?
And how did a war, declared to liberate Cuba, become an imperialist venture
with new territorial acquisitions? Contemporary anti-imperialists presented
their answers and arguments, but lost the debate. Historians are still debating
these issues.*

DOCUMENTS

In his War Message of April 11, 1898, reprinted as the first document, President
William McKinley explained why he thought the United States had to take up arms.
Congress granted his request on April 19 and var was officially declared two days
later. As the next two documents demonstrate, critics of the American imperial
course—evident in the absorption of the Philippines and the subsequent military
suppression of a Filipino Insurrection led by nationalist Emilio Aguinaldo—spoke
vigorously against what they considered a gross violation of American principles.
Philosopher William James's impassioned letter to the *Boston Evening Transcript*
(March 1, 1899) and the program of the American Anti-Imperialist League (October

17, 1899) condemn the McKinley administration's foreign policy. A defender of American imperialism, Senator Albert J. Beveridge of Indiana, gave an unabashed endorsement to overseas acquisitions in his 1900 "March of the Flag" speech, as the last document demonstrates.

William McKinley's War Message, 1898

Obedient to that precept of the Constitution which commands the President to give from time to time to the Congress information of the state of the Union and to recommend to their consideration such measures as he shall judge necessary and expedient, it becomes my duty to now address your body with regard to the grave crisis that has arisen in the relations of the United States to Spain by reason of the warfare that for more than three years has raged in the neighboring island of Cuba.

I do so because of the intimate connection of the Cuban question with the state of our own Union and the grave relation the course which it is now incumbent upon the nation to adopt must needs bear to the traditional policy of our Government if it is to accord with the precepts laid down by the founders of the Republic and religiously observed by succeeding Administrations to the present day.

The present revolution is but the successor of other similar insurrections which have occurred in Cuba against the dominion of Spain, extending over a period of nearly half a century, each of which during its progress has subjected the United States to great effort and expense in enforcing its neutrality laws, caused enormous losses to American trade and commerce, caused irritation, annoyance, and disturbance among our citizens, and, by the exercise of cruel, barbarous, and uncivilized practices of warfare, shocked the sensibilities and offended the humane sympathies of our people. . . .

Our people have beheld a once prosperous community reduced to comparative want, its lucrative commerce virtually paralyzed, its exceptional productiveness diminished, its fields laid waste, its mills in ruins, and its people perishing by tens of thousands from hunger and destitution. We have found ourselves constrained, in the observance of that strict neutrality which our laws enjoin and which the law of nations commands, to police our own waters and watch our own seaports in prevention of any unlawful act in aid of the Cubans.

Our trade has suffered, the capital invested by our citizens in Cuba has been largely lost, and the temper and forbearance of our people have been so sorely tried as to beget a perilous unrest among our own citizens, which has inevitably found its expression from time to time in the National Legislature, so that issues wholly external to our own body politic engross attention and stand in the way of that close devotion to domestic advancement that becomes a self-contained commonwealth whose primal maxim has been the avoidance of all foreign entanglements. All this must needs awaken, and has, indeed, aroused, the utmost concern on the part of this Government, as well during my predecessor's term as in my own. . . .

The war in Cuba is of such a nature that, short of subjugation or extermination, a final military victory for either side seems impracticable. The alternative lies in the physical exhaustion of the one or the other party, or perhaps of both—a condition which in effect ended the ten years' war by the truce of Zanjon. The prospect of such a protraction and conclusion of the present strife is a contingency hardly to be contemplated with equanimity by the civilized world, and least of all by the United States, affected and injured as we are, deeply and intimately, by its very existence.

Realizing this, it appeared to be my duty, in a spirit of true friendliness, no less to Spain than to the Cubans, who have so much to lose by the prolongation of the struggle, to seek to bring about an immediate termination of the war. To this end I submitted on the 27th ultimo, as a result of much representation and correspondence, through the United States minister at Madrid, propositions to the Spanish Government looking to an armistice until October 1 for the negotiation of peace with the good offices of the President.

In addition I asked the immediate revocation of the order of reconcentration, so as to permit the people to return to their farms and the needy to be relieved with provisions and supplies from the United States, cooperating with the Spanish authorities, so as to afford full relief.

The reply of the Spanish cabinet was received on the night of the 31st ultimo. It offered, as the means to bring about peace in Cuba, to confide the preparation thereof to the insular parliament, inasmuch as the concurrence of that body would be necessary to reach a final result, it being, however, understood that the powers reserved by the constitution to the central Government are not lessened or diminished. As the Cuban parliament does not meet until the 4th of May next, the Spanish Government would not object for its part to accept at once a suspension of hostilities if asked for by the insurgents from the general in chief, to whom it would pertain in such case to determine the duration and conditions of the armistice. . . .

With this last overture in the direction of immediate peace, and its disappointing reception by Spain, the Executive is brought to the end of his effort. . . .

The grounds for . . . intervention may be briefly summarized as follows:

First. In the cause of humanity and to put an end to the barbarities, bloodshed, starvation, and horrible miseries now existing there, and which the parties to the conflict are either unable or unwilling to stop or mitigate. It is no answer to say this is all in another country, belonging to another nation, and is therefore none of our business. It is specially our duty, for it is right at our door.

Second. We owe it to our citizens in Cuba to afford them that protection and indemnity for life and property which no government there can or will afford, and to that end to terminate the conditions that deprive them of legal protection.

Third. The right to intervene may be justified by the very serious injury to the commerce, trade, and business of our people and by the wanton destruction of property and devastation of the island.

Fourth, and which is of the utmost importance. The present condition of affairs in Cuba is a constant menace to our peace and entails upon this Government an enormous expense. With such a conflict waged for years in an island so near us and with which our people have such trade and business relations; when the lives and liberty of our citizens are in constant danger and their property destroyed and themselves ruined; where our trading vessels are liable to seizure and are seized at our very door by war ships of a foreign nation; the expeditions of filibustering that we are powerless to prevent altogether, and the irritating questions and entanglements thus arising—all these and others that I need not mention, with the resulting strained relations, are a constant menace to our peace and compel us to keep on a semi war footing with a nation with which we are at peace. . . .

In view of these facts and of these considerations I ask the Congress to authorize and empower the President to take measures to secure a full and final termination of hostilities between the Government of Spain and the people of Cuba, and to secure in the island the establishment of a stable government, capable of maintaining order and observing its international obligations, insuring peace and tranquillity and the security of its citizens as well as our own, and to use the military and naval forces of the United States as may be necessary for these purposes.

And in the interest of humanity and to aid in preserving the lives of the starving people of the island I recommend that the distribution of food and supplies be continued and that an appropriation be made out of the public Treasury to supplement the charity of our citizens.

The issue is now with the Congress. It is a solemn responsibility. I have exhausted every effort to relieve the intolerable condition of affairs which is at our doors. Prepared to execute every obligation imposed upon me by the Constitution and the law, I await your action.

Yesterday, and since the preparation of the foregoing message, official information was received by me that the latest decree of the Queen Regent of Spain directs General Blanco, in order to prepare and facilitate peace, to proclaim a suspension of hostilities, the duration and details of which have not yet been communicated to me.

This fact, with every other pertinent consideration, will, I am sure, have your just and careful attention in the solemn deliberations upon which you are about to enter. If this measure attains a successful result, then our aspirations as a Christian, peace-loving people will be realized. If it fails, it will be only another justification for our contemplated action.

William James on the Suppression of the Philippines, 1899

Here was a people towards whom we felt no ill-will, against whom we had not even a slanderous rumor to bring; a people for whose tenacious struggle against their Spanish oppressors we have for years spoken (so far as we spoke of them at all) with nothing but admiration and sympathy. Here was a leader who as the Spanish lies about him, on which we were fed so long, drop off, and as the truth gets more and more known, appears as an exceptionally fine specimen of the patriot and national hero; not only daring, but honest; not only a fighter, but a governor and organizer of extraordinary power. Here were the precious beginnings of an indigenous national life, with which, if we had any responsibilities to these islands at all, it was our first duty to have squared ourselves. Aguinaldo's movement was, and evidently deserved to be, an ideal popular movement, which as far as it had had time to exist was showing itself "fit" to survive and likely to become a healthy piece of national self-development. It was all we had to build on, at any rate, so far—if we had any desire not to succeed to the Spaniards' inheritance of native execration.

And what did our Administration do? So far as the facts have leaked out, it issued instructions to the commanders on the ground simply to freeze Aguinaldo out, as a dangerous rival, with whom all compromising entanglement was sedulously to be avoided by the great Yankee business concern. We were not to "recognize" him, we were to deny him all account of our intentions; and in general to refuse any account of our intentions to anybody, except to declare in abstract terms their "benevolence," until the inhabitants, without a pledge of any sort from us, should turn over their country into our hands. Our President's bouffé-proclamation was the only thing vouchsafed; "We are here for your own good; therefore unconditionally surrender to our tender mercies, or we'll blow you into kingdom come."

Our own people meanwhile were vaguely uneasy, for the inhuman callousness and insult shown at Paris and Washington to the officially delegated mouthpieces of the wants and claims of the Filipinos seems simply abominable from any moral point of view. But there must be reasons of state, we assumed, and good ones. Aguinaldo is evidently a pure adventurer "on the make," a blackmailer, sure in the end to betray our confidence, or our Government wouldn't treat him so, for our President is essentially methodistical and moral. Mr. McKinley must be in an intolerably perplexing situation, and we must not criticise him too soon. We assumed this, I say, though all the while there was a horribly suspicious look about the performance. On its face it reeked of the infernal adroitness of the great department store, which has reached perfect expertness in the art of killing silently and with no public squealing or commotion the neighboring small concern.

But that small concern, Aguinaldo, apparently not having the proper American business education, and being uninstructed on the irresistible character of our Republican party combine, neither offered to sell out nor to give up. So the Administration had to show its hand without disguise. It did so at last. We are now openly engaged in crushing out the sacredest thing in this great human world—the attempt of a people long enslaved to attain to the possession of itself, to organize its laws and government, to be free to follow its internal destinies according to its own ideals. War, said Moltke, aims at destruction, and at nothing else. And splendidly are we carrying out war's ideal. We are destroying the lives of these islanders by the thousand, their villages and their cities; for surely it is we who are solely responsible for all the incidental burnings that our operations entail. But these destructions are the smallest part of our sins. We are destroying down to the root every germ of a healthy national life in these unfortunate people, and we are surely helping to destroy for one generation at least their faith in God and man. No life shall you have, we say, except as a gift from our philanthropy after your unconditional submission to our will. So as they seem to be "slow pay" in the matter of submission, our yellow journals have abundant time in which to raise new monuments of capitals to the victories of Old Glory, and in which to extol the unrestrainable eagerness of our brave soldiers to rush into battles that remind them so much of rabbit hunts on Western plains.

It is horrible, simply horrible. Surely there cannot be many born and bred Americans who, when they look at the bare fact of what we are doing, the fact taken all by itself, do not feel this, and do not blush with burning shame at the unspeakable meanness and ignominy of the trick?

Why, then, do we go on? First, the war fever; and then the pride which always refuses to back down when under fire. But these are passions that interfere with the reasonable settlement of any affair; and in this affair we have to deal with a factor altogether peculiar with our belief, namely, in a national destiny which must be "big" at any cost, and which for some inscrutable reason it has become infamous for us to disbelieve in or refuse. We are to be missionaries of civilization, and to bear the white man's burden, painful as it often is. We must sow our ideals, plant our order, impose our God. The individual lives are nothing. Our duty and our destiny call, and civilization must go on.

Could there be a more damning indictment of that whole bloated idol termed "modern civilization" than this amounts to? Civilization is, then, the big, hollow, resounding, corrupting, sophisticating, confusing torrent of mere brutal momentum and irrationality that brings forth fruits like this! It is safe to say that one Christian missionary, whether primitive, Protestant or Catholic, of the original missionary type, one Buddhist or Mohammedan of a genuine saintly sort, one ethical reformer or philanthropist, or one disciple of Tolstoi would do more real good in these islands than our whole army and navy can possibly effect with our whole civilization at their back. He could build up realities, in however small a degree; we can only destroy the inner realities; and indeed destroy in a year more of them than a generation can make good.

It is by their moral fruits exclusively that these benighted brown people, "half-devil and half-child" as they are, are condemned to judge a civilization. Ours is already execrated by them forever for its hideous fruits.

Shall it not in so far forth be execrated by ourselves? Shall the unsophisticated verdict upon its hideousness which the plain moral sense pronounces avail nothing to stem the torrent of mere empty "bigness" in our destiny, before which it is said we must all knock under, swallowing our higher sentiments with a gulp? The issue is perfectly plain at last. We are cold-bloodedly, wantonly and abominably destroying the soul of a people who never did us an atom of harm in their lives. It is bald, brutal piracy, impossible to dish up any longer in the cold pot-grease of President McKinley's cant at the recent Boston banquet—surely as shamefully evasive a speech, considering the right of the public to know definite facts, as can often have fallen even from a professional politician's lips. The worst of our imperialists is that they do not themselves know where sincerity ends and insecurity begins. Their state of consciousness is so new, so mixed of primitively human passions and, in political circles, of calculations that are anything but primitively human; so at variance, moreover, with their former mental habits; and so empty of definite data and contents; that they face various ways at once, and their portraits should be taken with a squint. One reads the President's speech with a strange feeling— as if the very words were squinting on the page.

The impotence of the private individual, with imperialism under full headway as it is, is deplorable indeed. But every American has a voice or a pen, and may use it. So, impelled by my own sense of duty, I write these present words. One by one we shall creep from cover, and the opposition will organize itself. If the Filipinos hold out long enough, there was a good chance (the canting game being already pretty well played out, and the piracy having to show itself hence-forward naked) of the older American beliefs and sentiments coming to their rights again, and of the Administration being terrified into a conciliatory policy towards the native government.

The programme for the opposition should, it seems to me, be radical. The infamy and iniquity of a war of conquest must stop. A "protectorate," of course, if they will have it, though after this they would probably rather welcome any European Power; and as regards the inner state of the island, freedom, "fit" or "unfit," that is, home rule without humbugging phrases, and whatever anarchy may go with it until the Filipinos learn from each other, not from us, how to govern themselves. Mr. Adams's programme—which anyone may have by writing to Mr. Erving Winslow, Anti-Imperialist League, Washington, D.C.— seems to contain the only hopeful key to the situation. Until the opposition newspapers seriously begin, and the mass meetings are held, let every American who still wishes his country to possess its ancient soul—soul a thousand times more dear than ever, now that it seems in danger of perdition—do what little he can in the way of open speech and writing, and above all let him give his representatives and senators in Washington a positive piece of his mind.

Program of the American Anti-Imperialist League, 1899

We hold that the policy known as imperialism is hostile to liberty and tends toward militarism, an evil from which it has been our glory to be free. We regret that it has become necessary in the land of Washington and Lincoln to reaffirm that all men, of whatever race or color, are entitled to life, liberty and the pursuit of happiness. We maintain that governments derive their just powers from the consent of the governed. We insist that the subjugation of any people is "criminal aggression" and open disloyalty to the distinctive principles of our Government.

We earnestly condemn the policy of the present National Administration in the Philippines. It seeks to extinguish the spirit of 1776 in those islands. We deplore the sacrifice of our soldiers and sailors, whose bravery deserves admiration even in an unjust war. We denounce the slaughter of the Filipinos as a needless horror. We protest against the extension of American sovereignty by Spanish methods.

We demand the immediate cessation of the war against liberty, begun by Spain and continued by us. We urge that Congress be promptly convened to announce to the Filipinos our purpose to concede to them the independence for which they have so long fought and which of right is theirs.

The United States have always protested against the doctrine of international law which permits the subjugation of the weak by the strong. A self-governing state cannot accept sovereignty over an unwilling people. The United States cannot act upon the ancient heresy that might makes right.

Imperialists assume that with the destruction of self-government in the Philippines by American hands, all opposition here will cease. This is a grievous error. Much as we abhor the war of "criminal aggression" in the Philippines, greatly as we regret that the blood of the Filipinos is on American hands, we more deeply resent the betrayal of American institutions at home. The real firing line is not in the suburbs of Manila. The foe is of our own household. The attempt of 1861 was to divide the country. That of 1899 is to destroy its fundamental principles and noblest ideals.

Whether the ruthless slaughter of the Filipinos shall end next month or next year is but an incident in a contest that must go on until the Declaration of Independence and the Constitution of the United States are rescued from the hands of their betrayers. Those who dispute about standards of value while the foundation of the Republic is undermined will be listened to as little as those who would wrangle about the small economies of the household while the house is on fire. The training of a great people for a century, the aspiration for liberty of a vast immigration are forces that will hurl aside those who in the delirium of conquest seek to destroy the character of our institutions.

We deny that the obligation of all citizens to support their Government in times of grave National peril applies to the present situation. If an Administration may with impunity ignore the issues upon which it was chosen, deliberately create a condition of war anywhere on the face of the globe, debauch the civil service for spoils to promote the adventure, organize a truth-suppressing censorship and demand of all citizens a suspension of judgment and their unanimous support while it chooses to continue the fighting, representative government itself is imperiled.

We propose to contribute to the defeat of any person or party that stands for the forcible subjugation of any people. We shall oppose for reëlection all who in the White House or in Congress betray American liberty in pursuit of un-American ends. We still hope that both of our great political parties will support and defend the Declaration of Independence in the closing campaign of the century.

We hold, with Abraham Lincoln, that "no man is good enough to govern another man without that other's consent. When the white man governs himself, that is self-government, but when he governs himself and also governs another man, that is more than self-government—that is despotism. Our reliance is in the love of liberty which God has planted in us. Our defense is in the spirit which prizes liberty as the heritage of all men in all lands. Those who deny freedom to others deserve it not for themselves, and under a just God cannot long retain it."

We cordially invite the cooperation of all men and women who remain loyal to the Declaration of Independence and the Constitution of the United States.

Senator Albert J. Beveridge on the "March of the Flag," 1900

Fellow citizens, It is a noble land that God has given us; a land that can feed and clothe the world; a land whose coast lines would enclose half the countries of Europe; a land set like a sentinel between the two imperial oceans of the globe, a greater England with a nobler destiny. It is a mighty people that he has planted on this soil; a people sprung from the most masterful blood of history; a people perpetually revitalized by the virile, man-producing workingfolk of all the earth; a people imperial by virtue of their power, by right of their institutions, by authority of their heaven-directed purposes—the propagandists and not the misers of liberty. It is a glorious history our God has bestowed upon his chosen people; a history whose keynote was struck by Liberty Bell; a history heroic with faith in our mission and our future; a history of statesmen who flung the boundaries of the Republic out into unexplored lands and savage wildernesses; a history of soldiers who carried the flag across the blazing deserts and through the ranks of hostile mountains, even to the gates of sunset; a history of a multiplying people who overran a continent in half a century; a history of prophets who saw the consequences of evils inherited from the past and of martyrs who died to save us from them; a history divinely logical, in the process of whose tremendous reasoning we find ourselves today. . . .

Shall the American people continue their resistless march toward the commercial supremacy of the world? Shall free institutions broaden their blessed reign as the children of liberty wax in strength, until the empire of our principles is established over the hearts of all mankind?

Have we no mission to perform, no duty to discharge to our fellowman? Has the Almighty Father endowed us with gifts beyond our deserts and marked us as the people of his peculiar favor, merely to rot in our own selfishness, as men and nations must, who take cowardice for their companion and self for their Deity—as China has, as India has, as Egypt has?

Shall we be as the man who had one talent and hid it, or as he who had ten talents and used them until they grew to riches? And shall we reap the reward that waits on our discharge of our high duty as the sovereign power of earth; shall we occupy new markets for what our farmers raise, new markets for what our factories make, new markets for what our merchants sell—aye, and, please God, new markets for what our ships shall carry?

Shall we avail ourselves of new sources of supply of what we do not raise or

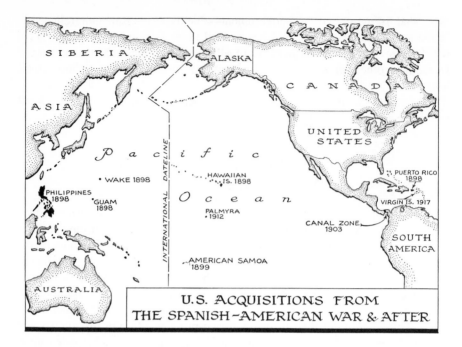

U.S. ACQUISITIONS FROM
THE SPANISH-AMERICAN WAR & AFTER

make, so that what are luxuries to-day will be necessities to-morrow? Shall our commerce be encouraged until, with Oceanica, the Orient, and the world, American trade shall be the imperial trade of the entire globe? . . .

For William McKinley is continuing the policy that Jefferson began, Monroe continued, Seward advanced, Grant promoted, Harrison championed, and the growth of the republic has demanded. Hawaii is ours; Porto Rico is to be ours; at the prayer of the people Cuba will finally be ours; in the islands of the East, even to the gates of Asia, coaling-stations are to be ours; at the very least the flag of a liberal government is to float over the Philippines, and I pray God it may be the banner that Taylor unfurled in Texas and Fremont carried to the coast—the Stars and Stripes of glory. . . .

The Opposition tells us that we ought not to govern a people without their consent. I answer, The rule of liberty that all just government derives its authority from the consent of the governed, applies only to those who are capable of self-government. I answer, We govern the Indians without their consent, we govern our territories without their consent, we govern our children without their consent. I answer, How do you assume that our government would be without their consent? Would not the people of the Philippines prefer the just, humane, civilizing government of this republic to the savage, bloody rule of pillage and extortion from which we have rescued them?. . .

And, now, obeying the same voice that Jefferson heard and obeyed, that Jackson heard and obeyed, that Monroe heard and obeyed, that Seward heard and obeyed, that Ulysses S. Grant heard and obeyed, that Benjamin Harrison heard and obeyed, William McKinley plants the flag over the islands of the seas, outposts of commerce, citadels of national security, and the march of the flag goes on! . . .

Distance and oceans are no arguments. . . .

Steam joins us; electricity joins us—the very elements are in league with our destiny. Cuba not contiguous! Porto Rico not contiguous! Hawaii and the Philippines not contiguous! Our navy will make them contiguous. Dewey and Sampson and Schley have made them contiguous, and American speed, American guns, American heart and brain and nerve will keep them contiguous forever. . . .

To-day, we are raising more than we can consume. To-day, we are making more than we can use. To-day, our industrial society is congested; there are more workers than there is work; there is more capital than there is investment. We do not need more money—we need more circulation, more employment. Therefore we must find new markets for our produce, new occupation for our capital, new work for our labor. And so, while we did not need the territory taken during the past century at the time it was acquired, we do need what we have taken in 1898, and we need it now.

Think of the thousands of Americans who will pour into Hawaii and Porto Rico when the republic's laws cover those islands with justice and safety! Think of the tens of thousands of Americans who will invade mine and field and forest in the Philippines when a liberal government, protected and controlled by this republic, if not the government of the republic itself, shall establish order and equity there! Think of the hundreds of thousands of Americans who will build a soap-and-water, common-school civilization of energy and industry in Cuba, when a government of law replaces the double reign of anarchy and tyranny! —think of the prosperous millions that Empress of Islands will support when, obedient to the law of political gravitation, her people ask for the highest honor liberty can bestow, the sacred Order of the Stars and Stripes, the citizenship of the Great Republic!

What does all this mean for every one of us? It means opportunity for all the glorious young manhood of the republic—the most virile, ambitious, impatient, militant manhood the world has ever seen. It means that the resources and the commerce of these immensely rich dominions will be increased as much as American energy is greater than Spanish sloth; for Americans henceforth will monopolize those resources and that commerce. . . .

Fellow Americans, we are God's chosen people. Yonder at Bunker Hill and Yorktown his providence was above us. At New Orleans and on ensanguined seas his hand sustained us. Abraham Lincoln was his minister and his was the Altar of Freedom, the boys in blue set on a hundred battlefields. His power directed Dewey in the East and delivered the Spanish fleet into our hands on the eve of Liberty's natal day, as he delivered the elder Armada into the hands of our English sires two centuries ago. His great purposes are revealed in the progress of the flag, which surpasses the intentions of Congresses and Cabinets, and leads us like a holier pillar of cloud by day and pillar of fire by night into situations unforeseen by finite wisdom, and duties unexpected by the unprophetic heart of selfishness. The American people cannot use a dishonest medium of exchange; it is ours to set the world its example of right and honor. We cannot fly from our world duties; it is ours to execute the purpose of a fate that has driven us to be greater than our small intentions. We cannot retreat from any soil where Providence has unfurled our banner; it is ours to save that soil for Liberty and Civilization. For Liberty and Civilization and God's promise fulfilled, the flag must henceforth be the symbol and the sign to all mankind—the flag!—

> Flag of the free heart's hope and home,
>   By angel hands to valor given,
> Thy stars have lit the welkin dome,
>   And all their hues were born in heaven!
> Forever wave that standard sheet,
>   Where breathes the foe but falls before us,
> With freedom's soil beneath our feet
>   And freedom's banner streaming o'er us.

ESSAYS

Richard Hofstadter's essay places the war and imperialism in the context of a "psychic crisis" in the 1890s, wherein tumultuous events such as the depression created a compulsion to lash out overseas. Walter LaFeber of Cornell University also sees the 1890s as a watershed, but places more emphasis on the quest for foreign markets as a major stimulant to war and imperialism. On the other hand, in his essay, Ernest R. May of Harvard University does not find the causes of war in the United States itself. Rather, he argues that American leaders temporarily borrowed ideas from European imperialists. One question, then, is whether foreign policy is influenced more by events abroad than by careful thinking and planning in Washington. Just how self-conscious, rational, and deliberate were Americans in their imperial thrust?

The Psychic Crisis of the 1890s

RICHARD HOFSTADTER

The taking of the Philippine Islands from Spain in 1899 marked a major historical departure for the American people, a breach in their traditions and a shock to their established values. To be sure, from their national beginnings they had constantly engaged in expansion, but almost entirely into contiguous territory. Now they were extending themselves to distant extra-hemispheric colonies. They were abandoning a strategy of defense hitherto limited to the continent and its appurtenances, in favor of a major strategic commitment in the Far East. Thus far their expansion had been confined to the spread of a relatively homogeneous population into territories planned from the beginning to develop self-government; now control was to be imposed by force on millions of ethnic aliens. The acquisition of the islands, therefore, was understood by contemporaries on both sides of the debate, as it is readily understood today, to be a turning point in our history.

To discuss the debate in isolation from other events, however, would be to deprive it of its full significance. America's entrance into the Philippine Islands was a by-product of the Spanish-American War. The Philippine crisis is inseparable from the war crisis, and the war crisis itself is inseparable from a larger constellation that might be called "the psychic crisis of the 1890's."

Central in the background of the psychic crisis was the great depression that broke in 1893 and was still very acute when the agitation over the war in Cuba began. Severe depression, by itself, does not always generate an emotional crisis as intense as that of the nineties. In the 1870's the country had been swept by a depression of comparable acuteness and duration which, however, did not give rise to all the phenomena that appeared in the 1890's or to very many of them with comparable intensity and impact. It is often said that the 1890's, unlike the 1870's, form a "watershed" in American history. The difference between the emotional and intellectual impact of these two depressions can be measured, I believe, not by the difference in severity, but rather by reference to a number of singular events that in the 1890's converged with the depression to heighten its impact upon the public mind.

First in importance was the Populist movement, the free-silver agitation, the heated campaign of 1896. For the first time in our history a depression had created a protest movement strong enough to capture a major party and raise the specter, however unreal, of drastic social convulsion. Second was the maturation and bureaucratization of American business, the completion of its essential industrial plant, and the development of trusts on a scale sufficient to stir the anxiety that the old order of competitive opportunities was approaching an eclipse. Third, and of immense symbolic importance, was the apparent filling up of the continent and the disappearance of the frontier line. We now know how much land had not yet been taken up and how great were the remaining possibilities for internal expansion both in business and on the land; but to the mind of the 1890's it seemed that the resource that had engaged the energies of the people for three centuries had been used up. The frightening possibility suggested itself that a serious juncture in the nation's history had come. As Frederick Jackson Turner expressed it in his famous paper of 1893: "Now, four centuries from the discovery of America, at the end of one hundred years of life under the Constitution, the frontier has gone, and with its going has closed the first period of American history."

To middle-class citizens who had been brought up to think in terms of the nineteenth-century order, the outlook seemed grim. Farmers in the staple-growing region had gone mad over silver and Bryan; workers were stirring in bloody struggles like the Homestead and Pullman strikes; the supply of new land seemed at an end; the trust threatened the spirit of business enterprise; civic corruption was at a high point in the large cities; great waves of seemingly unassimilable immigrants arrived yearly and settled in hideous slums. To many historically conscious writers, the nation appeared overripe, like an empire ready for collapse through a stroke from outside or through internal upheaval. Acute as the situation was for all those who lived by the symbols of national power—for the governing and thinking classes—it was especially poignant for young people, who would have to make their careers in the dark world that seemed to be emerging.

The symptomatology of the crisis would record several tendencies in popular thought and behavior that had previously existed only in pale and tenuous form. These symptoms were manifest in two quite different moods. The key to one of them was an intensification of protest and humanitarian reform. Populism, utopianism, the rise of the Christian Social gospel, the growing intellectual interest in socialism, the social settlement movement that appealed so strongly to the college generation of the nineties, the quickening of protest and social criticism in the realistic novel—all these are expressions of this mood. The other mood was one of national self-assertion, aggression, expansion. The motif of the first was social sympathy; of the second, national power. During the 1890's far more patriotic groups were founded than in any other decade of our history; the naval theories of Captain Mahan were gaining in influence; naval construction was booming; there was an immense quickening of the American cult of Napoleon and a vogue of the virile and martial writings of Rudyard Kipling; young Theodore Roosevelt became the exemplar of the vigorous, masterful, out-of-doors man; the revival of European imperialism stirred speculation over what America's place would be in the world of renewed colonial rivalries, and in some stirred a demand to get into the imperial race to avoid the risk of being overwhelmed by other powers. But most significant was the rising tide of jingoism, a matter of constant comment among observers of American life during the decade.

Jingoism, of course, was not new in American history. But during the 1870's and 1880's the American public had been notably quiescent about foreign relations. There had been expansionist statesmen, but they had been blocked by popular apathy, and our statecraft had been restrained. Grant had failed dismally in his attempt to acquire Santo Domingo; our policy toward troubled Hawaii had been cautious; in 1877 an offer of two Haitian naval harbors had been spurned. In responding to Haiti, Secretary of State Frelinghuysen had remarked that "the policy of this Government . . . has tended toward avoidance of possessions disconnected from the main continent." Henry Cabot Lodge, in his life of George Washington published in 1889, observed that foreign relations then filled "but a slight place in American politics, and excite generally only a languid interest." Within a few years this comment would have seemed absurd. In 1895, Russell A. Alger reported to Lodge, after reading one of Lodge's own articles to a Cincinnati audience, that he was convinced by the response that foreign policy, "more than anything else, touches the public pulse of today." The history of the 1890's is the history of public agitation over expansionist issues and of quarrels with other nations. . . .

Since Julius W. Pratt published his *Expansionists of 1898* in 1936, it has been obvious that any interpretation of America's entry upon the paths of imperialism in the nineties in terms of rational economic motives would not fit the facts, and that a historian who approached the event with preconceptions no more supple than those, say, of Lenin's *Imperialism* would be helpless. This is not to say that markets and investments have no bearing; they do, but there are features of the situation that they do not explain at all. Insofar as the economic factor was important, it can be better studied by looking at the relation between the depression, the public mood, and the political system.

The alternative explanation has been the equally simple idea that the war was a newspapers' war. This notion, once again, has some point, but it certainly does not explain the war itself, much less its expansionist result. The New Deal period, when the political successes of F.D.R. were won in the face of overwhelming newspaper opposition, showed that the press is not powerful enough to impose upon the public mind a totally uncongenial view of public events. It must operate roughly within the framework of public predispositions. Moreover, not all the papers of the nineties were yellow journals. We must inquire into the structure of journalistic power and also into the views of the owners and editors to find out what differentiated the sensational editors and publishers from those of the conservative press.

There is still another qualification that must be placed upon the role of the press: the press itself, whatever it can do with opinion, does not have the power to precipitate opinion into action. That is something that takes place within the *political* process, and we cannot tell that part of the story without examining the state of party rivalries, the origin and goals of the political elites, and indeed the entire political context. We must, then, supplement our story about the role of the newspapers with at least two other factors: the state of the public temper upon which the newspapers worked, and the manner in which party rivalries deflected domestic clashes into foreign aggression. Here a perennial problem of politics under the competitive two-party system became manifest again in the 1890's. When there is, for whatever reason, a strong current of jingoism running in the channels of public sentiment, party competition tends to speed it along. If the party in power is behaving circumspectly, the opposition tends to beat the drums. For example, in 1896, with Cleveland still in office, the Republican platform was much more exigent on the Cuba issue. When McKinley came into office and began to show reluctance to push toward intervention, the Democratic party became a center of interventionist pressure; this pressure was promptly supplemented by a large number of Republicans who, quite aside from their agreement on the issue, were concerned about its effect on the fate of their party.

When we examine the public temper, we find that the depression, together with such other events as the approaching completion of the settlement of the continent, the growth of trusts, and the intensification of internal social conflict, had brought to large numbers of people intense frustrations in their economic lives and their careers. To others they had brought anxiety that a period of stagnation in national wealth and power had set in. The restlessness of the discontented classes had been heightened by the defeat of Bryan in 1896. The anxieties about the nation's position had been increased among statesmen and publicists by the revival of world imperialism, in particular by the feeling that America was threatened by Germany, Russia, and Japan. The expansionist statesmen themselves were drawn largely from a restless upper-middle-class elite that had been fighting an unrewarding battle for conservative reform in domestic politics and looked with some eagerness toward a more spacious field of action.

Men often respond to frustration with acts of aggression, and allay their anxieties by threatening acts against others. It is revealing that the underdog forces in American society showed a considerably higher responsiveness to the idea of war with Spain than the groups that were satisfied with their economic or political positions. Our entry into the Philippines then aroused the interest of conservative groups that had been indifferent to the quixotism of freeing Cuba but were alert to the possibility of capturing new markets. Imperialism appealed to members of both the business and the political elites as an enlargement of the sphere of American power and profits; many of the underdogs also responded to this new note of national self-assertion. Others, however, looked upon our conduct in the Philippines as a betrayal of national principles. Anti-expansionists attempted to stir a sense of guilt and foreboding in the nation at large. But the circumstances of the period 1898–1900—the return of prosperity and the quick spectacular victories in war—made it difficult for them to impress this feeling upon the majority. The rhetoric of Duty and Destiny carried the day. The anti-expansionists had neither the numbers nor the morale of their opponents. The most conspicuous result of their lack of drive and confidence can be seen in the lamentable strategy of Bryan over the ratification of the treaty.

Clearly this attempt to see the war and expansion in the light of social history has led us onto the high and dangerous ground of social psychology and into the arena of conjecture. But simple rationalistic explanations of national behavior will also leave us dissatisfied. What I have attempted here is merely a preliminary sketch of a possible explanatory model. Further inquiry might make it seem more plausible at some points, more questionable at others.

Preserving the American System

WALTER LAFEBER

The "splendid little war" of 1898, as Secretary of State John Hay termed it at the time, is rapidly losing its splendor for those concerned with American foreign policy in the 1960s. Over the past decade few issues in the country's diplomatic history have aroused academics more than the causes of the Spanish-

American War, and in the last several years the argument has become not merely academic, but a starting point in the debate over how the United States evolved into a great power, and more particularly how Americans got involved in the maelstrom of Asian nationalism. The line from the conquest of the Philippines in 1898 to the attempted pacification of Vietnam in 1968 is not straight, but it is quite traceable, and if Frederick Jackson Turner was correct when he observed in the 1890s that "The aim of history, then, is to know the elements of the present by understanding what came into the present from the past," the causes of the war in 1898 demand analysis from our present viewpoint.

Historians have offered four general interpretations to explain these causes. First, the war has been traced to a general impulse for war on the part of American public opinion. This interpretation has been illustrated in a famous cartoon showing President William McKinley, in the bonnet and dress of a little old lady, trying to sweep back huge waves marked "Congress" and "public opinion," with a very small broom. The "yellow journalism" generated by the Hearst-Pulitzer rivalry supposedly both created and reflected this sentiment for war. A sophisticated and useful version of this interpretation has been advanced by Richard Hofstadter. Granting the importance of the Hearst-Pulitzer struggle, he has asked why these newspaper titans were able to exploit public opinion. Hofstadter has concluded that psychological dilemmas arising out of the depression of the 1890s made Americans react somewhat irrationally because they were uncertain, frightened, and consequently open to exploitation by men who would show them how to cure their frustrations through overseas adventures. In other words, the giddy minds of the 1890s could be quieted by foreign quarrels.

A second interpretation argues that the United States went to war for humanitarian reasons, that is, to free the Cubans from the horrors of Spanish policies and to give the Cubans democratic institutions. That this initial impulse resulted within ten months in an American protectorate over Cuba and Puerto Rico, annexation of the Philippines, and American participation in quarrels on the mainland of Asia itself, is explained as accidental, or, more familiarly, as done in a moment of "aberration" on the part of American policy-makers.

A third interpretation emphasizes the role of several Washington officials who advocated a "Large Policy" of conquering a vast colonial empire in the Caribbean and Western Pacific. By shrewd maneuvering, these few imperialists pushed the vacillating McKinley and a confused nation into war. Senator Henry Cabot Lodge, of Massachusetts, Captain Alfred Thayer Mahan, of the U.S. Navy, and Theodore Roosevelt, Assistant Secretary of the Navy in 1897–1898, are usually named as the leaders of the "Large Policy" contingent.

A fourth interpretation believes the economic drive carried the nation into war. This drive emanated from the rapid industrialization which characterized American society after the 1840s. The immediate link between this industrialization and the war of 1898 was the economic depression which afflicted the

Walter LaFeber, "That 'Splendid Little War' in Historical Perspective," *Texas Quarterly,* 11 (1968), 89–98.

nation in the quarter-century after 1873. Particularly important were the 1893–1897 years when Americans endured the worst of the plunge. Government and business leaders, who were both intelligent and rational, believed an over-supply of goods created the depression. They finally accepted war as a means of opening overseas markets in order to alleviate domestic distress caused by the overproduction. For thirty years the economic interpretation dominated historians' views of the war, but in 1936 Professor Julius Pratt conclusively demonstrated that business journals did not want war in the early months of 1898. He argued instead the "Large Policy" explanation, and from that time to the present, Professor Pratt's interpretation has been pre-eminent in explaining the causes of the conflict.

As I shall argue in a moment, the absence of economic factors in causing the war has been considerably exaggerated. At this point, however, a common theme which unites the first three interpretations should be emphasized. Each of the three deals with a superficial aspect of American life; each is peculiar to 1898, and none is rooted in the structure, the bed-rock, of the nation's history. This theme is important, for it means that if the results of the war were distasteful and disadvantageous (and on this historians do largely agree because of the divisive problems which soon arose in the Philippines and Cuba), those misfortunes were endemic to episodes unique to 1898. The peculiarities of public sentiment or the Hearst-Pulitzer rivalry, for example, have not reoccurred; the wide-spread humanitarian desire to help Cubans has been confined to 1898; and the banding together of Lodge, Mahan, and Roosevelt to fight for "Large Policies" of the late 1890s was never repeated by the three men. Conspiracy theories, moreover, seldom explain history satisfactorily.

The fourth interpretation has different implications. It argues that if the economic was the primary drive toward war, criticism of that war must begin not with irrational factors or flights of humanitarianism or a few stereotyped figures, but with the basic structure of the American system.

United States foreign policy, after all, is concerned primarily with the nation's domestic system and only secondarily with the systems of other nations. American diplomatic history might be defined as the study of how United States relations with other nations are used to insure the survival and increasing prosperity of the American system. Foreign policymakers are no more motivated by altruism than is the rest of the human race, but are instead involved in making a system function at home. Secretary of State, as the Founding Fathers realized, is an apt title for the man in charge of American foreign policy.

Turning this definition around, it also means that domestic affairs are the main determinant of foreign policy. When viewed within this matrix, the diplomatic events of the 1890s are no longer aberrations or the results of conspiracies and drift; American policymakers indeed grabbed greatness with both hands. As for accident or chance, they certainly exist in history, but become more meaningful when one begins with J. B. Bury's definition of "chance": "The valuable collision of two or more independent chains of causes." The most fruitful approach to the war of 1898 might be from the inside out (from the domestic to the foreign), and by remembering that chance is "the valuable collision of two or more independent chains of causes."

Three of these "chains" can be identified: the economic crisis of the 1890s which caused extensive and dangerous maladjustments in American society; the opportunities which suddenly opened in Asia after 1895 and in the Caribbean and the Pacific in 1898, opportunities which officials began to view as poultices, if not cure-alls, for the illnesses at home; and a growing partnership between business and government which reached its nineteenth-century culmination in the person of William McKinley. In April 1898, these "chains" had a "valuable collision" and war resulted.

The formation of the first chain is the great success story of American history. Between 1850 and 1910 the average manufacturing plant in the country multiplied its capital thirty-nine times, its number of wage-earners nearly seven times, and the value of its output by more than nineteen times. By the mid-1890s American iron and steel producers joked about their successful underselling of the vaunted British steel industry not only in world markets, but also in the vicinity of Birmingham, England, itself. The United States traded more in international markets than any nation except Great Britain.

But the most accelerated period of this development, 1873–1898, was actually twenty-five years of boom hidden in twenty-five years of bust. That quarter-century endured the longest and worst depression in the nation's history. After brief and unsatisfactory recoveries in the mid-1880s and early 1890s, the economy reached bottom in 1893. Unparalleled social and economic disasters struck. One out of every six laborers was unemployed, with most of the remainder existing on substandard wages; not only weak firms but many companies with the best credit ratings were forced to close their doors; the unemployed slept in the streets; riots erupted in Brooklyn, California, and points in between, as in the calamitous Pullman Strike in Chicago; Coxey's Army of broken farmers and unemployed laborers made their famous march on Washington; and the Secretary of State, Walter Quentin Gresham, remarked privately in 1894 that he saw "symptoms of revolution" appearing. Federal troops were dispatched to Chicago and other urban areas, including a cordon which guarded the Federal Treasury building in New York City.

Faced with the prospect of revolution and confronted with an economy that had almost ground to a stop, American businessmen and political officials faced alternative policies: they could attempt to re-examine and reorient the economic system, making radical modifications in the means of distribution and particularly the distribution of wealth; or they could look for new physical frontiers, following the historic tendency to increase production and then ferreting out new markets so the surplus, which the nation supposedly was unable to consume, could be sold elsewhere and Americans then put back to work on the production lines.

To the business and political communities, these were not actually alternatives at all. Neither of those communities has been known historically for political and social radicalism. Each sought security, not new political experiments.

Some business firms tried to find such security by squashing competitors. Extremely few, however, searched for such policies as a federal income tax. Although such a tax narrowly passed through Congress in 1894, the Supreme Court declared it unconstitutional within a year and the issue would not be resurrected for another seventeen years. As a result, business and political leaders accepted the solution which was traditional, least threatening to their own power, and (apparently) required the least risk: new markets. Secretary of the Treasury John G. Carlisle summarized this conclusion in his public report of 1894: "The prosperity of our people, therefore, depends largely upon their ability to sell their surplus products in foreign markets at remunerative prices."

This consensus included farmers and the labor movement among others, for these interests were no more ingenious in discovering new solutions than were businessmen. A few farmers and laborers murmured ominously about some kind [of] political and/or economic revolution, but Richard Hofstadter seems correct in suggesting that in a sense Populism was reactionary rather than radical. The agrarians in the Populist movement tended to look back to a Jeffersonian utopia. Historians argue this point, but beyond dispute is the drive by farmers, including Populists, for foreign markets. The agrarians acted out of a long and successful tradition, for they had sought overseas customers since the first tobacco surplus in Virginia three hundred and fifty years before. Farmers initially framed the expansionist arguments and over three centuries created the context for the growing consensus on the desirability of foreign markets, a consensus which businessmen and others would utilize in the 1890s.

The farmers' role in developing this theme in American history became highly ironic in the late nineteenth century, for businessmen not only adopted the argument that overseas markets were necessary, but added a proviso that agrarian interests would have to be suppressed in the process. Industrialists observed that export charts demonstrated the American economy to be depending more upon industrial than agrarian exports. To allow industrial goods to be fully competitive in the world market, however, labor costs would have to be minimal, and cheap bread meant sacrificing the farmers. Fully comprehending this argument, agrarians reacted bitterly. They nevertheless continued searching for their own overseas markets, agreeing with the industrialist that the traditional method of discovering new outlets provided the key to prosperity, individualism, and status.

The political conflict which shattered the 1890s revolved less around the question of whether conservatives could carry out a class solution than the question of which class would succeed in carrying out a conservative solution. This generalization remains valid even when the American labor movement is examined for its response to the alternatives posed. This movement, primarily comprised of the newly-formed American Federation of Labor, employed less than 3 per cent of the total number of employed workers in nonfarm occupations. In its own small sphere of influence, its membership largely consisted of skilled workers living in the East. The AFL was not important in the West or South, where the major discontent seethed. Although Samuel Gompers was known by some of the more faint-hearted as a "socialist," the AFL's founder never dramatized any radical solutions for the restructuring of the economy. He was concerned with obtaining more money, better hours, and improved working conditions for the Federation's members. Gompers refused, moreover, to use direct political action to obtain these benefits, content to negotiate within the corporate structure which the businessman had created. The AFL simply wanted more, and when overseas markets seemed to be a primary source of benefits, Gompers did not complain. As Louis Hartz has noted, "wage consciousness," not "class consciousness," triumphed.

The first "chain of causes" was marked by a consensus on the need to find markets overseas. Fortunately for the advocates of this policy, another "chain," quite complementary to the first, began to form beyond American borders. By the mid-1890s, American merchants, missionaries, and ship captains had been profiting from Asian markets for more than a century. Between 1895 and 1900, however, the United States for the first time became a mover-and-pusher in Asian affairs.

In 1895 Japan defeated China in a brief struggle that now appears to be one of the most momentous episodes in the nineteenth century. The Japanese emerged as the major Asian power, the Chinese suddenly seemed to be incapable of defending their honor or existence, Chinese nationalism began its peculiar path to the 1960s, and European powers which had long lusted after Asian markets now seized a golden opportunity. Russia, Germany, France, and ultimately Great Britain initiated policies designed to carve China and Manchuria into spheres of influence. Within a period of months, the Asian mainland suddenly became the scene of international power politics at its worst and most explosive.

The American reaction to these events has been summarized recently by Professor Thomas McCormick: "The conclusion of the Sino-Japanese War left Pandora's box wide open, but many Americans mistook it for the Horn of Plenty." Since the first American ship sailed to sell goods in China in 1784, Americans had chased that most mysterious phantom, the China Market. Now, just at the moment when key interest groups agreed that overseas markets could be the salvation of the 1890s crisis, China was almost miraculously opening its doors to the glutted American factories and farms. United States trade with China jumped significantly after 1895, particularly in the critical area of manufactures; by 1899 manufactured products accounted for more than 90 per cent of the nation's exports to the Chinese, a quadrupling of the amount sent in 1895. In their moment of need, Americans had apparently discovered a Horn of Plenty.

But, of course, it was Pandora's box. The ills which escaped from the box were threefold. Least important for the 1890s, a nascent Chinese nationalism appeared. During the next quarter-century, the United States attempted to minimize the effects of this nationalism either by cooperating with Japan or European powers to isolate and weaken the Chinese, or by siding with the most conservative groups within the nationalist movement. Americans also faced the competition of European and Japanese products, but they were nevertheless confident in the power of their newly-tooled industrial powerhouse. Given a "fair field and no favor," as the Secretary of State phrased the wish in 1900, Americans would undersell and defeat any competitors. But could fair fields and no favors be guaranteed? Within their recently-created spheres of influence European powers began to grant themselves trade preferences, thus effectively shutting out American competition. In 1897, the American business community and the newly-installed administration of William McKinley began to counter these threats.

The partnership between businessmen and politicians, in this case the Mc-Kinley administration, deserves emphasis, for if the businessman hoped to exploit Asian markets he required the aid of the politician. Americans could compete against British or Russian manufacturers in Asia, but they could not compete against, say, a Russian manufacturer who could turn to his government and through pressure exerted by that government on Chinese officials receive a prize railroad contract or banking concession. United States businessmen could only compete against such business-government coalitions if Washington officials helped. Only then would the field be fair and the favors equalized. To talk of utilizing American "rugged individualism" and a free enterprise philosophy in the race for the China market in the 1890s was silly. There consequently emerged in American policy-making a classic example of the business community and the government grasping hands and, marching shoulder to shoulder, leading the United States to its destiny of being a major power on a far-Eastern frontier. As one high Republican official remarked in the mid-1890s: "diplomacy is the management of international business."

William McKinley fully understood the need for such a partnership. He had grown to political maturity during the 1870s when, as one Congressman remarked, "The House of Representatives was like an auction room where more valuable considerations were disposed of under the speaker's hammer than in any other place on earth." Serving as governor of Ohio during the 1890s depression, McKinley learned firsthand about the dangers posed by the economic crisis (including riots in his state which he terminated with overwhelming displays of military force). The new Chief Executive believed there was nothing necessarily manifest about Manifest Destiny in American history, and his administration was the first in modern American history which so systematically and completely committed itself to helping businessmen, farmers, laborers, and missionaries in solving their problems in an industrializing, supposedly frontierless America. Mr. Dooley caught this aggressive side of the McKinley administration when he described the introduction of a presidential speech: "Th' proceedin's was opened with a prayer that Providence might r-remain undher th' protection iv th' administration."

Often characterized as a creature of his campaign manager Mark Hanna, or as having, in the famous but severely unjust words of Theodore Roosevelt, the backbone of a chocolate eclair, McKinley was, as Henry Adams and others fully understood, a master of men. McKinley was never pushed into a policy he did not want to accept. Elihu Root, probably the best mind and most acute observer who served in the McKinley cabinets, commented that on most important matters the President had his ideas fixed, but would convene the Cabinet, direct the members toward his own conclusions, and thereby allow the Cabinet to think it had formulated the policy. In responding to the problems and opportunities in China, however, McKinley's power to exploit that situation was limited by events in the Caribbean.

In 1895 revolution had broken out in Cuba. By 1897 Americans were becoming increasingly belligerent on this issue for several reasons: more than $50,000,000 of United States investments on the island were endangered; Spaniards were treating some Cubans inhumanely; the best traditions of the Monroe Doctrine had long dictated that a European in the Caribbean was a sty in the eye of any red-blooded American; and, finally, a number of Americans, not only Lodge, Roosevelt, and Mahan, understood the strategic and political relationship of Cuba to a proposed isthmian canal. Such a canal would provide a short-cut to the west coast of Latin America as well as to the promised markets of Asia. Within six months after assuming office, McKinley demanded that the island be pacified or the United States would take a "course of action which the time and the transcendent emergency may demand." Some Spanish reforms followed, but in January 1898, new revolts wracked Havana and a month later the "Maine" dramatically sank to the bottom of Havana harbor.

McKinley confronted the prospect of immediate war. Only two restraints appeared. First, a war might lead to the annexation of Cuba, and the multitude of problems (including racial) which had destroyed Spanish authority would be dumped on the United States. Neither the President nor his close advisers wanted to leap into the quicksands of noncontiguous, colonial empire. The business community comprised a second restraining influence. By mid-1897 increased exports, which removed part of the agricultural and industrial glut, began to extricate the country from its quarter-century of turmoil. Finally seeing light at the end of a long and treacherous tunnel, businessmen did not want the requirements of a war economy to jeopardize the growing prosperity.

These two restraints explain why the United States did not go to war in 1897, and the removal of these restraints indicates why war occurred in April 1898. The first problem disappeared because McKinley and his advisers entertained no ideas of warring for colonial empire in the Caribbean. After the war Cuba would be freed from Spain and then ostensibly returned to the Cubans to govern. The United States would retain a veto power over the more important policy decisions made on the island. McKinley discovered a classic solution in which the United States enjoyed the power over, but supposedly little of the responsibility for, the Cubans.

The second restraint disappeared in late March 1898, exactly at the time of McKinley's decision to send the final ultimatum to Madrid. The timing is crucial. Professor Pratt observed in 1936 that the business periodicals began to change their antiwar views in mid-March 1898, but he did not elaborate upon this point. The change is significant and confirms the advice McKinley received from a trusted political adviser in New York City who cabled on March 25 that the larger corporations would welcome war. The business journal and their readers were beginning to realize that the bloody struggle in Cuba and the resulting inability of the United States to operate at full-speed in Asian affairs more greatly endangered economic recovery than would a war.

McKinley's policies in late March manifested these changes. This does not mean that the business community manipulated the President, or that he was repaying those businessmen who had played vital roles in his election in 1896. Nor does it mean that McKinley thought the business community was forcing his hand or circumscribing his policies in late March. The opinions and policies of the President and the business community had been hammered out in the furnace of a terrible depression and the ominous changes in Asia. McKinley and pivotal businessmen emerged from these unforgettable experiences sharing a common conclusion: the nation's economy increasingly depended upon overseas markets, including the whole of China; that to develop these markets not only a business-government partnership but also tranquillity was required; and, finally, however paradoxical it might seem, tranquillity could be insured only through war against Spain. Not for the first or last time, Americans believed that to have peace they would have to wage war. Some, including McKinley, moved on to a final point. War, if properly conducted, could result in a few select strategic bases in the Pacific (such as Hawaii, Guam, and Manila) which would provide the United States with potent starting-blocks in the race for Asian markets. McKinley sharply distinguished between controlling such bases and trying to rule formally over an extensive territorial empire. In the development of the "chains of causes" the dominant theme was the economic, although not economic in the narrow sense. As discussed in the 1890s, business recovery carried most critical political and social implications.

Some historians argue that McKinley entered the war in confusion and annexed the Philippines in a moment of aberration. They delight in quoting the President's announcement to a group of Methodist missionaries that he decided to annex the Philippines one night when after praying he heard a mysterious voice. Most interesting, however, is not that the President heard a reassuring voice, but how the voice phrased its advice. The voice evidently outlined the points to be considered; in any case, McKinley numbered them in order, demonstrating, perhaps, that either he, the voice, or both had given some thought to putting the policy factors in neat and logical order. The second point is of particular importance: "that we could not turn them [the Philippines] over to France or Germany—our commercial rivals in the Orient—that would be bad business and discreditable. . . ." Apparently everyone who had been through the 1890s knew the dangers of "bad business." Even voices.

Interpretations which depend upon mass opinion, humanitarianism, and "Large Policy" advocates do not satisfactorily explain the causes of the war. Neither, however, does Mr. Dooley's famous one-sentence definition of American imperialism in 1898: "Hands acrost th' sea an' into somewan's pocket." The problem of American expansion is more complicated and historically rooted than that flippancy indicates. George Eliot once observed, "The happiest nations, like the happiest women, have no history." The United States, however, endured in the nineteenth century a history of growing industrialism, supposedly closing physical frontiers, rapid urbanization, unequal distribution of wealth, and an overdependence upon export trade. These historical currents clashed in the 1890s. The result was chaos and fear, then war and empire.

In 1898 McKinley and the business community wanted peace, but they also sought benefits which only a war could provide. Viewed from the perspective of the 1960's, the Spanish-American conflict can no longer be viewed as only a "splendid little war." It was a war to preserve the American system.

Influence from Abroad

ERNEST R. MAY

In 1898–99 the United States suddenly became a colonial power. It annexed the Hawaiian Islands. Humbling Spain in a short war, it took Puerto Rico and the Philippines. In quick sequence it also acquired Guam and part of Samoa and, if the Danish Rigsdag had consented, would have bought the Virgin Islands. In an eighteen-month period it became master of empires in the Caribbean and the Pacific.

Viewing America's tradition as anticolonial, historians have found these events puzzling. The legislative resolution for war with Spain seemingly expressed this tradition. Calling for independence for Spain's Cuban colony, Congress disclaimed "any disposition or intention to exercise sovereignty, jurisdiction, or control over" Cuba. That the same body should have ended the war by annexing Puerto Rico and Spanish islands in the Pacific appears a paradox, and many historians see 1898–99 as, in Samuel Flagg Bemis' phrase, a "great aberration."

To be sure, Americans of the time were hustled along by events. The first battle of the war took place not in Cuba but in Spain's more distant Philippine colony. A spectacular success, in which Admiral Dewey's squadron overcame all opposition without losing a single ship or life, it surprised many Americans into their first awareness that the Philippine Islands existed and that Spain owned them. Soon, however, following reports that Dewey's victory had shaken Spain's control, American troops sailed to seize the colonial capital, Manila. On the ground that these troops would need a support base in mid-Pacific, Congress annexed the Hawaiian Islands. By war's end, therefore, the United States already had one Pacific colony, and debate centered on whether to acquire another in the Philippines.

Both Americans and Europeans assumed that the United States could dispose of the Philippines as it chose. Seeming alternatives included handing the islands back to Spain, arranging for transfer to a European power, insisting on independence, or annexing. Most Americans saw the first alternative as giving up a hard-won prize and, moreover, returning the Filipinos to virtual slavery; the second as throwing an apple of discord among European states, perhaps even

From *American Imperialism* by Ernest R. May. Copyright © 1967, 1968 by Ernest R. May. Reprinted by permission of Atheneum Publishers.

leading to general war; and the third, given the low level of Philippine development, as infeasible. Annexation appeared the least unattractive course.

American politicians could reason so, however, only by assuming that annexation would not cost votes at home. The historical puzzle rises from the
fact that politicians then in power apparently did not expect to pay a price at
the polls. Why not? With anticolonialism as strong as the Congressional war
resolution suggests, how could politicians conclude that a colonialist policy
could safely be pursued?

In *Expansionists of 1898* Julius W. Pratt offers part of an answer.[1] He shows
that, after Dewey's victory, religious journals changed tone. The Baptist *Standard,* the Presbyterian *Interior* and *Evangelist,* the Congregationalist *Advance,*
and the *Catholic World* all spoke of rule over the Philippines as America's
Christian duty. Methodist, Episcopalian, and Campbellite organs said the
same. Only Quaker and Unitarian papers stood unitedly in opposition.

Pratt also shows the business press following a similar pattern. Having in
the past either opposed or said nothing about acquisition of new territory,
business journals now talked of the advantages of expansion. . . .

Before finally making up his mind, President McKinley toured the Midwest.
Standing before large audiences, he delivered equivocal speeches. Some lines
hinted at a decision to annex the Philippines; other lines hinted the opposite.
His staff took notes on the relative levels of applause and reported that proannexation words drew louder handclaps. Other public figures presumably had
similar experiences. Politicians thus had before them persuasive evidence of a
dramatic swing in public opinion.

Such evidence explains their behavior partly but not entirely. In the past
they had had plenty of evidence of antiexpansionist feeling. Though knowing in
1890 that minor tariff changes could encourage Canadians to seek annexation,
congressmen found so little public enthusiasm that they failed to enact the
changes. When voting the war resolution, they evidently felt that the people
would not want Cuba. One might suppose that politicians would have anticipated the public's recovery from a momentary fancy for Pacific colonies and
its repudiation of the officeholders who had pandered to such a perversion. That
politicians showed no such fear must mean that they had some basis for believing the whim would endure. They must have seen some impulse stronger
than momentary excitement over victories in far-off places. What can it have
been? What conditions existed conducive to a lasting popular movement in
favor of imperialism?

This question has challenged historians. Setting aside versions that stress
Providence, the westward trend, or inherent tendencies in capitalism, one can
single out four major efforts to answer it. Each emphasizes a different factor.

Frederick Merk, the preeminent historian of American expansion in the
1840s, argues that a long-lived Manifest Destiny tradition offset the anticolonial tradition.[2] In *Manifest Destiny and Mission in American History* he describes two schools of thought existing at the time of the Mexican War. One,
he says, favored the acquisition of territory in order to increase the nation's
wealth and power. The other laid more stress on America's mission as the ex-

emplar of democracy and individual liberty. After the victories of Taylor and Scott, men in the first school favored taking all or most of Mexico. Those in the second school wanted only sparsely inhabited tracts which settlers could easily turn into other Kentuckys and Ohios. In an epilogue on the 1890s Merk suggests that the ideas of the first, or Manifest Destiny, school reappeared later as imperialism, while the idea of Mission persisted as anti-imperialism. The two traditions had had equal hardihood, and the circumstances of 1898-99 gave the expansionist tradition an edge.

Explaining the actions of McKinley and other politicians would be an awareness of the expansionist tradition and an assumption that the balance had tipped toward it and away from the tradition of Mission. For parallels one might think of politicians concluding in 1913 that the protectionist tradition had lost out to the free-trade tradition or, in 1964, that states' rights had lost out to civil rights. In Merk's view the Manifest Destiny tradition provides the key to understanding what happened in 1898–99.

Julius Pratt emphasizes Social Darwinism. In *Expansionists of 1898* and elsewhere Pratt describes the expansionism of the 1890s as having a different rationale from that of pre–Civil War days. It took from Herbert Spencer and other writers the idea of an endless struggle testing each nation's fitness to survive. On this premise the United States had to seize whatever share of the earth it could, for not to do so would give advantages to rivals and in the long run would lead to defeat, decay, and decline. Expansion presented itself not as an open choice but as a necessity dictated by stern scientific law.

The premise already had wide acceptance. Dealing with domestic economic and social issues, writers and clergymen commonly invoked such formulae as "struggle for survival" and "survival of the fittest." At an early point some Americans progressed to conclusions about how the United States should behave internationally. Pointing to the navy's shift from sail to steam, they argued that the United States would stand at a dangerous disadvantage without coaling stations in distant seas. The Spanish War then created opportunities for acquiring such stations, far out in the Pacific as well as in the Caribbean. It also placed in America's grasp territories which, if not seized, could go to potential rivals. And it offered a seeming chance for Protestant Christianity (also a species, by Social Darwinist canons) to score a gain in its struggle for survival against Catholicism and heathenism. In Pratt's view these Social Darwinist theses captured American public opinion. The anticolonial tradition would not have intimidated politicians, because they would have expected these new ideas to dominate future public thinking about foreign policy.

In *The New Empire,* a more recent book than either Merk's or Pratt's, Walter LaFeber stresses economic forces.[3] Like Pratt, he regards post–Civil War expansionism as different from that of the prewar era, but different because businessmen now captained the country and set their sights on markets rather than land. Whether manufacturers, merchants, or investors, they feared lest America's multiplying factories produce more than Americans could buy. As European states laid on protective tariffs, their thoughts turned to colonies and spheres of influence. Politicians behaved as they did in the 1890s, LaFeber suggests, because they put the interests of business ahead of all else, assumed the electorate would do the same, judged colonial expansion to serve business, and counted on the public's coming to the same conclusion and endorsing their actions.

A fourth major interpretation of the period, that of Richard Hofstadter, describes expansionism as merely one manifestation of a widespread "psychic crisis."[4] The rise of bigger, more powerful, and more bureaucratized business organizations produced protest in strikes such as those at Homestead and Pullman and political movements such as those of the Populists and Bryanite Democrats. These forms of protest failed. Meanwhile, with such savants as Frederick Jackson Turner warning that the free land frontier no longer existed to drain off the discontented, members of the urban middle class took alarm not only at the growth of big business but at the radicalism of the protesters. For Americans in all these groups, Hofstadter argues, war with Spain and annexation of distant islands represented an escape from reality—madcap behavior comparable to that of disturbed adolescents. Politicians presumably counted on the public's remaining in this state of mind and applauding the acquisition of new frontiers rather than swinging back to disapproval of expansion.

The interpretations of Merk, Pratt, LaFeber, and Hofstadter can be reconciled. One could picture LaFeber's businessmen as borrowers of the Manifest Destiny tradition, differing from expansionists of the 1840s in questing for consumers rather than resources and quoting Herbert Spencer instead of the Book of Genesis, and one could explain their success in the 1890s as due to the "psychic crisis." But even such a blend of interpretations leaves two questions unanswered.

The first has to do with process. Merk does not say how the Manifest Destiny tradition came temporarily to outbalance the tradition of Mission. Pratt does not show how the Social Darwinist prescription won acceptance. LaFeber fails to explain how businessmen came to see expansion as in their interest. Hofstadter offers no reason why men caught in a "psychic crisis" concluded that Pacific islands would be good things to have. No one charts the phases through which the individuals making up the public might have passed as they changed their convictions about colonies.

The second open question has to do with timing. Why did the change take place when it did?

Through the 1870s and 1880s the tradition of Mission, as Merk interprets it, appeared to hold the field. The influence of Social Darwinism did not extend to thought about foreign policy, and businessmen gave few signs of seeing colonial expansion as an answer to overproduction. At the end of the eighties, reports that Germany was about to take over Samoa produced some discussion of America's interest in the islands. Though no one spoke as a full-fledged expansionist, not everyone adopted the doctrinaire view that the United States could not consider taking part of the archipelago.

When Americans in Hawaii overthrew the native ruler in 1893 and appealed for annexation by the United States, politicians and newspaper reporters detected a surprising degree of public support for such a step. Some historians have concluded that if President Grover Cleveland had been of a mind to acquire the islands, he could have carried Congress and the country with him. Thus, despite the public's show of disinterest in annexing Canada and despite the language in Congress' 1898 war resolution, some shift away from anticolonialism could be observed even before Dewey's victory and its sequel. Circumstances created by the war will not account entirely for the estimates of public opinion formed by McKinley and other politicians. One has to ask why an apparent change in public attitudes should have set in around the beginning of the nineties.

Merk does not deal with this question. Pratt does so only indirectly. Describing books and essays by Josiah Strong, John Fiske, John W. Burgess, Alfred Thayer Mahan, and Henry Cabot Lodge that appeared after 1885, he implies that these writings had continuing and growing influence.[5] LaFeber has at least a partial answer. According to his reconstruction, the idea of colonial expansion as a partial solution to overproduction gained ground after 1879, when European states began putting up protective tariffs, and became much more attractive when the domestic market suddenly shrank in the panic of 1893. Hofstadter responds to the question by saying, in effect, that the turn to expansionism originated in the "psychic crisis" and that, since the "psychic crisis" occurred in the 1890s, it could only have come at that time.

But the timing of American imperialism has an aspect that neither LaFeber nor Hofstadter adequately explains. Change occurred after 1898 as well as before. After annexing the Philippines and negotiating treaties for acquisition of part of Samoa and all of the Danish West Indies, McKinley stood for reelection. He won by a larger margin than in 1896, in a contest characterized by his Democratic opponent as a referendum on imperialism. After his assassination in 1901 the presidency went to Vice President Theodore Roosevelt, who had been an ardent champion of colonial expansion. Yet the United States did not continue a career as an imperial power.

Not only did the American government make no efforts after 1900 to acquire new islands in the Caribbean or Pacific, it deliberately spurned opportunities to do so. Theodore Roosevelt rebuffed Haitians and Dominicans who dropped proannexation hints, and during nearly eight years as President he acquired only one piece of real estate—the ten-mile-wide Canal Zone in Panama. Though one may cite the Platt Amendment, as applied to Cuba, the acquisition of the Canal Zone, and the Roosevelt Corollary to the Monroe Doctrine as evidence that the United States still had a mild case of imperialism, the nation's expansion as a colonial power effectively came to an end as of 1899 or 1900.

After that date, moreover, politicians reverted to the working assumption they had employed before 1898. McKinley and Roosevelt took it for granted that public opinion would not approve keeping Cuba as a colony. They judged that acquisition of a leasehold in China or annexation of Haiti, Santo Domingo, or a portion of Central America would be unpopular. And no evidence contradicted these judgments. After 1900 scarcely a congressman or newspaper editor raised his voice in favor of further colonial extension. Imperialism as a current in American public opinion appeared to be dead.

None of the theories concerning the rise of the imperialist movement satis-factorily explains its sudden demise. While Merk may be right that, over the long term, Mission had more power than Manifest Destiny, such a hypothesis does not in itself explain why, in this instance, Manifest Destiny enjoyed such short-lived ascendancy. Social Darwinism, the factor stressed by Pratt, had as much currency in 1902 as in 1898, yet seemed not to work the same effect on thought about foreign policy. LaFeber's businessmen had the same standing as before and regarded overproduction with only a little, if any, less concern. No apparent economic factor would account for their having different feelings about colonies. If a "psychic crisis" actuated imperialism, then it must have been literally a crisis, followed by quick recovery.

None of these comments depreciates the work of Merk, Pratt, LaFeber, and Hofstadter: all historians leave some questions unanswered. Nor does the pres-ent essay pretend to prove any of the four wrong. To the factors they have stressed, it adds a fifth—the impact on Americans of English and European examples. It does not, however, assert that this influence dominated. As much synthesis as reinterpretation, this study endeavors to portray the public that would have had opinion about expansion and to indicate how tradition, Social Darwinism, market hunger, psychological turmoil, *and* awareness of foreign fashions combined to cause a shift away from the anticolonial tradition at about the beginning of the 1890s, an upsurge of genuine imperialism in 1898–99, and then an abrupt return to the earlier faith. . . .

Owing to historic factors, the pretensions of its old families, and an essen-tially mercantile economy, Boston and its suburbs had many residents equipped by education, attainments, and connections to lead opinion on the colonial issue.

Thomas Jefferson Coolidge typified this comparatively large foreign policy elite. His autobiography and collected private papers tell us a good deal about him, and from recent historical studies by Barbara Solomon, Arthur Mann, and Geoffrey Blodgett we know that he had little to do with molding public opinion on domestic issues.[6] He thus exemplifies the specialized opinion leader —a prototype member of what today we call the foreign policy establishment.

Born in 1831 into a securely rich family, Coolidge took his primary and secondary schooling in England and Switzerland and then attended Harvard. Entering business, he became, by his late forties, president of the Merchants Bank of Boston and a heavy investor in railroads, serving at one time as presi-dent of the Sante Fe and, at another, as a director of the Chicago, Burlington, and Quincy. Owning land in the center of Birmingham, Alabama, he built stores that prospered from Birmingham's sudden boom. Not all his gambles succeeded. An electric-light plant in Topeka, Kansas, for example, resulted in a loss. Its optimistic manager wrote, "A coupon cutter and a Dividend payer, are the next inventions I look for in connection with this versatile agent"; but he proved unable to deliver.[7] Nevertheless, in association with other financiers, Coolidge made many a dollar from well-timed purchases and sales of bonds, stocks, lands, and buildings.

Owning most if not all the characteristics of a robber baron, Coolidge could write the following record of a conversation with a rental agent: "He said the woman who occupies the Anderson property cannot pay rent. I directed him to turn her out and I would make the house into two tenements which could be rented." On another occasion Coolidge advised a friend not to accept a certain mortgage, cautioning, "It is very hard to collect either interest or capital from the Church without putting your hand in your pocket to help the good cause." Property in Birmingham attracted him because of "the endless supply of black labor." When profit beckoned he speculated in any commodity, including opium.[8]

In domestic politics Coolidge also showed the temper of a robber baron. One of his letters gave marching orders for the senators and representatives from Nebraska who "are obeying the C.B.&Q." As the largest shareholder in the Amoskeag Cotton Mills, he maintained an agent in Manchester, New Hampshire, who labored to prevent "radical legislation." He himself spent time in Washington lobbying for protective duties on textiles.[9]

Yet the press quoted him, and politicians sought his views and estimates of public feeling only on foreign policy problems, and not even on cotton tariffs. Reporters for Boston papers and for the Springfield *Republican* sought him out during a crisis with Chile of 1891–92, a crisis with Britain four years later over the Venezuela-Guiana boundary, the blowing up of the *Maine,* war with Spain, and the question of whether or not to annex the Philippines. James G. Blaine, when Secretary of State for Benjamin Harrison, expressed interest in Coolidge's views on possible complications with Germany in the Pacific. Both of Massachusetts' senators solicited his reactions to their positions on other foreign policy issues, including colonial expansion. Journalists in his home community and politicians in Washington evidently attached special weight to Coolidge's views on foreign policy.

He possessed unusually wide knowledge of the world. Fluent in French and familiar with English and European culture from his early education, he subsequently traveled much, not only in Europe but also in out-of-the-way places, such as Alexandria and Port au Prince, which most Americans discovered only as datelines on crisis reports. In 1889 he served as a delegate to the first Pan American Conference. In 1892–93 he spent a year as United States Minister to France.

Partly as a result of his travels and his diplomatic experience, Coolidge knew leading figures abroad. He could speak familiarly of such English and French statesmen as Joseph Chamberlain, Arthur Balfour, Jules Ferry, and Gabriel Hanotaux. He could name for President Harrison the men in England who would hold the keys to an international agreement on bimetallism and advise Massachusetts' Senator George F. Hoar on whether a proposed emissary would have the proper entree to this group.[10] Interested citizens and politicians probably looked to Coolidge as an opinion leader primarily because of his firsthand knowledge of foreign places and inside knowledge of foreign politics.

Coolidge's near contemporary, William C. Endicott, possessed comparable qualifications. A noted lawyer, onetime judge and holder of large and profitable railroad investments, he had been Secretary of War during Cleveland's first administration, and his daughter had married the celebrated English politician,

Joseph Chamberlain. When in England, he met the great and near great, and through his daughter and her friends received inside news of British and European political developments. Like Coolidge, Endicott could set Washington straight as to who pulled strings in London, and both politicians and newspapermen looked upon him as an authority on foreign affairs.

Richard Olney did not have quite the background of Coolidge or Endicott. Though of an old family, he came from western Massachusetts, and he had a bachelor's degree from Brown rather than Harvard. A hardworking, somewhat solitary railroad lawyer, he traveled little and gained none of Coolidge's or Endicott's firsthand knowledge of foreign statesmen. Before the 1890s he could have qualified as a leader of opinion on certain domestic issues, but hardly on foreign policy. In Cleveland's second administration, however, Olney served first as Attorney General and then, for two years, as Secretary of State. Coupled with his professional distinction, this experience caused him too to become a target of reporters' questions and of inquiring letters from politicians.

The circle of foreign policy leaders in Boston probably included also President Charles W. Eliot of Harvard. Of a high-caste family and equipped, of course, with a Harvard diploma, Eliot had lived in France and Germany and made many trips to England. He could claim friendship with Bryce and other eminent Englishmen, and he could speak with authority not only on European education but also on English government and the English colonial system. . . .

Men such as Coolidge, Endicott, and Eliot had a sense of the nation's complex traditions. Most had some acquaintance with Darwinian ideas as applied to current problems, and two, Fiske and Savage, were leading Social Darwinist writers. As capitalists or corporation lawyers, Coolidge, Endicott, Olney, and Elder watched out not only for the interests of their own companies or clients but for the general welfare of American business. And some at least participated in what Holstadter calls the "psychic crisis." In 1891, when workingmen and agrarians had only begun to agitate, Coolidge prophesied darkly, "communism will in time destroy not only the stock capital, but the bonds which are . . . the accumulation of labor."[11] The distinction between these men and others sensitive to tradition, imbued with Darwinism, concerned about business, or irrationally anxious about the future, lay chiefly in their having special familiarity with, even inside knowledge of, European politics. . . .

By focusing on leaders of opinion we do not necessarily commit ourselves to the proposition that only an elite counted. If, however, only a relatively small public concerned itself with foreign policy issues, its members would have known the special qualifications of certain individuals, and these individuals would have functioned in some sense as opinion leaders. By examining the influences working on these leaders we can perhaps come somewhat closer to understanding why opinion within the foreign policy public changed during the 1890s. . . .

Primarily the object of this essay is to set forth a synthetic interpretation of a single episode. Trying to take account of the easily forgotten fact that public opinion is seldom if ever opinion among more than an interested minority of the electorate, it has emphasized the small group of opinion leaders that gave this minority some guidance and, perhaps more importantly, provided political leaders with evidence as to how the interested public might bend.

Though these opinion leaders seemed for an interval not to be directing or representing the public, that interval was short. Most of the time the men whom we have described as members of the foreign policy establishment served as the voices of effective opinion, and their expressed views underwent changes. Through the 1870s and 1880s they opposed America's acquiring colonies. By 1893 they had adopted a different outlook and, by and large, approved of annexing Hawaii. Only from the outbreak of the Spanish war in 1898 to some point in 1900 or 1901 did they not either concur or divide along clear lines corresponding to party lines. After 1901 they agreed once again that the United States did not need and should not want colonial possessions. . . .

International fashions in thought and events on the world scene could have had a decisive influence on men of the establishment. Not that they attached more importance to keeping step with Europeans than to preserving tradition, furthering trade, obeying scientific laws, or preventing domestic upheaval. Quite the contrary. But knowledge of foreign thought affected their ideas about America's world mission and their understanding of Social Darwinism. Observation of foreign experience suggested to them alternative methods of promoting national prosperity and dealing with social discontent. Above all, the foreign scene provided models for imitation (reference groups and reference idols, in social science jargon). The well-traveled and well-read American could select a position on the colonial issue by identifying it with, on the one hand, Bright, Gladstone, Morley, and Richter or, on the other, Rosebery, Chamberlain, Ferry, Bismarck, or Wilhelm II. Neither the American past nor an assessment of American economic needs nor Social Darwinism nor the domestic political scene offered such guidance.

Men of the establishment belonged both to their own country and to a larger Atlantic community. Ordinarily they defined opinion for an interested public, most of whom had less familiarity with currents abroad. Probably this fact explains in part why, when the establishment ceased to be coherent and leadership dispersed, apparent public opinion on colonies became so simplistic and emotional. It may also explain why, when the interested public appeared to be expanding, many politicians took an antiestablishment tack: they realized that a gulf separated the citizen of the Atlantic community from the citizen whose outlook comprehended only his county or state. Currents running within the larger community help to account for American public opinion not so much because they influenced a large number of Americans as because they influenced the few who set styles within a normally small foreign policy public.

As stated in the beginning, this essay does not dispute what other historians have said. On the contrary, it seeks to draw together previous interpretations by means of hypotheses about late nineteenth-century public opinion, its manifestations, and the play within it of tradition, economic interest, Social Darwinism, and psychological malaise, together with awareness of ideas and events abroad. I hope others will advance alternative hypotheses, for my aim is not to close debate but rather to reopen it by prompting new questions about this and other episodes. In the literal meaning of the term, this work is an essay.

Notes

1. Julius W. Pratt, *Expansionists of 1898: The Acquisition of Hawaii and the Spanish Islands* (Baltimore, 1936), pp. 230–316.
2. Frederick Merk, *Manifest Destiny and Mission in American History: A Reinterpretation* (New York, 1963), pp. 228–266.
3. Walter LaFeber, *The New Empire: An Interpretation of American Expansion, 1860–1898* (Ithaca, 1963).
4. Richard Hofstadter, "Manifest Destiny and the Philippines," in Daniel Aaron, ed., *America in Crisis* (New York, 1952), pp. 173–200, and *The Paranoid Style in American Politics and Other Essays* (New York, 1966), pp. 145–187.
5. Pratt, *Expansionists of 1898*, pp. 1–22.
6. Barbara Solomon, *Ancestors and Immigrants* (Cambridge, Mass., 1956), Arthur Mann, *Yankee Reformers in the Urban Age* (Cambridge, Mass., 1954), and Geoffrey Blodgett, *The Gentle Reformers: Massachusetts Democrats in the Cleveland Era* (Cambridge, Mass., 1966). Basic information on Coolidge is taken from Thomas Jefferson Coolidge, *Autobiography* (Boston, 1902) and Allen Johnson and Dumas Malone, eds., *Dictionary of American Biography*, 20 vols. and two supplementary vols. (New York, 1928–58)—hereafter cited as *DAB*—IV, 395.
7. E. Wilder to Coolidge, May 24, 1887, Private Papers of Thomas Jefferson Coolidge, Massachusetts Historical Society.
8. Coolidge to A. D. Paton, Oct. 11, 1888; to John Codman, June 3, 1889; to W. H. Edwards, Dec. 8, 1887; to Dabney, Simmons, and Co., April 19, 1887, *ibid.*
9. Coolidge to C. E. Perkins, April 18, 1888; H. F. Straw to Coolidge, Nov. 6, 1886; Coolidge to P. M. Moon, April 4, 1890, *ibid.*
10. Coolidge to Benjamin Harrison, June 29, 1891; to Hoar, July 11, 1891, Coolidge Papers.
11. Coolidge to C. E. Perkins, March 4, 1891, Coolidge Papers.

FURTHER READING

Howard K. Beale, *Theodore Roosevelt and the Rise of America to World Power* (1956)

Robert L. Beisner, *From the Old Diplomacy to the New* (1975)

Robert L. Beisner, *Twelve Against Empire* (1968)

Charles S. Campbell, *The Transformation of American Foreign Relations, 1865–1900* (1976)

Philip S. Foner, *The Spanish-Cuban-American War and the Birth of American Imperialism* (1972)

Henry F. Graff, ed., *American Imperialism and the Philippine Insurrection* (1969)

John A. S. Grenville and George B. Young, *Politics, Strategy, and American Diplomacy* (1967)

David Healy, *U.S. Expansionism* (1970)

Walter LaFeber, *The New Empire* (1963)

Margaret Leech, *In the Days of McKinley* (1959)

Gerald F. Linderman, *The Mirror of War: American Society and the Spanish-American War* (1974)

Ernest R. May, *Imperial Democracy* (1961)

H. Wayne Morgan, *America's Road to Empire* (1965)

R. G. Neale, *Great Britain and United States Expansion, 1898–1900* (1966)

Thomas G. Paterson, ed., *American Imperialism and Anti-Imperialism* (1973)

Bradford Perkins, *The Great Rapprochement* (1968)

Julius Pratt, *Expansionists of 1898* (1936)

Daniel B. Schirmer, *Republic or Empire* (1972)

E. Berkeley Tompkins, *Anti-Imperialism in the United States* (1970)

M. M. Wilkinson, *Public Opinion and the Spanish-American War* (1932)

William A. Williams, *The Roots of the Modern American Empire* (1969)

William A. Williams, *The Tragedy of American Diplomacy* (1962)

11

The Open Door Policy and China

In late nineteenth-century China, when Japan and the great powers of Europe began to carve the Celestial Empire into leaseholds and spheres of influence, America's traditional trading policy of commercial equality was challenged. The imperial powers practiced discrimination in tariff rates and other fees, to the detriment of American economic interests. China was too weak to halt this assault upon its sovereignty or to insist on uniform, non-discriminatory trading behavior. The British, who heretofore had dominated Asian markets, hoped America would protest the dismemberment of China and the economic restrictions. Shortly after the Spanish-American War, Secretary of State John Hay issued two notes that became known as the "Open Door Policy." What prompted the United States to intervene verbally in the Asian tumult? British influence? American business interests? The China market? Ideals of self-determination and equal trade opportunity?

DOCUMENTS

In the first Hay note of September 6, 1899, the Secretary of State appealed for an end to discrimination against foreign commerce in the various Chinese spheres and leaseholds. The responses from the great powers were evasive. The second note, dated July 3, 1900, written during the Boxer Rebellion and the threat of partition by the imperial powers, argued for the preservation of Chinese independence.

The Open Door Note, 1899

At the time when the Government of the United States was informed by that of Germany that it had leased from His Majesty the Emperor of China the port of Kiao-chao and the adjacent territory in the province of Shantung, assurances were given to the ambassador of the United States at Berlin by the Imperial German minister for foreign affairs that the rights and privileges insured by treaties with China to citizens of the United States would not thereby suffer or be in anywise impaired within the area over which Germany had thus obtained control.

More recently, however, the British Government recognized by a formal agreement with Germany the exclusive right of the latter country to enjoy in said leased area and the contiguous "sphere of influence or interest" certain

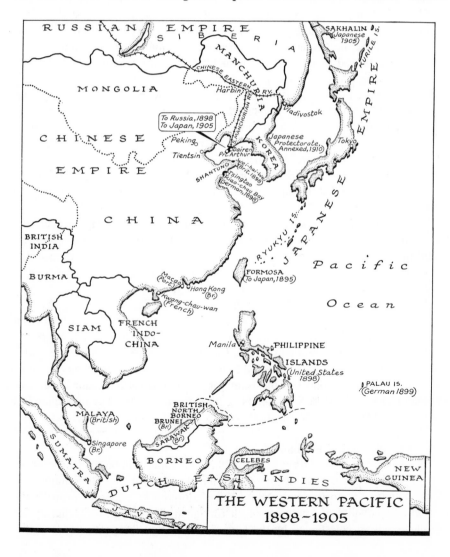

THE WESTERN PACIFIC
1898–1905

privileges, more especially those relating to railroads and mining enterprises; but as the exact nature and extent of the rights thus recognized have not been clearly defined, it is possible that serious conflicts of interest may at any time arise not only between British and German subjects within said area, but that the interests of our citizens may also be jeopardized thereby.

Earnestly desirous to remove any cause of irritation and to insure at the same time to the commerce of all nations in China the undoubted benefits which should accrue from a formal recognition by the various powers claiming "spheres of interest" that they shall enjoy perfect equality of treatment for their commerce and navigation within such "spheres," the Government of the United States would be pleased to see His German Majesty's Government give formal assurances, and lend its cooperation in securing like assurances from the other interested powers, that each, within its respective sphere of whatever influence—

First. Will in no way interfere with any treaty port or any vested interest within any so-called "sphere of interest" or leased territory it may have in China.

Second. That the Chinese treaty tariff of the time being shall apply to all merchandise landed or shipped to all such ports as are within said "sphere of interest" (unless they be "free ports"), no matter to what nationality it may belong, and that duties so leviable shall be collected by the Chinese Government.

Third. That it will levy no higher harbor dues on vessels of another nationality frequenting any port in such "sphere" than shall be levied on vessels of its own nationality, and no higher railroad charges over lines built, controlled, or operated within its "sphere" on merchandise belonging to citizens or subjects of other nationalities transported through such "sphere" than shall be levied on similar merchandise belonging to its own nationals transported over equal distances.

The liberal policy pursued by His Imperial German Majesty in declaring Kiao-chao a free port and in aiding the Chinese Government in the establishment there of a custom-house are so clearly in line with the proposition which this Government is anxious to see recognized that it entertains the strongest hope that Germany will give its acceptance and hearty support.

The recent ukase of His Majesty the Emperor of Russia declaring the port of Ta-lien-wan open during the whole of the lease under which it is held from China to the merchant ships of all nations, coupled with the categorical assurances made to this Government by His Imperial Majesty's representative at this capital at the time and since repeated to me by the present Russian ambassador, seem to insure the support of the Emperor to the proposed measure. Our ambassador at the Court of St. Petersburg has in consequence been instructed to submit it to the Russian Government and to request their early consideration of it. A copy of my instruction on the subject to Mr. Tower is herewith inclosed for your confidential information.

The commercial interests of Great Britain and Japan will be so clearly served by the desired declaration of intentions, and the views of the Governments of these countries as to the desirability of the adoption of measures insuring the benefits of equality of treatment of all foreign trade throughout China are so similar to those entertained by the United States, that their acceptance of the propositions herein outlined and their cooperation in advocating their adoption by the other powers can be confidently expected. I inclose herewith copy of the instruction which I have sent to Mr. Choate on the subject.

In view of the present favorable conditions, you are instructed to submit the above considerations to His Imperial German Majesty's Minister for Foreign Affairs, and to request his early consideration of the subject.

Copy of this instruction is sent to our ambassadors at London and at St. Petersburg for their information.

Circular Note to the Great Powers, 1900

In this critical posture of affairs in China it is deemed appropriate to define the attitude of the United States as far as present circumstances permit this to be done. We adhere to the policy initiated by us in 1857, of peace with the Chinese nation, of furtherance of lawful commerce, and of protection of lives and property of our citizens by all means guaranteed under extraterritorial treaty rights and by the law of nations. If wrong be done to our citizens we propose to hold the responsible authors to the uttermost accountability. We regard the condition at Pekin as one of virtual anarchy, whereby power and responsibility are practically devolved upon the local provincial authorities. So long as they are not in overt collusion with rebellion and use their power to protect foreign life and property we regard them as representing the Chinese people, with whom we seek to remain in peace and friendship. The purpose of the President is, as it has been heretofore, to act concurrently with the other powers, first, in opening up communication with Pekin and rescuing the American officials, missionaries, and other Americans who are in danger; secondly, in affording all possible protection everywhere in China to American life and property; thirdly, in guarding and protecting all legitimate American interests; and fourthly, in aiding to prevent a spread of the disorders to the other provinces of the Empire and a recurrence of such disasters. It is, of course, too early to forecast the means of attaining this last result; but the policy of the Government of the United States is to seek a solution which may bring about permanent safety and peace to China, preserve Chinese territorial and administrative entity, protect all rights guaranteed to friendly powers by treaty and international law, and safeguard for the world the principle of equal and impartial trade with all parts of the Chinese Empire.

ESSAYS

The essay by A. Whitney Griswold, selected from his *The Far Eastern Policy of the United States,* emphasizes British influence on the Open Door Notes. Thomas J. McCormick of the University of Wisconsin, on the other hand, points to the self-conscious quest by American leaders for the China market. The question, as in the case of the Spanish-American War and imperialism and other issues, is whether external or internal factors were most important in stimulating Hay's notes. In the final selection, Paul A. Varg argues that the China market was a myth and that Americans evinced little concrete interest, despite their rhetoric, in China's economic fortunes.

The Open Door Notes and British Influence

A. WHITNEY GRISWOLD

Business and diplomacy were not the only forces impelling Hay toward his fateful decision. American missionaries in the Far East had also been thrilled by the conquest of the Philippines. In 1899 there were between one thousand and fifteen hundred of them in China where they, and their predecessors, had early assumed a political importance out of all proportion to their numbers. Now their situation was very comparable to that of American businessmen in China. Just as they were rejoicing in the annexation of the Philippines for the aid and comfort they thought it would give their cause, they found themselves confronted by an anti-foreign movement stirred up partly by the concessions-scramble, partly by their own proselytizing, that was to culminate in the Boxer Rebellion. In 1899 they, too, wished the United States to show a strong hand in China.

So far the McKinley Administration had adhered strictly to precedent in the Far East. It had kept free of alliances or understandings with foreign powers. It had called the attention of Europe to the long-established interest of the United States in the open door and the preservation of existing treaty rights. From the two particular nations that caused it most alarm it had obtained assurances. The President had declared himself satisfied with these, and proved it by rejecting Pauncefote for the second time within a year. In spite of the concessions-scramble, American trade with China, small though it was, was actually increasing. If it appeared likely to certain business groups that Russia would some day close them out of Northern China, others contemplated great profit in the sale of products to Russia in the development of that region. As yet Germany had been no less hospitable to American trade and capital in Shantung than England had been in the Yangtse Valley. American fears of exclusion, like American hopes of gain, were all in the future. Up to the summer of 1899 neither had been strong enough to cause a departure from the diplomatic traditions and precedents of the past hundred years.

Then, in July and August, through informal, personal channels, the British influence was once more turned on Hay, this time with success.

Like most Secretaries of State, John Hay had only a superficial knowledge of conditions in the Far East. To advise him on this complicated subject he had chosen a friend and, as it happened, one of the best-informed authorities on China of his generation, William W. Rockhill. Born in Philadelphia in 1854, Rockhill's early youth was spent in France, where he completed his education at the military school at Saint Cyr, and where he acquired an interest in the Chinese language and literature. After three years of service as lieutenant in the French Foreign Legion in Algeria, he returned to the United States, and in 1884 procured an appointment as Second Secretary of the Peking Legation. The next year he was promoted to First Secretary. During the winter of 1886–1887 he served as Chargé d'Affaires at Seoul, Korea. He had entered the diplomatic service as a means of pursuing his Chinese studies. He resigned because of personal incompatibility with Denby. After two famous journeys of exploration through Mongolia and Tibet (1888–1889 and 1891–1892) he returned to the diplomatic service as Chief Clerk of the State Department in 1893. From February 14, 1896, to May 10, 1897, he served as Assistant Secretary of State under Olney, during part of which period (March 4 to May 10, 1897) he filled the gap between Olney and Sherman as Acting Secretary.

By this time Rockhill's scholarly writings and explorations had brought him membership in learned Oriental societies and scientific institutes all over the world. His wide experience in the Far East and in the Department of State had established his reputation as an expert on China and earned him the friendship and admiration of influential Republicans including Roosevelt, Lodge and Hay. When it became evident that Denby was to be replaced, Rockhill's friends urged McKinley to appoint him Minister to China, a post his training pre-eminently qualified him to fill. They were disappointed. Rockhill was sent to Athens as Minister to Greece, Roumania and Servia. It was from this post that Adee and Hay rescued him in April, 1899, by helping to secure his appointment as Director of the Bureau of American Republics in Washington, presumably in order to have the benefit of his counsel on affairs in Eastern Asia. In any event, Rockhill had no sooner assumed his new office (May 22) than the Secretary of State began to solicit his advice.

Rockhill, too, had his confidential adviser in Alfred E. Hippisley, a British subject and a member of the Chinese Imperial Maritime Customs Service. Hippisley was an old China hand. It should be recalled that the Chinese customs service was administered by the British, a privilege ultimately sanctioned by treaty in 1898 for as long as England's share of China's foreign trade should exceed that of any other nation. A member of this service since 1867, Hippisley had long followed political affairs in China with a sharp, intelligent eye. His acquaintance with Rockhill dated from the autumn of 1884 when the latter first joined the staff of the American legation in Peking. "In a small community such as that of Peking," wrote Hippisley many years later, "acquaintance quickly ripens into intimacy between persons who have similar tastes, and both Rockhill and I were deeply interested in China and Chinese politics, and in my case the intimacy was made the closer by my marriage in the following year with Miss Howard, a friend of long standing of Mrs. Rockhill's, who had accompanied the latter and her husband from Baltimore." What Rockhill was to Hay, Hippisley was to Rockhill: an old friend and trusted adviser on the Far East.

Mutual friendship—and fate—drew the three men together in the early summer of 1899. Simultaneously with Rockhill's inauguration as Director General of the Bureau of American Republics, a periodic leave of absence brought Hippisley to the United States on his way home to England. From about the middle of June to the end of July the Englishman visited his wife's family in Baltimore. He was pleased to renew his acquaintance with Rockhill, whom he had not seen for over ten years. "Naturally," he remembers, "I went over as frequently as I could to Washington to discuss the conditions in China with him and especially what could be done to maintain the 'open door' or equality of opportunity for all nations in that country." On one of these occasions Rockhill, deeply impressed by his friend's ideas, introduced him to the Secretary of State. Hay heard him expound, in outline, the scheme ultimately comprehended by the open door notes.

Throughout the informal negotiations of that summer, Hippisley was clearly the prime mover. Hay, though disposed to cooperate with England, was waiting for Rockhill to find a way to do it. Rockhill, who had been absent from China for seven years, was rusty on China. Hippisley came fresh from the scene, his mind brimming with images and theories of the concessions-scramble and how to deal with it. It was he who took the initiative, who supplied the concrete plans; nor did he lack encouragement. "China is, and will remain, the one absorbing subject," Rockhill told him, "so I am awfully anxious to have all the data you can give me on the subject, that I may not make any mistake, and that my conclusions shall be practicable."

When, about August first, Hay left Washington for his summer home in New Hampshire, and Hippisley departed Baltimore on a leisurely journey, *via* Lenox and Bar Harbor to Quebec (whence he would sail for England September seventh), Hippisley opened an active correspondence with Rockhill. "As I shall not now have an opportunity of seeing you before we start for Europe," he wrote July 25, "I write these lines to ask you to use your influence towards, if possible, inducing the govt. to do what it can to maintain the open door for ordinary commerce in China." . . .

Rockhill passed Hippisley's recommendations on to Hay after adding to their weight his own authoritative *imprimatur*. The same day he replied to Hippisley:

> You know what my views are about the position the United States should take in China; I would like to see it make a declaration in some form or other, which would be understood by China as a pledge on our part to assist in maintaining the integrity of the Empire. I fear, however, that home politics and next year's elections will interfere with this, for it might be interpreted by a large part of the voting population of the United States, especially the Irish and the Germans, as an adoption of the policy advocated by England, and any leaning towards England on the part of the administration would, at this time and for the next year to come, be dangerous, and might lose the President his nomination. I consequently fear that he will do absolutely nothing either on the lines you indicate, and which are clearly those most beneficial to our interests in China, or in any other which will commit us. We will simply continue drifting along.

Hay confirmed these doubts. "I thank you for your letter inclosing Mr. Hippisley's," he wrote, August 7. "I am fully awake to the great importance of what you say, and am more than ready to act. But the senseless prejudices in certain sections of the 'Senate and people' compel us to move with great caution."

Hippisley did not give up hope. His reason for "urging *prompt* action" along the lines of his last note was, he explained, "precisely to forestall any suggestion likely to prove injurious to the Administration that it was following the lead of or leaning towards England by inducing it to take the initiative itself; then if England took similar action, she would follow America's lead." The Englishman had developed a remarkable solicitude for the welfare of the United States. "I think it would be suicidal for America to drift and do nothing for another year," he warned.

> My latest advices from Peking say: "the activity of the Russians in Manchuria is simply wonderful. . . . The Russification of Peking and of North China will proceed as rapidly as has that of Manchuria." These are precisely the districts which are the great consumers of American textile fabrics, and I don't for a moment believe that American manufacturers will sit by with folded hands and see these districts closed without making an effort to retain them. Pressure will therefore be brought to bear upon the Administration and it may then have no option but to take such action as I have suggested, with possibly however the difference of following instead of leading England.

This time Rockhill's response was more encouraging. He had received "today," he wrote on the eighteenth, "pretty clear assurances from the State Department that it may take some action sooner than could be anticipated from the position it held until within a few weeks and which I gave you in my last letter." But Rockhill was not over-sanguine. Once more he showed himself to be in advance of Hippisley: he favored securing "tangible" assurances from the powers "as to their desire to maintain and insure the integrity of the Chinese Empire. . . ." This, he still believed the Administration was unwilling to consider; the best he and Hippisley could do was to "keep pegging away at it." The next day he submitted to Adee long extracts from Hippisley's last two letters.

Meanwhile two things had come to Hippisley's support. Almost simultaneously came the news of the return to the United States of Dr. Jacob Gould Schurman, Chairman of the President's Philippine Commission, and the Czar's ukase of August 15 declaring Talienwan a free port. All that restrained Hay from embarking on the policy advocated by Hippisley, apparently, was the opposition to it of the President himself. Whatever the true source of this opposition—respect for tradition, the lingering influence of Sherman, sincere conviction or mere partisan expediency—it had tied the Secretary's hands since his assumption of office. Undoubtedly Hay had been converted as early as June, 1898, when he had written McKinley a personal letter from the London embassy, urging him to reconsider the first Pauncefote overture. More lately he had professed to be "more than ready to act" and lamented the "senseless prejudices" that restrained him. It is probable that, for the past year, whenever the occasion had offered, he had urged on the President some such policy as that now in the making. Dr. Schurman and the Czar seem to have knocked the last props from under McKinley's resistance. . . .

The Rockhill memorandum (dated August 28, 1899) appears to have been the final instrument of McKinley's conversion. For, on September 5, Rockhill composed the actual drafts of the open door notes themselves, which, after a few corrections by Adee, were despatched the following day, over the signature of the Secretary of State, to the American ambassadors in London, Berlin and St. Petersburg. The notes, like the memoranda from which they were written, and as their authors had privately agreed, eschewed the subject of China's territorial integrity. This Rockhill felt to be "still such a complex question that I do not think we have it in anything like a shape to discuss it advantageously . . . so awfully big, that I think for the time being we had better not broach it over here." But, he believed, the notes would have the desired effect of giving China breathing space, of promoting "a general line of policy which may be favorable to the maintenance and the strengthening of the Peking Government."

The notes were carefully worded. Their authors were aware of the exigencies of American politics that restrained their own personal desires. Accordingly they recognized the spheres of influence as existing facts, omitted any reference to mining and railway concessions, and the whole perplexing problem of capital investment, and specifically asked only for equal commercial opportunity within each sphere. Each power addressed was requested to give its formal assurances that it would observe the regulations presented by the notes *mutatis mutandis*. But that is not all the notes requested. In addition to its own assurances, each power was urged to cooperate with the United States in obtaining the assurances of all the other powers concerned. Thus the notes invoked not only the time-honored American principle of the open door, but also the so-called "cooperative policy." The combination of the two, applied to the current situation in China, made the notes something more than a mere iteration of the traditional Far Eastern policy of the United States. It made them a foray into World politics, an attempt to influence the foreign policies of the European powers in such a way as to establish free commercial competition in the region of Eastern Asia. It was an unusual thing for the United States to seek to influence the dispensations of international politics in regions outside its own hemisphere. . . .

A careful perusal of the replies to the open door notes shows Rockhill's assumptions, both as to the influence of the United States in the Far East and the effectiveness of the notes themselves, to have been unfounded. The replies to the notes were uniformly evasive and non-committal. The first and most satisfactory reply was the British, but even this left much to be desired. Though Lord Salisbury professed his enthusiasm for the open door principle, he was loath to apply it either to Hongkong or to Weihaiwei, contending that the former was a colony, the latter a leased territory, and opposing the application of the principle to areas in either of these categories.

The Prime Minister's attitude was "rather disappointing in view of his first reception of your proposition," Ambassador Choate wrote Hay. Moreover, Salisbury was of the opinion that "we are a little too sanguine in our expectations of obtaining Declarations from the other Powers." Nearly three months elapsed before Salisbury was willing to compromise, which he did grudgingly. Great Britain agreed to the application of the open door principle to Weihaiwei, and to all British leased territory and spheres of interest in China, present or future, the United States acquiesced in the exemption of Kowloon [Hongkong] from this rule. The entire British declaration was then emasculated by the proviso that it was "to be considered as dependent on similar assent by the other Powers in like circumstances."

The replies of the other powers were full of loopholes, Russia's amounting to a thinly disguised rejection of the whole proposition. Each of them, like the British, made its acceptance contingent upon the acceptance of all the others, which reduced everyone to the least common denominator, the Russian. Rockhill and Hay realized the situation perfectly and tried to meet it with bluff. Rockhill privately admitted to Hippisley that the Russian reply "has what we call in America a string attached to it"; but he thought it "prudent" to accept it none the less. "Our object," Hay wrote Tower, "is now to give the widest significance to the Russian reply of which it is capable. Without running the risk of bringing upon ourselves a contradiction of our assumptions, we want to take it for granted that Russia has acceded to our proposals without much qualification." At length, on March 20, the Secretary of State cavalierly announced that he had received satisfactory assurances from all the powers addressed, and that he regarded each as "final and definitive."

Hay had not long to wait to discover just how "final and definitive" they were. In June, not three months after his expression of satisfaction, a Chinese patriotic society known to the West as the "Boxers" stirred up an armed rebellion against foreign missionaries and concession-hunters and the Manchu Government that had truckled with them. Ripping up portions of the Tientsin-Peking Railway and destroying telegraph lines, the rebels cut off Peking from the outside world, murdered the secretary of the Japanese legation, and the German minister, and besieged the foreign legations in the city. An allied military force was hastily dispatched to the relief of the legations. From June 20 until August 14, the day the siege was lifted, the foreigners in Peking lived under fire in the legation compound, menaced by starvation and disease, their fate unknown either to their governments or to the troops marching to their rescue.

It was apparent to Hay from the outset that the disorders had provided certain of the powers not unwelcome pretexts for enlarging their spheres and extending their influence in China. Russia and Germany were on the march. Hay sensed the need—or opportunity—for more extensive measures than mere participation in the allied relief expedition. "We have no policy in China except to protect with energy American interests, and especially American citizens, and the legation," he had wired Conger, June 10. "There must be nothing done which would commit us to future action inconsistent with your standing instructions. There must be no alliances." When the Boxers moved on Peking he showed his hand more fully. On July 3, with the approval of McKinley, he despatched to the powers another circular defining American policy. Unlike the notes of the previous September, this circular asked for no assurances and, indeed, elicited none; it was merely submitted to the consideration of each of the powers addressed. Taking cognizance of the "virtual anarchy" existing in China it set forth the purpose of the United States to "act concurrently with the other powers" in restoring order and protecting the lives and property of its nationals and "all legitimate American interests." In its concluding sentence, however, it added to this purpose a momentous new objective, namely, "to seek a solution which may bring about permanent safety and peace to China, *preserve Chinese territorial and administrative entity,* protect all rights guaranteed to friendly powers by treaty and international law, and safeguard for the world the principle of equal and impartial trade with all parts of the Chinese Empire."

The United States had always stood for the "territorial and administrative entity" of China but in a purely subjective way. It had observed the principle itself; it had not assumed the function of persuading others to observe it. The notes of September 6, as we have seen, had accepted the impairment of China's territorial integrity as a *fait accompli.* They had taken it for granted that foreign spheres of influence and territorial concessions in China would continue to exist, and even to expand, as is proved by the fact that the notes asked for most-favored-nation treatment for American commerce in all future as well as present spheres and leased territories. But the circumstances attending the Boxer Rebellion, following the unfavorable reception of the September notes, led Hay to the conclusion that the maintenance of the open door in China depended on the maintenance of China's complete sovereignty over her own territories. In his circular of July 3, 1900, therefore, he went further than reiterating America's traditional policy of respect for China's integrity, further than asking the powers to observe the principle of equal commercial opportunity. He suggested a collective guarantee of both these conditions. To "preserve" Chinese integrity was something different from merely respecting it. Assuming, as did Hay himself, that the chief end of America's Far Eastern policy remained commercial, the circular of July 3 and the subsequent adherence of the United States to the principles it contained, appreciably altered the means to that end. He had committed the United States to the policy of striving to deter its competitors for the Chinese market from violating the territorial and administrative integrity of the Chinese nation.

Only Great Britain made response to Hay's circular, and this in the most casual manner. The other powers proceeded with their independent plans for obtaining satisfaction from, or taking advantage of, China. Russia continued to pour troops into Manchuria. That England had no faith in the Hay policy, and had decided to rely on means other than American note-writing to defend her interests in China, seems obvious. She had never banked wholly on American co-operation in the Far East, but had used this only as one of three instruments, the other two being outright participation in the concessions-scramble, and bilateral agreements with her rivals.

Hay need not have been puzzled (as he was) by Pauncefote's uncommunicative attitude during the summer of 1900; by Salisbury's intrigues with the other powers to permit Japan to send an expeditionary force into northern China; by the Anglo-German declaration of October 16, 1900, in favor of the open door and the territorial integrity of China. What these signs indicated was that Great

Britain had turned to Japan as her partner in the Far East, her ally against Russia, and had resorted to bilateral negotiations to stay the advance of Germany.

It was in this manner that the partitioning of China was halted, temporarily, in 1900. The Boer War, the German navy, the maneuverings of the hostile European coalitions, the Czar, the Kaiser, Delcassé and Salisbury—these were the factors and agents that called the halt, not the diplomacy of John Hay. It was a case of political stalemate rather than conversion to principle. No power dared move further for fear of precipitating the universal *débâcle* that was destined to come a decade later, and so China was granted a brief respite.

Experience was disillusioning to the authors of the open door notes, as it was to Roosevelt in the case of the Philippines. No sooner had the rescue of the legations been effected than McKinley began to press for the withdrawal of the American troops from China. He feared their continued residence there as a political liability at home. Rockhill, who had done so much to launch the United States on its new policy, and who, in July, 1900, was sent to China as special commissioner to investigate the rebellion and represent his country at the peace settlement, readily confessed his discouragement. So did Hippisley. The excessive indemnities demanded of China, the latter wrote, after a long silence, in March, 1901, would have to be "liquidated by territorial concessions leading to partition and so ultimately to war among the Powers.

> The soldiers have committed atrocities horrible beyond description, and the Ministers of their nationals are all engaged in looting. While [*sic*] Russia working independently on her own account places Manchuria, Mongolia, and Turkestan under a protectorate, and throws the treaty rights of other nations into the dustbin. Right and reason disappear, and we return to the ethics of the Dark Ages. To an outsider it is all very sad and shows utter demoralisation."

Rockhill replied in the same gloomy vein. He was, he said, "sick and tired of the whole business and heartily glad to get away from it.

> I have been able to do something for commercial interests, and in a number of points have been able to carry out the Secretary's views, but have been practically alone in the negotiations. England has her agreement with Germany, Russia has her alliance with France, the Triple Alliance comes in here, and every other combination you know of is working here just as it is in Europe. I trust it may be a long time before the United States gets into another muddle of this description."

Hay's disillusionment, though less outspoken, was if anything more complete. For in November, 1900, under pressure from the War and Navy Departments, he executed the surprising *volte face* of instructing Conger to endeavor to obtain for the United States a naval base and territorial concession at Samsah Bay in the Chinese maritime province of Fukien. The erstwhile champion of Chinese integrity, still outwardly loyal to the policy of his notes, had actually forsaken that policy and tried to enter the concessions-scramble. As it happened Fukien had already been pre-empted as a sphere of influence by Japan, whose treaty right in the province would be infringed by the American venture. Japan had to be consulted. It must have been embarrassing for Hay to read the Japanese reply, reminding him of his own admonitions against using the Boxer Rebellion as the opportunity for territorial aggrandizement, and reaffirming the Imperial Government's adherence to that principle.

Thereafter the Secretary of State trimmed the sails of his Far Eastern policy ever more closely to the wind. As Russia strengthened her hold on Manchuria, he gradually retreated to the position of his first open door notes, accepting the fact that Manchuria was no longer an integral part of the Chinese Empire, but rather a Russian province, in which open door treatment was to be bargained for with the Czar. "I take it for granted," he told Roosevelt in April, 1903, "that Russia knows as we do that we will not fight over Manchuria, for the simple reason that we cannot. . . . If our rights and interests in opposition to Russia in the Far East were as clear as noonday, we could never get a treaty through the Senate, the object of which was to check Russian aggression." To all intents and purposes Hay had abandoned the doctrine of the territorial integrity of China, at least to the extent of recognizing Manchuria as beyond the Chinese pale.

What, then, had the open door notes accomplished? They had not invented, or even promoted, a "co-operative" policy. There never had been a co-operative policy in Eastern Asia that rose above joint military expeditions, such as the Shimonoseki and Boxer, or identic notes of protest at anti-foreign riots. Only in common defense of their nationals did the powers stand together. As for co-operating among themselves, in the interest of collective security, fair play, free competition, equal opportunity, there was none of that; there never had been any. Japanese, Russian, British, German, French and American soldiers could all march together to Peking. But once the siege was raised and the diplomats had taken charge, every semblance of co-operation vanished.

It has been suggested that the Hay notes were part of a diplomatic trade by which the United States gained supremacy in the Caribbean, in return for co-operating with England in the Far East. But, in spite of intensive search, no evidence has been discovered that would remove the idea from the realm of conjecture. Chronology alone makes it plausible. By the Hay-Pauncefote Treaty of 1900 the United States gained from England the right to construct and maintain a canal across the Isthmus of Panama. At approximately the same time, America came to England's assistance in China. History abounds, however, with examples of the *post hoc* fallacy. Rockhill and Hippisley, at pains to exhaust every possible argument that might further their designs, never mentioned the connection between the Caribbean and the Far East, which Hippisley has since called "the product of lively but ill-balanced imagination."

England was scarcely in a position to exact any such price as that supposed to have been paid by Hay for her strategic retreat from the Caribbean. The Boer War, the growing power of the United States, not to recapitulate more of the many international factors already reviewed, were sufficient to account for that. Months before the open door notes were written, Salisbury had informed Hay (through Henry White) in so many words that he realized the United States would build the canal, that he approved, and that "the canal is of comparatively little importance to England now that they have the Suez Canal. . . ." Pauncefote and Salisbury did not receive the open door notes or the circular on China's territorial integrity as if they were collecting payment for value received.

Hay's claim that he had "accomplished a good deal in the East, but thus far without the expense of a single commitment or promise" is no less difficult to validate. Hay was technically correct: nothing had been "put in writing." Legally the United States was no more bound to pursue the policy of the notes than the powers which had, in varying degrees, evaded their demands. It was the style of the notes, the fact that they were promulgated in a manner deliberately contrived to mobilize public opinion and create the impression of an international commitment, and most important of all, the way Hay's successors practiced what he preached that molded American policy. It may be conceded that the Secretaries of State who followed John Hay did not adhere to the principles of the open door and the preservation of China's territorial integrity solely because he had done so, and at the same time, that tradition and precedent exert a powerful influence on foreign policy.

One thing is clear: Hay had not secured anything approaching an international guarantee of the open door or the "territorial and administrative entity" of China. He had merely oriented American policy toward a more active participation in Far Eastern politics in support of those principles. In so doing he had kept pace with the expansionist forces (of which he was as much product as cause) that had propelled the United States into the conquest and annexation of the Philippines.

The China Market

THOMAS J. MCCORMICK

One year after the armistice with Spain, America sent forth into the world the then-famous, now-denigrated Open Door Notes. In and of themselves, they established no new policy lines. Both Cleveland's response to the Sino-Japanese War and McKinley's stance during peace talks with Spain make it abundantly clear that the open door in China was already cardinal American policy long before the 1899 notes appeared.

But the promulgation of the Hay Doctrine did pass the sceptre of open door champion from Great Britain to the United States. For a half-century the British had successfully used an open door policy to create and sustain their economic (and diplomatic) supremacy in the Chinese Empire; the Americans, as "hitchhiking imperialists," gathered the commercial leavings. Now, as Britain's power wavered—and with it her commitment to the open door, the United States made a concerted effort to adapt the nineteenth-century policy to the expansive needs of a twentieth-century industrial America.

This dramatic departure and its timing have long been the source of interpretive controversy. For example, George F. Kennan, in a capsule version of A.

Whitney Griswold's work, has viewed the Open Door Notes as a rather haphazard product, sold by an English member of the Chinese Customs Service indirectly to a somewhat disinterested and quickly disillusioned Secretary of State. On the other hand, Charles S. Campbell, Jr., has stressed the midwife role played by special business interests in bringing the policy to life. Yet each analysis, in its own way, has trivialized an event of enormous importance. The first grossly overestimates the influence of a quite peripheral figure, whose ideas were wholly unoriginal (and well known to every journeyman diplomat) and whose efforts in no way affected the timing of the Open Door Notes. The other bases its provocative interpretation upon a too narrow segment of the national community. Both inadequately appreciate that the Open Door Policy accurately reflected the widely shared assumptions and analyses of most social elements in America (including many without special vested interests); that both individual and group pressures were at best minor catalytic factors. Both, by focusing on the particular, miss the really substantive thing about the Open Door Policy—that it represented America's basic response to the methodological question of how to expand. Instead of closed doors, open markets; instead of political dominion, economic hegemony; instead of large-scale colonialism, informal empire. In short, a most interesting hybrid of anti-colonialism and economic imperialism.

On October 19, 1898, President McKinley told a Citizens' Banquet of Chicago that "territorial expansion is not alone and always necessary to national advancement" and the "broadening of trade." Before another year had passed, his State Department was feverishly at work trying to transform this unilateral sentiment into a universally accepted tenet—at least so far as the Chinese Empire was concerned. Behind this belated effort to make the open door a multilateral vehicle were two seemingly contradictory factors: a sense of power and a sense of impotence.

Latter-day critics of the Open Door Policy have managed to evade one central truth—that the policy was one of strength as well as weakness. A less confident nation might easily have joined in the partitioning scramble in China, content to have an assured but fragmentary slice of the market. But America wanted more, much more than that, and was certain of her ability to get it. When Brooks Adams wrote in 1899 that "East Asia is the prize for which all the energetic nations are grasping," few of his readers doubted who would win that prize. When William McKinley told Congress in that same year that "the rule of the survival of the fittest must be . . . inexorable" in the "rivalry" for "mastery in commerce," most of his listeners were doubtless sure who would be the fittest. In each instance, the certitude grew from that sense of American economic supremacy born in the export revival of 1897, nourished by the retooling and refinancing of American industry, and confirmed by the return of full prosperity. Viewed from this vantage, the open door became appropriate means for the most advanced and competitive industrial nation to grab the lion's share of the China market instead of settling for a pittance. No one saw this more clearly or said it more forcefully than the influential *Bankers' Magazine,* when it exclaimed that "without wars and without military aggression that nation will secure the widest and best markets which can offer the cheapest and best goods." "If China was open to trade with all the world . . . the United States and England need not be afraid of any competitors. But Russia, Germany and France . . . are more or less at a disadvantage when they meet either English or American goods. They therefore do not take the philosophical view at all."

The analysis was hardly an isolated one. In the private sector, for example, the Riverside, New York, Republican Club assured Secretary Hay that "the Chinese market . . . rightfully belongs to us and that in free and untrammeled competition we can win it." Old war-horse Joseph C. Wheeler, musing on his belief that "eight thousand miles of ocean could not stay the destinies of mankind," prophesied to President McKinley that the ultimate volume of American exports to China would reach $5.4 billion a year. The International Commercial Congress (an *ad hoc* meeting of Eastern manufacturers and merchants) wrote Far Eastern expert W. W. Rockhill that "no other market in the world [i.e., China] offers such vast and varied opportunities for the further increase of American exports." The NAM's journal, *American Trade,* reported authoritatively that "millions after millions are being invested in Southern mill property, solely in the faith of a continuation of trade . . . in the Chinese empire." Later *The Nation* nicely summarized general sentiments by predicting that "An open door and no favor infallibly means . . . the greater share and gain in the commercial exploitation of China."

Likewise, public officials expressed optimism about America's open door penetration of the China market. Cushman K. Davis, chairman of the Senate Foreign Relations Committee, proclaimed that our position in the orient was now such "that we can commercially [do] what we please" and predicted that the China trade "would put 18 millions of people on the Pacific coast within not many years and give its cities a preponderance like that of Tyron." Charles E. Smith, Secretary of Agriculture and informal adviser on foreign affairs, reported his impression that "the people of the West regard the Pacific as an American lake which should be covered with ships carrying the American flag" and added that "I don't know but they are about right." Administration trade expert Worthington C. Ford noted (with some reservations) that "the commercial future" of the China trade "is wonderful to think of"—a view based on an independent analysis that China could both double its population and living standards, "and this without any revolutionary change." Finally, even the cautious John Hay, in a public letter that coincided with the dispatch of the Open Door Notes, exclaimed that "in the field of trade and commerce we shall be the keen competitors of the richest and greatest powers, and they need no warning to be assured that in that struggle, we shall bring the sweat to their brows."

In view of subsequent developments, such glowing optimism about the future of the China trade appears naive, misguided, and grotesquely overdrawn— much flap about nothing. But the *potential* for trade expansion was real, and it remained so (enough to exercise vast impact upon American policy-makers for the four decades that preceded Pearl Harbor). In 1899 there were signs— however small—that the penetration of the China market was already underway. For one thing, in the relative sense, manufactured products began to account for more than 90 per cent of American exports to China—a fact of some significance to those preoccupied with *industrial* overproduction. (By 1906, 96 per cent of all United States exports to China were finished products, as compared to 27 per cent for Europe.) The absolute volume of manufactured exports also experienced a sharp rise (albeit from a small base), multiplying four times between 1895 and 1899, from $3.2 million to $13.1 million. (Seven years later, despite a Chinese boycott and persistent obstacles from both Russia and Japan, the total had reached nearly $42 million.) Particularly blessed were the iron and steel industry and cotton textile enterprises, both key elements in the American economy. The latter's exports to China, for example, grew from less than $2 million in 1895 to almost $10 million in 1899 (and reached $30 million by the Panic of 1907, accounting for 56.5 per cent of all American cotton textile exports). The figures lent an air of credence to one southern group's assessment that "[the China trade] is everything." All these facts were, to be sure, small straws in the wind and easily written off in retrospect. But in the expansionist psychology of the 1890's they were eagerly seized upon to bolster the widespread expectation that given equal, open door access, the United States could and would win economic dominion in China.

If American commercial ascendancy made the Open Door Policy a fruitful one, American weaknesses made it nearly unavoidable.

Political power was the prime deficiency. The Far East was no Latin America, where, after 1895, American hegemony was seldom challenged and usually acknowledged. In China the United States faced all the handicaps of the latecomer to a game already in play with a full lineup of great powers. America did have the capacity to play a significant role in Chinese affairs, and its words and acts now carried substantially more weight, thanks to the Spanish-American War. As the American Ambassador to France reported to McKinley: "we did in three months what the great powers of Europe had sought in vain to do for over a hundred years . . ." and "the most experienced statesmen here envy our transcendent achievements and see clearly the future benefits." Still, heightened power and all, the United States was in no position to issue any Olney Corollaries for the Chinese Empire; to make American word fiat; to manipulate with relative impunity and success. Here more subtle methods would be demanded.

The instances are many (and well known) of America's inability to control events in the western Pacific. Significantly, these failures came despite "the President's most serious consideration" of Chinese instability; despite Secretary Hay's "serious attention" to the famous petition of cotton textile spokesmen, exhorting that something be done to keep the door open in northern China; despite Hay's assurances to Paul Dana of the *New York Sun* that "we are keenly alive to the importance of safeguarding our great commercial interests in that Empire." For all this accumulated anxiety, America's newly won status in the Pacific could not prevent Germany's acquisition of Spain's old insular empire in Micronesia. It could not prevent Japan from occupying Marcus Island (a cable point upon which the American Navy had tentative designs) or from establishing an extraterritorial settlement in Amoy (important for its geographic relationship to Manila). It could do little to stop Russia's apparent drift toward trade discrimination in Manchuria. It could do nothing, one way or another, about the rumored impending war between Russia and Japan. Finally, it could not block Italy's far-reaching demands for a sphere of influence in San Mun Bay and Che-Kiang province—demands that ominously had the support of Great Britain; that threatened to set off another whole round of partitioning in China; that led the *New York Times* to conclude that the disintegration of China (and the open door) was "inevitable," and the *Chicago Inter-Ocean* to guess that "the end may be at hand." All the administration did was to watch, wait, and hope—a policy (better, a stance) that offered little hope for the future.

Financial weakness, another marked American liability, was in part an extension of political weakness. Simply put, American commercial expansion could not encompass financial expansion. In the realm of investments (chiefly railroads and mines) no open door existed, and no American syndicate seemed likely to compete on equitable grounds with its European peers. None of this was exactly new, of course; the move toward a "modified" open door (one that concerned only commerce, not investment) had begun in 1895 and, as already noted, accelerated sharply in 1898. But it did not reach its climax until the Anglo-Russian agreement of April 1899. In effect, Great Britain promised not to compete for railroad concessions north of the Great Wall, while Russia made a similar pledge for the Yangtze basin. All that remained between them for open competition was a buffer zone between the Russian and British spheres— and much of this was already covered by the earlier Anglo-German agreement.

This tightly constricted area of activity left American investors with little more than hope of a junior partnership with the British. This would be by no means inconsequential, and in early 1899 there was some optimism along these general lines. On February 1 the American China Development Company and the British and Chinese Corporation agreed on paper to share in each other's future concessions. One day later the *New York Times* reported that yet another British syndicate had agreed to give American capital a one-quarter share of investments in the railroads and mines of Szechwan province. But in fact British support was seldom vigorous, and American financiers fared poorly in competition with their politically and financially subsidized opponents. A prime example was the glaring failure of the American China Development Company to secure the Hankow-Canton concession, despite initially high hopes. The syndicate's inability to meet the rigorous Chinese terms was probably the major reason for the contract loss, but the company, in its frustration, blamed it on inadequate governmental support. In the end the concession "went thataway" while the State Department and the company engaged in futile backbiting as to why. Overall the episode was more souring than cathartic and played no small role in the administration's later attitude toward American investment in China.

A realistic foreign policy is an exact blend of means and ends—it knows what is vital to the national interest, whether that interest can be fulfilled within the framework of national power and ideology, and precisely how. By 1899 the makers of American foreign policy had long since defined marketplace expansion into China as an important element in their variegated effort to stabilize the political economy. But they had to adopt means that would make the best use of American commercial power while minimizing American liabilities: a still inadequate power base and financial frailty.

There were only three viable choices, and the McKinley administration considered them all. One obvious alternative was to accept the disintegration of China as inevitable (even beneficial) and join in the partitioning. In 1899 there were repeated rumors that the United States would take precisely this course. The *New York Times,* during the San Mun Bay crisis, reported that the administration had already determined to have Pechihli province for an American sphere, while at the same time the actions of the American Consul in Amoy seemed designed to convert that port and its environs into an American entrepôt. But the rumors were untrue and the American Consul's efforts repudiated, and both for the same reason: the administration felt that partitioning was an ineffectual vehicle for American trade expansion. For one thing, it would intensify anti-imperialist criticism while adding bureaucratic and military burdens that McKinley wished to avoid (a view shared with his anti-imperialist critics). For another, American sales and arteries of distribution were largely centered in zones controlled by Russia and Germany, and to relocate these in an American sphere would be expensive and time consuming—far better to keep open existing channels if possible. And finally, to re-emphasize an earlier point, a small slice of the pie (which is all partitioning could offer) held little attraction for men who wanted (and thought they could get) the major share of the market.

The second policy possibility was to make common cause with other open door supporters, presumably England and Japan, and use force if necessary to keep trade entrées open. This was the method that Theodore Roosevelt later tried informally, and it did have the merit of reflecting one vital truth—that in the last analysis only force could make the open door work. But this technique also raised basic objections which ultimately made it an impractical choice for the administration. To begin with, no military alliance (especially one with the English) was likely to enhance the political popularity of the McKinley administration. Moreover, such a formal commitment would deprive the United States of complete freedom of action, and the President (far more than his Anglophile Secretary of State) disliked tying American national interests too rigidly to the foreign policies of countries whose own shifting interests might not always coincide with those of the United States. He already had sufficient evidence (and more was to come) of British and Japanese ambivalence toward the Open Door Policy—enough to make them seem somewhat uncertain allies. Finally, any policy predicated upon the *possible* use of force might eventually require its *actual* use, and the use of force in China (save against Chinese themselves) was considered out of the question. A Far Eastern war would be an unpopular war; it might lead to the very consequence one wished to avoid—the fragmentation of China; and it might ignite the general world holocaust that all the great powers feared at the turn of the century. No, this would not do. What the United States wanted was not force but coexistence and economic competition for open markets; an "eat-your-cake-and-have-it-too" policy of peace and market domination. That America could not have both was, again, the certain fallacy of informal marketplace expansionism and the insoluble dilemma that American policy-makers vainly struggled with for the first half of the twentieth century.

There was of course some informal tripartite consultation and cooperation, and some public figures (generally outside the government) did refer to an "open door entente" of Great Britain, Japan, and the United States. But such collusion never aimed at the use of force, and moreover it was generally an on-again-off-again sort of thing, a tactical strategem employed when it was advantageous to American interests and ignored when it was not—which was frequently.

The third policy alternative—and the one embodied in the Open Door Notes—was to gain common agreement among a concert of powers that China would be exempted from imperial competition. This course obviously begged the whole question of force and has been rightly criticized on that ground. But, on the other hand, it was hardly the legalistic-moralistic anachronism that some have made it seem. On the contrary, as we shall see, it tried to make use of two very real and interrelated factors: (1) the *de facto* balance of power that existed between the Russo-French entente and the emerging Anglo-Japanese bloc; and (2) the intense fear of possible world war that preoccupied the foreign offices of Europe. In this framework of balance and fear, the policies of each power were likely to be flexible and even a bit tentative, for rigidity could be disastrous. (Certainly British action was chameleonic, and students of Russian policy in the Far East at the turn of the century find it so baffling and contradictory that there is doubt one existed.) Furthermore, any changes in the status quo were likely to be cautious ones, undertaken on a quid pro quo basis, lest imbalance lead to conflict. Under these circumstances, if a third force dramatically insisted that the status quo (the open door and Chinese sovereignty) be universally accepted, and if that force had the capacity to upset the delicate equilibrium of power (as the United States certainly had in Europe's eyes after 1898), then there was a good chance the powers would acquiesce. The agreement might be more rhetorical than real, but it would (and did) offer useful leverage in exploiting Europe's fears and occasionally manipulating the scale of power.

These were the realities that produced the Open Door Notes. Neither partitioning nor military alliance offered practical means to realize the desired American ends; only the consensus neutralization held any glimmer of hope. That such hope was illusory, that indeed it *had* to be illusory, is worth analyzing later at length. But for the moment it ought to be emphasized that, given America's commitment to economic penetration in China, given the peculiar combination of American strengths and weaknesses, the Open Door Policy was the most *realistic* one at hand.

The Myth of the China Market

PAUL A. VARG

The thrust into Asia owed much to that segment of the business community interested in the China market and to the publicists who linked prosperity with sales to China's four hundred million customers. The ardent proponents talked about the future rather than the present. Exports to China had increased sufficiently to provide a basis for their argument and those who wrote about the future never failed to cite statistics that supported their cause. Exports of cotton goods had increased dramatically, and most of these went to North China and southern Manchuria, the area threatened by Russian expansion. But there, sales, never more than a miniscule portion of total American exports, became the indices for measuring the potential of the China market for manufactured goods.

From the middle of the 1890's to 1906, exports to China showed only a modest rate of growth but were sufficient to maintain faith in the earlier predictions. No one challenged this optimistic view. However, from 1906 to the Chinese Revolution of 1911, when annual export figures moved both up and down, there were some second thoughts. Declines were readily explained as caused by temporary phenomena. In 1906, the unsettling effects of the Russo-Japanese War and the piling up of supplies in warehouses during the hostilities received much attention. In the next few years, the difficulties were explained as due to the instability of the Chinese currency. Both, unquestionably, did hamper trade but conditions in China of a more permanent character were of greater importance.

In this period, too, it became apparent that there was reason to question the generally accepted assumption that the nations establishing leaseholds and spheres of influence would utilize them to favor their own exporters. Therefore, these should be opposed as hostile to the commercial interests of the United States. Other Governments did favor their own nationals, but in some cases, American sales increased within the spheres of influence due to the economic development fostered by the controlling nation. Sales of railroad equipment to Japan's South Manchuria Railway offered the best illustration.

The facts notwithstanding, the prospect of a large market for manufactured goods lost but little of its luster prior to the Chinese Revolution. This continued to serve as one of the major reasons for the United States to make its influence felt in Chinese affairs. But there is also cause for reflection as to the real meaning of the repeated reliance of the Department of State on the commercial argument whenever it confronted a development in the China crucible that it found objectionable. It was undoubtedly convenient to object to a particular move on the part of other nations on the ground that it would violate the rights of American business to an equality of commercial opportu-

Paul A. Varg, *The Making of a Myth: The United States and China, 1897–1912* (East Lansing, Mich.: Michigan State University Press, 1968), pp. 36–40, 40–42, 43–47, 48–52, 53.

nity, but the argument served more than business interests. It provided a suitable basis for those responsible for the conduct of foreign relations to assert an interest and to convey to other Powers that the United States was an interested party. Not until 1909, when Philander Knox became Secretary of State, did the United States make a determined effort to initiate arrangements which would enlarge the prospects of American business. Even then, the political aim seems to have been as important as the commercial. However, these reflections pertain only to the thinking of statesmen. A segment of the business community entertained the prospect of a growing market in China and it was interested in business, not the political future of East Asia.

The most elementary facts contradicted the dream that China would, before long, provide a large market. The first of these was that only a small part of China, the coastal cities and a few ports on the rivers, was open to trade. In 1899, Rounseville Wildman, the U.S. Consul-General in Hongkong, wrote:

> Another great point that American exporters overlook is that 99 percent of China is still closed to the world. When the magazine writer refers in glowing terms to the 400,000,000 inhabitants of China, he forgets that 350,000,000 are a dead letter so far as commerce is concerned.

Burlingame Johnson, the Consul in Amoy, in 1901, called for treaty revisions which would permit businessmen to reside in the interior. Such action, he believed, would open the markets as far away "as 150 to 200 miles . . . whereas now even kerosene and flour seldom get further than fifty miles from open ports and few other goods that far."

The lack of a transportation system restricted the influx of western goods. Except for river traffic, transport was almost nonexistent. The Grand Canal, which, in the time of Marco Polo, carried large vessels over a six hundred and fifty mile stretch between Peking and Hangchow, was in disrepair and small junks now navigated it with difficulty. Of the roads, the U.S. Consul in Shanghai in 1895 reported:

> Their condition is such that passage over them is virtually stopped as the holes and ruts that deface them force travelers to desert them for the tracks by the sides, although these in wet weather are but quagmires, and in dry weather, several inches in dust.

A survey of the roads in 1890 by the China branch of the Royal Asiatic Society led to this conclusion:

> Probably no country in the world, certainly none aiming at civilization even of the most rudimentary nature, has paid so little attention to roads and means of communication as had the Chinese empire; and it may be remarked at the outset that no road in the European acceptance of the term, as an artificially constructed viaduct, laid out with engineering skill even of the crudest description, exists from one end of China to the other.

Given these conditions, only a small part of the country was accessible to foreign goods.

Another formidable barrier stood in the way. Western goods fitted neither ancient Chinese preferences nor Chinese pocketbooks. Flour, cotton goods, kerosene and lumber jibed with the native consumer habits and did find a growing market, but the great variety of western goods ran counter to long-established ways of work and customs. In 1906, James L. Rodgers, the Consul-General in Shanghai, wrote: "It is perhaps needless to call attention to the antiquity of Chinese methods and habits, to the fact that traders have for centuries been trying to introduce new things, and that beyond some modern devices for using and making the necessities of life, one sees very few inroads upon established customs." Rodgers stated that the Chinese did buy foreign oil, flour, leather, lamps, clocks and some food stuffs, but, he warned, "it does not follow that there is a market for a foreign shoe, for an agricultural implement, for machinery of various kinds and for the infinite variety of manufactured goods which distinguish the industry of the United States, Great Britain, and Germany." A certain Occidental, Rodgers reported, had written home that there was a great market for windmills. Such an opinion ignored the fact that the Chinese had been raising water from one level to another by means of pumps and water wheels long before the Christian era began and they were not likely to change their methods. Even more important than the reluctance to change, he declared, was the fact that "a windmill would cost many rice crops, or perhaps the savings of a lifetime. . . ."

Rodgers, after an examination of the markets in the Chinese cities near Shanghai, noted that there were few foreign products and "you will hunt for a day before you will find in this section of China an agricultural implement of foreign make." He concluded: "Numberless instances might be cited to show how limited a Chinese market is for things which encroach upon their customs or which will supplant the articles handed down from generation to generation. . . ." In conclusion, he offered these words: "And all this is written not to discourage but to place that which is conceived to be plain truth before the minds of those who nowadays read in the newspapers glowing prophecies about the oriental trade, who then remember that there are said to be four hundred million Chinese and who are straightway moved to attempt an export business to China. . . ." Given the "present scheme of civilization" whereby the Chinese "are practically sufficient unto themselves," he warned, "China, even under the reformation now beginning, will take at first only in a small way of those things she does not seem to need. . . ."

The poverty of the Chinese constituted a further obstacle. When the Department of State, in 1898, instructed Consuls throughout the world to report on the possible outlets for the surplus products of soap manufacturers, E. T. Williams, then Vice-Consul-General in Shanghai, wrote:

> The people of China are extremely poor. Their wages are paid in copper cash, one of which equals one-twentieth of a cent. One hundred to one hundred and fifty of these cash, that is, from five to seven and a half cents, form the average daily wage of the ordinary working man. It is evident that such an article as soap, which from the Chinese point of view, is an article of luxury rather than necessity, however, much desired, can be purchased only when furnished at a very low price. . . .

Another deterrent to a market for American goods was the rapid development after 1894 of an unfavorable trade balance. Exports to China did increase but exports from China did not. A study of China's long-term trade developments made by the Imperial Maritime Customs Service in 1904 showed that China's imports had increased until they were a third greater than exports. Indemnities incurred as a result of the war with Japan and the Boxer Revolt had necessitated foreign loans thereby increasing the outflow of gold. These foreign loans, in 1904, called for payments upwards of forty-five million haikwan taels a year.

Within this market, so circumscribed by inaccessibility to the interior, by aversion to western style products, by poverty, and by an unfavorable balance of international payments, a dog-eat-dog fight for sales and contracts raged. Germany, Great Britain, France, Russia, and Japan were more dependent upon foreign markets than the United States; the Governments of these nations gave their business enterprises greater support than did the United States, and, most important, the business enterprises of these countries demonstrated greater energy and initiative in China. Consequently, American companies found the going rough.

The Standard Oil Company, oriented to foreign markets by long experience and by the fact that since the 1860's more than half of its major product, kerosene, was exported, eyed the Far East. As early as 1882, the company sent William Herbert Libby to explore possible markets in that part of the world. He made a careful study of the China situation and more particularly of the barriers to greater sales of kerosene. Beginning in 1890, Standard Oil, anxious to expand sales, departed from the practice of selling to merchants on the Atlantic Seaboard who then handled sales in China. Under the new system, it distributed its products through its British affiliate, the Anglo-American Oil Company. In the next two decades, sales increased but Standard Oil's hopes of dominating the market never came even close to realization. Russian oil enjoyed the advantages of lower production costs, shorter transportation routes, and benefited by the tariffs levied on value as opposed to volume. The competition of the Dutch operating out of the East Indies also cut seriously into Standard Oil's sales in China. Standard Oil, more than any other American company, adopted a system of distribution and sales that was efficient and well suited to success in China, but although sales became important, the competition of the Russians and the Dutch was so effective that, in the words of the historians of the company, its "efforts in the Far East proved relatively ineffectual."

These barriers to trade, although not readily surmountable, sometimes appeared minor in comparison to inveterate Chinese hostility toward the foreigner. Indeed, the one characteristic quality of the Chinese in relations with the outside world—whether political, economic, or religious—was an intractable opposition. The missionaries, more often exposed to antagonism because their efforts touched upon matters subject to deep emotional response and because they were often in the interior, were the most frequent targets of antiforeign disturbances. Business and government representatives enjoyed the protection of treaty ports, but they could not be protected from the Chinese aversion to them that found expression in delayed negotiations, the placing of obstacles in the way of land purchases, and the playing of one foreigner against another. . . .

Turning our attention to a second major aspect of the problem, the willingness of the Government in Washington to lend assistance to American business, we find that the support was usually little more than an expression of goodwill. Beginning in the late 1880's, the Department of Commerce and the Department of State were vigorous in asking their officers for reports on commercial opportunities for many different types of manufactured goods. Bulletins including the reports were issued in great numbers.

Both Denby and Conger believed that the investment of American capital would spur the sale of American goods and they therefore supported their fellow countrymen when they presented proposals. In April, 1898, Denby reported to Secretary of State Sherman that he had "devoted a great deal of time and labor to the promotion of railroad projects" presented by his countrymen. His successor, E. H. Conger, later in the same year wrote: "So long as I am at this legation, its aid will be cheerfully and actively given along these lines so far as is wise and proper; but experience has long since proven that neither legislation nor official aid can take the place of business enterprise in business affairs." It was also true "that one of the chief elements of foreign potency, is the leverage obtained from actual occupation or ownership of territory." This was Conger's observation in August of 1898. During the next few years, the reverse was also true on occasion. Americans received some advantage because their schemes were considered to be free of political ambitions. In the period 1894 to 1906, Washington, through its representative in Peking, struck the boldest pose at the time that the Chinese Government cancelled the contract of the American China Development Company for building the railroad from Hankow to Canton. The cancellation led to sharp diplomatic notes and the Minister, W. W. Rockhill, questioned the chief of China's Foreign Office in a most peremptory tone.

However, the promotion of economic interests was generally the function of the Consular Service rather than the Legation in Peking. If the degree of government support of the Consular Service is a fair measure of how seriously Washington took the promotion of interests in China, the conclusion can only be that interest approximated apathy. For years, the Consul-General in Shanghai protested that the American consular offices in that city were not only inadequate but reflected unfavorably upon the United States. As late as 1905, Consul-General Rodgers declared that they were the poorest of any foreign nation except Portugal. The inadequacy of consular offices had its parallel in a very small staff. Rodgers compared the failure to provide an adequate group of American officers with the elaborate efforts of Great Britain, Germany, France and Japan. In September, 1905, he reported:

> They know for instance that Great Britain has a force of Englishmen in the various departments of its representation; that Germany has not only a large

number here, but also has men traveling on trade matters; that France is likewise provided and that Japan is represented elsewhere. They know that absolute count will show that in Shanghai where the United States has one employee, Great Britain and Germany have six, France about four and Japan counting only those in evidence, three.

All of the districts found reason to complain but no one demonstrated greater impatience than Edward Bedloe who was appointed Consul in Canton in the latter part of 1897. On arrival, he found the offices so inadequately furnished that he carried on business from his hotel room. When facing the necessity of giving a reception in the offices for Chinese officials and other Consuls, he borrowed furnishings from several friendly parties.

The importance of the Canton district seemed to justify better quarters and a more adequate staff. Eighty million people lived in the area. Some seven cities had been made into treaty ports in 1897 and both the British and Germans had an official at each. Consul Bedloe was the only officer representing the United States. When he first took over, he had no Vice-Consul or clerk. During his first several months he employed a clerk and paid him out of his own pocket. A Vice-Consul was appointed late in 1898 after a missionary group petitioned the Department of State. The inadequacy of staff, particularly the absence of Consuls in the interior, meant there was no official to protest against a variety of types of interference with shipments of American goods or to promote American commercial interests.

The U.S. Consulate in Amoy typified the general neglect and apathy. In the early 1890's Edward Bedloe, previous to his transfer to Canton, occupied the office. A German resident served for several months after Bedloe was transferred. Then Delaware Kemper took over. In June, 1897, Burlingame Johnson, an energetic young man from Colorado, replaced Kemper. Johnson immediately reported to the Department of State "that the condition in which the work of the office has been found is very unsatisfactory." The "property," he declared, "is in a most dilapidated condition." He added: "The verandas are falling, posts have rotted off, plastings (sic!) falling, and the roof needs thorough repairs." An official reading the letter noted: "He may have the flagstaff painted at once." Within a year seventeen hundred dollars were spent on renovations.

The work of the Amoy Consulate harmonized with the dismal surroundings. Burlingame Johnson informed the Department of State: "Notwithstanding this I find that absolutely no attention was given to the opening for American products by my predecessor and that for three years there has not been a single trade report to the Department calling attention of exporters to existing conditions." Johnson's initial enthusiasm found expression in a detailed report on missionary work, praising its philanthropic aspects and as an activity that opened the door to commerce, but his efforts in behalf of trade do not appear to have measured up to his own high hopes.

In April, 1906, the Consul in Hankow, William Martin, complained "that all the force in this office at present, capable of doing clerical work, consists of Mr. W. B. Hull, Student Interpreter, Mr. Kong Chen-ren, the Chinese writer and myself." He asked for a stenographer and a typewriter. He based his request on the sharp increase of Standard Oil's business but acknowledged that his plea had a more important basis, the great numbers of missionaries scattered over the district and the voluminous correspondence carried on with them. Samuel Gracey, after many years of service, in 1902, requested restoration of his salary to what it was previously, namely, thirty-five hundred dollars. John Fowler, a veteran officer stationed in Chefoo, one of the more important posts from the point of view of sale of cotton goods, received a raise to thirty-five hundred dollars in 1905. He noted: ". . . it is the smallest salary any professional Consul or Vice-Consul is receiving at this port, and all of my colleagues in course of time will retire on a pension larger than the salary of $3500." Fowler, a short time later, protested that his allowance of $1775 for contingent expenses fell far short of the average annual $3209.85 contingency expenses of the previous five years. He met the difference by dipping into his own pocket.

Of course, this penurious policy resulted in a rapid turnover of personnel and in much incompetence. The interest in foreign markets led to agitation for reform, but there was long delay because appointments to foreign service assignments were an important source of patronage for members of Congress. Not until 1906 did Congress provide for improvements. In a final speech in the House of Representatives supporting the bill, Robert Adams, of Pennsylvania, cited the fact that for "sixteen years efforts have been made to secure the proposed legislation." "The new legislation," he agreed, "will go a long way in the movement that is now occupying the time of our merchants for the enlargement of our foreign commerce, for these are our advance pickets, sent throughout the world to furnish the merchants the necessary information to enlarge their business abroad."

The new law establishing five categories of consular posts based on estimates of the commercial importance of the foreign city did indicate a degree of serious purpose concerning China. Shanghai and Hongkong were placed in the second category, Tientsin and Canton in the fourth and Amoy and Fuchow in the fifth among the Consul-General posts.

The improved Consular Service reflected the Government's increasing awareness of the importance of foreign trade. The importance of export markets in the eyes of Washington is also evidenced in the strong support given to economic interests in Cuba, Santo Domingo, and the Philippines after the war with Spain. The building of the Panama Canal was likewise, in part, an extending of the helping hand of government to commercial interests. Others have discussed the role of economic considerations in the move of the Taft Administration to neutralize the railroads of Manchuria. These were important but compared to the actions of some other Governments, Washington scarcely played the game in a daring manner.

We are here dealing with the market for goods rather than for investment, but the first cannot be treated without some reference to the other. The lack of investments, especially in railroads, was quite correctly viewed by contemporaries as one of the reasons why the sale of American goods was not greater. . . .

The policy of government aid certainly rested on wide agreement on the importance of exports, but its implementation fell somewhere beyond half-heartedness and considerably short of boldness. Wide agreement did not produce aggressiveness because the very economic interests that might be expected to spur government action were now concerned with other matters: expanding the tremendous home market and gaining tariff protection. In 1909, John Barrett, Director of the Bureau of American Republics, in an address before the National Association of Manufacturers, bemoaned the fact that in all the speeches in Congress over the new tariff bill, and in almost all the discussions in the newspapers, "there has been an absolute neglect of the effect the tariff may have on our export trade." In brief, in spite of a consensus of opinion on the importance of foreign trade, government action was moderated by concerns that evoked a much greater response.

Having examined the two questions of the strengths and weaknesses of the China market at the turn of the century, and the degree of support provided by the Government in Washington in efforts to capture this market, the next question is whether the American business community demonstrated energy and imagination. Some of the Consuls stationed in major ports took a deep interest in the business activities of their fellow nationals and they prepared lengthy reports and wrote frequent letters containing detailed observations on commerce, the opportunities at hand, the factors making for success and failure, and the nature of the competition. In the 1890's, a majority of them filed optimistic reports and heralded even minor advances in sales of American goods, but throughout the hundreds of these reports and letters there is a common complaint of the lack of assertiveness on the part of American business concerns.

The apathy of American business concerns showed itself in a variety of ways. Consul John Fowler, stationed in the port of Chefoo, complained of the failure of American concerns to provide credit facilities, of the failure to send representatives to promote sales, and of the poor packaging of American goods. These practices did not change. Eleven years later, in 1911, Consul George Anderson, in charge of the Consulate in Hongkong, attributed the decline in sales in recent years to the high prices of American goods, Japanese competition, failure to supply credit, poor packaging, and the lack of an effective sales organization. Another official cited the failure of Americans to invest in China and reminded his readers that trade follows investment. Vice-Consul-General Willard B. Hull, in Hankow, warned that American firms could not follow their present policies and hope to secure the business. "Nearly every American company represented in Hankow," wrote Hull, "has some European firm for its agent, and, naturally, American products will be sold only when these firms cannot secure the same things from their own country in Europe, thus keeping American goods, in most cases, as a second choice." Hull likewise advised that American manufacturers "must also count on giving longer credits if they wish to do business in this field." Vice-Consul-General Percival Heintzleman in Shanghai, in 1908, stated that the three greatest handicaps of U.S. trade were: (1) failure to extend credit; (2) failure to send representatives; and (3) failure to invest American capital. The Vice-Consul in Dalny, in 1909, deplored the failure to send representatives. American business, he observed, is in the hands of persons who are regarded as commercial rivals.

American business, with the notable exception of Standard Oil, made no great effort to do what was necessary to sell to China. One major reason seems to have been the greener pastures near at hand. Consul George Anderson reported:

> They state frankly here that the cotton-goods market in the United States is so great, its demands so steady, the prices it pays so good, and its consumption so broad, that American manufacturers will give no more than passing interest to any foreign market and will not make the effort necessary to secure foreign business until home conditions turn against them.

These observations lead to the conclusion that American business was apathetic or at least unimaginative in its methods.

United States Ministers in Peking often expressed regret over the lack of enterprise. In October, 1897, Charles Denby observed: "Unfortunately, our fellow-citizens have made no serious effort to avail themselves of the good will of China." Two years before a loan of one hundred million dollars had been offered to Americans, but he recorded: "I could find nobody in the United States that would touch it." American banking representatives had come to China but they were without authority to make a contract. Denby advised: "To accomplish anything here we must imitate the European powers and have fully authorized agents on the ground."

Denby's successor, E. H. Conger, reported that Europeans were active in studying opportunities for railroads and mines. "If our capitalists," wrote Conger, "really desire a share they must have brains and money here."

The apathy of American business in the China market did not correspond to their behavior elsewhere if we may assume that success in sales was a result of their initiative. Exports of manufactured goods increased dramatically. In 1890, they constituted only 12.48 percent of total exports; in 1900, they represented 31.65 percent of the total. In 1910, the value reached $767 million compared to $122 million in 1880.

An examination of figures on the China trade shows that it was limited to a very few commodities. Illuminating oil and cotton goods led the way by a wide margin. Tobacco and tobacco products ranked third and lumber was fourth. Analyzing these further, we find that unbleached cloth constituted the bulk of textiles. In the peak year, 1909, unbleached cloth exports totaled $6,983,774; bleached cloth was valued at $908,681 and colored cloth at $111,402. The total exports of these three varieties in 1910 were $10,098,985 of unbleached, $1,351,040 of bleached and $8,521,466 of colored; of the total, China took $5,762,318 or approximately twenty-seven percent. However, cotton textiles ranked eleventh among the exports of the United States in 1910 and accounted for only 1.95 percent of the value of all exports.

Sales of illuminating oil totaled $1,251,201 in 1900, reached a peak for this period of $8,499,279 in 1908, and declined again to $5,016,397 in 1910. In the latter year, total exports of illuminating oil were valued at $62,477,527 and the Chinese market accounted for eight percent.

The next most important item in the trade fell far below cotton cloth and oil. Exports to China of leaf tobacco amounted to $639,369 in 1906; dipped to $273,687 in 1909; and advanced to a peak of $653,496 in 1910. Exports of cigarettes reached a high of $1,393,051 in 1907 and then slipped to $793,381 in 1908. The chief lumber products exported to China were boards, deals and planes. These totaled $976,629 in 1907 but declined by fifty percent in 1909 and then recovered in part, amounting to $748,026 or two percent of total exports of these lumber items in 1910.

These major exports represent the great bulk of the trade, $13,003,470 of a total of $16,181,670 in 1910. Sales of other important items were either trivial or nonexistent. Railway cars, carriages and other equipment varied; totaling only $382 in 1906, mounting to $137,439 in 1909 and then falling to $17,204 in 1910. Sales of railway equipment to Japan in her sphere in China were greater. The rebuilding of the South Manchuria Railway, destroyed by the Russians during the war, was done largely with American-made equipment and in 1908 the sales totaled almost two million dollars. Rails, considered a separate item, were sold to Japan for use in China to the extent of $1,121,199. But in the case of both equipment and rails, sales were trivial in most years. Locomotives, also considered a separate item, likewise were sold in large numbers ($2,404,619 worth in 1910) in one year and scarcely any in most years.

The point that the sales of most manufactured items were small is well illustrated by the statistics for 1900. In that year, American manufacturers sold $292 worth of cash registers, $6,345 of electrical supplies, $2,102 of laundry machinery, $17,520 of pumps and pumping machinery, and $7,769 of sewing machines. These were not the only items sold but they are representative. Obviously, these sales were scarcely adequate to excite the interest of the industrialists.

Contemporary observers of the China trade saw that the availability of credit and investment of American dollars were necessary for increasing sales. Recognition of this interdependence of trade and investment eventually encouraged bankers to show an interest in China but they found domestic American opportunities—and a few selective foreign ones—more promising. That the United States remained a debtor nation until World War I was, of course, of primary importance in explaining the absence of American capital in China. . . .

Measured against these actualities, the rhetoric concerning the China market was so wild as to suggest that it was in the nature of a myth. Indeed, the gap between the rhetoric and the actualities attained dimensions of such scope that one may assume that the sheer joy of the discussion and not facts sufficed as a propellant.

FURTHER READING

Charles S. Campbell, *Special Business Interests and the Open Door Policy* (1951)
Charles S. Campbell, *The Transformation of American Foreign Relations, 1865–1900* (1976)
Warren I. Cohen, *America's Response to China* (1971)
Michael Hunt, *Frontier Defense and the Open Door: Manchuria in Chinese-American Relations, 1895–1911* (1973)
Akira Iriye, *Across the Pacific* (1967)
George F. Kennan, *American Diplomacy, 1900–1950* (1951)
Robert McClellan, *The Heathen Chinee: A Study of American Attitudes Toward China, 1890–1905* (1971)
Paul A. Varg, *Missionaries, Chinese, and Diplomats* (1958)
Paul A. Varg, *Open Door Diplomat: The Life of W. W. Rockhill* (1952)
Marilyn Blatt Young, "American Expansion, 1870–1900: The Far East," in Barton J. Bernstein, ed., *Towards a New Past* (1968)
Marilyn Blatt Young, *The Rhetoric of Empire* (1968)

12

Intervention in the Caribbean

In the years after the Spanish-American War, the Caribbean became an American "lake." Through the acquisition of Puerto Rico, the building of the Panama Canal, strong commercial links, Pan-Americanism, governance of Cuba, financial protectorates, reiterations of the Monroe Doctrine, and interventions—military, political, and economic—in the affairs of many Latin American states, the United States substantiated Richard Olney's 1895 dictum that America's word was fiat in the Western Hemisphere. The administrations of Theodore Roosevelt, William Howard Taft, and Woodrow Wilson, although sometimes differing in means, pursued the same goal of United States hegemony. Why the United States intervened—economic profit? humanitarianism? mission? security?—was a topic of vigorous debate among contemporaries as it still is among scholars today.

DOCUMENTS

In a 1903 treaty with Cuba, the United States placed restrictions on Cuban independence and gave Washington the right to intervene in Cuban internal affairs. This "Platt Amendment" was not abrogated until 1934 and, to generations of Cubans, stood as a symbol of their subordinate status. The Treaty of 1903 with Panama came after the United States encouraged Panamanian independence from Colombia. The pact granted the United States canal rights. Panama, like Cuba, became an American satellite. A year later, President Roosevelt announced a "corollary" to the Monroe Doctrine in his Annual Message to Congress in December. The United States, he declared, would exercise "police power" among its neighbors to thwart "chronic wrongdoing."

American financial management of Santo Domingo and military intervention in other states soon followed. In a State of the Union message in December 1912, President Taft summarized his administration's Caribbean policy as a substitution of "dollars for bullets." And in October 1913, President Wilson, a critic of "dollar diplomacy," suggested that Latin American nations could expect more United States "understanding" and more emphasis on "constitutional liberty" in the future. Like many Latin American nationalists, Francisco García Calderón, a Peruvian diplomat and writer who later represented his nation at the Paris Peace Conference of 1919, resented United States interventions, as his modest critique indicates.

The Platt Amendment, 1903

Article I. The Government of Cuba shall never enter into any treaty or other compact with any foreign power or powers which will impair or tend to impair the independence of Cuba, nor in any manner authorize or permit any foreign power or powers to obtain by colonization or for military or naval purposes, or otherwise, lodgment in or control over any portion of said island.

Article II. The Government of Cuba shall not assume or contract any public debt to pay the interest upon which, and to make reasonable sinking-fund provision for the ultimate discharge of which, the ordinary revenues of the Island of Cuba, after defraying the current expenses of the Government, shall be inadequate.

Article III. The Government of Cuba consents that the United States may exercise the right to intervene for the preservation of Cuban independence, the maintenance of a government adequate for the protection of life, property, and individual liberty, and for discharging the obligations with respect to Cuba imposed by the Treaty of Paris on the United States, now to be assumed and undertaken by the Government of Cuba. . . .

Article V. The Government of Cuba will execute, and, as far as necessary, extend the plans already devised, or other plans to be mutually agreed upon, for the sanitation of the cities of the island, to the end that a recurrence of epidemic and infectious diseases may be prevented, thereby assuring protection to the people and commerce of Cuba, as well as to the commerce of the Southern ports of the United States and the people residing therein. . . .

Article VII. To enable the United States to maintain the independence of Cuba, and to protect the people thereof, as well as for its own defense, the Government of Cuba will sell or lease to the United States lands necessary for coaling or naval stations, at certain specified points, to be agreed upon with the President of the United States.

The Panama Canal Treaty, 1903

Article I. The United States guarantees and will maintain the independence of the Republic of Panama.

Article II. The Republic of Panama grants to the United States in perpetuity the use, occupation and control of a zone of land and land under water for the construction, maintenance, operation, sanitation and protection of said Canal of the width of ten miles extending to the distance of five miles on each side of the center line of the route of the Canal to be constructed. . . .

Article III. The Republic of Panama grants to the United States all the rights, power and authority within the zone mentioned and described in Article II of this agreement and within the limits of all auxiliary lands and waters mentioned and described in said Article II which the United States would possess and exercise if it were the sovereign of the territory within which said lands and waters are located to the entire exclusion of the exercise by the Republic of Panama of any such sovereign rights, power or authority. . . .

Article XIV. As the price or compensation for the rights, powers and privileges granted in this convention by the Republic of Panama to the United States, the Government of the United States agrees to pay to the Republic of Panama the sum of ten million dollars ($10,000,000) in gold coin of the United States on the exchange of the ratification of this convention and also an annual payment during the life of this convention of two hundred and fifty thousand dollars ($250,000) in like gold coin, beginning nine years after the date aforesaid. . . .

Article XVIII. The Canal, when constructed, and the entrances thereto shall be neutral in perpetuity, and shall be opened upon the terms provided for by Section I of Article three of, and in conformity with all the stipulations of, the treaty entered into by the Governments of the United States and Great Britain on November 18, 1901. . . .

Article XXIII. If it should become necessary at any time to employ armed forces for the safety or protection of the Canal, or of the ships that make use of the same, or the railways and auxiliary works, the United States shall have the right, at all times and in its discretion, to use its police and its land and naval forces or to establish fortifications for these purposes. . . .

Article XXV. For the better performance of the engagements of this convention and to the end of the efficient protection of the Canal and the preservation of its neutrality, the Government of the Republic of Panama will sell or lease to the United States lands adequate and necessary for naval or coaling stations on the Pacific coast and on the western Caribbean coast of the Republic at certain points to be agreed upon with the President of the United States.

The Roosevelt Corollary, 1904

It is not true that the United States feels any land hunger or entertains any projects as regards the other nations of the Western Hemisphere save such as are for their welfare. All that this country desires is to see the neighboring countries stable, orderly, and prosperous. Any country whose people conduct themselves well can count upon our hearty friendship. If a nation shows that it knows how to act with reasonable efficiency and decency in social and political matters, if it keeps order and pays its obligations, it need fear no interference from the United States. Chronic wrongdoing, or an impotence which results in a general loosening of the ties of civilized society, may in America, as elsewhere, ultimately require intervention by some civilized nation, and in the Western Hemisphere the adherence of the United States to the Monroe Doctrine may force the United States, however reluctantly, in flagrant cases of such wrongdoing or impotence, to the exercise of an international police power. If every country washed by the Caribbean Sea would show the progress in stable and just civilization which with the aid of the Platt amendment Cuba has shown since our troops left the island, and which so many of the republics in both Americas are constantly and brilliantly showing, all question of interference by this Nation with their affairs would be at an end. Our interests and those of our southern neighbors are in reality identical. They have great natural riches, and if within their borders the reign of law and justice obtains, prosperity is sure to come to them. While they thus obey the primary laws of civilized society they may rest assured that they will be treated by us in a spirit of cordial and helpful sympathy. We would interfere with them only in the last resort, and then only if it became evident that their inability or unwillingness to do justice at home and abroad had violated the rights of the United States or had invited foreign aggression to the detriment of the entire body of American nations. It is a mere truism to say that every nation, whether in America or anywhere else, which desires to maintain its freedom, its independence, must ultimately realize that the right of such independence can not be separated from the responsibility of making good use of it.

William Howard Taft on Dollar Diplomacy, 1912

The diplomacy of the present administration has sought to respond to modern ideas of commercial intercourse. This policy has been characterized as substituting dollars for bullets. It is one that appeals alike to idealistic humanitarian sentiments, to the dictates of sound policy and strategy, and to legitimate commercial aims. It is an effort frankly directed to the increase of American trade upon the axiomatic principle that the Government of the United States shall extend all proper support to every legitimate and beneficial American enterprise abroad. How great have been the results of this diplomacy, coupled with the maximum and minimum provision of the tariff law, will be seen by some consideration of the wonderful increase in the export trade of the United States. Because modern diplomacy is commercial, there has been a disposition in some quarters to attribute to it none but materialistic aims. How strikingly erroneous is such an impression may be seen from a study of the results by which the diplomacy of the United States can be judged.

Woodrow Wilson on Latin American Policy, 1913

The future, ladies and gentlemen, is going to be very different for this hemisphere from the past. These States lying to the south of us, which have always been our neighbors, will now be drawn closer to us by innumerable ties, and

I hope, chief of all, by the tie of a common understanding of each other. Interest does not tie nations together; it sometimes separates them. But sympathy and understanding does unite them, and I believe that by the new route that is just about to be opened, while we physically cut two continents asunder, we spiritually unite them. It is a spiritual union which we seek.

I wonder if you realize, I wonder if your imaginations have been filled with the significance of the tides of commerce. Your governor alluded in very fit and striking terms to the voyage of Columbus, but Columbus took his voyage under compulsion of circumstances. Constantinople had been captured by the Turks and all the routes of trade with the East had been suddenly closed. If there was not a way across the Atlantic to open those routes again, they were closed forever, and Columbus set out not to discover America, for he did not know that it existed, but to discover the eastern shores of Asia. He set sail for Cathay and stumbled upon America. With that change in the outlook of the world, what happened? England, that had been at the back of Europe, with an unknown sea behind her, found that all things had turned as if upon a pivot and she was at the front of Europe; and since then all the tides of energy and enterprise that have issued out of Europe have seemed to be turned westward across the Atlantic. But you will notice that they have turned westward chiefly north of the Equator and that it is the northern half of the globe that has seemed to be filled with the media of intercourse and of sympathy and of common understanding.

Do you not see now what is about to happen? These great tides which have been running along parallels of latitude will now swing southward athwart parallels of latitude, and that opening gate at the Isthmus of Panama will open the world to a commerce that she has not known before, a commerce of intelligence, of thought and sympathy between north and south. The Latin American States, which, to their disadvantage, have been off the main lines, will now be on the main lines. I feel that these gentlemen honoring us with their presence to-day will presently find that some part, at any rate, of the center of gravity of the world has shifted. Do you realize that New York, for example, will be nearer the western coast of South America than she is now to the eastern coast of South America? Do you realize that a line drawn northward parallel with the greater part of the western coast of South America will run only about 150 miles west of New York? The great bulk of South America, if you will look at your globes (not at your Mercator's projection), lies eastward of the continent of North America. You will realize that when you realize that the canal will run southeast, not southwest, and that when you get into the Pacific you will be farther east than you were when you left the Gulf of Mexico. These things are significant, therefore, of this, that we are closing one chapter in the history of the world and are opening another, of great, unimaginable significance.

There is one peculiarity about the history of the Latin American States which I am sure they are keenly aware of. You hear of "concessions" to foreign capitalists in Latin America. You do not hear of concessions to foreign capitalists in the United States. They are not granted concessions. They are

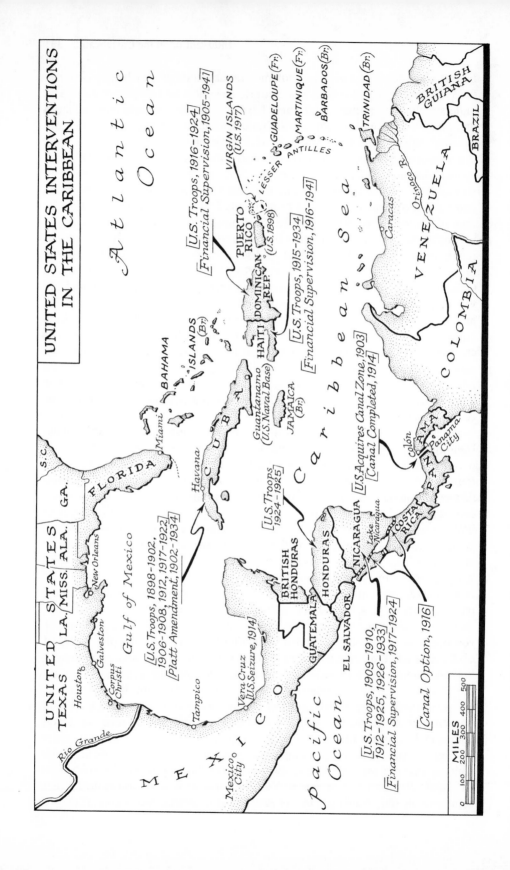

UNITED STATES INTERVENTIONS
IN THE CARIBBEAN

Atlantic Ocean

UNITED STATES

TEXAS   LA. MISS. ALA. GA.   S.C.

FLORIDA

New Orleans
Galveston
Houston
Corpus Christi
Rio Grande

M E X I C O

Tampico
Mexico City
Vera Cruz
(U.S. Seizure, 1914)

Pacific Ocean

Gulf of Mexico

Miami

BAHAMA

ISLANDS (Br.)

Havana   C U B A

Guantanamo
(U.S. Naval Base)

JAMAICA (Br.)

U.S. Troops, 1898–1902,
1906–1908, 1912, 1917–1922,
[Platt Amendment, 1902–1934]

U.S. Troops
1924–1925

BRITISH
HONDURAS

GUATEMALA

HONDURAS

EL SALVADOR

NICARAGUA
Lake
Nicaragua

COSTA RICA

U.S. Troops, 1909–1910,
1912–1925, 1926–1933,
[Financial Supervision, 1917–1924]

[Canal Option, 1916]

PANAMA
Colón
Panama City

U.S. Acquires Canal Zone, 1903
[Canal Completed, 1914]

HAITI   DOMINICAN REP.
(U.S. 1898)

PUERTO RICO

U.S. Troops, 1916–1924
[Financial Supervision, 1905–1941]

U.S. Troops, 1915–1934
[Financial Supervision, 1916–1941]

VIRGIN ISLANDS
(U.S. 1917)

LESSER ANTILLES

GUADELOUPE (Fr.)
MARTINIQUE (Fr.)
BARBADOS (Br.)
TRINIDAD (Br.)

Caribbean Sea

Caracas
Orinoco R.

V E N E Z U E L A

COLOMBIA

BRITISH
GUIANA

BRAZIL

MILES
0 100 200 300 400 500

invited to make investments. The work is ours, though they are welcome to invest in it. We do not ask them to supply the capital and do the work. It is an invitation, not a privilege; and States that are obliged, because their territory does not lie within the main field of modern enterprise and action, to grant concessions are in this condition—that foreign interests are apt to dominate their domestic affairs, a condition of affairs always dangerous and apt to become intolerable. What these States are going to see, therefore, is an emancipation from the subordination, which has been inevitable, to foreign enterprise, and an assertion of the splendid character which, in spite of these difficulties, they have again and again been able to demonstrate. The dignity, the courage, the self-possession, the self-respect of the Latin American States, their achievements in the face of all these adverse circumstances, deserve nothing but the admiration and applause of the world. They have had harder bargains driven with them in the matter of loans than any other peoples in the world. Interest has been exacted of them that was not exacted of anybody else, because the risk was said to be greater; and then securities were taken that destroyed the risk—an admirable arrangement for those who were forcing the terms! I rejoice in nothing so much as in the prospect that they will now be emancipated from these conditions, and we ought to be the first to take part in assisting in that emancipation. I think some of these gentlemen have already had occasion to bear witness that the Department of State in recent months has tried to serve them in that wise. In the future they will draw closer and closer to us because of circumstances of which I wish to speak with moderation and, I hope, without indiscretion.

We must prove ourselves their friends and champions upon terms of equality and honor. You can not be friends upon any other terms than upon the terms of equality. You can not be friends at all except upon the terms of honor. We must show ourselves friends by comprehending their interest, whether it squares with our own interest or not. It is a very perilous thing to determine the foreign policy of a nation in the terms of material interest. It not only is unfair to those with whom you are dealing, but it is degrading as regards your own actions.

Comprehension must be the soil in which shall grow all the fruits of friendship, and there is a reason and a compulsion lying behind all this which is dearer than anything else to the thoughtful men of America. I mean the development of constitutional liberty in the world. Human rights, national integrity, and opportunity as against material interests—that, ladies and gentlemen, is the issue which we now have to face. I want to take this occasion to say that the United States will never again seek one additional foot of territory by conquest. She will devote herself to showing that she knows how to make honorable and fruitful use of the territory she has, and she must regard it as one of the duties of friendship to see that from no quarter are material interests made superior to human liberty and national opportunity. I say this, not with a single thought that anyone will gainsay it, but merely to fix in our consciousness what our real relationship with the rest of America is. It is the relationship of a family of mankind devoted to the development of true constitutional liberty.

We know that that is the soil out of which the best enterprise springs. We know that this is a cause which we are making in common with our neighbors, because we have had to make it for ourselves.

Francisco García Calderón on American Imperialism, 1913

To save themselves from Yankee imperialism the American democracies would almost accept a German alliance, or the aid of Japanese arms; everywhere the Americans of the North are feared. In the Antilles and in Central America hostility against the Anglo-Saxon invaders assumes the character of a Latin crusade. Do the United States deserve this hatred? Are they not, as their diplomatists preach, the elder brothers, generous and protecting? And is not protection their proper vocation in a continent rent by anarchy?

We must define the different aspects of their activities in South America; a summary examination of their influence could not fail to be unjust. They have conquered new territories, but they have upheld the independence of feeble States; they aspire to the hegemony of the Latin continent, but this ambition has prevented numerous and grievous conflicts between South American nations. The moral pressure of the United States makes itself felt everywhere; the imperialist and maternal Republic intervenes in all the internal conflicts of the Spanish-speaking democracies. It excites or suppresses revolutions; it fulfills a high vocation of culture. It uses or abuses a privilege which cannot be gainsaid. The better to protect the Ibero-Americans, it has proudly raised its Pillars of Hercules against the ambition of the Old World.

Sometimes this influence becomes a monopoly, and the United States take possession of the markets of the South. They aim at making a trust of the South American republics, the supreme dream of their multi-millionaire *conquistadores*. Alberdi has said that there they are the "Puerto Cabello" of the new America; that is to say, that they aim, after the Spanish fashion, at isolating the southern continent and becoming its exclusive purveyors of ideas and industries.

Their supremacy was excellent when it was a matter of basing the independence of twenty republics of uncertain future upon a solid foundation. The neo-Saxons did not then intervene in the wars of the South; they remained neutral and observed the peace which Washington had advocated. They proclaimed the autonomy of the continent, and contributed to conserve the originality of Southern America by forbidding the formation of colonies in its empty territories, and by defending the republican and democratic States against reactionary Europe.

But who will deliver the Ibero-Americans from the excess of this influence? *Quis custodiet custodem?* An irresponsible supremacy is perilous. . . .

Interventions have become more frequent with the expansion of frontiers. The United States have recently intervened in the territory of Acre, there to found a republic of rubber gatherers; at Panama, there to develop a province and construct a canal; in Cuba, under cover of the Platt amendment, to maintain order in the interior; in Santo Domingo, to support the civilising revolution and overthrow the tyrants; in Venezuela, and in Central America, to enforce upon these nations, torn by intestine disorders, the political and financial tutelage of the imperial democracy. In Guatemala and Honduras the loans concluded with the monarchs of North American finance have reduced the people to a new slavery. Supervision of the customs and the dispatch of pacificatory squadrons to defend the interests of the Anglo-Saxon have enforced peace and tranquility: such are the means employed. The *New York American* announces that Mr. Pierpont Morgan proposes to encompass the finances of Latin America by a vast network of Yankee banks. Chicago merchants and Wall Street financiers created the Meat Trust in the Argentine. The United States offer millions for the purpose of converting into Yankee loans the moneys raised in London during the last century by the Latin American States; they wish to obtain a monopoly of credit. It has even been announced, although the news hardly appears probable, that a North American syndicate wished to buy enormous belts of land in Guatemala, where the English tongue is the obligatory language. The fortification of the Panama Canal, and the possible acquisition of the Galapagos Islands in the Pacific, are fresh manifestations of imperialistic progress.

The Monroe doctrine takes an aggressive form with Mr. Roosevelt, the politician of the "big stick," and intervention *à outrance*. Roosevelt is conscious of his sacred mission; he wants a powerful army, and a navy majestically sailing the two oceans. His ambitions find an unlooked-for commentary in a book by Mr. Archibald Coolidge, the Harvard professor, upon the United States as a world-power. He therein shows the origin of the disquietude of the South Americans before the Northern peril: "When two contiguous States," he writes, "are separated by a long line of frontiers and one of the two rapidly increases, full of youth and vigor, while the other possesses, together with a small population, rich and desirable territories, and is troubled by continual revolutions which exhaust and weaken it, the first will inevitably encroach upon the second, just as water will always seek to regain its own level."

He recognises the fact that the progress accomplished by the United States is not of a nature to tranquillise the South American; "that the Yankee believes that his southern neighbours are trivial and childish peoples, and above all incapable of maintaining a proper self-government." He thinks the example of Cuba, liberated "from the rule of Spain, but not from internal troubles, will render the American of the States sceptical as to the aptitude of the Latin-American populations of mixed blood to govern themselves without disorder," and recognises that the "pacific penetration" of Mexico by American capital constitutes a possible menace to the independence of that Republic, were the death of Díaz to lead to its original state of anarchy and disturb the peace which the millionaires of the North desire to see untroubled.

Warnings, advice, distrust, invasion of capital, plans of financial hegemony —all these justify the anxiety of the southern peoples. . . . Neither irony nor grace nor scepticism, gifts of the old civilisations, can make way against the plebeian brutality, the excessive optimism, the violent individualism of the [North American] people.

All these things contribute to the triumph of mediocrity; the multitude of primary schools, the vices of utilitarianism, the cult of the average citizen, the transatlantic M. Homais, and the tyranny of opinion noted by Tocqueville; and in this vulgarity, which is devoid of traditions and has no leading aristocracy, a return to the primitive type of the redskin, which has already been noted by close observers, is threatening the proud democracy. From the excessive tension of wills, from the elementary state of culture, from the perpetual unrest of life, from the harshness of the industrial struggle, anarchy and violence will be born in the future. In a hundred years men will seek in vain for the "American soul," the "genius of America," elsewhere than in the undisciplined force or the violence which ignores moral laws. . . .

In seeking to imitate the United States we should not forget that the civilisation of the peoples of the North presents these symptoms of decadence.

Europe offers the Latin-American democracies what the latter demand of Anglo-Saxon America, which was formed in the school of Europe. We find the practical spirit, industrialism, and political liberty in England; organisation and education in Germany; and in France inventive genius, culture, wealth, great universities, and democracy. From these ruling peoples the new Latin world must indirectly receive the legacy of Western civilisation.

Essential points of difference separate the two Americas. Differences of language and therefore of spirit; the difference between Spanish Catholicism and the multiform Protestantism of the Anglo-Saxons; between the Yankee individualism and the omnipotence of the State natural to the nations of the South. In their origin, as in their race, we find fundamental antagonisms; the evolution of the North is slow and obedient to the lessons of time, to the influences of custom; the history of the southern peoples is full of revolutions, rich with dreams of an unattainable perfection.

The people of the United States hate the half-breed, and the impure marriages of whites and blacks which take place in Southern homes; no manifestation of Pan-Americanism could suffice to destroy the racial prejudice as it exists north of Mexico. The half-breeds and their descendants govern the Ibero-American democracies, and the Republic of the [sic] English and German origin entertains for the men of the tropics the same contempt which they feel for the slaves of Virginia whom Lincoln liberated.

In its friendship for them there will always be disdain; in their progress, a conquest; in their policy, a desire for hegemony. It is the fatality of blood, stronger than political affinities or geographical alliances. . . .

The Monroe doctrine, which prohibits the intervention of Europe in the affairs of America and angers the German imperialists, the professors of external expansion, like Münsterberg, may become obsolete. If Germany or Japan were to defeat the United States, this tutelary doctrine would be only a melancholy memory. Latin America would emerge from the isolation imposed upon it by the Yankee nation, and would form part of the European concert, the combination of political forces—alliances and understandings—which is the basis of the modern equilibrium. It would become united by political ties to the nations which enrich it with their capital and buy its products.

ESSAYS

Lloyd C. Gardner of Rutgers University, in surveying United States relations with Latin America in the early twentieth century, points to markets and investments as the primary motives for the imperial intrusion in the sovereign affairs of other countries. Dana G. Munro, for years a specialist in Latin American affairs in the State Department, disagrees. Denying the existence of North American imperialism, he argues that the interventions sprang from a United States desire to preserve the independence of the Caribbean states from European threat and to protect United States security.

A Haven for Markets and Investments

LLOYD C. GARDNER

Banker involvement in American foreign policy was greatest in the Caribbean and Central America. Each succeeding Administration in the years from 1900 to 1921 eventually found itself relying upon the bankers to carry the burden, although the government never made policy simply in response to their wishes. Theodore Roosevelt was concerned that someday a European power would seize upon a "bad debt" as an excuse to demand, China fashion, a naval base in one of the Caribbean countries, or even on the coast of some South American country. To prevent such a possibility in the former area, the United States adopted policies that, when Europeans practiced them, were called "administrative imperialism." These started with the Platt Amendment to the Cuban Constitution. Imposed by the United States on the new Cuban government, the amendment supposedly made it impossible for any other country to obtain military or economic footholds on the island. Cuba was prohibited from granting any nation but the United States military or naval bases or from contracting public debts that could not be discharged by ordinary revenues (a complicated way of saying that the Cubans could not borrow without American approval). Finally, the Cuban government was required to consent to a further constitutional provision that "the United States may exercise the right to intervene for the preservation of Cuban independence, the maintenance of a government adequate for the protection of life, property, and individual liberty," and for other unspecified reasons connected with America's "obligations" under the Treaty of Paris ending the war with Spain.

"The people ask me what we mean by a stable government in Cuba," wrote General Leonard Wood from Havana in early 1900. "I tell them that when money can be borrowed at a reasonable rate of interest and when capital is willing to invest in the Island, a condition of stability will have been reached." That, in sum, was the rationale for the Platt Amendment. It was developed in response to a need to work out a satisfactory solution to the Cuban problem, since outright annexation had been ruled out, but it soon became the model for resolving other problems in the Monroe Doctrine area. None of the later arrangements were spelled out so fully, but like the Platt Amendment they led to military interventions on a regular basis, and in some cases, to semipermanent military occupations.

When viewed from the perspective of the Platt Amendment, TR's intervention in support of the November 1903 Panamanian "revolution" against Colombia appears to have been prompted by more than a temporary setback dealt to the United States when the Colombian Senate refused to ratify the Hay-Herran Treaty covering rights to build a canal across the Isthmus of Panama in return for $10 million. Long before that crisis, Roosevelt had warned Germany not to seek a permanent foothold in Venezuela; at one point, he even ordered the fleet to make ready to sail from Puerto Rico to display the flag near the area. He recalled much later that he had become convinced that "Germany intended to seize some Venezuelan harbor and turn it into a strongly fortified place of arms, on the model of Kiaochow, with a view to exercising some measure of control over the future Isthmian Canal, and over South American affairs generally."

Roosevelt wanted that control and influence for the United States; his intervention in the Panamanian affair assured the United States complete dominance over the canal route, but he also seized upon the opportunity presented when the Colombian Senate defied American wishes to secure an American Kiaochow, as it were, "a strongly fortified place of arms" on the South American continent. TR could then issue his general pronouncement, commonly referred to as the "Roosevelt Corollary" to the Monroe Doctrine, with the confidence that he could stand behind every word with military force. In his Annual Messages of both 1904 and 1905, Roosevelt asserted the right to intervene between *any* "American Republic" and the rest of the world whenever it became necessary to prevent even a "temporary" seizure of a customs house by a nation seeking to satisfy a foreign debt.

To make the Corollary work, Roosevelt found it necessary to apply something like a Platt Amendment solution to the situation in Santo Domingo. Since 1899 that half of the Island of Hispaniola, which it shared with Haiti, had been in a state of permanent revolution. Small-scale troop landings from European and American naval vessels had become an almost commonplace event. Beginning in 1903, the State and Navy Departments showed considerable interest in completing negotiations for a naval base at Samana Bay and for financial control of at least that half of the island. The problem became finding a way to keep a government in power long enough to sign the agreements. "I have about the same desire to annex it," Roosevelt confided to a close friend, "as a gorged boa constrictor might have to swallow a porcupine wrong-end to."

But every report TR received insisted that the only way to put an end to the revolutions and perpetual disorder was to take away the legalized plunder of the customs houses by each succeeding regime. An American planter suggested how this might be done: After the people had elected their next President, the United States should step in and say, "All right, you have elected a president. We will not permit any lawless revolutions against this government. This policy would insure lasting peace and would not require the landing of a marine or soldier on that island." This proposal, as it turned out, was strikingly similar to those later advanced by Woodrow Wilson as his own solution to the dilemma of the 1913 Mexican situation as well as to his lesser problems in the Caribbean.

Finally, in December 1904, a protocol was signed by Carlos Morales requesting the United States to take over and to administer Santo Domingan customs houses. The agreement was signed under the watchful guns of American navy ships, primarily to make sure that Morales was protected from his own people. The circumstances surrounding these events provoked serious opposition in Congress and delayed its formal approval. In fact, Root's first assignment when he succeeded John Hay was to get the legislative branch to act favorably on the protocol. He accomplished this feat by removing those items in the treaty that had stirred up the most comment and then enlisting the business community in its support. "Our treatment of Santo Domingo," Root told the National Committee for the Extension of Foreign Commerce, "is but a part of a great policy which shall in the years to come determine the relations of this vast country, with its wealth and enterprise, to the millions of men and women and the countless millions of trade and treasure of the great world to the south."

The "great policy" the Secretary spoke about was underlined in an extended tour Root undertook in 1906 to all the major South American cities. The message he left with them was that the United States had no intention or desire to take additional territory. "Our surplus energy is beginning to look beyond our own borders," he affirmed upon his return, but it was looking "to find opportunity for the profitable use of our surplus capital, foreign markets for our manufacturers, foreign mines to be developed, foreign bridges and railroads and public works to be built, foreign rivers to be turned into electric power and light. As in their several ways England and France and Germany have stood, so we in our own way are beginning to stand and must continue to stand toward the industrial enterprise of the world." Now was the time, he went on, perhaps our only chance, to take advantage of another development. Latin America had risen out of the "stage of militarism" and had moved on into the "stage of industrialism." If the United States failed to take full advantage of this development, its rivals surely would—and soon. He ended by listing particulars for capturing the Latin American market, giving special emphasis to the need for new steamship lines, subsidized, if need be, by the federal government.

Root was anxious to help Latin American evolution along by moving disputes between Central American countries off the battlefield into an international tribunal. "Those people are as anxious to fight as your highland clans used to be," the Secretary wrote to Andrew Carnegie (who he hoped might contribute funds to build a Central American Court of Justice), "but we have been working in harmony with Mexico to keep the peace, and representatives of the disturbing element are now on their way to Washington pursuant to suggestions that the whole matter shall be submitted to arbitration. . . ." Carnegie came through with money to build the Courthouse, but neither Taft nor Wilson was spared difficult decisions on military intervention.

Indeed, the Cuban protectorate had already collapsed. Unaware of how serious the situation had become in Havana by June 1906, Secretary Root recommended to Harvard President Charles Eliot that the university grant Cuban President Tomas Estrada Palma an honorary degree. The Cubans were an "affectionate, sensitive people, easily impressed by marks of consideration and courtesy, and they are too frequently treated with rudeness by Americans," he said; anything, "which tends to increase their respect for their own government, and make them proud of the man they have chosen for their leader, is good for them."

Estrada Palma soon required a more forcible demonstration of Root's affection. Instead of a sound democracy, protected from outside storms by the Platt Amendment, the Cuban political structure had turned out to be, as Taft would put it, nothing more than a "house of cards." The only real goal of a Cuban politician had become to stay in office, since the Platt Amendment determined the more important matter of what to do with power. As the principal interpreter of that document, the American Minister in Havana quickly became "the second most important man in Cuba; sometimes even more important that the President." As Ambassador Earl T. Smith thus indicated in 1959, that situation persisted down to the time when Fidel Castro came to power, though the Platt Amendment itself was formally abrogated in 1933. Ironically, American planners had unknowingly built into the Cuban situation a revolutionary impetus: Those "out" of power could not gain much by attacking their opponents for failing to develop the island politically and economically, for it was well known that the Cuban President was sometimes only the "second most important" man in Havana. Serious political discussion, therefore, had to begin with the nature of Cuba's relationship to the United States.

Estrada Palma tried to explain the relationship to Roosevelt's special emissaries in September 1906. A member of the conservative elite, the Cuban President had arrived at the conclusion that the only way to avoid perpetual disorder and revolution was annexation. Secretary of War Taft had no power to grant his request and tried to persuade Estrada Palma to stick out the situation, using what he thought was the best argument: "There is no difference in the political or economic principles of the two [Cuban] parties. The only difference is personal." Taft had put his finger on the Cuban-American predicament, but he seemed unaware of the implications of the situation he had so accurately described. It was already too late for more words. American troops were landed to pick up the pieces and start the Cuban government again. They left in 1909, but a cycle of interventions had begun. Each time it came around, the "revolution" was pushed farther to the left: in 1917, 1933, and then, 1961, when it culminated in the Bay of Pigs.

"I am anxious to get away from here," Taft exclaimed to Elihu Root, "out of this atmosphere which is one of disappointment, intrigue and discouragement." He found things little more to his liking in the White House. Taft had inherited a full carpetbag of troubles in Central America. Exasperated by the steady deterioration of law and order in that area, he once demanded of his Secretary of State that he supply him with the means to compel peace there, even if it meant someone had to "knock their heads together." The State Department gave him an unequivocal answer: eliminate Nicaraguan President José Santos Zelaya and the Central American problem would shrink at once to manageable proportions. As usual, however, such advice proved more complicated in execution than in theory, and Taft found himself deeply embroiled in the conflicting schemes of several aspirants to Zelaya's rule, none of whom could guarantee the peace. Then one of these, Adolfo Díaz, finally asked openly for the same kind of assistance "which had resulted so well in Cuba." Díaz had figured out the Americans, and what they offered was better than risking a short reign and quick profits. He ordered his Foreign Minister, Salvador Castrillo, to sign a convention providing for a $15 million loan in exchange for United States management of Nicaraguan customs houses. Neither Taft nor Díaz expected trouble from the United States Senate, but it turned down the convention three times, despite special pleading from the White House.

When the smoldering revolution flared up again in 1912, Taft smothered the flames with troops sent from the Panama Canal Zone. The State Department had advised him that the situation was "analogous to the Boxer trouble in China." The comparison was a striking, if unintended, confirmation of Roosevelt's foresight in seizing a "fortified place of arms" in Central America, as well as of his understanding of how his successors would define future situations and remedies. "We think that if the United States did its duty promptly, thoroughly and impressively," said the State Department, "it would strengthen our hand and lighten our task, not only in Nicaragua itself in the future, but throughout Central America and the Caribbean and would even have some moral effect in Mexico." This memorandum leaves the reader with an eerie sense of things to come, but it also stands out as strong evidence that American policy makers knew what they were about and did not resemble the caricatures drawn by "realist" critics of "Dollar Diplomacy" and "Moral Imperialism."

Taft had good reason to resent the Senate's double standard in foreign policy. On the one hand, it refused to ratify the Knox-Castrillo Convention, yet it insisted that American property rights be protected against the depredations of revolutionaries and bandits. Moreover, it was filled with bellicose oratory at the least sign of "foreign intervention" in the Monroe doctrine preserve. If the President tried to satisfy one group in the Senate, he faced a rising chorus of "progressive insurgents" who denounced him from the other side. This cacophony obscured the few clear-cut successes Taft could claim for "Dollar Diplomacy," though these presaged the nation's economic foreign policy in years to come. The most impressive gain was made in Argentina, a traditional stronghold of British capitalists. Knox mobilized a "very strong group" of bankers, "headed by J. P. Morgan and Company," to offer Buenos Aires a large loan to seal an American bid for battleship contracts. "It is the first time in our history," declared shipbuilder Charles Schwab when the $22 million contract was consummated, "that the United States has received a contract of this magnitude and description. . . . It is, to my mind, the best step ever made towards the further development of America's commercial relations with foreign countries." This "consortium" had been organized before the China offensive in 1909; it demonstrated that the idea of close banker-exporter cooperation originated not simply in response to a desire "to play the game" in Manchuria, whether for prestige's sake or for some other psychological satisfaction, but also from general policy and in answer to national need. The *London Times* indicated the awareness of what lay behind the American challenge: "The recent complete American defeat of all competitors for Argentine awards for battleships seems to [indicate] . . . the approaching American commercial absorption of the southern continent, which will be assisted by the opening of the Panama Canal. In my opinion our American cousins can only be amicably combatted by the resolute combination of . . . enormous British financial interests." . . .

The long reign of Mexican dictator Porfirio Díaz came to an end in 1910. During his time foreign investors had enjoyed easy access to Mexican resources —too easy, claimed the followers of the liberal reformer Francisco Madero, who replaced Díaz. Madero never pacified the countryside, nor brought under his control the revolutionary forces dividing Mexico. Americans had invested $2 billion in Mexican enterprises, Taft once explained to his wife, adding that if the country went to pieces he (or his successor) would have to intervene. During Madero's three-year rule, 1910–1913, American investors tried to work out a private arrangement with Mexico City, over the objections of the American Ambassador Henry Lane Wilson, who openly disparaged Madero and encouraged his enemies by aligning himself with the most reactionary elements of Mexican society and the foreign community. Nevertheless, American bankers received Secretary Knox's blessings for a plan to advance Mexico a $10 million loan, conditioned on Madero's turning over certain financial controls. But the internal situation disintegrated so rapidly that these efforts were abandoned in the fall of 1912.

In February 1913 Madero was overthrown by a coalition of reactionary forces led by the old dictator's nephew, Felix Díaz, and one of his own generals, Victoriano Huerta. Their "compact" was actually signed under Henry Lane Wilson's benevolent gaze in the American Embassy. It provided that Huerta was to assume the presidency on a provisional basis; Díaz was to name the cabinet; and then, at a later election, Huerta would support Díaz's candidacy. Thus the old regime would be restored. But the "compact" triggered a new phase of the revolution that did not come to an end for nearly a decade. Moreover, for most of those ten years, Mexican-American relations verged on collapse.

Relieved that the crisis had come so near the end of his term, William Howard Taft did not grant Huerta diplomatic recognition, since he could leave that question (and whatever else followed) to his successor. Secretary Knox's final instructions directed Ambassador Henry Lane Wilson to keep his fingers on the situation in the interim: "It is left to you to deal with this whole matter of keeping Mexican opinion, both official and unofficial, in a salutary equilibrium between a dangerous and exaggerated apprehension and a proper degree of wholesome fear."

Woodrow Wilson came into office convinced that Huerta's *coup* constituted a serious setback for constitutional rule in the hemisphere. Special agents that he sent into Mexico confirmed this impression and added other reasons for not recognizing the usurper. Most important, they reported, Huerta did not then and probably could not ever exercise control over the Mexican countryside. Because Great Britain and other European nations had extended Huerta's regime full diplomatic recognition, how to proceed from these conclusions was another matter. It was suggested by some presidential advisers that this hasty action was linked to British oil policy.

Meanwhile, representatives of the large American investors in Mexico contacted Wilson's closest adviser and confidante, Colonel Edward M. House. "It was the general belief" in Mexico, explained E. N. Brown, head of the Mexican Railways, "that if this Government could not maintain itself, no other could." Brown went over the Huerta-Díaz compact point by point, urging House to persuade the President not to recall Ambassador Wilson until Huerta kept his word to Felix Díaz. House noted in his diary that President Wilson agreed to wait for the promised elections. The investors saw that, even if it was not yet clear to the new President, deep social questions were involved here, not merely another changing of the customs-house guard in a "banana republic."

Over the next few weeks a growing sense of urgency characterized Cabinet discussions of the Mexican situation. Reports had come to Washington that Huerta, having fallen out with Felix Díaz, had set out to gain financial backing in Europe. Wilson took these reports and other rumors back to Colonel House in early May when he went to see him in New York. House repeated his original advice, but suggested that the President do something positive to convince Huerta to hold an election "supporting Díaz for the Presidency."

Wilson selected the former governor of Minnesota, John Lind, to do the convincing. Some years later, in 1920, Lind testified that he had been instructed to bring the factions back together so that "there should be an election at which, under his own contract with Díaz, [Huerta] . . . should not be a candidate. . . ." A government would have emerged from this election which the United States could recognize and support financially. Huerta responded to these carefully laid plans by calling down on Lind all the pent-up forces of Mexican nationalism, forcing him to retreat to the safety of the American fleet stationed off Vera Cruz. There he made contacts with the "Constitutionalist" leader Venustiano Carranza, who welcomed any aid in his fight against Huerta.

Months passed, but the tighter the United States tried to pull the economic noose, the more Huerta seemed to prosper. Angered by British support for the dictator, Wilson began to look for a reason to intervene. In February 1914, the American naval commander confided to a friend that "conditions are gradually drifting into a more complex condition." He had good reason to know. Then, in early April, Wilson seized upon the arrest and brief (a few hours) detention of a small number of American sailors in Tampico to justify interrupting an arms shipment intended for Mexico City. Next came the order to occupy Vera Cruz and Tampico, which was accomplished only after the Mexican naval academy was bombarded and a large number of cadets killed.

At that point, the next logical step for either of the capitals would have been a declaration of war. A timely mediation offer from the ABC powers (Argentina, Brazil, and Chile) may have prevented that tragedy, for it made possible Huerta's retirement without his having appeared to surrender to the United States. Unhappily, his departure did little to resolve Mexican-American differences. Numerous claimants turned up to take charge of the revolution. Wilson tried to keep tabs on them all, but the task frustrated him and the State Department at every turn. In 1915 Carranza controlled Mexico City, but he refused to give assurances to American representatives of his willingness to observe Anglo-Saxon sanctions against interference with legitimate property rights. Wilson looked around for an alternative, even picking out Pancho Villa for a brief moment. No one showed the capacity to take charge of the revolution, at least as Wilson would have liked, except Carranza. The principal reason for not extending the "constitutionalist" leader diplomatic recognition, maintained Secretary of State Lansing, was to keep American options open in case some other figure might arise, and to bring pressure on Carranza. Lansing proposed a plan for bringing about such a change late in the summer of 1915 but backed off when Wilson indicated his opposition to the idea.

The Secretary of State would propose several other intervention plans over the next four years. Each time the President opposed the scheme, but each time he offered no alternative for coming to terms with the revolution. In 1917 Carranza promulgated a new Mexican Constitution, containing explicit restrictions on the operations of foreign capitalists. Of these, the most vexing was Article 27, which placed the ownership of subsoil minerals in the hands of the central government.

Lansing responded to the document with a further admonition. Article 27, he told a special agent, seemed "to indicate a proposed policy toward foreigners which is fraught with possible grave consequences affecting the commercial and political relations of Mexico with other nations. You will point out that the Government of the United States cannot, of course, acquiesce in any direct or indirect confiscations of foreign-owned properties in Mexico." The President approved the State Department's continued refusal to grant Carranza even de facto recognition, but the wheels of diplomacy, still stalled in a position of "Watchful Waiting," refused to turn for the President. Some months after the United States entered the war, Wilson received a group of Mexican newspaper editors. Their country, he began, was a "storehouse of treasure," but as long as he was President of the United States, no one would be permitted to exploit those resources solely to the advantage of foreigners. After the war all nations would be held to strict standards of honor and fair dealing, "because so soon as you [Mexicans] can admit your own capital and the capital of the world to the free use of the resources of Mexico, it will be one of the most wonderfully rich and prosperous countries in the world." Like McKinley and Hay, Woodrow Wilson presumed that most of the contradictions and tensions in Adam Smith's vision of the "Great Society" could be reconciled by honesty and fair dealing among the great powers. Carranza (and other "revolutionaries" yet to come) held that the problem was more complex than that. A conservative landowner himself, Carranza saw that limits had to be put upon capitalism. What seemed prudent to him, appeared revolutionary to Americans. A corollary to Marx's prophecy that "At a certain stage of their development the material productive forces of society come into contradiction with the existing productive relationships," seemed to be emerging from Mexican-American relationships: An essentially conservative effort to rectify that contradiction takes on revolutionary implications in an international setting, perhaps forcing radical changes in the policies of both countries at once.

Secretary of State Bryan had been eager to try out a new approach to America's relations with Caribbean area countries, in an effort to anticipate and resolve similar contradictions. Convinced that European bankers (and some American investors, too) exploited the poor credit standing of these governments to gain economic control through usurious loans (a situation familiar to him from his personal experience in western politics and economics in the 1890s), Bryan suggested to Wilson that the United States government "loan" the Caribbean countries its credit standing. Put another way, he was proposing that the United States co-sign and guarantee their "notes." The savings would be twofold: Economically, the borrowers would no longer have to pay out in interest rates and initial charges a large percentage of their money; politically, the fewer defaults there were the less chance there would be of complications and disagreements between governments.

Wilson thought the idea too radical, but he allowed his Secretary of State ample room to achieve his goal by alternative means. Blocked from trying out his original plan, Bryan fell back on earlier policies, for example, a renegotiated Nicaraguan Treaty containing clauses like those in the Platt Amendment to the Cuban Treaty of 1903. The Senate disapproved the first version of the Bryan-Chamorro pact, but finally agreed to a second one that guaranteed the United States an option on any Nicaraguan trans-isthmian canal, as well as options on strategically located naval bases. In exchange, the United States loaned Nicaragua $3 million. After the Senate acted, Secretary Bryan complained to Wilson that his original treaty "would have given us the right to do that which we might be called upon to do anyhow. We cannot escape the responsibilities of our position. . . ." Root and Knox had reached the same conclusion, and used the same words in discussing the issue. It was not just a matter of "Big Stick Diplomacy," or "Dollar Diplomacy," or "Moral Imperialism." As Bryan predicted, the treaty was used as justification for a series of interventions and occupations well into the next decade.

Wilson once observed to Colonel House that although Secretary of State Bryan "was always using the 'soft pedal' in negotiations with Germany he had to restrain him when he was dealing with Santo Domingo, Haiti, and such small republics." That was hardly fair. Bryan had proposed significant changes that the President had found too novel. In the Nicaraguan negotiations, the Secretary had overseen the contract writing between the bankers and the Nicaraguan representatives so as to assure himself that the terms were fair to both parties. Yet from the perspective of five decades, there seems very little difference in the terms of this contract—which allowed American investors to control that country's railroads as well as its finances—and those negotiated under previous Secretaries of State.

The dynamic of America's relations with the Caribbean area could not be changed simply by the election of an "idealist" to the White House, or by putting a "Great Commoner" in charge of the Department of State. Thus, when Theodore Roosevelt's Domingan customs receivership failed to prevent the outbreak of yet another revolution in that country, Bryan insisted upon firmer controls. Santo Domingo must be made to accept an enforced peace among all its rival factions, and supervised elections: the very solution Wilson tried to impose on Mexico at the same time. "No opportunity for argument should be given to any person or faction," Bryan instructed his representative in plain undiplomatic language. "It is desired that you present a plan and see that it is complied with." Once a new government had been elected, the United States would extend it diplomatic recognition and insist that all "revolutionary movements cease and that all subsequent changes in the Government of the Republic be effected by the peace processes provided in the Dominican Constitution." Almost word for word this was the plan offered to Theodore Roosevelt by an American planter in 1904 when the former decided to take over the customs house. But the Wilson Administration's 1914 warning was ignored by the "natives," leading to another intervention in November 1916. American troops stayed in Santo Domingo until 1924.

As early as June 1913 Bryan had suggested to the President that the United States obtain a naval base somewhere on the other side of Hispaniola, the island shared by Santo Domingo and Haiti. Negotiations never got off the ground because of a lack of stability in the latter. The Secretary's principal adviser on Haitian affairs was Roger L. Farnham, a vice president of the National City Bank. After one conversation in early 1914, Farnham left Bryan a memorandum detailing Haiti's supposed potential if "revolutionary disturbances" were brought to an end. For more than a year every attempt to complete a treaty containing financial provisions like those of other Caribbean pacts was thwarted at the last minute by some new uprising. Finally, one Haitian ruler suggested a counterproposal: He would grant special economic concessions to American private interests, but would not turn over semiprotectorate power to the United States government. This gambit offered Bryan a chance to explain what he had been attempting to do in the whole area. The United States, he began, was not disposed to bargain. Such practice was precisely what had been wrong in past policies: "While we desire to encourage in every proper way American interests in Haiti, we believe that this can be better done by contributing to stability and order than by favoring special concessions to Americans. American capital will gladly avail itself of business opportunities in Haiti when assured of peace and quiet necessary for profitable production."

After several fruitless attempts to reach agreement on "some such arrangement as we have in Santo Domingo," the Administration finally decided "to take the bull by the horns and restore order" once and for all in July 1915. Because of the European war situation, military intervention was easy to justify, and it could be made to seem that the United States was only pre-empting some future attempt by one or more of the warring nations to invade and to occupy Haiti. Bryan's successor, Robert Lansing, assured the Haitians that the United States did indeed have positive aims as well. "Haiti should appreciate," he explained, "that means for economic and industrial development cannot come from within and that foreign capital must be sought and secured, and this cannot be expected unless there is reasonable assurance against internal dissensions."

Among Wilson's advisers, Robert Lansing was always the first to sense German malevolence behind every adverse development in the hemisphere. But a memorandum he wrote *before* the outbreak of the European war demonstrated an ability to go beyond immediate problems. The future challenges to the Monroe Doctrine, he predicted, would not be military. Nor could political, economic, and strategic factors be separated. America's competition would come "in the construction of railways, the establishment of mines, the cultivation of cotton, fruit, and other agricultural products, and the operations of various industrial enterprises." He summed up the situation this way: "With the present industrial activity, the scramble for markets, and the incessant search for new opportunities to produce wealth, commercial expansion and success are closely interwoven with political domination over the territory." Lansing's summation could just as easily have been written by any one of the Secretaries of State or Presidents in that period.

In Search of Security

DANA G. MUNRO

To many observers the policy which culminated in the military occupation of Haiti and the Dominican Republic and interference to a lesser degree in the internal affairs of other nearby countries seemed little different from the imperialism of European powers in Africa and the Far East. The American intervention in the Caribbean aroused a hostility throughout Latin America that still affects our relations with the other countries of the hemisphere. What happened might have been forgotten after the repudiation of the intervention policy by Presidents Hoover and Franklin Roosevelt, had it not been

"Intervention and Dollar Diplomacy in Retrospect," in Dana G. Munro, *Intervention and Dollar Diplomacy in the Caribbean, 1900–1921* (copyright © 1964 by Princeton University Press), pp. 530–546, ftns. deleted. Reprinted by permission of Princeton University Press.

for the belief that the policy was inspired by sinister and sordid motives, which might well reassert themselves at some future time. This belief has contributed materially to the myth of North American imperialism, political and economic, which is assiduously kept alive today by hostile propaganda.

The persistence of this belief in Latin America is not surprising, because the same ideas about the motives behind the intervention policy have often found expression in the United States. Many liberal North Americans were shocked when they realized that American marines were killing Haitians and Dominicans who resisted the occupation of their countries by foreign forces, and thought that the policy which led to such a situation must be wrong. Writing at a time when historians were prone to assume that all governments were unprincipled and that governmental actions must be explained by economic considerations, "anti-imperialist" authors assumed that the United States could only have been acting for the benefit of American financial interests, and they found enough in the story of dollar diplomacy to convince them that their assumption was correct. One still hears it said that the marines were sent to the Caribbean "to collect debts," an idea that seems somewhat incongruous when one reflects that it was Woodrow Wilson who ordered the more important interventions. For several years after 1920 most of the books written about Caribbean affairs, some of them the work of honest and competent historians, reflected this point of view.

It would be impossible to deny that many of the American government's actions were ill-judged and unfortunate in their results. As we look back on the story, however, it seems clear that the motives that inspired its policy were basically political rather than economic. What the United States was trying to do, throughout the period with which this study has dealt, was to put an end to conditions that threatened the independence of some of the Caribbean states and were consequently a potential danger to the security of the United States. Revolutions must be discouraged; the bad financial practices that weakened the governments and involved them in trouble with foreigners must be reformed; and general economic and social conditions, which were a basic cause of instability, must be improved. The Platt Amendment was an effort to achieve these purposes in Cuba, and the Roosevelt Corollary to the Monroe Doctrine meant that the United States would seek to achieve them in other Caribbean states.

The same purposes inspired the policy of successive administrations from Theodore Roosevelt to Woodrow Wilson. The methods used in attempting to achieve them varied from one administration to another, but more because of accumulating experience and increasing involvement than because of any difference in the ultimate goals. Each successive Secretary of State took up Caribbean problems where his predecessor had left them, in most cases making no abrupt change in the way in which they were being handled.

As time went on, there was more and more active interference in the internal affairs of some of the states that seemed most in need of help. When Roosevelt first took office, he certainly did not contemplate any extensive effort by the United States to better political and economic conditions in the Caribbean. The Cubans had already been compelled to accept the Platt Amendment, but this, as its sponsors conceived it, was essentially a negative measure, designed to give the United States a legal basis for any action that might some day prove necessary. It seems clear that neither Roosevelt nor Root, who had been chiefly responsible for the amendment, thought that it should serve as an excuse for any avoidable interference in the island's internal affairs. There were, moreover, special reasons why the United States felt responsible for the welfare of Cuba. It was not until after the Anglo-German attack on Venezuela that Roosevelt came to feel that European intervention in any Caribbean state must be prevented. With the formulation of his Corollary to the Monroe Doctrine, he committed the United States to a policy of helping its neighbors to correct conditions that exposed them to possible aggression.

Roosevelt offered such help only where it was urgently needed and usually avoided any appearance of coercion. By the time when he became president, he seems to have given up the somewhat imperialist ideas that he had expressed as a younger man. The Panama affair showed that he was capable of aggressive and arbitrary action in what he considered a good cause, but he thought that public opinion would not support him in any general policy of intervention in the Caribbean. He clearly seems to have been less willing than were his successors to assume responsibilities in connection with the internal affairs of Caribbean states. He apparently looked on the establishment of the customs collectorship in Santo Domingo as an unfortunate necessity, and he endeavored to avoid intervention in Cuba in 1906.

Root, who directed Latin American policy in Roosevelt's second administration, had helped to formulate the President's Corollary to the Monroe Doctrine and believed in its validity, but he realized that injudicious efforts to bring about more orderly conditions and better government in the Caribbean states would arouse opposition and resentment. In dealing with threats of war in Central America, he enlisted the cooperation of Mexico to avoid the suspicion that would have been aroused by unilateral North American intervention, and he encouraged the Central Americans to devise their own program for maintaining peace, instead of putting forward his ideas. In the Dominican Republic the permanent establishment of the customs collectorship and the adjustment of the foreign debt were carried out in friendly cooperation with the local government. Unfortunately, subsequent developments both in Central America and in Santo Domingo undid much of what he seemed to have accomplished, and the problems that confronted his successors were the more troublesome because of the new commitments which the United States had assumed under his leadership.

In Cuba, Central America, and Santo Domingo, Roosevelt and Root did not act until they were faced with emergencies where action seemed necessary to prevent further bloodshed or to ward off European intervention. Their successors began to urge fiscal and political reforms which would prevent such emergencies from arising. In the somewhat naïve belief that the chief goal of revolutions was the customs receipts, they hoped that the establishment of customs collectorships would give the Central American states the same stability and economic progress that the Dominican Republic enjoyed between 1907 and 1911. Their efforts to substitute North American for European financial influence were intended to do away with a potential source of conflict with European states. In Cuba, the purpose of the Taft administration's preventive policy was to correct conditions that threatened to bring on another intervention. Knox and Huntington Wilson were not very successful in what they attempted to do, partly because they did not have Root's sympathetic understanding of the people with whom they were dealing. Their dollar diplomacy miscarried when the United States Senate rejected the loan treaties. The Dominican Republic, where the customs receivership seemed to have had such good results, sank into anarchy, and the government with which they were working in Nicaragua was kept in office only by American armed intervention.

The problems that confronted the Taft administration, however, were to a considerable extent the logical consequence of what Roosevelt and Root had done. In Central America, after the United States' sponsorship of the 1907 treaties and its vigorous diplomatic efforts to persuade the Central American governments to respect them, it would have been difficult to tolerate Zelaya's blatant repudiation of his treaty obligations, even if he had not made himself still more offensive by murdering Cannon and Groce. In Santo Domingo the existence of the receivership made it impossible to remain indifferent when civil war occurred; and in Cuba there was real reason for concern about the possibility of a third intervention because the previous one had been profitable to the party whose revolt had forced the United States to act.

The Wilson administration also had to take up Caribbean problems where its predecessor left them. There was little immediate change in policy, but there was a still greater disposition to insist on peace and internal reform in the more disorderly states and to use force if necessary to compel the acceptance of measures that the United States thought beneficial. By 1913 it had become evident that some of the Caribbean governments could not maintain order by their own efforts and that even the establishment of customs collectorships did little to assure financial solvency if the local officials were free to spend the revenues as they [saw] fit. The new administration consequently began to urge more thoroughgoing reforms, to be carried out under the actual control of North Americans designated by the United States, and it resorted to the military occupation of Haiti and the Dominican Republic when the governments of those countries refused to accept such control.

Despite Wilson's emphasis on the duty of the United States to promote constitutional government in the Caribbean, the Roosevelt Corollary to the Monroe Doctrine, though rarely mentioned, was still the basis of American policy. President Wilson expressed his full agreement when Secretary Lansing wrote in November 1915:

"The possession of the Panama Canal and its defense have in a measure given to the territories in and about the Caribbean Sea a new importance from the standpoint of our national safety. It is vital to the interests of this country that European political domination should in no way be extended over these regions.

As it happens within this area lie the small republics of America which have been and to an extent still are the prey of revolutionists, of corrupt governments and of predatory foreigners.

"Because of this state of affairs, our national safety, in my opinion, requires that the United States should intervene and aid in the establishment and maintenance of a stable and honest government, if no other way seems possible to attain that end."

Throughout the period between 1901 and 1921, the first objective of American policy in the Caribbean was to discourage revolutions. Revolutions, and the interstate wars that often rose out of them, were the chief cause of controversies with European powers because they endangered foreign lives and property and disrupted the government's finances so that it could not meet foreign claims. Frequent civil wars were also an obstacle to any sort of material or social progress. A government that had to devote all of its resources simply to maintaining itself in power could do little road building and little for public education, and an atmosphere of insecurity discouraged private enterprise in agriculture or industry.

The improvement of economic conditions was a second objective. There could be little basic improvement in the political situation while the masses of the people were poverty stricken and illiterate. A part of the Dominican bond issue of 1908 was used for public works, though little was accomplished, and the proposed loan for Nicaragua was to have provided funds to build a railroad. In Haiti and the Dominican Republic the occupation authorities had ambitious programs of roadbuilding, port improvement, and sanitation. All economic development, however, had to be carried on with the limited funds available from the countries' own revenues or from loans, because it would hardly have been possible before 1921 to ask the United States Congress to make grants of aid to another country.

In discussing their policy, officials in the State Department sometimes held out the hope of increased trade and new fields for American investment as a third objective. It is doubtful, however, whether these considerations really had any great influence in the formulation of policy. There is little evidence that the American government made any important effort to promote trade, and with the exception of Cuba the countries which the United States tried particularly to help were too small and too poor in natural resources to offer attractive opportunities for foreign enterprises.

These objectives, whatever we may think of the way in which the American government tried to attain them, were neither sinister nor sordid. Many critics of the United States' policy, however, maintained that there was a fourth purpose: to forward the selfish interests of American businessmen and bankers. To what extent this charge is justified is one of the questions that must be considered in any study of dollar diplomacy and intervention.

Certainly many American citizens who lived in Caribbean countries did benefit from the establishment of more orderly conditions and from the increased influence and prestige of the United States, which made their lives and property more secure. The American government, like other governments, thought that it had a duty to intercede for its nationals when they were the victims of violence or injustice in a foreign country, and it showed somewhat more interest in protecting them after 1900 than it had in the past. Warships were sent to Caribbean ports not only to influence the local political situation but to prevent injury to Americans and other foreigners. The State Department also tried to bring about the settlement of American claims, and in Nicaragua, Haiti, and Santo Domingo it urged the establishment of mixed commissions for this purpose. The benefits derived from these, however, were dubious, for all claims, and especially those of Americans and other foreigners, were usually arbitrarily scaled down and many claimants were compelled to accept awards which they considered unfair. A study of the work of the claims commissions hardly supports the idea that the purpose of the Caribbean interventions was to collect debts.

It is also true that controversies between certain American companies and the local governments played an important part in the chain of events that led up to each intervention. The arbitral award in favor of the San Domingo Improvement Company helped to bring on the crisis that led to the establishment of the Dominican customs receivership, and the dispute over the Emery claim aggravated the already bad relations between the United States and Nicaragua. In Haiti the disputes between the government and the National Bank and the National Railroad made the situation more exasperating and helped to convince Wilson and Bryan that the United States should intervene. In each case, however, other considerations had far more weight in determining policy: the danger of European intervention, in Santo Domingo; the determination to make the 1907 treaties effective, in Central America; and the feeling that the United States must do something about the political chaos, in Haiti. It should be noted that the companies involved profited little from the interventions. The San Domingo Improvement Company was treated less kindly than many of the Dominican government's other creditors, and the Emery claim was paid only after a delay of several years and then because a legal technicality forced the State Department to agree to its payment. In Haiti the railroad never prospered, and the occupation compelled the National Bank to give up some of the privileges that it enjoyed under its concession.

Except in Cuba, little new American capital went into the countries where the United States intervened. The occupation in Santo Domingo and the treaty officials in Haiti tried to encourage investment in new agricultural or industrial enterprises, in Santo Domingo by setting up the land courts, which improved the chaotic state of land titles, and in Haiti by abrogating the constitutional provision against foreign land ownership. The results were not particularly impressive, though the sugar companies in Santo Domingo, some of which were American, found it easier to obtain new acreage and considerably increased their production. A few new foreign agricultural enterprises were started in Haiti, most of them after 1921, but only one or two of them were ever profitable. Little foreign capital went into Nicaragua.

Dollar diplomacy might have brought profits to American bankers if it had been more successful, but its purpose, under Taft as well as under Wilson, was purely political. Both administrations were interested in loans as a means of stabilizing Caribbean governments and bringing about the establishment of American customs collectorships, and as a way to provide funds for economic development. They also wished to eliminate European financial influence in the area. Disputes over unpaid debts were always likely to provide an excuse for European intervention, and it was thought that the exploitation of the Caribbean countries by European interests was one cause of their backwardness.

In most cases, it was the State Department that took the initiative in bringing forward projects for loans. The bankers, however, were usually glad to participate in them and sometimes competed for the privilege, because they assumed that they would be sound business ventures. At times, a desire to cooperate with the State Department and the fascination exerted by projects for the development of strange and distant countries led the bankers into ventures which at least cost them far more in time and trouble than the profits could justify, but they would have been subject to merited criticism if they had gone into transactions where there was not a prospect of a reasonable profit.

The State Department, as we have seen, endeavored to make sure that the profit was reasonable and not excessive. Knox, who realized that anything that savored of exploitation would invite criticism, insisted on a careful scrutiny of the proposed Honduras and Nicaragua loan contracts by a disinterested law firm to make sure that the interests of the borrowing government were properly safeguarded. Under the proposed contracts, the Morgan firm and its associates would have bought $7,500,000 5-percent bonds from Honduras at 88, and Brown Brothers and Seligman would have taken $12,000,000 5-percent Nicaraguan bonds at 90½. The bankers' profits would of course have depended on the spread between these prices and the figure at which they could have sold them to the public. Brazilian 5-percent bonds were selling around par on the stock exchange in the first months of 1911, and Cuban 5's between 102½ and 103½. If the bankers had been able to sell the Honduran and Nicaraguan bonds at these prices, they would have had a substantial profit, but perhaps not an unreasonable one in view of the smallness of the issues and the great amount of work involved in setting them up. It is impossible to say whether Central American bonds, even when secured by customs receiverships, would have been equally attractive to investors. It is at least clear that the two governments were obtaining better terms than they could have without the help of the United States, for the 6-percent bonds of the Ethelburga loan, contracted by Zelaya in 1909, were taken by the bankers at 75 and were offered to the public at 92 in London and 93½ in Paris.

In Honduras, the time and effort expended by the bankers in working out the contract were wasted. In Nicaragua, Brown Brothers and Seligman agreed to finance the very urgent currency reform without waiting for the loan treaty to be ratified, and their purchase of $1,500,000 in treasury bills was the first of a series of transactions that continued for many years. None of these, during the Taft administration at least, were unconscionably profitable. On the treasury bills and on the small loans made in 1912 Nicaragua paid 6 percent interest, with an additional commission of 1 percent on the two smaller loans. These terms were certainly not onerous in view of political and economic conditions in Nicaragua. Some of the bankers' transactions in Nicaragua after 1913 were probably somewhat more profitable, but hardly profitable enough to make the bankers feel that the Nicaraguan venture had been worthwhile from a purely financial standpoint.

If we dismiss as unfounded the charge that the purpose of dollar diplomacy was to enrich a few North American businessmen, we must still inquire whether the broader Caribbean policy of which it was a part was wise and profitable. The policy did eliminate, for the time being, the danger of European intervention. Perhaps neither Germany nor any other power seriously entertained the idea of territorial expansion in the Caribbean, but there is little doubt that European interference would have taken forms unacceptable to the United States and possibly dangerous to the independence of the countries involved if the American government had not acted as it did in Santo Domingo in 1905 and in Haiti after 1910. Before 1914 the vital importance of defending the approaches to the Panama Canal made any unfriendly activity in the Caribbean a much more serious matter than it seemed to be after the First World War, when the naval power of the United States was so much greater.

It is more difficult to assess the benefits and disadvantages to the Caribbean countries themselves. The policy of the United States certainly reduced, though it did not end, the bloodshed and turmoil that had kept the Caribbean states so backward before 1900. It stopped international wars between the five Central American states and made internal revolutions less frequent and destructive. Except for the *caco* uprising in Haiti, that country and the Dominican Republic had a long period of peace. Unless one has seen something of the terror and the misery caused by a civil war in a small Caribbean country, it is difficult to appreciate what peace meant to all classes of the people. It was certainly the first requisite for any sort of economic progress.

We have seen that the amount of economic progress actually achieved down to 1921 in the countries where the United States intervened was not very great. There were, nevertheless, some material benefits. The customs receiverships, which continued in Nicaragua, Haiti, and Santo Domingo for several years after 1921, helped commerce by eliminating favoritism and corruption in the customhouses and strengthened the financial position of the governments. These three countries were among the very few in Latin America that continued to pay interest on their foreign bonds during the depression. Some other administrative reforms introduced by American officials and advisers were of lasting value. Much-needed roads were built in Haiti and the Dominican Republic, and there was a notable improvement in sanitary conditions in the larger cities of both countries. More might have been achieved if the public works programs had not had to be financed entirely from the scanty resources of the local governments. For various reasons, the substantial foreign loans which the customs receiverships were to have made possible did not materialize, and the United States government could give little help.

The replacement of the old inefficient and corrupt armies by better-trained police forces, in Haiti and the Dominican Republic, helped to maintain peace but had unfortunate consequences after the American occupations ended. The efficiency and discipline of these organizations gave their officers a potential political power which only the ablest of the old style *caudillos* had had. In Santo Domingo, General Trujillo, the chief of the new force, took control of the government in 1930 and ruled the country despotically until 1961. In Haiti, too, the *Garde* has at times been the master of the government rather than its servant. It is perhaps less unpleasant to live under the tyranny of a comparatively efficient military force than under the equally tyrannical but irresponsible and inefficient rule of the old type of local *comandantes,* but the evolution of the constabularies was a disappointment to those who hoped that they would help to promote republican government.

It can hardly be said, in fact, that the American government's policy did very much to promote republican government in other ways, except insofar as the maintenance of peace and some economic progress created an atmosphere more conducive to the gradual development of democratic institutions. The support of constituted governments and the discouragement of revolutions meant in practice that one party might stay in power indefinitely. A government that felt secure in its position was less likely to mistreat its opponents or to curtail civil rights, and it could devote more energy and resources to constructive work; but it would be no more inclined to permit its opponents to win elections.

Roosevelt and Taft dealt with the governments in power without questioning how they had attained power and seemed to deprecate revolutions not so much on moral grounds as because of their harmful effects. They endeavored to find ways of making revolutions less frequent, and at times, as in Honduras and Santo Domingo, the Taft administration interposed to end a civil war by compromise. Wilson was much more emphatic in his denunciation of all revolutionary action on moral grounds. He effectively discouraged political uprisings in Central America and attempted to prevent them in Santo Domingo. His policy of refusing to recognize any government that came into office by force was difficult to enforce, but it greatly strengthened the position of governments that were already in power.

If Wilson did not always seem to inquire very closely into the character of the regimes that he was supporting against revolution, he did on several occasions attempt to see that changes of government took place in a democratic way. In 1914 he insisted on a free election in Santo Domingo, so that there would be a government there which the United States could consistently maintain in office by force if it needed such help. In 1916 and again in 1920 he tried, without great success, to see that fair elections were held in Cuba. On the other hand, governments that were obviously opposed by a majority of the people were kept in power in Nicaragua, where the American government decided who should be the president in 1916 and made only a feeble attempt to bring about a fair election in 1920. In Haiti, where real elections were obviously impossible, there was no pretense of consulting the voters after the plebiscite on the constitution of 1918.

The failure to insist on fair elections in Cuba and in Nicaragua unquestionably gave the opposition parties reason to feel that they were unfairly treated. The opposition parties in several other Caribbean states could likewise complain that the discouragement of revolutions and the policy of refusing recognition to governments coming into office by force was unreasonable when they had no other means of changing an unsatisfactory regime. Officials at Washington, however, might well have hesitated before committing themselves to any general policy of compelling the holding of fair elections. No supervision could be effective without assuming control of or supplanting the military forces and the civil authorities and the courts in all functions connected with the electoral process. The governments in power would have had to be coerced into accepting this sort of intervention, and this would be unfair because it would hurt the prestige and probably cause the defeat of the government party, even in cases where it might otherwise have majority support. It would be difficult to find qualified people to conduct the supervision, and there was a practical problem: the State Department had very little money which it could use for such purposes. It is not surprising that there was not a more strenuous effort to change the way in which the Caribbean governments had always conducted their elections, even though there was an inconsistency in preventing revolutions against governments that perpetuated their control in obviously undemocratic ways. It could be argued that the maintenance of peace was the first requisite for the sort of progress that would ultimately make real elections possible, and that it would be futile to try to force democratic practices on people who were not ready for them.

One unfortunate consequence of the American government's efforts to improve political conditions in the Caribbean was that the local leaders got into the habit of looking to Washington for the settlement of political problems. A belief that the faction favored by the United States would usually come out on top, and even that an established government which the United States disliked might not be able to stay in office, gave an excessive importance to every indication or fancied indication of the attitude of American officials. Rumors about American policy were fabricated and circulated for political effect, and even ordinary courtesies extended by the State Department or the American legations were given an exaggerated significance. Under such conditions, many of the local leaders tended to feel less responsibility for the settlement of their own problems.

The willingness of many political leaders to accept American help made it more difficult for the State Department and its representatives to appreciate the resentment their actions were causing. If the American government's policy after 1909, as we look back on it, seems increasingly callous in its disregard of local sentiment, we must remember that those who directed it thought that they had the support of important groups in the countries with which they were dealing. In the State Department's correspondence, one frequently encounters the idea that the truly patriotic leaders, and most of the solid and intelligent people, wanted peace and reform, and that the opposition came from "corrupt politicians" and "professional revolutionists." Had it not been for the belief that the United States must help the decent element against evil men who wished for their own selfish reasons to perpetuate anarchy and misgovernment, it would have been more difficult for Taft to send the Marines into Nicaragua in 1912 and for Wilson to order the military occupation of Haiti and Santo Domingo.

Important groups in the community often did welcome American interposition. In countries where there had been long periods of disorder, property owners and businessmen were glad to have peace restored, and many humbler citizens were glad to be free from the oppression and hardship that always accompanied civil strife. When the United States prevented a revolution, only those who had hoped to get possession of the government were really distressed. There were many patriotic people who approved of the reforms which the State Department urged and who wished for American help in roadbuilding and education and economic development. The spirit of economic nationalism, which had already made its appearance in Mexico after 1910, was much less evident in the smaller Caribbean republics, where many people hoped that the development of their natural resources by foreign capital would help them to emerge from the backward conditions that made their lives unattractive.

As the American policy developed, however, it met with increasing opposition. There had always been much distrust and traditional dislike of the United States and some suspicion of American motives. This suspicion grew stronger as the American government intervened more and more in purely internal affairs and began to seek actual control of important governmental functions. The use of force or the threat of force to settle political problems or to compel reforms was offensive to people who were jealous of their independence. The occupation of the country by American military forces, in Haiti and the Dominican Republic, was of course still more offensive.

The hostility and distrust that it aroused, not only in the Caribbean but throughout Latin America, was the worst result of the intervention policy. The full extent of this feeling was not apparent until after the First World War, when Haitian and Dominican opponents of the American occupations began to carry on a propaganda campaign in South America and in the United States. A realization of the reaction in Latin America and of the unpopularity of intervention at home led to a gradual change of policy at Washington after 1921, but suspicion of North American "imperialism" continued to be a major obstacle to inter-American cooperation throughout the 1920's. Even today the recollection of what happened in the first decades of the century provides useful material for anti-American propaganda.

The American government was necessarily interested in what happened in the Caribbean, especially after the decision to build the Panama Canal, and it had sound reasons for wishing to do away with the internal disorder and financial mismanagement that endangered the independence of some of the Central American and West Indian republics and the security of the United States. In trying to correct these conditions the statesmen who directed the policy of the United States in the Roosevelt, Taft, and Wilson administrations were dealing with exasperatingly difficult situations, where their best efforts were often defeated by the unpredictable and irresponsible conduct of local *caudillos* and their followers. We may well hesitate to criticize them too severely, but since it is clear that their policies had bad results, and since we are still faced with similar problems, it would be regrettable if we did not learn something from the story.

One fact that stands out is the inadvisability of sending incompetent diplomatic representatives to countries where the United States had great interests and heavy responsibilities. No policy could succeed when its implementation was in the hands of ministers who were too ignorant or too senile to command respect. The State Department repeatedly had to make decisions on the basis of information and recommendations received from persons who knew little about what was really happening, and it had to entrust these same persons with the conduct of its negotiations. Several of its representatives were, of course, not so incompetent, but few of them, especially after 1913, were fitted for their positions by training or experience. Many mistakes and unfortunate incidents could have been avoided if there had been able ministers at each post.

The bad results of the American government's policy, however, cannot be attributed wholly to diplomatic ineptitude. What made the policy offensive, in the Caribbean and in South America, was the use of coercion to compel the acceptance of American control in internal affairs and to obtain reforms that the United States considered desirable. Imposition of this sort would have been intolerable, however efficiently and tactfully it was carried out. Knox, Bryan, and Lansing might have achieved more, with less bad feeling, if they had attempted, as Root did, to help the people of the Caribbean states to solve their problems in their own way, instead of insisting that they place their financial administration and their military forces under the direction of foreign officials. With a policy of persuasion and cooperation the moral influence of the United States might have accomplished more than attempted compulsion did.

Had it not been for the effort to impose controls unacceptable to any people who prized their independence, there would have been less resentment of the vast influence which the United States necessarily exercised, and less resentment even when the American government used force to back up its efforts to end armed strife and to protect foreigners. Natives, as well as foreigners, were usually glad to see a warship appear at a port where fighting was imminent, and a show of force to stop a war caused little lasting bad feeling if it led to a fair settlement with no continuing offensive American interference in the government's affairs.

With tactful persuasion, much could have been done to promote better administration and economic progress. Caribbean governments often voluntarily accepted the help and advice of foreign experts, though they naturally resisted efforts to give experts authority over their own officials. Aid in roadbuilding and education and sanitation would have been welcome if it was not accompanied by efforts to impose foreign control. In Haiti and Santo Domingo there would probably have been less progress in these fields than there was under the military occupations, but the gains that were made might have been more lasting. If the American government could have provided funds for economic development, as it does today, a great deal could have been accomplished.

A policy that relied on cooperation rather than compulsion would have required patience and self-restraint. Its success would have depended on the quality of the American diplomatic representation in the Caribbean, but the diplomats would not have had to be supermen. A minister or even a young chargé d'affaires could exercise a great influence in a Caribbean country simply because he was the representative of the United States, and this influence was still greater if he was liked and respected. It was dangerous to have an incompetent man in such a position, but a moderately able man could accomplish a great deal, both for his own government and for the people of the country where he was serving.

Such a policy would also have required a willingness to accept and to live with situations in some Caribbean countries that were far from satisfactory from the American point of view. American influence could not bring about free and fair elections in countries where the people had not learned to demand them and to run them; and so long as elections were not satisfactory governments would inevitably be ousted by force or threats of force from time to time. Other evils, like corruption and oppression of political opponents, would have continued to exist. The United States could have exercised a very great influence for better and more democratic government and for the peaceful settlement of political conflicts, but in countries which were and must remain independent political progress had to be made primarily through the efforts of the people themselves. Stable democratic government cannot be imposed by exhortation or outside pressure.

FURTHER READING

Richard Abrams, "United States Intervention Abroad: The First Quarter Century," *American Historical Review*, 79 (1974), 72–102

Howard K. Beale, *Theodore Roosevelt and the Rise of America to World Power* (1956)

John M. Blum, *The Republican Roosevelt* (1954)

Kenneth J. Grieb, *The United States and Huerta* (1969)

William H. Harbaugh, *The Life and Times of Theodore Roosevelt* (1975)

David Healy, *Gunboat Diplomacy in the Wilson Era: The U.S. Navy in Haiti, 1915–1916* (1976)

Lester Langley, *The Cuban Policy of the United States* (1968)

Arthur S. Link, *Wilson*, 3 vols. (1960–1965)

Arthur S. Link, *Wilson the Diplomatist* (1963)

David McCullough, *The Path Between the Seas: The Creation of the Panama Canal, 1870–1914* (1977)

Allan R. Millett, *The Politics of Intervention: The Military Occupation of Cuba, 1906–1909* (1968)

Dwight C. Miner, *The Fight for the Panama Route* (1940)

Dexter Perkins, *The Monroe Doctrine, 1867–1907* (1937)

Dexter Perkins, *The United States and the Caribbean* (1947)

Frederick B. Pike, *The United States and the Andean Republics* (1977)

Julius Pratt, *America's Colonial Experiment* (1950)

Robert E. Quirk, *An Affair of Honor: Woodrow Wilson and the Occupation of Veracruz* (1962)

J. Fred Rippy, *The Capitalists and Colombia* (1931)

Ramon Ruiz, *Cuba: The Making of a Revolution* (1968)

Hans Schmidt, *The United States Occupation of Haiti, 1915–1934* (1971)

Karl M. Schmitt, *Mexico and the United States, 1821–1973* (1974)

Arthur P. Whitaker, *The United States and the Southern Cone: Argentina, Uruguay, and Chile* (1976)

1 2 3 4 5 6 7 8 9 0